MY CHINESE DREAM

我的中国梦

From Red Guard to CEO

Liu Ping

chinabooks.com

Published in the United States of America by
China Books
360 Swift Avenue, Suite 48
South San Francisco, CA 94080
www.chinabooks.com

Editor: Yu Ling, Xu Mingqiang, Yang Chunyan, Liu Fangnian
Book and Cover Design: Liu Yi and Liu Ping

ISBN : 978-0-8351-0040-3

Printed in China
First Edition

谨将此书献给我的家人、朋友和经历过中国改革开放全过程的我的同龄人。
　　本书讲述了五十年来作者本人、家族和普通中国人的故事，反映了国家和人民在半个世纪里发生的巨大变化。请读者不要对号入座。

This book is dedicated to my family, my friends and people of my contemporaries who have experienced the full period of China's reform and opening-up.

It tells the stories of myself, my family and the common Chinese people which happened in the past 50 years to reflect the great change the country and the people experienced in that period.

The stories told in this book are true, but names have been changed in order to protect the people concerned.

Acknowledgements

My book is finally completed and it would not have been done without the support from many others. I would like to take this opportunity to acknowledge my family members and friends who shared special insight and advice. Their guidance, support and encouragement proved invaluable throughout this process and helped me to realize my Chinese dream.

I am indebted to my parents and all of my family members, especially those from my hometown in northeast China. They willingly shared their recollections, including many that evoked painful memories. I cannot thank them enough for allowing me to tell their stories. This book is a tribute to their hard work, sacrifice and perseverance.

I owe a special debt of gratitude to my cousin, Liu Fu. She grew up with our grandmother and captured first hand accounts from the older generations of Liu Family. This precious history provided me with the perspective and inspiration to complete my book.

I am also grateful to my childhood friends, Julin, Juhua, Shaofan and my university schoolmate, Yang Shengming. We all lived through the Cultural Revolution, a profound period in Chinese history. This was a hectic time in my life and my story would not be complete without their vivid depictions of many events.

My neighbors, Bai Nanfeng and Wang Hong, and my sister and brother-in-law, Liu Hua and Ye Bin, have greatly contributed to this book. The knowledge and insight they provided were instrumental when I reached a critical impasse while writing my book. Their reassurance gave me the confidence to forge ahead. They deserve my heartfelt thanks for making a seemingly overwhelming process fun and rewarding.

I would be remiss if I didn't also thank my son, Zheng Han. I wasn't quite sure how my story would resonate with younger generations. Han was born in the late 1980s and his interest in the book alleviated my concerns. I'm incredibly proud of him. My hope is that my story lives on through him and future generations.

I am also grateful to a young man I have never met. His name is E Peng and he is a postgraduate of Harbin Institute of Technology. Peng stayed up for several nights to read all my blog entries. He left me a message to say how much he was inspired and touched by my stories. Peng motivated me to share my story. He helped me to realize that I could inspire others to realize their dreams.

My book was originally written in Chinese in an effort to portray events and emotions accurately. My colleague, Xiao Chun, accepted the unenviable challenge of translating the book with me. It was an arduous but worthwhile process. I'm extremely grateful for Chun's help and expertise.

Writing a book of hundreds of pages is nearly a full time job. I spent many hours away from the office over the last year while completing my book. This would not have been possible without the support of my entire team at Xin Xin Yi Xiang (China Star). I am especially grateful to my trusted friend, business partner and confidant, Liu Yanxiang (David Liu), president of China Star.

The enthusiastic interest of my Western friends has been a perpetual source of encouragement. To all of them, I am indebted. I have received particular help from Peter Ueberroth, Jeffrey Thomas, Stephanie Quesada, Martin Sirk, Kees van Galen, Martin Lewis, Gail Small, Sean Mahoney, Ray Bloom, Paul Flackett and Jonar Nader.

Finally, I give my special thanks to Yu Ling, editor of the book and my contemporary. Her understanding and appreciation of my story was instrumental throughout the editing process. Ling corrected my mistakes and contributed to a compelling finished product.

Liu Ping
Beijing, China
July, 2011

Contents

Preface

Two years ago, Liu Ping told me that she was writing a book. When I asked her why she wanted to write the book, she said she was very disappointed with the Westerners' prejudice against China and Chinese people. She thought there were underlying reasons behind many phenomena in China and many Westerners didn't understand China's today because they knew little about China's past. So she wanted to write a book about what happened to herself, her family and her friends in the past 50 years and hoped the book could help Westerners know more about China and learn how to understand China and Chinese people. Liu Ping was confident that her experience from a Red Guard to a CEO was very convincing.

When I received her manuscript of hundreds of pages, I was amazed and convinced that I should look at this Chinese woman with new eyes.

The stories in her book are true and believable. You can feel how hard it was for her to write this book when reading the stories which are told in a simple direct way. She tried hard to tell the stories from a standpoint that was acceptable to both the East and West, with no whitewash or criticism. Ping hoped Westerners could understand her, but she didn't want to impose her feelings on others. Worried to see the detours China has taken, yet proud to see the achievements China has made. Although she doesn't express directly her love for her country in the book, the strong feelings of her passion to her motherland can be found between the lines. The stories focus on the comparison between old and new and emphasize the close connection between the destiny of individuals and that of the country. No matter how many twists and turns there are in the stories, the ending is always positive and inspiring. What's more commendable, Liu Ping also talks about some sensitive topics such as religion, democratic parties, ethnic minority and family planning policies, Taiwan issue and Tibet issue, etc. from her own perspectives. She hopes Westerners can understand the true feelings of most ordinary Chinese people, and distinguish them from the biased views of some Western politicians and media or the Chinese government's high-sounding propaganda. These are exactly what we Westerners want to know.

Beyond the above comments about the book, I'm compelled to share my personal opinion and observation about Liu Ping. I've had the opportunity to watch her leadership skills and entrepreneurial vision. Ping could be the CEO of a company on any continent. She knows how to pick the best associates and they accept her leadership in achieving the highest performance on all fronts.

Along with being a loyal and devoted citizen of China, Ping has the talent and drive to make her company a regional and global player.

She is an exceptional woman and our friend.

Peter V. Ueberroth
President, Los Angeles Olympic Games 1984
Chairman, United States Olympic Committee
2004-2008 Beijing Olympic Games

Liu Family Tree

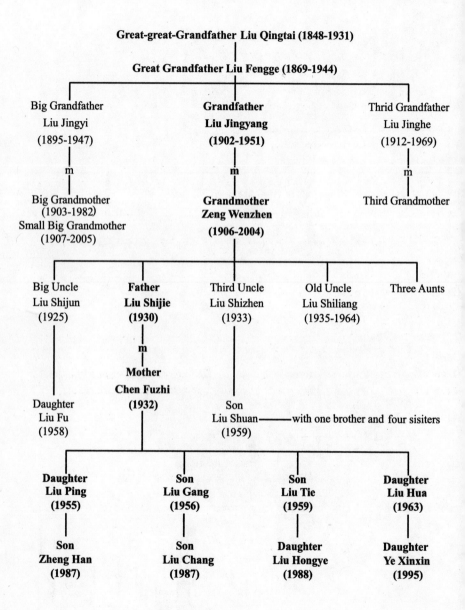

Great-great-Grandfather Liu Qingtai (1848-1931)

Great Grandfather Liu Fengge (1869-1944)

Big Grandfather
Liu Jingyi
(1895-1947)

**Grandfather
Liu Jingyang
(1902-1951)**

Thrid Grandfather
Liu Jinghe
(1912-1969)

m

m

m

Big Grandmother
(1903-1982)
Small Big Grandmother
(1907-2005)

**Grandmother
Zeng Wenzhen
(1906-2004)**

Third Grandmother

Big Uncle
Liu Shijun
(1925)

**Father
Liu Shijie
(1930)**

Third Uncle
Liu Shizhen
(1933)

Old Uncle
Liu Shiliang
(1935-1964)

Three Aunts

m

**Mother
Chen Fuzhi
(1932)**

Daughter
Liu Fu
(1958)

Son
Liu Shuan————with one brother and four sisiters
(1959)

**Daughter
Liu Ping
(1955)**

**Son
Liu Gang
(1956)**

**Son
Liu Tie
(1959)**

**Daughter
Liu Hua
(1963)**

**Son
Zheng Han
(1987)**

**Son
Liu Chang
(1987)**

**Daughter
Liu Hongye
(1988)**

**Daughter
Ye Xinxin
(1995)**

IV

Chen Family Tree

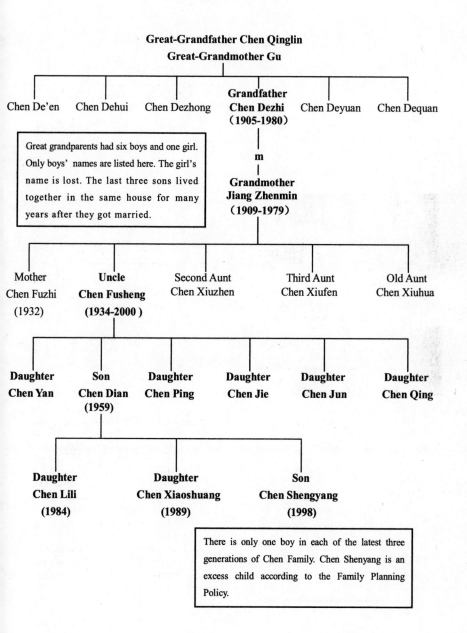

Great-Grandfather Chen Qinglin
Great-Grandmother Gu

Chen De'en   Chen Dehui   Chen Dezhong   **Grandfather Chen Dezhi** (1905-1980)   Chen Deyuan   Chen Dequan

Great grandparents had six boys and one girl. Only boys' names are listed here. The girl's name is lost. The last three sons lived together in the same house for many years after they got married.

m

Grandmother Jiang Zhenmin (1909-1979)

Mother Chen Fuzhi (1932)   **Uncle Chen Fusheng** (1934-2000)   Second Aunt Chen Xiuzhen   Third Aunt Chen Xiufen   Old Aunt Chen Xiuhua

Daughter Chen Yan   **Son Chen Dian** (1959)   **Daughter Chen Ping**   **Daughter Chen Jie**   **Daughter Chen Jun**   **Daughter Chen Qing**

Daughter Chen Lili (1984)   **Daughter Chen Xiaoshuang** (1989)   **Son Chen Shengyang** (1998)

There is only one boy in each of the latest three generations of Chen Family. Chen Shenyang is an excess child according to the Family Planning Policy.

V

Chapter One

My Family

I have been thinking about writing something about my home for many years. Several years ago, when my grandma was still alive, I made a special trip to my hometown in northeast China to listen to her stories of our family.

More and more family members of my generation have left the countryside. Now only two of my cousins stay in the villages of my hometown. The younger generation has all moved to live in the city.

Stories of my old home would be drowned in the long river of history without trace if nobody writes them down.

Liu Family

Liu Family has lived in a small village named Liu Family River in Liaoning Province in northeast China since the generation of my great-great-grandfather. Liu Family River is just a name, nothing to do with a river. I guess that the name came from an ancient *fengshui* master who believed that the place needed more water to be luckier though there was a river named Cao River not far from our house.

Liu is a big family name in China. The Chinese put the family names before the given names.

The history of my family dates back to five generations before my great-great-grandfather Liu Qingtai. They were Liu Chaofu, Liu Shangren, Liu Ying, Liu Defeng and Liu Wanjin, whose names were found on the gravestones in ruins.

Liu Fengge was my great-grandfather. He had three sons, Liu Jingyi, Liu Jingyang and Liu Jinghe. The second son Liu Jingyang was my grandfather.

I should call Liu Jingyi Big Grandfather and Liu Jinghe Third Grandfather as required by family rules.

In 1923, my grandmother Zeng Wenzhen was married to my grandfather Liu Jingyang. She was 17 years old, two years younger than my grandfather.

Liu Family used to be a big rich family. Great-great-grandfather Liu Qingtai was a doctor of traditional Chinese medicine and ran a herbal medicine shop in the village. The family had dozens *mu* (15 *mu* equals one hectare) of good land and hired two long-term laborers. Old and young generations lived a comfortable life together. My grandmother and her sisters-in-law could have some private savings.

Big Grandfather Liu Jingyi was a talented and good-looking young man. He was so capable and warm-hearted that people in the neighboring villages would come to seek his help whenever they had a problem, big or small. He was also the most hardworking one of the three brothers. The wife of Big Grandfather, whom I called Big Grandmother, was a literate woman. She gave birth to three daughters after she was married. Big Grandfather was extremely unhappy about it because he wanted a son to carry on the family line. He was on the thought of having a concubine. Big Grandmother, blaming herself for not bringing the family a son, offered to find a girl for Big Grandfather. Big Grandfather took a fancy to a girl living in the neighboring village. Big Grandmother went to the girl's home to propose a marriage. The girl refused. Big Grandmother didn't give up. She tried and tried with her silver tongue. Finally the girl changed her mind. Soon came the wedding.

I called Big Grandfather's concubine Small-Big-Grandmother. Not long after the wedding, Big Grandmother and Small-Big-Grandmother got pregnant at about the same time. They both gave birth to a lovely boy. But the two boys died at the age of five or six. Small-Big-Grandmother later had another boy named Liu Shixun, who was mentally retarded. Big Grandfather felt a great shame and couldn't lift his head up.

Big Grandmother's eldest daughter Dongmei stealthily fell in love with a hired laborer of the family and got pregnant. When Big Grandmother found it out, she beat Dongmei and cursed her with the filthiest words. Dongmei committed suicide by drinking bittern right before her mother's eyes. During the whole process, Big Grandmother was looking on coldly as a bystander, no trace of regret could be found on her face. Big Grandfather hurried back home to see her daughter for the last time and said, "My daughter has backbone. Her death is worth it."

Big Grandfather died of illness at the age of 50. Big Grandmother moved to live with her second daughter. Small-Big-Grandmother alone brought up her retarded son Liu Shixun, receiving help from my grandmother from time to time. She died peacefully in her late nineties in 2005, and her son Liu Shixun died of diabetes in his early seventies one year earlier in 2004.

In 1925, my grandmother had her first child, a boy. He was my Big Uncle. Later she gave birth to another six children: my father, Third Uncle, Old Uncle and three daughters (in north China, the youngest one is called OLD, such as old aunt, old uncle, old son, old daughter), altogether seven children, named respectively Liu Shijun, Liu Shijie, Liu Shizhen, Liu Shiliang, Liu Cui'e, Liu Yu'e and Liu Shi'e.

When my Big Uncle was four years old, my grandfather was addicted to opium and gambling and hardly did any work. Both my Big Grandfather and Third Grandfather sold opium, so my grandfather turned to them to buy opium on credit and asked my grandmother for money to pay up his debt at the end of the year. Soon, my grandmother's private savings had all been extracted and the family was plunged into heavy debt. Life was getting more and more difficult.

Despite his bad habits, my grandfather was kind-hearted and honest and good to my grandmother. My grandmother never scolded him, just pleaded with tactful words. There was only one time when my grandmother couldn't bear it anymore and threatened my grandfather with death by drinking bittern. My grandfather was deadly frightened, but he still couldn't get rid of opium.

In order not to be a burden to other two brothers, my grandmother suggested dividing the family property up and living apart. They got a shabby house with a mill at one end and a *kang* at the other, a piece of small land on the hillside, a horse and two heads of cattle.

Kang, which is made of bricks and clay, is a heatable bed used in rural areas in north China. There is a flue beneath *kang* connecting *kang* with a stove which is also made of brick and clay. *Kang* is warmed up by the flue connected with a wood or coal burning stove.

My great-grandfather Liu Fengge lived with my Third Grandfather Liu Jinghe's family. Third Grandmother was born in a rich landlord family, so they lived a comfortable life with enough food to eat and enough clothes to wear. Seeing that my grandmother was living a hard life with so many children, Third Grandfather did not want to tie up with this poor family and decided to move to a neighboring village. My great-grandfather refused to move. Third Grandfather quietly took his family away at middle night. When great-grandfather woke up the next morning, he realized that he was abandoned. My grandmother took him home and said she would look after great-grandfather as long as he didn't mind the too many kids and the poverty of the family. Great-grandfather nodded his head. When it came to bedtime at night, grandmother helped great-grandfather undress and found his cotton-padded coat full of lice. She caught the lice one by one and threw them into the fire-pan. The whole family took good care of great-grandfather and would leave it to him whenever they had something nice to eat. Great-grandfather died a few months later, at the age of 75.

Although Third Grandmother was born in a rich family, she died of illness young, leaving three little children motherless. With no woman at home to take care of the young, Third Grandfather moved with his children to his brother—my grandfather's house and lived for two years. Grandmother did their sewing, laundry and cooking.

My grandfather was still indulged in gambling and smoking opium day and night. He didn't return home to sleep. The horse and cattle were taken away to pay the debt. Life was harder year after year. Grandmother shed tears all day long, but for her children, she had to clench her teeth and bear it.

My grandmother was a good wife and kind mother. She went through countless hardships and sufferings all her life. She never really hated her husband for his gambling and opium smoking. There was one time when she was pulling out weed in the vegetable garden, an elder of the village passed by and asked "Second daughter-in-law (my grandfather was the second child of the three boys), is Jingyang not back yet?" Grandfather was out somewhere gambling and hadn't returned home for several days. Angry grandmother replied without thinking "He is dead and will never come back." Grandmother told us many years later that she regretted having said something like that for the rest of her life. She always believed that grandfather was a good man and it was the old society to blame for his acquiring the bad habits. After liberation (when People's Republic of China was founded in 1949), with the help of the Communist Party, grandfather gave up gambling and opium smoking. He changed to a new man. Grandmother was grateful to the Party, and treated grandfather even better. Once, grandfather needed to go out early the next morning. It was early winter, and grandfather had no cotton-padded trousers. Grandmother stayed up the whole night making a pair of cotton-padded trousers from two pairs of old trousers under the kerosene lamp. When she finished with the trousers, it was already dawn. Then she had to prepare breakfast. When grandfather got up, wearing his warm cotton-padded trousers and eating steaming hot breakfast, he said to my grandmother thankfully, "I will repay you for what you have done for me in the future. I will buy you a fur coat when I earn money." Having a fur coat of one's own was something to be quite proud of at that time.

My grandfather passed away without having realized his promise. He died at 49 in 1951, probably of lung cancer judging from the symptoms. Long years' opium smoking damaged his health. He had frequently suffered from lung pain, and had no money to see a doctor. When approaching his end, my grandfather held my father and Old Uncle's hands, "I have no time to pay your mother my debt of gratitude. You two must do it for me." That year, my grandmother was 45 years old.

My Grandmother

My grandmother endured all hardships all her life. A poverty-stricken family in her youth, losing husband and a son in middle age, eldest son being jailed for 13 years, all these were unbearable pains for ordinary people. However, she survived them, brought up her children, her grandchildren, and died peacefully at the age of 98.

My grandmother, Zeng Wenzhen, was born in 1906. She was

adopted right after she was born by a couple surnamed Zeng.

The Zeng couple had three children, all of whom died several days after birth. The third child died the third day after birth. The mother was heart broken. My grandmother's family and the Zeng family lived in the same village. About half a month after the death of their third child, my grandmother was born. Touched by the bereaved parents, the elders of the village talked to my grandmother's parents and suggested that if it was a girl, it be given to the Zeng couple. They agreed.

On the day my grandmother was born, the Zeng husband was sitting outside waiting. The minute he heard the midwife yelling "It's a girl", he dashed into the room, held the wrapped baby girl in his arms and left. He was afraid that the mother would change her mind at the sight of the baby. Zeng's wife, waiting anxiously at home, was overjoyed when she saw her husband walking in with a baby in his arms. She took the baby and breastfed her. The Zeng couple became my grandmother's foster parents. They treated her as the apple of their eyes.

When my grandmother was five, her foster mother gave birth to a boy, who grew up healthily. Her foster parents considered it a blessing brought by my grandmother, and treated her even better.

When my grandmother was 14, her foster mother died of illness. Since then, she took over the responsibility of taking care of her little brother and foster father. Her foster father doubled his love for the two children, and the sister and brother built up intimate relationship with each other. Later my grandmother was married to Liu Family. Her younger brother would travel a dozen kilometers' mountain road to visit his sister, until he was too old to walk.

After my grandmother's foster mother died, her birth parents wanted to be close to her. But she ignored them. She hated them for giving her out when she was still a new-born baby. Deep in her heart, foster parents were her real parents. It was not until later she became a mother herself that she began to understand her birth parents. She regretted that she had estranged herself from her parents and hurt their feelings. From then on, my grandmother would abstain from eating meat on her birthday in memory of the pain her mother suffered in giving her life.

My Big Uncle

Liu Shijun is my Big Uncle. He is now 85 years old. He suffered many a setback in his life. My heart still aches whenever I think of him.

When Big Uncle was a little child, my grandfather squandered all the family property on gambling and opium smoking. Life was very difficult for the family.

One day, my grandmother was doing sewing on the *kang* weeping. Five-year-old Big Uncle was sitting beside her. He asked,

"Ma, why are you crying?"

"Your father smokes opium and gambles and he doesn't care if we have no money for food. I can't bear it anymore."

"I will earn a lot of money and give it to you when I grow up."

"Think about the long years. Why don't I just die?"

"Where shall I bury you after you die?"

"Put me in a coffin and bury it in Cornfield Ditch." Cornfield Ditch is the name of the place where our ancestors are buried.

"Then I will go to Cornfield Ditch and sit beside your coffin to keep you company."

My grandmother looked up and saw Big Uncle's face soaked in tears. She held him tight in her arms and said, "Don't cry. Mama will not die. Mama will live and wait for you to earn money."

Big Uncle started to do all kinds of hard and dirty jobs at the age of 15 to support the family, building houses, working in the field, feeding pigs, and walking cattle to pasture. Because the family was poor, he had no shoes to wear, even in winter, so he had to put his bare feet into the dung to keep them warm when the cold became unbearable. Big Uncle found a job loading and unloading coal at the Benxi railway station when he was 17 years old. My grandmother went to see him and could hardly recognize her son. Big Uncle was covered with coal dust all over, except his white teeth when he opened his mouth. My grandmother was heartbroken.

Big Uncle fell ill due to overwork and couldn't get up from the *kang* for over 30 days. He couldn't even turn over by himself during the most serious period. His life was in danger. The family couldn't afford to send him to hospital, so my grandfather asked a necromancy master to come home to cure the illness. Grandfather was not superstitious, but there were no other choices. The master practiced her magic power for three days and said that Big Uncle's soul was a monkey who ran into the mountain. Fortunately it didn't run far away and could be called back. She also said that there would be no way to save Big Uncle if two days had been delayed. She swang the horsewhip in the air, to and fro, up and down, murmuring something in her mouth. She didn't stop until she sweated all over. "It's done now. Not easy for me to catch the monkey back. Luckily it hasn't passed the mountain; otherwise there would be nothing I could do."

Three days later, when my grandmother was turning the mill at the courtyard, Big Uncle amazingly got up by himself and walked out of the room leaning on the wall. Grandmother ran over to embrace him, "Thank goodness! My son is really recovered."

Most of the money earned by Big Uncle was used to pay my grandfather's debts on gambling and opium smoking.

When Big Uncle was 20 years old, he was introduced to a girl in the neighboring village. They got along well and became engaged. The next spring, my grandfather took Big Uncle to the girl's home to propose a marriage. The girl's family refused because Liu Family was poor. Shortly afterwards, my grandmother took Big Uncle again to the girl's home. Finally her parents agreed to the marriage. The wedding was to be held in that autumn. Liu Family borrowed usurious money to prepare the wedding. However, the ill-fated girl died of malaria before autumn came.

Big Uncle was captured in March, 1945 by the Japanese army and was forced to join their troops. He joined Kuomintang forces of Chiang Kai-shek after Japan surrendered. He joined People's Liberation Army with Kuomintang forces defecting to the Communist Party in November of 1948. He became a Communist Party member in 1951 and joined the War to Resist US Aggression and Aid Korea in 1952. He stayed in North Korea for another two years after the war ended in 1953. He returned triumphantly with a hero's badge pinned to his chest in 1955. It was the most glorious moment in Big Uncle's life. When my father, together with then pregnant mother, went to visit Big Uncle, who was in his uniform and had just returned from North Korea, Big Uncle said, "We are in peace now. Name the child Heping (Heping means peace in Chinese) after it's born." Heping is me. I am the first child of my father's generation.

Before long, Old Uncle was demobilized from the army and was assigned a job at Dandong cement plant. He worked hard there and was soon appreciated by the leaders and respected by his colleagues. He was chosen as a model worker every year.

Big Uncle was in his thirties when he was introduced to a widow with two children. They got married and had a daughter, my cousin Liu Fu.

During the Great Leap Forward (1958-1959), not only agriculture and industry, but also the public security sector was actively involved in the movement. They wanted to catch all the "bad people" as soon as possible and finished their task faster and better. They started to search for "bad people" desperately.

One day in 1958, several policemen suddenly appeared in the workshop where Big Uncle was working, and arrested him. He was convicted of being a counter-revolutionary for he killed someone when he served in the Chiang Kai-shek's army.

Big Uncle lost everything in one day. He was expelled from the

Party and discharged from public employment. His wife divorced him, abandoned their little daughter and left the family. From then on, Liu Fu depended on grandma for a living. She was only two years old.

Big Uncle was sentenced to 15 years' imprisonment as an active counter-revolutionary.

Living conditions were extremely harsh in the prison. Tens of men slept in a work shed, on hard wooden bed with a rice straw mattress and pillow. They had to sleep with their clothes on all the year round.

Food was bad and scanty. During the "three famine-stricken years" (1959-1961), everyone was rationed to two *kaoliang* porridge meals every day, and soon all of them fell ill because of hunger. There was someone dying almost every day. Lying in bed on the verge of death, Big Uncle thought to himself "Dying like this is not a completely bad thing. All my troubles will end with my death. But what about my family? Old mother has to bring up my daughter for me, brothers and sisters are under the accusation of being a counter-revolutionary's family because of me." Big Uncle felt as if a knife had stabbed his heart when thinking of his family.

When Big Uncle was almost starved to death in prison, Old Uncle Liu Shiliang went to see him and saved his life with some fried maize flour he brought from home. Seeing Big Uncle lying there with only breath out and no breath in, Old Uncle thought Big Uncle wouldn't survive the day when he was released. He went back home crying all the way. Old Uncle discussed it over with my father and Third Uncle: If Big Uncle dies, they shall do everything possible to get the body back.

We had a relative who worked as a salesman in the commune store. Big Uncle wrote him a letter asking for some biscuit crumbs when he was too hungry to get up. He was hopeful because it was not something difficult for the relative to do. Besides, it wouldn't cost him any. Big Uncle was anxiously waiting for the life-saving biscuit crumbs to come, but no reply came.

In 1971, Big Uncle was released two years before the sentence expired for his good performance in prison. He returned to Liu Family River commune and became a peasant, living together with his daughter and old mother.

Although Big Uncle was freed, he suffered all kinds of discrimination and the whole family was involved in the trouble. Big Uncle was a kind person. He did the hardest work without complaint and had developed good skills at bricklaying when in prison. But he had to behave himself by tucking his tail between his legs. If his chicken ran to other's garden, such cursing would be heard "Even the chicken of a counter-revolutionary is counter-revolutionary." Usually the dirtiest and most tiring job with the lowest work points (work credits which determined one's pay) in the production team would be assigned to Big Uncle. He had to swallow humiliation and live on.

The building site where Big Uncle worked was roughly 20 kilometers away. He couldn't afford to eat in the canteen, so he had to walk three or four hours after work to get home for supper, usually at nine or 10 in the evening, then get up at two after midnight to go back to the work site with the day's lunch my grandmother cooked for him.

What Big Uncle worried about most was the bad influence his jail experience brought to the family. My father was the only child in the big family that had escaped from the countryside and got a job in a state-owned mine in 1950. Whenever there was a political movement, my father would be undoubtedly investigated and criticized. Sometimes, it even involved me, although I had never met Big Uncle. In order to draw a clear line with Big Uncle, my father didn't write to him or meet him for over 10 years. Although he never said it, I could tell deep inside he felt guilty. In fact, we all felt guilty and heartache for Big Uncle.

My cousin Liu Fu's marriage was nearly spoiled because of her father. Liu Fu's boyfriend He Wu was a PLA (People's Liberation Army) officer. To be a soldier's wife, you had to go through the background investigation by the army and only those with proper class origins could match soldiers. The troop where He Wu served questioned Liu Fu's family background. They asked him to think twice before making the decision which might destroy his future. He wavered, but finally he managed to overcome himself and married Liu Fu. They have had a happy life since they got married.

Big Uncle's case was redressed in 1978. Although Big Uncle used to serve in the Japanese army, he was forced. He killed people on the battlefield when serving in the Kuomintang army, but he was just following orders as a soldier. Even if he was guilty, his heroic deeds in the War to Resist U.S. Aggression and Aid Korea enabled him to make amends.

Soon he regained his status as a demobilized soldier, a Communist Party member and his former employment. My cousin Liu Fu was also assigned a job. Big Uncle worked even harder after he was given a new life. He was again chosen as a model worker every year.

Big Uncle was retired for many years with a monthly pay of over 1,800 yuan, living happily with his mother, daughter and son-in-law. My grandmother died at the age of 98 in 2004. Big Uncle still lives with his daughter and his son-in-law today, enjoying a happy life in his old age. His pension has been increased to 3,000 yuan a month.

Big Uncle has not remarried after Liu Fu's mother left the family.

Old Uncle Dies Young

Old Uncle was the most knowledgeable son of Liu Family. His big brother and third brother hadn't been in school for a single day. His second brother, my father, only finished primary school. Being the youngest son of the family, Old Uncle was able to finish his high school, which was quite something at that time.

When in senior high school, Old Uncle fell in love with a girl named Qu Ping in his class. They were very close and both ranked first or second academically. They were looking forward to a happy life together. The girl did well in the college entrance examination and was admitted to a university as expected. Old Uncle didn't do himself justice in the examination and failed. He made up his mind to break up with the girl. He felt heartbroken to see the girl crying. He didn't want to part with her. But thinking the gap between them would become wider and wider, he made the decision to end their relationship.

Old Uncle came back after graduation and became a teacher in the village primary school. Teaching was a well-paid job then, and Old Uncle became the main breadwinner of the family. He had knowledge, could play the *erhu* (a Chinese traditional musical instrument) and dearly loved the children. It was Old Uncle who sent for the doctor and took care of the children when they fell ill. He was very popular among the children.

Once, Third Uncle Liu Shizhen's son Liu Shuan was ill, but the careless father didn't take any notice of it. When Old Uncle rushed home from school, it was already dark. He flew into a rage when he found that Liu Shuan had a fever. "How come you haven't sent him to see a doctor when he is having such a high fever? What kind of father you are!" He yelled. With these words, he carried the boy and ran out of the house towards the hospital which was a long distance away. When they came back, it was already past midnight. Old Uncle was single then, but he threated all the children as his own.

My parents joined the labor force the year New China was founded. Later they were transferred to southwest China to make contributions to the remote regions there. When I was five in 1960, my mother took me and my two brothers to our hometown. I still remember that Old Uncle would always sit in the courtyard, playing his *erhu*, looking melancholy. My brothers and I were not used to the climate there and easily got sick. When the doctor came to give us shots, I would always cry and scream loudly and run to Old Uncle for help.

Old Uncle's love life didn't go smoothly since he broke up with the girl in senior high school. He reluctantly married a primary school teacher of another village at the age of 29. Most of the country fellows got married at 18 or 19 then.

Their marriage was not a happy one. Conflicts were common. On the wedding night, the bride refused to go to bed, and Old Uncle sat beside her till daybreak. Nobody knew that Old Uncle and his wife, whom I should call Old Aunt-in-law, didn't get along well. It was not until after Old Uncle died that one of his colleagues told my grandmother about it. She was terribly sad with her heart broken into pieces.

Old Uncle died within half a year after he got married. Superstitious elders in the village said that there had been an omen for Old Uncle's death.

It happened on the day of Old Uncle's wedding. On the morning of the wedding day, someone got a message that the cattle of the production team in the bride's village had been infected with some disease. The cart driver on the groom's side was a bad element of the Four Categories of the landlord, rich peasant, counter-revolutionary and bad element, the classes created in the political climate of the 1960s. He didn't dare to drive the groom there to pick up the bride for he was afraid that the horse would be infected. Cattle were the commune's property and he didn't want to take the responsibility. Everyone was worried. An auspicious time had been chosen for the wedding. It would be ominous if it was delayed. One of the neighbors Old Sun, a poor peasant, was on good terms with Liu Family. He volunteered to drive the cart to pick up the bride and said that he would take all the responsibility if something went wrong. They arrived at the bride's home. The bride and groom performed the wedding ceremony. After that the groom carried his bride onto the cart. According to the custom on the groom's side, the bride should sit cross-legged at the front of the cart facing ahead. But the bride insisted sitting at the back facing back with her legs straightened. Old Sun told her it was inauspicious to sit like that, which meant "kick the groom". "I just want to kick him to death", said the bride.

Old Uncle drowned. On the day, the Cao River not far from our house had gone up wildly. Old Aunt-in-law's younger sister and one of her friends came to visit her and had stayed for several days. It was time for them to go home. They asked my Old Uncle to escort them across the river. My grandmother tried to stop them, "It has been raining for days. It's too dangerous to cross the river now." But the two guests insisted. Old Uncle escorted them safely to the other side of the river. He was carried away by the flood on his way back.

My grandmother was cooking lunch when she suddenly heard someone yell out, "Elder sister, Liu Shiliang was gone when crossing the river. His wife is standing at the river bank and doesn't dare to come back home." The words hit like a thunderbolt. Everyone dashed to the river. Old Aunt-in-law was standing there with Old Uncle's clothes in her arms, trembling with fear. "Liu Shiliang sent them across the river. When he was walking back halfway, he was washed down by the water and never got up." At these words, my poor grandmother just said, "How could we explain to their parents if it were the other two kids who had been drowned?" She said not even one word of complaint to her daughter-in-law.

The whole family and the village people ran along the river, "Son, Shiliang, elder brother, younger brother, Old Uncle…" The river banks were reverberated with heart-rending shouts.

My grandmother went out searching Old Uncle's body accompanied by her two unmarried daughters. Seven-year-old Liu Fu, whose father was in prison, followed them. Every day, Third Uncle would search down-stream along the river almost to its end, but only in vain. Grandmother was worried that another accident might happen, so she told Third Uncle to stop searching. Third Uncle wouldn't listen to her. He said he wouldn't give up unless he found the body.

One week later when the river receded, the body surfaced in the river a kilometer away. It was carried home. My grandmother cried bitterly, and then she sat against the wall smiling. Someone said that she was bewitched. She told us later, "The one who said something like that doesn't understand the pain a mother suffers from the loss of her son. How could I smile? I had cried all my tears out and only smiling could make me feel alive."

Third Uncle abandoned all his work those days. He had lost confidence in life. Every day, he would take a bottle of liquor to Old Uncle's grave, light a cigarette and fill a cup of liquor for him. He cried every day. My grandmother was worried to see Third Uncle in such low spirits. She told herself that she had to be strong, otherwise the family would collapse. She encouraged Third Uncle to stop thinking about it. Those who were deceased couldn't come back to life, and those who were alive have to continue their lives. She began to work in the field and take care of her vegetable garden. Third Uncle, inspired by my grandmother, returned to farm work too.

Old Aunt-in-law was already pregnant when Old Uncle died. She secretly had an abortion and left the family.

Every year on the date of Old Uncle's death, the whole family would go to his grave and cry loudly and bitterly.

When Old Uncle died, my family was in southwest China over 3,000 kilometers away. One day, my father came home with a letter in his hand and said, "Shiliang died." It was the first time for me in my childhood to cry over the loss of a family member.

Big Uncle was in jail when Old Uncle died. Most of the family letters to Big Uncle had been written by Old Uncle. My father wrote a letter to Third Uncle "If big brother knows about Shiliang's death, he will die too. We may just tell him that Shiliang has decided to break off brotherly relationship with him for his political progress and will never write to him again."

Old Uncle died in the summer of 1964.

Chen Family

Chen Family lived in a village called Little River Bank, about 15 kilometers away from Liu Family River Village.

Chen Qinglin was my great-grandfather on my mother's side. My great-grandmother's surname was Gu. Nobody remembers her name. People in the old society married young. If 20 years was a generation, great-grandpa and great-grandma should have been born in the 1870s.

They had altogether seven children, six boys and one girl. In the feudal society where sons were valued only, it was a great honor to one's ancestors to have six boys in the family. I found the names of the six boys: Chen De'en, Chen Dehui, Chen Dezhong, Chen Dezhi, Chen Deyuan and Chen Dequan. No one knows the girl's name. All they know about her is that she was married to a family surnamed Che.

The fifth son Chen Deyuan was my maternal grandfather. He married a girl named Jiang Zhenmin from Grass River Mouth Town, who was my maternal grandmother. They had five children, four daughters and one son, Chen Fuzhi, Chen Fusheng, Chen Xiuzhen, Chen Xiufen and Chen Xiuhua. The second child Chen Fusheng was the only son.

Chen Fuzhi is my mother. Another girl was born before her, but she died of illness at the age of one. My mother became the eldest child of the family. My grandparents gave my mother a childhood name "Lingxiaozi" (taking a boy to the family) in the hope that she would bring along a boy. Two years later, my grandmother gave birth to a boy. Her mother came to see her with a duck. It was the local custom to give a duck as a gift when a son was born, wishing the son would grow up healthy and sound. This was how my uncle Chen Fusheng got his childhood name "Yadezi"(the duck hopefully would take another boy to the family).

My grandparents wanted more sons. When my second aunt was born, my grandmother cried out when she saw it was a girl. My second aunt's childhood name was "Huixiongzi", meaning meeting another younger brother. But my grandmother gave birth to another two girls. My mother was 18 years older than her youngest sister. My mother had been recruited by Grass River Mouth Pyrite Mine and worked as a physical worker when the youngest girl was born. She knew how badly her parents had expected a boy. She was praying and asking God to give her one more brother on the way back home from work. When she reached home, she saw a baby lying on the *kang*. Without asking, she knew it was a girl. The village had a custom that if a boy was born, a hole should be dug in the ground of the room and the placenta be buried deep in it; if a girl was born, the placenta should be thrown away in the wild. Seeing no hole in the ground, she knew it was another girl.

In rural China, boys were preferred to girls because girls wouldn't stay in the family after they were married to other families. Sons lived with parents in a big family after they married. Chinese people are proud of having a big family. My grandfather and his five brothers got married one after another. The house was too small, so the eldest, second and third brothers moved out and built their own houses nearby after they were married. The fourth, fifth and sixth brothers still lived together in the big family. When my mother was 16 years old in 1949, the big family had 23 members.

It's hard for people nowadays to imagine life like that in the old days. One big house had three *kangs*, one for each brother.

Each *kang* was a small family, and each small family carried on the family line in the big family where there was no privacy. They slept on the *kang*, ate on the *kang*, and their children played on the *kang*. My great-grandparents had already died. In the old society, parents controlled the family finance which would be taken over by the eldest son after the parents died. In the big family, it was the fourth son Chen Dezhi who managed the family finance since the three elder brothers had moved out with their families.

Chen Dezhi and his wife gave birth to boys one after another on their *kang*. My grandmother gave birth to four girls and one boy on the *kang* opposite to theirs. Having only one son was the biggest regret all the lives of my maternal grandparents.

Chen Family was poor and only sent boys to school. My mother hadn't been to school. Her three younger sisters went to primary school after 1949 when New China was founded. The youngest sister Chen Xiuhua was born in 1950 in the new society. She graduated from a normal school, with the highest educational level in Chen Family. She is now an English teacher.

During the Land Reform in northeast China (1946-1948), Chen Family was categorized into the middle peasant class.

One of the important tasks in the Land Reform was to divide rural population into different classes of farm laborers, poor peasants, middle peasants, rich peasants and landlords. Poor peasants and farm laborers were the target to depend on, middle peasants were the target to unite, rich peasants were the target to neutralize, and landlords as the exploiting class were the target to crack down.

In his famous article "Analysis of China's Different Social Classes", Mao Zedong divided the society into the capitalist class, the middle class, the petty bourgeoisie class, the half proletariat class and the proletariat class. Upper-middle peasants belonged to the class of petty bourgeoisie and lower-middle peasants belonged to the class of half proletariat. Middle peasants were not categorized. I thought they should be between petty bourgeoisie and half proletariat.

Mao also said that all warlords, bureaucrats, the comprador class and landlords that collaborated with imperialism and reactionary intellectuals that worked for them were our enemies. Industrial proletariat was the leading force in our revolution, and all half proletariat and petty bourgeoisie were our closest friends.

Chen Family was half proletariat. It should be "our closest friends" according to what Mao said in his article. But the family suffered attack in the early stage of the Land Reform.

Chen Family was categorized as middle peasant because the family owned some land and a horse-drawn cart, which was all the family property earned by the three brothers through hard work.

One day, the Land Reform work team, leading some poor peasants, rushed into the house and confiscated everything, including food and bedding. My third aunt was only an infant wrapped in a quilt. The quilt survived. With nothing to eat and nothing to wear, the whole family lived in hunger and cold. The children had to go out begging.

My mother hid a pair of relatively good trousers by wearing them under her cotton-padded trousers. It was found out by her friend, a poor peasant's daughter who forced my mother to take off the trousers in the latrine and took the trousers away.

The whole family was escorted to watch the landlord to be criticized and punished.

The target of criticism was the landlord's wife, an old woman with bound feet. She was tied up and hanged under the roof beam. The punishment executor hanged her up and down, down and up, over and over again. The old woman vomited, and what she threw up were bean dregs!

My mother and her family stood there watching the whole process, scared to death.

When the Communist Party realized the mistakes they had made in the Land Reform, they carried out the "correction movement" and narrowed down the scope of attack. Middle peasants became the class that could be depended on and united. So the family got some land and property back from the Land Reform work team.

My Maternal Grandparents

I only met my maternal grandparents twice in my life, at the age of five and 23 respectively.

When I was five in the summer of 1960, my mother took me and my two younger brothers to her old home in northeast China to see our sick grandmother.

My parents had been transferred to a phosphate mine in Kaiyang County, Guizhou Province, which was more than 3,000 kilometers away from our hometown in the northeast. It took my mother with three kids a whole week by train, bus and carriage to arrive home in Little River Bank Village.

My grandparents were in their late forties, but they looked like very old people in my memory. My grandmother was getting better when she saw her daughter.

By the mid 1950s, the old house was getting smaller and smaller with the increase of family members. A small house was built near the old house. Family property was divided equally among the fourth, fifth and sixth brothers. Land was divided per capita. The youngest brother Chen Dequan moved to live in the small house with his family. The fourth and fifth brothers stayed at the old house.

Two families lived in the old house, each occupying two *kangs*.

My grandfather's family had nine members: grandfather, grandmother, uncle, uncle's wife, their two children, and three unmarried aunts. Uncle, his wife and their two children slept on a *kang*. My grandparents and three unmarried aunts slept on the other.

The year 1960 was during the "three famine-stricken years". The whole country was suffering from the lack of food. People's commune canteen

22

was set up in the village, and everyone had to eat there. With four more mouths to feed, life was even more difficult for the family. My grandparents made dumplings with maize flour and elm tree leaves for me and my younger brothers. They told us to eat the dumplings secretly, not to be seen by others, including the family of my grandfather's brother who lived in the same house. They also avoided us when they had something to eat.

My three aunts were young and the youngest aunt was only 11. They saved from their ration of food for us. Both of my uncle's children were younger than me. The family could hardly survive.

We were about to return home after we stayed there for a month. My uncle and three aunts were very sad. My grandparents felt it almost unbearable to part with us. They knew it would be a long time to see us again. They and my second aunt sent us to the railway station and we took a photo there at Grass River Bank Town. It was the summer of 1973 when my mother visited her hometown again, with my 10-year-old younger sister. It had been 13 years since my mother met her parents, brother and sisters. I still feel painful in my heart when I am writing their stories. But their situation was not uncommon in China at that time.

In the Chinese New Year of 1979 when I was 23, my mother and I went back to our hometown. She had got a letter which said that my grandmother was seriously ill. What she suffered from was heart attack. She just took some pain-killers when she didn't feel well. She never saw a doctor because the family couldn't afford it. I bought two bottles of pills for her, one at three yuan and the other one yuan. My grandmother told me that the three yuan pill was very effective and she felt much more comfortable after taking it. We were poor at that time and couldn't afford to buy the pill on long terms even if it only cost three yuan a bottle. My mother sent my grandmother some money from time to time. But my grandmother hated to part with the money for medicine.

My grandfather got gastrointestinal disease and suffered from indigestion. It was not serious at the beginning. Like other people in the countryside, my grandparents didn't see a doctor when they were sick.

My heart ached when I visited them.

My grandmother couldn't do much work because of her poor health. My uncle was spoiled since childhood and was averse to working. He was fond of drinking, even gambled sometimes. My grandfather had to do all the heavy work in the field and feed animals although he was nearly 70 years old. Once, my uncle lost nearly 100 yuan a night. When he left the gambling house early in the morning, he ran into my grandfather, who was picking up horse droppings one by one from the ground with a manure basket on his back. For the first time, my uncle was shaken deep in his heart. When he came back home, he said to my grandmother, "How many horse droppings old daddy has to pick up to earn 100 yuan?"

My grandfather was a man who worked hard with few words. Though he didn't say anything, he looked very worried every time my grandmother had an attack of her illness. I always thought to myself: If grandmother died before him, how could he live alone?

My grandmother was happy to see us and was getting a little better. She passed away a few months later. My grandfather also died not long after my grandmother died.

The illnesses of my grandparents were not hard to diagnose and to cure. If the financial circumstances had been as good as today's, they should have been able to live at least 10 more years.

In my memory, my grandparents were both very kind people. They lived in poverty all their lives. They passed away at the end of the 1970s, in their early seventies.

The Eldest Daughter of Chen Family

Chen Family was too poor to send my mother to school. The whole family lived frugally to save money to send the only boy to school.

24

But the only dearer boy was not fond of study. My mother sent my uncle to school and was listening stealthily outside the classroom. She had mastered what the teacher taught, while my uncle learned nothing.

Being the eldest child of the family, my mother took on the responsibility of taking care of her younger sisters and brother since childhood.

When my mother was a teenager, northeast China was hit by cholera. Almost every household in the village had lost one or two family members. More and more people got sick and died and the village even didn't have enough healthy people to carry the corpses. My grandmother was also infected with cholera. She suffered from vomiting and diarrhea and was running a high fever. With no money to see a doctor, all she could do was lying on the *kang* struggling with death. She was then five months pregnant and had a miscarriage when in a coma for days and nights. Seeing no hope of life, the family began to prepare for a funeral. They dressed my grandmother in her grave clothes and waited her to breathe her last.

There were three children in the family, my mother, my uncle and my second aunt, at that time. They sat at my grandmother's side crying desperately. They couldn't believe their mother was dying. Their tears moved Heaven. My grandmother woke up. She murmured my uncle's name "Yadezi" the minute she opened her eyes.

Her teeth became loosened after she recovered from the illness. She lost all her teeth before she was 40.

In 1949, when my mother was 16 years old, she started to work at a pyrite mine which was about five kilometers away from home. The work conditions there were very harsh and she had to stand in the ice-cold water selecting ores in winter. This was probably how she got severe varicose vein in youth.

My mother spent 40 yuan, the first sum of money she saved after work, on my grandmother's artificial teeth. My grandmother was not used to them in the first few days. She was sad and cried. She thought the money her daughter had spent for her was wasted. Forty yuan was a big fortune at that time. Later she was happier as she became used to the teeth. She said proudly whenever she met someone in the village, "I can bite crisp radish now."

In rural China, it is the son who provides for parents in their old life. After the daughters were all married, my grandparents lived with my uncle and his family. Chen Family's daughters changed their lives through hard work, education or marriage. Though they were not rich, they had better life than my uncle's.

My mother started to learn to read and write by herself when she had her first job. She joined the Communist Party at the age of 19. Later she became a confidential secretary of Kaiyang Phosphate Mine.

My uncle, the only boy of the family, was the one who lived the hardest life. He had been living in the countryside all his life, doing farm work, odd jobs and driving horse-drawn carts. My mother often sent him some money to support his family. I remember that once my uncle's only son Xiaodianzi wrote a letter to my mother, asking for five yuan to buy a pair of big-head shoes.

Due to the hard living conditions and lack of money, my uncle fell ill and didn't see a doctor timely. He died of cerebral haemorrhage before he reached 70. His wife died of brain tumor not long after his death. My mother continues her financial help to my uncle's son Xiaodianzi who still lives in the countryside.

My mother is now nearly 80 years old. She and my father have been living with me since they retired. As the eldest child of the family and with certain level of economic capability, I take over the responsibility from my mother and try my best to help the family in my hometown.

Chapter Two

My Childhood

I was the first child of my family. Traditionally Chinese people, especially those who lived in northeast China, looked up to men and down on women and they also preferred that the first child was a boy. So I once asked my mother if she was disappointed when she saw I was a girl. She said no. I thought my parents didn't care if the first child was a boy or a girl because they could have as many children as they wanted at that time. When I was one year old, my first brother was born.

Our neighbors and my parents' colleagues admired them of a happy family with both a son and a daughter. My parents also tried their best to dress us neatly and lovely. We moved to Kaiyang Phosphate Mine in Guizhou Province in 1958. When the single young people and young couples saw my parents taking me and my two-year-old brother, they would always say that they would be contented if they had such a son and a daughter.

At the age of three, I started my childhood in the big mountains in Guizhou Province.

Do Whatever the Party Has Told Us to Do

My father and my mother started to work at the pyrite mine in Grass River Mouth Town, Benxi County, Liaoning Province in northeast China in 1949 and 1950, respectively. New China was just founded, and the government needed large young labor force for the industrial construction. As a result, my parents turned from peasants into workers. They met and married at their work place.

I was born in July 1955 and my younger brother was born in July 1956, both at the mine, not far from the villages of Liu Family and Chen Family.

In 1957, my parents were transferred to Jinping Phosphate Mine in Lianyungang City, Jiangsu Province in the east, over 1,000 kilometers away. The construction of the mine just began. There was no housing, and all the families had to live in a large warehouse. Some children got measles. My brother and I were infected. My brother wasn't taken good care of in his illness, so he has suffered from tracheitis all his life as a result.

One year later, my parents were transferred to Kaiyang Phosphate Mine in Guizhou Province in southwest China some 3,000 kilometers away from Liaoning Province. They were going farther and farther away from their hometown.

Both the pyrite mine and the phosphate mine were subordinate units under the Ministry of Chemical Industry. So it was an internal transfer within the same industry. My parents and their contemporaries couldn't choose their careers. As Communist Party members, they would absolutely accept the job the Party assigned to them. The most popular slogan at that time was: Do whatever the Party has told us to do.

Guizhou was located in the Yunnan-Guizhou Plateau, a place difficult of access with extremely poor transport infrastructure. Bandits were rampant there since ancient times. In 1958 when my father was 28 and my mother 26, they came from the better-developed Jiangsu Province to the backward and poverty-stricken Guizhou Province, taking me and my two-year-old brother.

My parents had worked there up to their retirement and had never changed their jobs again.

I was only three then, and couldn't remember how we traveled from Jiangsu to Guizhou. From the photo I could tell we traveled by train. We had a photo taken at the Yangtze River Bridge when we transferred trains in Wuhan City in the downstream of the Yangtze River.

Wuhan Yangtze River Bridge was the first dual-purpose bridge built over the Yangtze River. According to statistics, the construction of the bridge started on September 1, 1955, and was finished on October 15, 1957. Our country received help from the Soviet Union government whose experts provided substantial guidance in the design and construction of the bridge.

Wuhan Yangtze River Bridge was the pride of the whole nation. People who had the chance to come here would take a photo as a life-long memory.

After we arrived in Guiyang, the capital city of Guizhou Province, we changed to a truck bumping for hours on the rough mountain road, then changed to a horse-drawn cart before we reached our destination, the Kaiyang Phosphate Mine.

The scenes of the bridge and the horse-drawn cart constantly came into my dreams later.

Childhood Memory

At what age do we begin to have memory? I always believe my

memory began since I was very young.

The first memory I had was my legs were wrapped in white gauze; my father or my mother carried me in arms, walking on a small path, seeing no end...

Later I knew the memory was real. I was two years old. One day my parents were cooking supper, they put a pot of steaming hot porridge on the ground. My brother just learned to walk and we two little kids were chasing each other in the narrow room. All of a sudden, I fell and happened to sit in the porridge pot. My father quickly lifted me out and put me into the cold water vat. Luckily it was winter and I was heavily dressed. But still, my legs were scalded. In the following month, my legs were wrapped in white gauze and my parents carried me shuttling between home and hospital.

My mother was then seven months pregnant. She gave birth to a premature baby girl due to all the walking between home and hospital. The baby didn't cry, even if the nurse took her upside down and patted her on the bottom. She died. I couldn't help thinking if that younger sister had survived what kind of girl she would have been.

Most of the Chinese women didn't know much about birth control.

One day, I saw my mother get on a truck alone. I wondered where she was going. Several days later, one of our neighbors said to me, "Heping, your mother is back with your new brother." Then I knew the other day my mother was going to the hospital in the capital city to give birth to a baby. I was too young and didn't know she was pregnant. When I grew up, I couldn't imagine a pregnant woman traveling alone in a bumpy truck for hours to the hospital to give birth to her child, and coming back alone with the new-born baby in a few days.

Although my memories before six were vague, they were warm because I was always with my parents.

My younger brother and I were always dressed neatly, even fashionable sometimes. I had a red corduroy parka and I looked cute in it. Later it was passed down to my younger sister and our neighbors' kids. All our clothes and shoes were made by my mother, whose handwork was as good as that of a sewing machine.

We lived in single storey houses surrounded by large stretches of wasteland overgrown with weeds. Our house had two rooms, a bedroom and a kitchen. The bedroom was small and the whole family had to sleep on one bed. There was hardly any furniture. My father asked someone to make two camphorwood trunks, 20 yuan for each. It was a real luxury at that time.

The latrine was about 50 meters away. We peed outside the house instead of going there at night. I was too young and was afraid of the dark. I trembled with fear every time I went out to pee. There was a pile of coal in front of the house. Once when I was squatting there, I saw someone standing on the pile shoveling coal nonstop. I felt more and more scared and I started to cry. My parents ran out of the house at my crying. "There is someone there," I pointed to the pile of coal. But my parents didn't see anything. I still believe that some children can see things that can't be seen by adults.

There was another time my father took me and my brother to see a movie in the open air. It was dark. I saw a spot of light dancing up and down. I thought it was the cigarette end in someone's hand who passed by. But it looked more and more like something else as I walked closer and I saw more of them flying around us. I was scared and cried out. My father told me they were fireflies. I had no idea what a firefly was and I insisted going back home. After we arrived home, my father went out alone. Soon he came back holding a small bottle filled with fireflies.

Winter was cold. With no heating in the house, it was as cold as the outside when we stayed indoors. There is a scene which always makes me feel warm whenever I think of it. Every morning when we were waken up, there would be a stove burning wood shavings in the middle of the house. My parents would warm our cotton-padded trousers above the stove, wake us up and dress us one by one.

Later, my parents had less and less time with us. They had to work in the daytime and take part in meetings or political study sessions in the evening. There had been political movements one after another since then, which didn't finish until after 1976 when the Cultural Revolution ended. One night, I got sick. I vomited and had diarrhea. My parents had a quarrel over who should send me to the hospital. It ended with a fight. I cannot remember whether or not I was sent to the hospital in the end. They were too exhausted with life's tortures.

I Was Always Hungry

When I was about four, my brother and I were sent to the full-time kindergarten. We had meals in the kindergarten and my parents had meals in the public canteen.

It was during the "three famine-stricken years". There were huge numbers of unnatural deaths in China during the period. Most of them died of starvation.

In the kindergarten, every child could have a small bowl of rice for each meal. There was a snack time in the morning and afternoon, two pieces of biscuits for each child, which were made of wheat bran and rice husk powder. The children would have hard and dry motions after they had the biscuits. Sometimes the biscuits had already gone moldy. This was probably why I was to know many years later that not all biscuits tasted like that.

School children were less lucky.

The top requirement the government had for factories and mines was not about production but no starvation.

Both grown-ups and children went to the mountains to dig wild herbs and pick wild fruits. The first idea that came into their mind whenever they saw green buds was if it was edible or not. In the spring, people couldn't wait to put it into their mouths when they found sprouted grass. Bamboos were growing all over the mountains and plains. New bamboo leaves had hardly come out before they were plucked and put into mouths. People were so hungry that they ate anything they could find. Food poisoning was common.

There were lots of ferns growing in the mountains. People went to the mountains to pick ferns and dig their roots. The root contained some white fluid which could be used to make starch. They mixed the starch with the root dregs and ate it. This kind of food caused serious constipation. During the 10-minute break between classes, the latrine was full of moaning students who squatted there having difficulty pooing. When the bell rang, there were still some students squatting there crying. They helped each other digging the shit out with small sticks.

I remember we frequently had a kind of vegetable called "oxhide vegetable". It was normally used as forage to feed pigs, cattle, rabbits, ducks or geese. It was easy to grow and had high yield. So, large quantities of "oxhide vegetable" were planted at the mine. It didn't taste bad, but think about eating it every day! Afterwards, even the sight of "oxhide vegetable" would make us feel sick.

Grown-ups became dropsy because of hunger. Young children all looked lean and haggard with bony arms, bony legs and bloated stomachs.

In order to prevent starvations, the whole mine, from students to workers and cadres, were mobilized to open up wasteland and grow crops, raise pigs, chicken, ducks and geese.

Our neighbor's two daughters Julin and Juhua were several years older than me. They were in primary school. They had days off from time to time. Students were organized to grow crops. Every inch of arable land was utilized. Land was divided among classes and crops were planted based on seasons, corns, potatoes, sweet potatoes, peas, wheat…, anything that could be planted was planted.

33

All the time after class was spent in the field, digging earth, sowing seeds, applying fertilizer and reaping. The fertilizer was manure. Each class was assigned manure buckets, carrying poles and manure ladles. The students first ladled out manure from the latrine, then made compost in a pond dug beforehand by the side of the field. After the compost was done, they spread it to the crops. The manure buckets and ladles were placed just outside the classroom. The students were reading and writing in the classroom filled with foul odor. Nobody complained because those who complained would be considered as having bourgeois ideas and severely criticized. We have been educated since childhood that "working people are the most fragrant and the capitalist class is the most stinking".

The manure bucket was made of wood and there was a bamboo ring at the handle of the bucket used to fix the carrying pole. The pole went through the bamboo ring, and was carried by two students, each at an end. Julin was among the tallest in her class and usually she was the one who walked behind when carrying manure. Once she and another classmate were carrying a bucket full of manure up a hill. The weight tilted backwards and the bucket slid along the pole. The full bucket of manure poured down onto Julin all over her body. She charged down the hill and jumped into the Yang Water River, which was running through the mine, to wash the dirt off. But the smell didn't go off, so she had to run home to change her smelly clothes.

Harvest time was the happiest moment for both grown-ups and children.

When the corn harvest came, all the students went to the mountains to collect firewood, and then put up simple stoves in the school courtyard with bricks and boiled corn cobs in big woks which some students brought from home. The whole school was busy boiling corn cobs. When the corn cobs were done, everyone quickly grabbed one and began eating regardless it was still burning hot. They swallowed without chewing. Cornstalks were not wasted and were carried in bundles to the school. The fresh cornstalk had sweet juice and we called it "sweet cane".

Little kids were often seen putting out their hands when they saw other kids eating. They would beg piteously, "Give me some, give me some." In most cases, the kid who had been asked would share it with others; otherwise he would be called a niggard by other kids.

The "three famine-stricken years" seemed far more than three years to Chinese people. When people are suffering, they feel they pass a day as if it were a year, with no end to it.

On the weekend when my younger brother and I came back home from the kindergarten, we always saw my parents making the mixture of fern powder and dregs. If they came to take us home on a weekday, there must have been something good to eat. For example, if one kilogram flour was allotted, my parents would make dumplings and come to take us home. After we finished our dumplings, they would send us back to the kindergarten.

One day, a young girl who was about 10 years old came to the kindergarten. I just got my portion of biscuit and I gave it to her. Since then, her face would appear outside the classroom window every biscuit time. She would make hand gestures asking for biscuit whenever she saw me. If I pretended not to see her, she would try her best to attract my attention. She would jump up nervously if she saw me put the biscuit into my mouth. Almost all of my biscuit had been eaten by her. I heard she was from Sichuan, a neighboring province of Guizhou. A lot of people in her hometown died of starvation and the place was hit by a flood. She was the only one that survived in her family, and she came to depend on her sister who worked at the mine.

China was still in a severe scarcity of material resources after the "three famine-stricken years", and improvement in people's living conditions was only relative and very limited.

One day, I went to a little friend's home to play with her. She was eating an apple which her father brought from Beijing when he was on a business trip there. Apples were a rarity at that time. I asked for a bite while her parents were not around. She gave me the apple one moment and then changed her mind the other moment. I asked unremittingly, "Give me one bite, just one bite." The reason why it still remains fresh in my memory is that she later married a boy who had wooed me. I have been wondering whether she has told the boy I once asked her for her apple.

One of our playmates had a jar of honey in her home. The honey always came into my mind, and I frequently went to her home in the hope of getting some of it. Every time, she would dig a small spoon of honey, lick it and let me take a lick. The honey was getting less and less in the jar and finally her mother found it out and gave her a good spanking.

What people usually had for food then was chaff and wild plants; they could hardly get any meat. But we once had the meat of a leopard. It happened 50 years ago, and is still talked about a lot today.

Kaiyang Phosphate Mine was in the early stage of development. There were dense forests all around in the mountains and sometimes there were wild animals. When you were walking on the mountain road, suddenly some colorful wild birds would fly out from the bushes, flapping their wings. In the spring, all kinds of wild flowers, among which most of them were azalea, were blooming all over the mountains. Several years later, storeyed buildings were built. In the morning, we could often see some people gather in front of or behind the building, studying the strange footprints of some animals.

Large groups of military men were transferred to civilian work in Guizhou Province to support its construction. A regiment came to our mine, all in uniform. The political commissar was surnamed Zhang. He was equipped with a gun and a jeep, and became the Party secretary of the mine.

The residential area was haunted by a leopard, which destroyed large sects of vegetable plot and sometimes hid outside the windows of residential houses peeking inside. Though there had been no injury, people were frequently scared and would turn pale at the mention of the leopard.

One of my father's colleagues Wang Yufa placed a trap near the haunt of the leopard. The leopard got caught and tried to run into the mountain dragging the trap. Commissar Zhang, together with Wang Yufa and a group of men, was pursuing rigorously after the leopard and finally drove it behind a big rock. Being cornered, the wounded leopard suddenly leapt from behind the rock and jumped at Wang Yufa. At that moment, Commissar Zhang took out his gun. With a shot, the leopard dropped on the ground, dead.

The dead leopard was carried to the residential area. A lot of people came to see the trophy.

Part of the leopard meat was sent to the public canteen and the rest of it was sent to the kindergarten.

My younger sister always said that I was bold because I had eaten leopard meat.

My Teacher Lu Jinghua

I went to primary school when I was seven years old. On the first day of school, I was elected as the monitor of the class. Everyone voted for me. I didn't know why.

The teacher in charge of our class was Lu Jinghua. She had high prestige in the school. She, her husband and two daughters all liked me very much and I always went to her home to play. I did very well in my studies, so I was her favorite student.

When I was in the third grade, one day I heard mother saying to father, "Lu Jinghua is a rich peasant."

I knew "rich peasant" was not good, but I had no idea what severe consequences it would mean to a Chinese. I told it to one of my best friends in the class and told her again and again not to tell anyone else.

One day when I walked into the classroom, I was besieged by the whole class. One of them, the tallest and eldest boy, even tried to strike me. I was totally puzzled. I had been popular among the class. What happened?

The bell rang to signal the beginning of the class. Teacher Lu came in.

"What was all the noise about?" asked she.

"Heping said that you are a rich peasant," replied the tallest boy.

Then I knew what it was about.

There was a complete silence. All of us stared at teacher Lu, who immediately put on a grave expression.

"I am a rich peasant," she said with a long face.

Since that day, I lost favor. Teacher Lu would find fault with me no matter how well I behaved. I listened attentively to her and followed her all the time in the class, but she would still constantly find her opportunity to criticize me. In one class, she was teaching us the Chinese character "zhu" (pillar). She pointed to a pillar under the roof of the classroom and said, "That is a pillar." I looked up and took a look at the pillar along the direction of her finger.

She cast a glance at me, "Some student is not listening carefully in class and is looking around absent-mindedly."

All my classmates didn't know who she was talking about. But I knew. I was too young to bear the mental pressure. I began to retrogress in my studies and I was removed from the position of monitor.

I never told my parents about it.

Soon afterwards, the Cultural Revolution began. So did Ms. Lu's misfortune.

Great-grandfather Liu Fengge.

My grandfather Liu Jingyang was trained in the local army in the early 1920s. He left the army not long after because he was very homesick.

Grandfather Liu Jingyang in his 40s.

Grandmother Zeng Wenzhen in her 50s.

The very first photo of my family after I was born, taken in 1956. I was about 16 months old and my brother was several months old. The three standing from left to right are big aunt, mother, father and the two sitting are my maternal grandmother (left) holding me and paternal grandmother (right) holding my brother. After this photo was taken, my parents left their hometown in northeast China and moved to the east about 1000 km away, following the call of the Communist Party.

My parents in their late 20s and the two kids, my brother and I. A lot of families in China have this kind of photos taken in the 1950s in photo studio with the backdrop of Tian'anmen Rostrum.

My father Liu Shijie (left) with Big Uncle Liu Shijun (right) who was arrested in 1958. The photo on the left shows my Third Uncle Liu Shizhen, the only one taken when he was young, so he treasures it very much. Of my father's generation in Liu Family, Third Uncle is the only one still staying in Liu Family River Village.

A group of illiterate or semilliterate country girls joined the construction of New China in 1950. The first one from right in the back row is my mother.

This photo of me always arouses my younger sister's envy. She took her first photo when she was already over three.

My brother Liu Gang (left), my cousin Zhang Liang (right; we share the same maternal great-grandparents) and I (middle) in Jinping Phosphate Mine in Lianyungang City, Jiangsu Province. The photo was taken on April 21,1958.

From left to right: my two aunts (cousins of my mother who came to the east from northeast China together with my family) and my mother. My two aunts and their families stay in Jiangsu Province and have never moved. From left to right of the front row, my two cousins, my brother Liu Gang and I. A few days after this photo was taken on August 4, 1958, my family left Jiangsu Province in eastern China for Guizhou Province in southwest China.

The photo was taken in Wuhan, downstream of the Yangtze River on the way from eastern to southwestern China in 1958. Chinese people were so proud of Wuhan Yangtze River Bridge that they would take a photo in front of the bridge whenever they had the opportunity to visit Wuhan.

In the summer of 1960, my maternal grandmother got sick and asked my mother to come back for the last meet. My mother took us three children and traveled one week about 3,000 km from the southwest to the northeast. We took truck, train and finally horse carriage to reach Little River Bank, the village of Chen Family. I was five, my younger brother was four and my youngest brother, who was born in the southwest, was only one. My grandmother got recovered soon after she saw my mother. The photo was taken in a photo studio near the railway station on the day we left. My mother didn't see her family again since then until 13 years later in 1973.

My Old Uncle with his girl friend Qu Ping. He broke up with the girl when she went to university. She cried her heart out when she got to know my Old Uncle died in 1964.

My grandmother and Liu Fu, Big Uncle's daughter. Liu Fu was brought up by grandmother alone when Big Uncle Liu Shijun was in prison. Since Big Uncle was released in 1971 after 13 years in prison, the three generations had lived together till my grandmother passed away in 2004.

My father (first right) working in the geological prospecting team in 1958.

This leopard was shot in 1960 when Chinese people suffered the "three famine-stricken years". Part of the meat of the leopard was sent to the kindergarten for the children. Both my brother and I ate the leopard meat.

This is the first picture of my younger sister taken in 1966 when the Cultural Revolution began. I was 11, my two brothers Liu Gang and Liu Tie were 10 and seven and my sister Liu Hua was three.

Neglected Children

When I was eight years old, my younger sister was born. There were four children in my family, two boys and two girls.

Like most of the Chinese, we all have our names with meanings. My name Liu Heping means "peace", my first brother's name Liu Gang means "steel", my second brother's name Liu Tie means "iron" and my younger sister's name Liu Hua means "China".

Life was getting more difficult, and my parents were too busy to take care of us. The house was always in a mess. I began to have lice in the hair, like many other children in the class.

One day, we were doing morning exercises on the school playground, warm and comfortable bathed in the sunshine. Suddenly a boy screamed out, "Look, there is a louse moving in Heping's hair." I felt stunned by a blow, but I still stood straight. I wished there were a hole in the ground to hide myself.

There was only one public bathhouse at the mine. It was dirty and smelly with slippery floor covered with sticky filth. Taking a bath became a torture for me. Once I slipped over and had a cerebral concussion. I was lying in the bed under a dirty quilt. Some of my friends came to see me. Although I could hardly open my eyes because of my splitting head, I was ashamed of the dirty quilt. Afterwards I heard that they had talked everywhere, "Heping's quilt is really dirty."

When I was old enough to do housework, I began to do the cleaning and laundry like mad. I wanted to change our house into a neat and tidy place. My younger sister and brothers would make trouble when I was cleaning. I was driven crazy and cried out with anger. I continued with my cleaning while tears were running down my cheeks. We had cement floor in the house. If I just swept the floor, I would stop my family from walking on it until it was completely dry. I often got scolded by my parents for it. Through my efforts, my home became the cleanest home throughout the mine.

Due to the neglect of our parents, we have never been intimate with them or acted as spoiled children in our childhood.

One day, trying to show off my horizontal bar skill to the other children, I fell off the horizontal bar and hurt my right eyebrow. The cut got infected because the doctor hadn't handled it properly. My face was badly swollen and my head was as big as a basketball squeezing my eyes into slits. One night, I was tossing and turning unable to sleep from pain. Suddenly the light was turned on and my father stood at my bed looking at me. It was the first time he was worried since I hurt myself. He thought I was dying. The dazzling light made me even more uncomfortable. I screamed, "Turn off the light! Turn off the light!" My father immediately turned it off.

My younger sister who was born in 1963 later told me that she felt very lonely when she was around five or six. Parents, elder brothers and sister were all busy themselves in the Cultural Revolution. There was no one to take care of her. She played outside with other children and didn't come back home until very late in the evening. Nobody was home if she returned earlier. Sometimes, when she got home at night, there was still no one at home. Lonely and frightened, she stood outside the door crying loudly. When I think of the past, I find it hard to understand parents' neglect of their children. But the fact is almost every child at that time had the similar experience as my younger sister's.

When I was a teenage girl, I worked on a farm a dozen kilometers away from the mine to temper myself through physical labor. I went back home only on weekends, on foot to and fro. My parents had never asked me with whom I walked the mountain road. One time, for some reason, I had to go back to the farm with a strange man. Young though

I was, I realized the danger of walking alone on the mountain road with a strange man. I was worried and upset, but didn't know what to do. On the morning of that Sunday, I looked out of the window and saw a village girl who lived near the farm passing by. I didn't know her, only met her a few times near the farm. I immediately ran out to catch up with her. I was running so fast that I tripped and fell. Stars were dancing before my eyes, but I got up and continued to run. When I found her at the market, I felt relieved all at once. I invited her to have lunch with me at my home. I still remember clearly what we had for lunch that day was deep-fried dough cake I bought from a restaurant and she was grateful for it. That afternoon, we two girls went back to the farm together with joy and she collected some reed leaves on the way. She made some *zongzi* (a pyramid-shaped dumpling made of glutinous rice wrapped in bamboo or reed leaves) after she got home and sent some to my dormitory.

Talking about parents' neglect of their children during that time, my contemporaries share the same feeling.

Four Clean-ups Movement

The Four Clean-ups Movement which started in 1963 was the first political movement I could remember. I was turning eight that year.

Mao Zedong believed there had been severe class struggle in the Chinese society and capitalism and feudalism had launched furious attack against the Communist Party. He sought to reorganize the revolution ranks and remove the reactionary elements.

Mao said that if class struggle was not emphasized, there would unavoidably be nationwide restoration of the counterrevolution within a few years or decades at most. The party of Marxism-Leninism would become the party of revisionism and Fascism. The nature of the whole China would change by then.

He also said, "There is someone among us who could be bought over for one and a half kilos of pork or several packs of cigarettes. Only through socialist education can we prevent revisionism."

The Four Clean-ups Movement was an important part of the socialist education movement.

The goal of the Four Clean-ups Movement in rural areas was "to cleanse work points, accounts, warehouses and property" and "to cleanse ideology, politics, organization and economy" in cities and towns.

The masses were mobilized to expose unclean cadres. Cadres were encouraged to admit their faults, to "have a bath or wash their hands" to clean themselves and to return or compensate defalcated stuff on their own initiative.

A Four Clean-ups work team from Beijing came to the phosphate mine.

As soon as the team started their work, my parents became busy all day long, work in the day and political movement in the evening. All the cadres of the mine were racking their brains to find their faults. They would land themselves in a passive position if it was exposed by others.

As an eight-year-old child, I had no idea what the Four Clean-ups Movement was about. The reason why it was etched in my memory was that my father was involved in it. Once a group of children followed me and yelled repeatedly "Liu Shijie is afraid of the hot water when having a bath". Liu Shijie was my father's name. I didn't know what happened and why they laughed at me. My father was then head of the mine construction team and was in charge of part of the financial affairs. He reviewed himself over and over again and didn't find any economic problems in himself such as corrupt eating and taking.

The Four Clean-ups work team thought my father was dishonest. They mobilized the public to criticize him and made a couplet to satirize him and his colleague Pang Hongkui.

The first line was "Liu Shijie is afraid of the hot water when having a bath" and the second line was "Pang Hongkui plays tricks when making self-criticism" with a title "Twin Brothers". The couplet was deriding that my father was stubborn and did not want to admit his fault and Pang Hongkui tried to cover his faults by beating around the bush.

The large-sized couplet was stuck at the entrance of the office building of the mine, where I had to pass by from home to school or from school to home. The couplet was written in black and white, the color of elegiac couplets in China for the dead. When I passed by, people would gesticulate and whisper "Look, she is Liu Shijie's daughter". I speeded up and ran away in dejection, followed by a group of jeering children.

The Four Clean-ups work team absorbed new members from the mine. My mother became one of them at the beginning of the movement. She spoke in defense of my father later and was immediately dismissed from the work team.

All the cadres of the mine had to drastically check themselves and tried to find any corruptive behaviors, even just trifles. The Four Clean-ups work team pressed my father to voluntarily confess his crime. But my father could think of nothing that he should confess. He was worried with knitted eyebrows all day long. Affected by his gloomy mood, I felt depressed myself, though I didn't know what was happening.

One day, my father came home and rummaged through chests and cupboards. After a long time searching, he sat on bed and heaved a deep sigh. I was doing my homework at the dining table and glanced at him from time to time, wondering why he was so worried.

Suddenly he asked me, "Heping, do you know who cut off the three blank pages in this account book?'"

"I did it. I made myself a small notebook. Look!" I said.

When my father handed in the account book for the Four Clean-ups work team to examine, they found three pages missing. They suspected my father had torn off the three pages to destroy the evidence of his crime.

No wonder he was relieved. I was happy that I could do something to make my father happy.

My father handed the small book to the Four Clean-ups work team. They took it apart and put pieces together into just three pages. His grievance was redressed.

Another ridiculous thing also happened during the period. One of my father's colleagues suffered loss by theft. The work team gathered all the workers and called a meeting trying to solve the case. There was no result, so they decided to vote for a "thief". One of my father's colleagues named Ma Qianfeng was short-tempered and offended a lot of people at the mine. Therefore, he was elected the "thief". But the man was firm and unyielding and wouldn't admit it. The case had to be left unsettled.

The Four Clean-ups Movement started in 1963 and lasted four years till 1966. Like the rest of the political movements in China, many unjust, false and erroneous cases occurred during that period.

Chapter Three

Years with Burning Passion

I call the 10 years of the Great Proletarian Cultural Revolution (Cultural Revolution hereafter) "years with burning passion".

The Cultural Revolution is definitely erroneous, but the passion, ideal and belief of our generation came from the bottom of our soul.

For years, I have been doing research on the Cultural Revolution to prepare for my book. I find it almost impossible to give a clear-cut description of the Cultural Revolution. It is so complex that anyone who has experienced it can interpret this unprecedented political movement from a different angle.

My book is targeted for international readers, but few of them could understand the historical background of the Cultural Revolution except those experts on Chinese history. So I have decided to tell the stories about myself, my family and what happened around me during the Cultural Revolution from my own point of view to make the stories easy to understand.

Readers may find that Mao Zedong and Chairman Mao are used alternately in the book. I am used to calling Mao Zedong Chairman Mao when I express my own feelings. We never directly called him Mao Zedong in our childhood.

Class Brand

Division of class status in China first appeared in the Land Reform that started in 1947 in the north part of China. The reform spread to the whole country in the winter of 1950 and finished in the spring of 1953.

We started to fill in the form of personal details since primary school. I was proud every time I wrote down "poor peasant" under the Family Origin column.

The family origin was hereditary in China. If the grandfather was a landlord, the father's family origin would be landlord, and so was the grandson's. My father's family origin was poor peasant, so my family origin was also poor peasant, although I was born in New China under the Red Flag and hadn't been a peasant for a day. Some forms had the column of "Individual Status", and my individual status was student.

The origin of my mother's family was middle peasant, which I felt regretful for. Why was it not poor peasant? The poorer, the prouder. Although the middle peasant was defined as the dependable class in the Land Reform, I thought a thorough revolutionary should be a poor peasant or farm laborer.

The difference between a poor peasant and a farm laborer was that the former had little land which could hardly produce enough crops to feed the family and the latter had no land at all and was hired by the landlord as a long-term farmhand. They were the poorest class in China. I wished that my family had been farm laborer.

I tried to avoid mentioning my mother's family origin, but it was not easy. I had to write both my father's and my mother's family origins every time I filled in a form. My mother's family origin of middle peasant cast a shadow in my heart. What inferiority the children of landlords and rich peasants must have felt then!

The family origin in China fell into two broad categories: the working people and the exploiting class. There were 99 sub classes, very complicated.

Many young people who were born from the exploiting class betrayed their families and joined in the revolution. Their family origin was still the exploiting class because they were brought up in exploiting families.

My childhood friend Jianhua's mother was born in a landlord family. She joined in the revolution when she was in school, but her family origin had been landlord, although her individual status was revolutionary army woman and she married a revolutionary army man whose family origin was poor peasant. She suffered a lot during the Cultural Revolution because of her landlord family origin. Jianhua's father came from a poor peasant family. He joined in the revolution and became an army man. His family origin was still poor peasant and his individual status was revolutionary army man. He was later promoted to deputy regimental commander. His final individual status became revolutionary cadre. Jianhua's family origin was revolutionary cadre, which was a family origin to be proud of.

During the Cultural Revolution, family origin became the main yardstick to differentiate people between good and evil. If someone's grandfather was a landlord, even if his grandfather had died before he was born, he would be involved in trouble and be politically discriminated because of his landlord family origin, which was the case of many of my classmates.

The discrimination began since kindergarten. When young children were quarreling, the child with good family origin would call the child with bad family origin names, "Your family is landlord," "Your family is rich peasant," "You bastard of landlord" or "You bastard of rich peasant."

From the founding of New China to the early 1980s, political examination of three generations was required for Chinese people to join the Communist Youth League, to join the Communist Party, to be assigned a job on graduation, to join the army, to be promoted and to go to college. If you were a descendant of the exploiting class, you were not entitled to these opportunities. Even if you had the opportunity, you were considered as "reformable children". The number of "reformable children" was proportional. Some young people with bad family origin placed righteousness above family loyalty or declared to break off with their families in order to be "reformable children".

People would even have difficulty finding a boyfriend or a girlfriend if they had a bad family origin. One of my college schoolmates was a soldier. He had dated with a girl for many years, who was born in a landlord family. He would return to the army and be promoted to an officer after graduation. But if he married a landlord's daughter, not only couldn't he get the promotion but he would also be dismissed from the army. He loved his girlfriend very much, but he had to make a hard choice between love and career. After torturous inner struggle, he broke up with his girlfriend. I remember that he was in a trance for a long time during that period.

My father's family was well-off before the land reform. My grandfather squandered the family fortune by smoking opium. So the family was classified poor peasant in the land reform. We children always said that fortunately our grandfather had ruined the family by smoking opium, otherwise we the young generation would suffer.

The "descent theory" derived from the class status in the Cultural Revolution. According to the theory, "If the father is a hero, the son must be a hero; if the father is a reactionary, the son must be a bastard."

Red Guards led by children of high-ranking officials called themselves "Five Red Categories", namely children of revolutionary cadres, revolutionary martyrs, revolutionary army men, workers and peasants. Their contrary was "Seven Black Categories", children of landlords, rich peasants, counter-revolutionaries, bad men, rightists, capitalists and the capitalist-roaders.

I was between "Five Red Categories" and "Seven Black Categories". My father was marked as a "capitalist-roader" for a short period of time in the Cultural Revolution and my Big Uncle had served in Chiang Kai-shek's army. I was always embroiled with my Big Uncle's history though I had never met him. So I was not counted as a 100 percent "Five Red Categories".

We were born in New China and growing up under the Red Flag. Even those who were a few years older than us and born in Old China were also growing up under the Red Flag and received the Communist education. But we were marked a class brand since we were born, which affected our whole life.

Red Guard

The Cultural Revolution started in May 1966. That year, I wasn't even 11.

In the Middle School Affiliated to "Tsinghua University", most of the students were children of high-ranking officials. These high-ranking officials had once fought side by side with Mao Zedong. After the founding of New China, many of them became leaders of ministries and commissions under the State Council as founding fathers of the country.

The children of high-ranking officials heard from their fathers that something was going wrong within the Central Committee and someone was against Chairman Mao and intended to stage a counter-revolutionary coup.

People of our generation could never tolerate anyone who was against Chairman Mao. We would shed our blood and lay down our lives to protect Chairman Mao. We had never doubted Chairman Mao or his thoughts. Whatever Chairman Mao said was 100 percent right. We would give our lives to uphold Mao Zedong Thought. We were taught to love Chairman Mao by our parents, our school and the Party since we were born. The idea of absolute loyalty to Chairman Mao was infused in our blood and soul.

The children of high-ranking officials went into action.

On May 29, 1966, they put up a Dazibao (Big-Character Poster) under the signature of "Red Guard" declaring "We are the Red Guards who protect the red political power. The Party Central Committee and Chairman Mao are our backing. It is our unshakable responsibility to emancipate all human beings". This day, the first Red Guard organization in China's history came into being.

Other middle schools in Beijing followed the example and organized their own Red Guard teams.

Chairman Mao wrote letters to the Red Guards to support their actions.

What Chairman Mao said was imperial edict to us. Therefore, students all over the country followed Beijing and established the Red Guards teams, the full name of which was "Red Guards of Mao Zedong Thought".

The Red Guard movement spread from the Middle School Affiliated to Tsinghua University to the whole country.

The characteristic of the first batch of Red Guards in Beijing was their pure descent. The "children of high-ranking officials" Red Guards were dressed in their fathers' old military uniforms, with wide military leather belts around the waists, sometimes even in heavy military boots, which became the Red Guard's symbolic wear. Many of the uniforms they wore were not uniforms for soldiers but for officers, with shoulder straps for military rank epaulette which indicated their "red noble" descent and made us children of ordinary families envious.

All the other Red Guards began to dress themselves in all kinds of green "military uniforms". Many of the "uniforms" were fake ones made by parents or tailors. If someone managed to get a real military uniform, he would be badly admired by everybody.

At the beginning, only children of the "Five Red Categories" could join the Red Guards. Children of the "Black Seven Categories" were not qualified to join them.

When the Red Guards swept across the whole country, there was no restraint on who could join the Red Guards. Even the children of the "Black Seven Categories" gathered together into Red Guard fighting teams. Several students gathered together and talked about setting up a Red Guard fighting team. They drew some members, thought of a name for themselves such as corps, fighting team or headquarters, and made red armbands and an official seal. Then a Red Guard organization came into being. Most of the names of the Red Guards came from Mao Zedong's poems or a famous event. The Red Guards I joined was named "Mao Zedong Thought Red Guard Invincible Fighting Team", which came from a poem Chairman Mao wrote in 1963:

The Four Seas are rising, clouds and water raging,
The Five Continents are rocking, wind and thunder roaring.
Our force is invincible,
Away with all pests!
...

The Red Guards also had a song.

We are Chairman Mao's Red Guards.
We steel our red hearts in great winds and waves.
We arm ourselves with Mao Zedong thought,
To sweep away all pests.
We have the courage to criticize and to fight.
There will be no end to our revolution.

51

We will utterly smash the Old World,
To keep the revolutionary landscape red forever.

We are Chairman Mao's Red Guards.
We are most steadfast in our proletarian stand.
We carry on the revolutionary cause,
To take on heavy responsibilities of the times.
We are Chairman Mao's Red Guards.
We are pioneers of the Cultural Revolution.
We unite with all forces that can be united,
To sweep away all pests.
We have the courage to criticize and to fight.
There will be no end to our revolution.
We will utterly smash the Old World,
To keep the revolutionary landscape red forever.

The Red Guard revolutionary rebellion expanded from secondary school students to the working class. When the Red Guard organizations sprang up like bamboo shoots all over the country, large groups of worker rebel factions also emerged.

Kaiyang Phosphate Mine was located in the Yunnan-Guizhou Plateau some 2,000 kilometers away from Beijing. The first batch of Red Guards at the mine was organized by the school, not initiated by the students. Red Guards outside Beijing didn't from the beginning have a clear political goal. All they knew was that Chairman Mao supported the Red Guards and that they must be right. Only the students who were good both in moral character and in scholarship were chosen from the whole school to be the first Red Guards. Our neighbor's two daughters Julin and Juhua were among them.

A Cultural Revolutionary Committee consisting of leaders of the mine, workers and Red Guard representatives was established. Julin was elected member of the committee as a Red Guard representative.

At that time I was a third-grade primary school student. There was no Red Guard in primary schools. Younger children also wanted to make revolution, so one of Beijing's primary schools set up the first Little Red Guard organization and spread it all over the country to replace the Young Pioneers. During that period, I was wearing both a red scarf of the Young Pioneers and a red armband of the Little Red Guards. Although it was weird, I felt very proud. Later I found in a picture that Chairman Mao was also wearing both a red scarf and a red armband.

Although I was a young child, I itched to take part in the revolution to defend Chairman Mao when I saw people around me carrying out revolution enthusiastically. I was thinking of setting up a team of my own. I had even decided on the name of my team "Mao Zedong Thought Red Guard 'Revolutionary Successor' Fighting Team". At that time, I was admitted by Kaiyang Phosphate Mine's Mao Zedong Thought Propaganda Team. So I gave up the idea of building my own Red Guard team.

In August 1966, the Red Guards vigorously started the "Break the Four Olds and Foster the Four News" movement.

Break the Four Olds and Foster the Four News

Two and a half months after the Cultural Revolution started, the 11th Plenary Session of the Eighth Central Committee of the Party passed its "Decision Concerning the Great Proletarian Cultural Revolution" (also known as "The 16 Points"). All the Red Guards, students, workers and cadres carried a book of "The 16 Points" with them wherever they went and studied it every day.

Point one: "Although the bourgeoisie has been overthrown, it is still trying to use the old ideas, culture, customs, and habits of the exploiting classes to corrupt the masses, capture their minds, and endeavor to stage a comeback. The proletariat must do just the opposite: It must meet head-on every challenge of the bourgeoisie in the ideological field and use the new ideas, culture, customs, and habits of the proletariat to change the mental outlook of the whole of society."

As a child, I had no idea what old ideas, old culture, old customs and old habits were. Judging from the targets attacked by Red Guards, I saw that all those who were well dressed, had their hair curled, used lotion, perfume and cosmetics, elegantly posed for pictures and wore high heels, dresses and tight pants were four olds; all books that were ancient, foreign or contained love stories and romantic content were four olds; all works of art and literature including films, dramas and dances that were foreign and before the Cultural Revolution were four olds; Chinese traditional culture and folk culture were also four olds.

Beijing No. 2 Middle School was the pioneer in the "break the four olds and foster the four news" movement. On August 20, 1966, more than 3,000 Red Guards of the school rushed to the main streets of the city and put up their revolutionary declaration "Declare war against the world" everywhere, which said that "We are the criticizer of the old world. We will smash all old ideas, old culture, old customs and old habits".

Chen Kaige, one of China and world's well-known movie directors, gave a vivid description of the "break the four olds" movement.

In the entire August, flocks of Red Guards rushed into the Catholic Church, destroyed everything, beat and drove out foreign nuns; they rushed into the painting and calligraphy store full of masterpieces, tore up all the paintings and smashed all the antiques; they rushed into hundreds-year-old ancient shops or restaurants such as "Quanjude", tore down the restaurant sign and ordered them to produce "people's menu"; they rushed into all kinds of libraries and committed innumerable valuable collections and rare editions to the flames. They rode bicycles and swaggered through the streets; they smashed the street sign where the Soviet Union's Embassy to China was located and declared the name of the street "Yangweilu" was changed into

"Fanxiulu" which means "anti-revisionism road"; they smashed the neon signs in front of the shops with iron rods; they ganged up in the streets with big scissors in their hands, cut the hair of men or women they thought was too long, twisted off the high heels with pinchers and shouted in loudspeakers "We have run the bourgeois down". Each time their action received thunderous applause from the crowds, which gave impetus to the Red Guards for the following actions.

The Red Guards from Beijing went to Qufu of Shandong Province to dig Confucius grave, demolish Confucius sculptures, burn Confucian books and destroy Confucius steles.

The "break the four olds" movement quickly spread all over the country from Beijing.

Kaiyang Phosphate Mine was in the remote mountainous area and the living conditions were harsh in the first place. It was established in 1958, so there were not so many "four olds" as in the big cities.

"Break the four olds" was a nationwide revolution. So the Red Guards at the mine also began to dig the earth to find the "four olds".

The Cultural Revolutionary Committee gave them a name list and asked them to ransack the homes of the people who were on the list. The people who were rebelled against during the Cultural Revolution roughly fell into nine categories: landlords, rich peasants, counter-revolutionaries, bad people, rightists, traitors, secret agents, capitalist-roaders and intellectuals. Intellectuals were the object of dictatorship because they either went to college before the founding of the People's Republic of China or had received 17 years' revisionist education before the Cultural Revolution. The nine kinds of people were all referred to as "monsters and demons-forces of evil".

Most of the people on the name list belonged to the nine categories.

It was a great ordeal for the Red Guards at the mine to rise in rebellion. All the people they rose against were someone they knew, their elders, teachers, classmates' parents or acquaintances. There were about 30,000 workers and their families living at the mine. They had

55

innumerable ties with and saw one another every day. But they had to cast aside personal considerations and move on bravely to defend Mao Zedong Thought.

Julin led a team of Red Guards to ransack Cao Ming's home.

Cao Ming's mother liked Julin very much. Cao Ming and Julin were good students at school, popular among the classmates and favored by the teachers. They both were leaders in the school Young Pioneers commission. Although they were not in the same class, they often organized meetings or activities together and became good friends. Their parents were also acquaintances. Julin and Cao Ming adored each other and kept the secret deep in their hearts. Cao Ming left the mine and went to study in a boarding high school of Kaiyang County before the Cultural Revolution. Cao Ming's younger brother Cao Ning was Julin's classmate.

Cao Ming's mother was surprised to see Julin. Julin felt embarrassed. When she thought she was defending Chairman Mao's revolutionary lines, she was at the same time ashamed of her selfish ideas.

The Red Guards started to rummage through chests and cupboards.

Cao Ming's parents worked for the government before the founding of New China. They had taken a lot of photos. Many of Cao Ming and his brothers' classmates and friends had seen those old photos. Cao Ming's mother was a beauty and his father was learned and graceful. Their wedding photo was very stylish with the bride dressed in snow-white wedding gown and the groom in a spotless Western suit and leather shoes. Whoever had seen the photo could never forget it.

But now, all the things became the "four olds". When Julin was searching Cao Ming's home, she still had selfish ideas. Whenever she found something that might bring trouble to the family, she dropped a hint to Cao Ming's mother to burn it. Julin was a kind girl. She felt sorry when she saw the beautiful photos being burnt to ashes. At the same

56

time, she was blaming herself for not being a thorough revolutionary. In fact, many of the Red Guards had the same struggle deep inside their hearts.

All the families at the mine that had the similar history as the Cao family were ransacked by the Red Guards.

The Red Guards not only rose against others, they also rose against their own families. Julin's mother had a bottle of face cream which her father brought back from Beijing. Julin asked her mother to throw it away. Her mother hid it in the chimney in the kitchen.

We at that time didn't use any face cream or body lotion. When I was a child, I always had chaps on the face in the winter. My skin was so rough in winter that a lot of dead skin would be shaken out when I took off my trousers before going to bed. There was no heating in the public bathhouse and it was as cold as an icehouse. Countless tiny cuts as thin as hair appeared like scales and covered my two legs before I put on my pants. Even so, we would never use face cream or body lotion which was used by the capitalist class and was hardly found in the market.

The mine recruited some girls who grew up in the city and used to live a better life. They had seen the world and were much more fashionable than the girls at the mine. They became the target of the Red Guards, who rushed to their dormitories and confiscated their photos, diaries, face cream and high-heel shoes.

The photos were put up together for all the workers and their families to criticize. I squeezed in the crowd to see the big-character posters and the photos and heard people commenting on the owner of the photos with insulting words.

The "four olds" also included our textbooks, what the teacher taught us and even what they said. Mao Zedong thought that what the Ministry of Education carried out during the 17 years since the founding of the People's Republic of China was counter-revolutionary revisionist line. It was bourgeois intellectuals who ruled our schools. The world outlook of most of the teachers was bourgeois and they were bourgeois intellectuals.

A college graduate named Rui was assigned to our school to teach politics after graduation. He was handsome, knowledgeable and conceited. He often talked wildly and made "decadent" remarks such as "the top responsibility of mankind is to raise up offspring", "marriage is the most important thing of one's life", etc. Rui was also on the "four olds" name list.

The Red Guards said that revolution was the top responsibility and the most important thing for all human beings. "How dare you say that marriage and reproduction are the most important things in one's life? You are absolutely reactionary," the Red Guards yelled at him. When Rui was being criticized, we young children followed and watched the fun. I remember that he spoke very standard mandarin and tried to defend himself. The Red Guards didn't listen to him. He lost his status as a teacher and had to accept the reform through labor, cleaning up the streets and public latrines. Big-character posters directed against him were posted all over the school.

Rui had another serious offense which was indecent behavior. We knew he was accused of being "a counter-revolutionary and rascal", but we didn't know why he was called a rascal. It was not until 2010 that I found out the truth and I did not know I should laugh or cry.

Rui had acute appendicitis and was sent to the worker's hospital for a surgery. He was lying on the operating table, the lower part of his body naked. When a young nurse was doing preoperative skin preparation for him, he had an erection. The nurse blushed, shouted "You rascal" and ran out of the room, crying loudly. A male nurse was sent instead to continue with the skin preparation. Rui became a "rascal" when the operation was finished.

During that period of time, Rui was often taken to the hospital to go through criticism of the doctors and nurses after he was criticized by the students at the school.

The Red Guards intended to sweep away all the "monsters and demons". Our neighbor Zheng who lived downstairs was also one of the "monsters and demons". His story was very legendary and romantic. He was attacked in the Cultural Revolution because of his wife.

Zheng's wife used to be the wife of a Kuomintang officer. In 1949 before the founding of New China, her husband escaped to Taiwan and left her behind. She was pregnant. In order to make a living, she had to find a job. Zheng's parents liked this beautiful and educated young woman and were sympathetic with her. They took her in and let her work as a housekeeper. They even let her give birth to her baby at their home.

Zheng was a college student then. He fell in love with the housekeeper and married her. He adopted her son and treated him as his own child.

What class stand does he have to marry a Kuomintang officer's wife?

Zheng became the target of criticism and humiliation. He did the job of sweeping the streets and public latrines for many years with a monthly pay of 15 yuan to support his family, a wife and three children. Zheng's wife was a housewife always in humble manners. She was also forced to sweep the streets without any pay. Life was too difficult and Zheng had to send their eldest son to his hometown and ask a relative to bring him up. Afterwards, they were driven out of their apartment and had to live in a shabby house covered with asphalt felt on the roof which was leaking all the time when it rained.

Teacher Lu whom I mentioned in the previous chapter was born in a rich peasant family and used to be a member of the Kuomintang Party. She suffered severe punishment as soon as the Cultural Revolution began.

Before New China was founded, the Kuomintang rigorously recruited new party members to expand their influence. Some Kuomintang Party members wrote down the names of their relatives and friends and handed in the name list. This was how a lot of people became the Kuomintang Party members without knowing it themselves.

Teacher Lu was an example.

Although Teacher Lu had retaliated against me, I didn't hate her. I often met her on the street. She was sweeping the street under the reform through labor. I felt sorry for her. The formerly respected teacher now has to sweep the street and bear the discrimination of her former students and their parents. She would smile whenever she saw me, looking at me as if she had something to say, but she said nothing.

Later, Teacher Lu and her husband were both sent back to their hometown, the village where they were born in Sichuan Province, to accept the reform through labor.

For us young children, the so-called new ideas, new culture, new customs and new habits were not hard to understand because we could see them every day.

What we read were Chairman Mao's works, what we sang were songs coming from *Quotations from Chairman Mao*, what we shouted was "Long live Chairman Mao" and what we fought for was Mao Zedong Thought. The most fanatic "break the four olds" campaign happened during the time when Chairman Mao received the Red Guards eight times. Revolutionary signs and words were seen everywhere, revolutionary languages and songs were heard everywhere. The red flag, Little Red Book, red armband, and red slogan, all these were new ideas, new culture, new customs and new habits in our understanding.

New ideas had a concrete manifestation which was hard work and simple living. We were proud of living in a plain and diligent way. All my clothes were either black or dark blue. I remember that I had almost no new clothes between the age of 11 and 16.

I often rummaged through chest drawers for parents' old clothes. I bought a bag of dye, placed a basin of water on the coal stove, poured in the dye and put the old clothes in the basin to dye.

Since my parents started to work, they kept all their old clothes. I made good use of them during the Cultural Revolution. I always put on my father's clothes without making any change to them, which were too large and hung loosely on me. I was often praised though. I was wearing my father's clothes and carried his old canvas bag used in the geological prospecting team when I went to college in 1973.

I had a good reputation at the mine for my hard work and simple living. One of my friends who knew me well said, "Heping is willing to wear her parents' old clothes because she looks good in them. Otherwise she wouldn't wear them! She actually has some bourgeois ideas in her heart." What she said was true. There were always some girls who wanted to trade for my old clothes with their own clothes.

Once I was performing on the stage. The trousers I was dressed in had big patches on the knees of the two legs. One of the audience said to my mother after the performance, "Make your daughter a pair of new trousers."

When we were in college, one of my good friends Yang often walked in the campus in a heavily patched military uniform. We were proud to have a plain living and liked to demonstrate that we were steadfast proletarian revolutionaries.

The hair style of our generation was "revolutionary" since childhood to the end of the Cultural Revolution. For girls, it was always short hair or either two pig's tails or two brushes bound by rubber loops.

Chairman Mao Receiving Red Guards

On August 18, 1966, a mass meeting was held on the Tian'anmen Square to celebrate the Great Proletarian Cultural Revolution. On top of the Tian'anmen Rostrum, Chairman Mao, in his military uniform, was receiving the Red Guards and masses from all over the country.

Song Binbin, a student from the Girls' High School Attached to Beijing Normal University, was most envied by the Red Guards.

Song Binbin's team of Red Guards was located very close to Chairman Mao. Song Binbin squeezed to the front of Chairman Mao and put a red armband of the Red Guard on Chairman Mao's arm.

"What is your name?" asked Chairman Mao.

"My name is Song Binbin."

"Does Binbin mean gentle?"

"Yes, it does."

"Um, yaowu ma!" (*yaowu* here means be warrior-like, i.e. not to be too gentle and bookish in the Cultural Revolution, and *ma* is just an interjection).

Song Binbin changed her name into Song Yaowu on the spot.

I was too young to go to Beijing to see Chairman Mao, which became my lifelong regret. We watched the grand occasion in a documentary film. We were excited even if we only saw Chairman Mao in a documentary film. Every child wished he or she were Song Binbin.

That day, *People's Daily* published Song Binbin's article "I Put on a Red Armband for Chairman Mao".

"It was the most unforgettable day in my life. I put on a Red Guard armband for Chairman Mao and Chairman Mao gave me a great new name. I couldn't calm down after I returned home. Chairman Mao's voice "Yaowu ma" echoed in my ears, which gave me quite a shake-up and made me realize I was still far away from Chairman Mao's expectations...Today, in the Great Proletarian Cultural Revolution, Chairman Mao has pointed out the direction for us. We will rise to rebel! We will fight!"

Chairman Mao encouraged the students all over the country to come to Beijing to visit and learn from the Red Guards in the capital city of China how to rebel. All their train fares, lodging and accommodation were covered by the state expenditure.

Between August 8 and November 26, 1966, Chairman Mao received rallies of 13 million Red Guards eight times. Chairman Mao's support greatly ignited the Red Guards' revolutionary passion, which gave impetus to the nationwide "big link-ups" (the mass nationwide travel of the Red Guards to exchange revolutionary experiences).

The Red Guards at Kaiyang Phosphate Mine were going to Beijing to see Chairman Mao. When the news spread, all the workers and families were excited and admired them. On the day of their departure, a grand farewell ceremony was held.

Through strict selection of the students and thorough examination of their family and political backgrounds, 20 students were chosen to form a group to go to Beijing to see Chairman Mao.

The life pace at the mine was much slower than that in Beijing. Unlike the voluntary activities initiated by the Red Guards in Beijing, most of the actions at the mine were organized by the school. The Red Guard group which was going to Beijing was organized by the school and a teacher was arranged to go with them. Julin and Juhua were both chosen. I thought they were the happiest girls in the world.

Juhua recalled that they got up and assembled at midnight the day before and walked for hours from where they lived to the Tian'anmen Square. When they reached there, it was at about 3:00 a.m. Juhua was young and short and was seated at the very front of the team. Her elder sister Julin was sitting right behind her. The square was packed with the Red Guards, waiting in the dark.

Many of them fell asleep. Juhua was sitting in the front, staring at the east of the Chang'an Avenue which was the direction Chairman Mao's jeep would come from.

Around 10:00 a.m., Juhua saw a row of jeeps drawing near from the distance, a tall and familiar figure standing imposingly in the first car. "Chairman Mao is coming! Chairman Mao is coming!" She screamed with excitement.

The moment finally came. The song *The East Is Red* was resounding at the square. The jeep was approaching nearer and nearer. The Red Guards all stood up and pushed forward. Those who fell asleep were frightened awake and struggled to rise. Some were pressed to the ground and couldn't get up.

Julin used all her strength to stand up. Chairman Mao's jeep was driving past and she only got a glimpse of Chairman Mao's side face.

Juhua was standing in the front line and took a clear view of Chairman Mao's face. She waved her Little Red Book in her hand and shouted at the top of her voice, "Long live Chairman Mao! Long live Chairman Mao!" with tears rolling uncontrollably down her cheeks.

When many of the Red Guards finally managed to get up, Chairman Mao's jeep had already passed.

The Red Guards who didn't see Chairman Mao beat their chest and stamped in agony, crying bitterly. They wouldn't leave and asked to be reviewed by Chairman Mao one more time. Julin also refused to go back and cried that she wanted to see Chairman Mao again. More and more Red Guards gathered on the Golden Water Bridge below the Tian'anmen Rostrum and insanely shouted with tears and hoarse voice "We want to see Chairman Mao! We want to see Chairman Mao!" The Red Guards thought that Chairman Mao's office was on the Tian'anmen Rostrum and he would come out of his office as long as they requested again and again.

Soon after that, Zhou Enlai appeared on the rostrum and shouted in the loudspeaker, "Our young Red Guard fighters, please leave. Our young Red Guard fighters, please leave."

The Red Guards stayed several hours longer. It was already dark when they left in despair.

I was singing and dancing in the Mao Zedong Thought Propaganda Team when the Red Guards were received by Chairman Mao in Beijing. When I was performing the Red Guards seeing Chairman Mao on the stage, I was excited as if I were seeing Chairman Mao myself. When I was shouting "Long live Chairman Mao!", I felt as if I were present on the scene and tears welled up in my eyes.

The Red Guards always gathered together after they were back home to recall over and over the moment they saw Chairman Mao. I often went to Julin's home, with great interest, to listen to their stories that were repeated countless times. Julin, Juhua and the rest of the Red Guards were so popular because they were the only ones who had met Chairman Mao. Grown-ups and children would ask them again and again the details of seeing Chairman Mao whenever they met them, as if they would never listen to enough of them.

Yang, my good friend of university time, had very typical stories tinted with an air of romance.

When she was only 15 in 1966, she went to Beijing to see Chairman Mao with some of her classmates.

She squeezed onto the train with her classmates carrying an infantry pack on her back in which there were a quilt, a pair of shoes and some clothes, a Little Red Book in her hand and 25 yuan in her pocket. Like a can with sardine fish, the carriage was so crowded with the Red Guards who were going to Beijing to see Chairman Mao. Even the aisle and the toilet were stuffed with people. Guiyang was the starting station, so Yang had a seat. A group of younger Red Guards who were on their way back to Beijing from Chairman Mao's hometown Shaoshan of Hunan Province got on the train halfway. Yang offered her seat to them. She had to stand all the way to Beijing the following days and nights.

The train stopped at every station. The toilets on the train were crowded with the Red Guards and couldn't be used. No food or water was provided. The platform was like a battlefield with the Red Guards scrambling for the toilet, food and drinking water. The train was getting more and more crowded with more Red Guards getting on along the way.

Yang got sick and was too tired to stand any longer. She lied down on the dirty floor under the seat and fell into sleep among people's smelly feet. When she opened her eyes, what she saw was numerous feet in dirty green rubber-soled shoes, white gym shoes or canvas shoes.

The train stopped in Liuzhou City of Guangxi Zhuang Autonomous Region. A Red Guard who didn't know Yang but was worried to see her suffering from illness and hunger, jumped out of the train from the window, rushed to the platform and returned with a bowl of rice noodle. He held the bowl of rice noodle to Yang and watched her finish it. Over 40 years have passed, Yang still clearly remembers the handsome face of the lovely Red Guard. Many pure and romantic stories happened during the period of nationwide "big link-ups". The Red Guards enjoyed the pleasures of recalling them all their lives.

Yang recovered after she had the bowl of rice noodle. She took on the responsibility of buying food for her companions. When the train was decelerating before pulling in a station, Yang would climb out of the window and hang on with her two hands gripping the window. She would immediately jump off when the train stopped and make a dash towards the food vendor. She was the breaststroke champion of Guizhou's Youth Swimming Team and physically strong. So she succeeded in getting some food every time.

The train stopped when it reached Fangshan District in Beijing's suburban area. All the Red Guards got off the train and waited there for the instruction from the central government. The city of Bejing was already crammed with the Red Guards and couldn't hold any more.

One day, at midnight, the instruction came that Chairman Mao would receive the Red Guards the next day. Dozens of military trucks came to carry the Red Guards to the Tian'anmen Square. Yang and her companions were seated on one side of the Square. It was three o'clock in the morning. After a few hours of almost unbearable anticipation, the moment came.

The form of parade was adopted this time. Part of the Red Guards stood in a queue and marched along the Chang'an Avenue from east to west. The rest of the Red Guards were seated on the ground on the north and south sides of the Square. Yang was sitting on the north side.

When Chairman Mao appeared on the Tian'anmen Rostrum, all the Red Guards surged forwards. The queue suddenly became a chaos. Those who had walked under the Tian'anmen Rostrum stopped and didn't' continue. All of them wanted to take one more look at Chairman Mao. More and more people gathered there and the path was blocked.

At that moment, Yang heard the voice of Premier Zhou Enlai "Young Red Guards, please keep going for the sake of larger interest".

Premier Zhou shouted over and over again, but nobody listened to him. The chaos continued till the end of the rally.

Tens of thousands of shoes, socks and bags were left on the ground of the Tian'anmen Square and it took several trucks to carry them away.

Yang didn't go back home. She wanted to see Chairman Mao one more time, so she stayed for the next opportunity. During the time of waiting, she visited almost all of the universities in Beijing. She read the big-character posters and made extracts. She also took part in the debate among the Red Guards and exchanged revolutionary ideas with them.

It was on October 15 of 1966 when Yang saw Chairman Mao for the second time. It was the fifth time that Chariman Mao received the Red Guards. Kaiyang Phosphate Mine's Red Guards were there at the square that day.

The lesson was taken from the chaos in the previous rally. This time the Red Guards were seated on both sides of the Chang'an Avenue and the Square. Chairman Mao's jeep was driving along the Chang'an Avenue from east to west, so all the Red Guards could see Chairman Mao. But there were still some of them who were pushed to the ground and didn't see Chairman Mao.

Chairman Mao received rallies of 13 million Red Guards in eight times. Each time had 1.6 million attendees on average, and the largest one had almost 2.5 million participants. There would be no surprise if anything unexpected happened.

For the first two times, the Red Guards who came to Beijing were strictly selected and well organized. Later more and more Red Guards came to Beijing spontaneously. All they needed was a letter of recommendation issued by the local authority or their student ID card.

It is said that the highest record of the Red Guards from other parts of China stuck in Beijing was 2.5 million.

Nationwide Travel of Red Guards

The Red Guards' swarming into Beijing from all over the country to see Chairman Mao was followed by the nationwide travel of them to exchange revolutionary experiences.

The Red Guards took public transportation for free across the country to exchange revolutionary ideas. Reception stations were set up along the way to provide free food and lodging to the Red Guards. All schools, from primary schools to colleges, were suspended. Many factories stopped production and some young workers also joined in the mass nationwide travel of the Red Guards.

The nationwide travel of the Red Guards caused great pressure on the railway transportation. That year was the 30th anniversary of the victory of the Long March. In October 1966, students from Dalian Maritime University in northeast China set out on a long march to carry forward the revolutionary tradition of the Red Army. They traveled on foot for around 900 kilometers to Beijing and saw Chairman Mao at the rally. When the news spread, middle schools, secondary schools and colleges followed the example and organized their own "long march" to travel on foot.

Inspired by the Red Guards from Dalian Maritime University, the Red Guards of Kaiyang Phosphate Mine formed a Red Guard Long March Team composed of 20 Red Guards most of whom had been to Beijing to see Chairman Mao.

But they had no military uniforms, caps and belts which were the symbolic wear of the Red Guards. They went to the retired soldiers for help. Although the soldiers treasured their military stuff left from their army career, they lent them to the Red Guards without hesitation.

The Red Guards set out on their long march dressed in borrowed military uniforms and leg wrappings. They carried infantry packs with washbasin, lunch boxes, water jugs and bamboo hats. In order to march without too much burden, they didn't bring clothes for change. Girls only brought a suit of underwear. Besides the Little Red Book, they also took along with them steel plate, engraving pens and waxed paper which were used to make leaflets to propagate Mao Zedong Thought.

Most of the Red Guards from other parts of the country headed for Beijing to see Chairman Mao. The Red Guards from Beijing and those who had seen Chairman Mao traveled to Yan'an, Mt. Jinggangshan, Daqing, Dazhai and Shaoshan, either places of Chairman Mao's revolutionary bases before New China was founded or the industrial or agricultural models set up by Chairman Mao during the Cultural Revolution. Shaoshan was Chairman Mao's hometown.

The long march team of the mine worked out their itinerary completely based on the Red Army's Long March route. They started from the mine through Wujiang River to Zunyi City, crossed the iron cable bridge, visited the site of Zunyi Meeting of the Red Army, and walked from Zunyi to Loushanguan Pass, where they recited a poem which was written by Chairman Mao during the Long March.

Fierce the west wind,
Wild geese cry under the frosty morning moon.
Under the frosty morning moon,
Horses' hooves clattering,
Bugles sobbing low.

Idle boast the strong pass is a wall of iron,
With firm strides we are crossing its summit.
We are crossing its summit,

The rolling hills sea-blue,
The dying sun blood-red.

Chairman Mao made a lot of revolutionary poems when he was fighting north and south on many fronts. The Red Guards could fluently recite all of Chairman Mao's published poems and pick out the right poem suitable for the occasion. Chairman Mao's poems were full of strength and vitality and revolutionary romanticism that could fully express the revolutionary enthusiasm of the Red Guards.

Whenever the Red Guards reached a place, they would go to see the big-character posters, join in the local revolutionary struggles and print leaflets to spread the seed of revolution to every corner.

Cultural Revolution Reception Stations were set up in every city and town to welcome the Red Guards. They were treated as "Chairman Mao's guests".

In most of the cases, the Red Guards lived in the classrooms of local schools. They slept on the desks or the floor covered with straw with other Red Guards from every corner of the country. Everyone's heart was filled with enthusiasm and a sense of mission, feeling that they were courageous and daring pathbreakers who were striving for the great cause of communism.

When the long-march team reached Sichuan Province, they intended to cross the grassland as originally planned. But they were dissuaded by the local villagers.

The boundless grassland was all swamp and mire. There was hardly any road. When the Red Army crossed the grassland, they had to leap forward or use a stick to feel the depth of the ground. If they failed to step on the meadow, they would get stuck in the swamp. The more one struggled out, the deeper he would sink and finally be devoured by the mud. There were many rivers and streams on the grassland. Some of the rivers were very wide and had rapid torrents. One would easily be washed away if he was not careful enough. When the Red Army was crossing the grassland, nearly 10,000 of them lost their lives during the seven days.

The Red Guards of the mine decided to adopt another long march route, which was to start from Dabashan in Sichuan Province, cross the Qinling Mountains in Shaanxi Province to Xi'an and walk from Xi'an to Yan'an, the sacred place of the revolution.

Not long after the long march team departed from the mine, Juhua fell lame. Their shoes and socks were not suitable for long walking. Besides, Juhua had flat foot which increased her difficulty in long distance walking. Dozens kilometers of walking every day made her feet full of blisters. She could scarcely walk any longer, only moved forward bit by bit when they reached Sichuan. She went to the hospital. The doctor told her that the ligamenta of her feet were broken because of too much walking and advised her to quit the long march. Other team members also tried to persuade Juhua to return home. But Juhua wouldn't give up and said, "I won't go back. If you don't take me, I will go by myself."

When they were crossing the Qinling Mountains, they found it was very desolate all the way. They could hardly see a reception station or even a person during a day's walking. Juhua was always left behind moving slowly in the mountains all by herself. A few days later they heard that some Red Guards were killed in the mountains and even some female Red Guards were raped. After that, two Red Guards were assigned every day to walk with Juhua for her security.

The long march team of Kaiyang Phosphate Mine traveled on foot for three months from November 1966 to February 1967. They endured the entire cold winter.

During the three months, they only took two baths. Their clothes were infested with lice. Every night before they went to bed, they took off their clothes and began to catch lice. The clothes were covered with lice and louse eggs and it was almost impossible to clear them off. They also had lice in their hair. When it was warm, the lice would come out of the hair.

Another challenge for the girls was menstruation.

There was no toilet paper or feminine napkin at that time. What most people used was newspaper, leaflets or used homework notebooks. What women used in menstruation was old cloth or rough straw paper. The cloth was not for one time use. It would be cleaned and dried for repeated use.

When the period came, the girls would find a piece of hard paper, fold it into a long and narrow strap, make a hole at each end of the paper, put two strings through the holes, put straw paper or cloth strip on the paper strap, fix it with the strings and finally put it under the crotch.

The home-made simple feminine napkin was very rough and uncomfortable. The girls got blisters on the inner sides of their thighs rubbed by the hard paper. They had to bear great pain when walking. It was inconvenient to wash the cloth, so the girls used straw paper. The straw paper was of poor quality and had no tenacity and would be torn easily when it was soaked in blood. The girls could do nothing when the menstruation streamed down and penetrated through the underpants and the cotton-padded trousers. The crotch of trousers was repeatedly wet and dry, dry and wet, and formed a heavy layer of hard blood scab. Wearing these uncomfortable stiff trousers, the girls finished the magnificent feat of long march.

When they were two days' walking distance from Yan'an, they received a notice that the central government had decided to put an end to the nationwide travel of the Red Guards and encouraged them to return home to carry out revolution locally.

Yan'an was the sacred place of the revolution and Chairman Mao lived there for 10 years from 1937 to 1947. Yan'an was the place all Chinese people yearned to come to. How could they return when they were so close to it?

They decided to break up the team and those who could get a lift should go first and they would assemble when they reached Yan'an.

Many other Red Guards from all over the country were also on their way to Yan'an. They wouldn't return home until they had reached the destination. The Red Guards tried to get a ride on trucks. It was freezingly cold standing on the truck, but the Red Guards were burning with great zeal with their heart filled with revolutionary enthusiasm.

The Red Guard Long March Team of Kaiyang Phosphate Mine traveled over 1,000 kilometers in three months and finished the great "link-up".

Juhua's feet got recovered after half a year's treatment and care, but they were never the same and often gave her problems in the years to come.

When I was 14 or 15 years old, what was popular among the Red Guards was learning from the PLA's camp and field training including long-distance marching. In 1971, we spent a week marching from the mine to Zunyi to commemorate the 36th anniversary of the Zunyi Meeting (the historical meeting held in Zunyi, Guizhou Province during the Red Army's Long March). All the way I was walking in the front of the team holding Chairman Mao's portrait in my hands.

Mao Zedong Thought Performing Arts Propaganda Team

When the Cultural Revolution began, to express our love for Chairman Mao, three of my good girl friends and I created and put on a dance performance at a mass assembly.

A brilliant sun rises on the golden hill of Beijing shedding its rays in all directions.

Chairman Mao is the golden sun.
How warm, how kind,
To light up our heart!
We are walking with strides on the broad road to socialism, Bazhahei!
…

Our performance was very successful. Our parents, sisters and brothers were among the audience when we were dancing on the stage. When I got back home, my parents couldn't wait to tell me how the audience enjoyed our dance.

We went to the countryside, workshops, schools and construction sites to give performances and propagate Mao Zedong Thought. Gradually we enjoyed some reputation and our team developed from four girls to more than ten, all girls.

I was also good at singing besides dancing. Although I had received no professional training, I loved to sing.

Kaiyang Phosphate Mine had a propaganda team, composed of all grown-ups. When they heard about us, they decided to recruit us. All of us 12 girls were taken over by the propaganda team.

It was the first propaganda team at the mine. The team was dissolved and re-organized several times in response to the need of the revolution. The team members kept changing all the time, but I remained the mainstay of the propaganda team since I was 11.

At that time, almost all factories, mines, schools, army units, communes and production teams all over the country organized a Mao Zedong Thought Propaganda Team, to propagate Mao Zedong Thought by means of singing and dancing.

Propaganda teams visited each other and exchanged performances. We went to the countryside, factories, construction sites and army units to give performances. The first performance given by all propaganda teams would be the dance "The East Is Red".

When the curtain was slowly drawn back (if there was a curtain) and the band started to play "The East Is Red", the performers in olive-green military uniform would dance gracefully full of love and passion on the stage. Our emotion was sincere. We were paying our tribute to Chairman Mao in our dance with our heart filled with boundless reverence for him.

When the music started, everyone of the audience rose up, held the Little Red Book to his bosom and sang the song together with the dancers.

The East is red, the sun is risen,
China has brought forth a Mao Zedong.
He works to bring us happiness,
He is the people's great savior.

Miao Qing, the person in charge of the propaganda team, was a leader at the mine responsible for cultural publicity. He often came to see us rehearsing.

He was an old revolutionary. His wife Xiuzhen was one of his comrades and both of them had worked in intelligence in Yan'an.

Once after Miao Qing heard me sing, he said, "This kid has a good voice. Work hard. We will send you to the Central Conservatory of Music and you will become a professional singer when you grow up."

We usually had our rehearsals in the primary school of the mine. One night, when we were having a rehearsal, a flock of Red Guards rushed into the classroom and shouted "Down with the royalists!" The reason was Miao Qing had been labeled a "capitalist-roader", and the propaganda team became the royalists. The Red Guards called us "Miao Qing Propaganda Team".

In the Cultural Revolution, those who didn't rebel, or didn't rebel actively or sympathized with the capitalist-roaders were "royalists".

Some of us vehemently argued with the Red Guards, "What we propagate is Mao Zedong Thought. How can you call us royalists?"

The Red Guards waved the book of "The 16 Points" in their hands and criticized the propaganda team with sharp words. Some even began to smash the musical instrument.

One of our team members was enraged and said bitterly, "What Red Guards! You are nothing but red sows."

Her words were like a bomb dropped in the Red Guards who all joined in attacking her. At that moment, someone turned off the lights and the classroom was plunged into confusion and chaos.

Big-character posters and caricatures were put up everywhere to criticize the propaganda team. They painted me into a tortoise. I was most severely criticized among the 12 children because I was the favorite of the "capitalist-roader" Miao Qing.

I can't remember how the elder sister who cursed the Red Guards "red sow" went through the trouble. She could have been put into prison for what she had done. Maybe the people in mountainous areas were comparatively unsophisticated and didn't intend to put her to death. I remember that she smiled humbly and made apologies to the Red Guards again and again. The Red Guards said that we, the 12 young girls, were deceived by the "royalists" because we were too young. They asked us to quit the propaganda team. The other 11 children did as they were told. I stayed because I couldn't understand how we became "royalists" by propagating Mao Zedong Thought.

I was particularly favored by the grown-ups because of my loyalty to the propaganda team. They took me whenever they went to give a performance and my singing skill was getting better and better, which incurred jealousy from some girls of my age. They conspired to damage my voice. They heard that earwax could make people dumb. Later, one of the girls asked her younger brother to put his earwax into a cup of water and coaxed me into drinking it.

The propaganda team was disbanded in the end. Miao Qing and his wife Xiuzhen were captured by the Red Guards and worker rebels. They put them into an illegal prison and tortured them cruelly. One of the Red Guards who guarded them recounted that the hemp rope used to bind them were stained with blood and had flesh in the fiber.

Father Was Paraded by Rebels Through the Streets

One day, big-character posters directed against my father were put up all over the bulletin board. I can't remember what he was accused of. All I remember was that he and some of his good friends often met in the home of an uncle surnamed Zhao drinking tea and chatting, expressing their discontent with the Cultural Revolution. Someone informed against them. Soon afterwards the rebels wrote big-character posters to criticize them for being anti-Party and counter-revolutionary. They also called them the "Zhao Family Teahouse Counter-revolutionary Gang".

One day, the rebels and Red Guards broke into our house to catch my father and parade him through the streets. My father was sitting at one corner of the bed holding my four-year-old younger sister. My mother was arguing with them and tried to stop them from taking my father away. My two younger brothers were sitting by the stove in the middle of the house, their head lowered. The rebels pushed over the stovepipe. The house was in a mess.

One of the Red Guards, a young girl, was my first younger brother's classmate. When the rebels and Red Guards were arguing heatedly with my parents, she was standing aside holding a red-tassel spear with her head lowered from the beginning to the end. She didn't dare to look at my family.

Neither my father nor the rebels would give in and the confrontation lasted a couple of hours. Our neighbor Grandma Shi, who was not afraid of getting involved in trouble, came to our home, went into the kitchen and began to do lunch for us. My two brothers said that Grandma Shi would always remain in their memory.

77

In the end, my father was taken away by the rebels and was paraded through the streets. My mother was afraid that my father would be beaten by them, so she took a cup of tea and went with parade side by side with my father. When my father was paraded through the streets, my mother passed him the tea cup from time to time. A friend of my father followed the parade too and passed my father a lit up cigarette.

At that time, people were divided into many factions. Those who were on my father's side voluntarily walked with him through the parade. So the rebels didn't dare to beat him from beginning to end.

The rebels intended to escort my father to the capital city Guiyang. Uncle Xiao Hanshan who was one of our neighbors warned him not to go to Guiyang. There was no one there to protect him, and he might not be able to come back alive. Therefore my father insisted on not going to Guiyang. His friends surrounded him to stop the rebels from taking him away. Finally, the rebels gave in.

I was standing on a truck with the rest of the propaganda team members. We were about to depart to a village to give performances. When the parade was walking past our truck, an adult immediately covered my eyes with his hands.

When I returned home from performance, my mother scolded me for running out for fun when the family was in trouble.

One midnight, some rebels came to our home to search for my father's counter-revolutionary evidence. My father was then detained in the "study class". My mother and I watched them searching. I found my mother's diary in one of the drawers and some words jumped into my eyes "Today, someone reported that so-and-so wrote a reactionary slogan 'Down with Chairman Mao'". I was so scared. My god, how could my mother repeat the reactionary slogan "Down with Chairman Mao"! My mother found out her mistake too and was very nervous. One of the rebels used to be her colleague whom I called uncle. My mother begged him to allow her to tear off that page. He agreed and we heaved a sigh of relief.

They also searched my case. There was a pair of ballet shoes which a friend gave me as a gift. I took the ballet shoes out and showed to them, "I perform revolutionary ballet in the Mao Zedong Thought Propaganda Team."

During the Cultural Revolution, the Red Guards and rebels had privilege. They could ransack anybody's home and bring down anybody as they liked.

The highest rank my father had held in his life was the head of a department. For some unknown reason, he was labeled a "capitalist-roader". As the children of a "capitalist-roader", we were discriminated and bullied. All of a sudden, other children didn't speak to me and kept a distance from me. Two of my best friends also became estranged from me and instigated other children not to play with me. One of them was the daughter of an old revolutionary and the other was the daughter of a veteran worker. Once they stood in my way in the street.

The daughter of the worker pointed to the daughter of the revolutionary and said, "Her father is an old revolutionary."

Then she pointed to herself, "My father is a veteran worker."

"Your father is a 'capitalist-roader'. We don't want to play with you," she shouted at me.

They chased me along the street to strike me. I ran to the hostel where the Red Guards of Guizhou Art School who traveled here to exchange revolutionary experiences lived and hid myself in their room.

The two girls pounded at the door, "Get out of the room, you daughter of a 'capitalist-roader'!"

They even threw something into the room through the louver above the door.

I was crying. One of the Red Guards shouted to stop them and said to her roommate, "I sympathize with children who have the same experience as Heping."

My father was straightforward and always stated his views frankly. His mistake was easily used by his opponent. I didn't understand why he frequently fell into trouble. I didn't know who was right and who was wrong. But there was one thing I believed without the slightest doubt: Chairman Mao was infallible. My father was a Communist Party member, so I copied a paragraph from *Quotations from Chairman Mao* on his notebook.

"A Communist should have largeness of mind and he should be staunch and active, looking upon the interests of the revolution as his very life and subordinating his personal interests to those of the revolution; always and everywhere he should adhere to principle and wage a tireless struggle against all incorrect ideas and actions, so as to consolidate the collective life of the Party and strengthen the ties between the Party and the masses; he should be more concerned about the Party and the masses than about any individual, and more concerned about others than about himself. Only thus can he be considered a Communist."

My Days as a Red Guard

In the spring of 1967, the children of the "Five Red Categories" and "Seven Black Categories" at Kayang Phosphate Mine formed their own Red Guard fighting teams. All of a sudden, more than 10 teams emerged at the mine, falling into "red" and "black" two camps.

A schoolmate of mine was a limp because of polio and was nicknamed "Cripple Xue". Xue belonged to the "Seven Black Categories" because his father had joined Kuomintang before the founding of New China. Xue organized a Red Guard team under the name of "Mao Zedong Thought Red Guards 'Weidong' Fighting Team". "Weidong" means to protect Mao Zedong. His team admitted children of "Seven Black Categories". Some of my good childhood friends, all pretty girls, joined the Weidong Fighting Team and followed a cripple boy to make revolution every day carrying red-tassel spears.

Not long after the dissolution of the "Miao Qing Propaganda Team", I joined the largest Red Guard organization at the mine "Mao Zedong Thought Red Guards Invincible Fighting Team". I became a Red Guard when I was 12 years old. The Invincible Fighting Team was basically composed of children of "Five Red Categories". Although I was sometimes "red" and sometimes "black", I was admitted mainly because I could sing and dance. I became a member of the Red Guard Propaganda Team.

The commander of the Invincible Fighting Team was a naughty boy surnamed Hou. He didn't do well in his study and repeated at least two years' work at school. He was the kind of student the teacher would frown upon. He found his place in the Cultural Revolution and made full use of his leadership talent. He won over all the children who were politically qualified under his flag. He was called "commander Hou".

The Invincible Fighting Team occupied some rooms of the hostel of the mine and set up a Red Guard headquarters. Commander Hou had 100 percent prestige among the Red Guards. All the Red Guards curried favor with him and tried to please him. All the young children were afraid of him. Hundreds of Red Guards were in perfect order under his leadership.

We were organized like military units to have a collective life. We enjoyed it very much because we didn't have to go home and were free from our parents' control. We held meetings to learn Chairman Mao's works, to sing revolutionary songs, to discuss the situation of our revolution, to print propaganda leaflets and to do military training.

We drilled every day carrying our weapons of red-tassel spears made by ourselves. We could walk in a queue as good as honor guards. We patrolled in the streets during the day to keep close watch on the class struggle. At night we huddled in an auditorium and slept there. There would be "military action" any time at night.

The auditorium was made a temporary warehouse and many sacks of rice were stored there. We slept on the rice sacks. Mice were rampant in the auditorium and there were everywhere litters of pink mice babies with eyes closed. When the Red Guards had nothing to do, they would jump up and down the sacks of rice for fun. They would also play the game of fighting by throwing mice babies at each other. What they did all day long was to rebel against the "monsters and demons". When I think about what we were doing during those days as Red Guards, I can hardly believe it was true.

One day, the Red Guards caught a thief, a boy somewhat between 18 and 19 years old. They shaved him a *yin yang* haircut (a humiliating punishment to shave only one half of the head), spread asphalt on his head and whipped him with a leather belt.

One night we were wakened up for emergency muster. Commander Hou said, "The thief has run away. We must catch him back."

Hundreds of Red Guards were divided into groups to guard every crossroad at the mine. I lay in ambush in the wild grass bushes for hours and got mosquito bites all over my body. When it was nearly dawn, the news of victory came to us: The thief had been captured.

More cruel punishment was waiting for him. They took turns to whip him. He was taken to the top floor of the Red Guard headquarters and two of the stronger Red Guards lifted him by his legs and let him hang upside down outside the balcony. They threatened him to confess his crime, "You'd better be honest. Otherwise we will let go of you." The thief was scared to death and screamed, "Spare me! Spare me!"

Some of the female Red Guards were extremely merciless when beating others, though they were as beautiful as flowers.

I was considered to have weak revolutionary will because I didn't dare to beat people.

The thief was led through the streets and was forced to make up a song to criticize himself "I am a thief. I steal. I was caught and I ran away...."

He couldn't stand the torture and confessed. He even admitted a lot of things which he didn't do. The Red Guards were satisfied and offered good treatment to their captive. They stopped beating him and gave him food and clothes. They used him as an example to educate those incorrigible bad people. They wouldn't let him go because he gave them a sense of accomplishment.

One day when I was at home, I heard bitter wailing coming out from one of the rooms on the third floor of the hostel where the Red Guard headquarters was located. I ran out to the balcony to see what was happening in the hostel opposite to our house. Suddenly one of the windows was broken and a person jumped out of it.

He started to cry miserably the moment he fell to the ground. I saw white bone poking out from his ankle and blood gushed out.

He was our neighbor Uncle Xiao Hanshan who had warned my father not to go with the rebels to Guiyang. At that time, factional struggle was carried out all over the country. He was in the faction opposed to the Invincible Fighting Team. He was imprisoned and interrogated by the Red Guards. He couldn't stand the torture and jumped out of the window.

Fortunately I wasn't there during the interrogation. Otherwise I didn't know how to face the man who had saved my father's life (My father thought so).

Xiao Hanshan has been disabled since then.

Hongling, a very beautiful woman at the mine cheated on her husband and had an affair with another man. The Red Guards raided her place at midnight and caught the two of them on the scene.

She was imprisoned and criticized all night. The next day, they shaved her a *yin yang* haircut and put a pair of broken shoes around her neck and paraded her through the streets.

It was the most cruel humiliation and punishment to call a woman "broken shoes", not to mention to put a pair of broken shoes around her neck to be exposed to people in the streets. In the old society, some low prostitutes would put up an embroidery shoe outside the door as a sign. As time passed, the shoe became broken due to exposure to the sun and rain. Thereupon, "broken shoes" became a synonym for prostitutes.

Once a girl and I were ordered to guard a "counter-revolutionary". When I got there, I found that it was someone I knew. He worked in the bank at the mine. There was only one bank, so a lot of people knew him. The bank was on the first floor under our apartment, so I often met him.

I didn't know what "crime" he had committed. He was sitting on the ground pitiably with bruises on his face. I felt sorry for him and was nice to him during the several hours when I watched him.

He fished some notes from his pocket and asked me, "Can you buy me a pair of socks and a pack of cigarettes?"

"No problem." I nodded without hesitation.

I ran to the shop and bought the socks and cigarettes. I was eager to do something for him to show him my sympathy.

Commander Hou found it out and flew into a rage. He called me "traitor" and swore to kick me out. His younger sister Xia, my good friend at the Red Guard Propaganda Team, went to plead for mercy for me, but her brother wouldn't listen to her. Some girls went with me to Commander Hou's office to beg him not to kick me out. I had hardly craned my head in when a cup flew at me. Seeing her brother so stubborn, Xia said angrily, "If you expel Heping, we will all quit and there will be nobody to dance for you." This was how I escaped from being expelled.

Fight to Defend Mao Zedong Thought

When I was a child, I was convinced that imperialists were trying to take China's socialism down the road of peaceful evolution towards capitalism and they placed their hopes on the third and fourth generations of the Chinese Communist Party. I believed it because it was said by Chairman Mao.

I was sure that I would join the Communist Party someday in the future. So I was the third generation of the Chinese Communist Party and it was our sacred responsibility to prevent such a peaceful evolution of China.

Why did Chairman Mao start the Cultural Revolution? Though I was a child, I firmly believed it was Chairman Mao's wise decision to prevent the restoration of revisionism and capitalism. Although I had no ideas about revisionism, capitalism or imperialism, I knew it must be something terrible. If revisionism and capitalism were restored in China, we would suffer for the second time and be enslaved and oppressed by the exploiting class like other toiling masses who were two thirds of the world's population. We were told since childhood that two thirds of the people in the world were living in the abyss of suffering.

We are children of the Communist Party. We are children of Chairman Mao. We will never let it happen. We are the Communist successors. When we grow up, we will emancipate the working masses in the world and let them live happy lives where there is no inequality, no exploitation and no oppression.

In May 1966 when Chairman Mao was 73 years old, he resolutely started the Cultural Revolution and a Central Cultural Revolution Leading Group was established to lead the revolution. As the Cultural Revolution advanced, the Central Cultural Revolution Leading Group became an authority of great power, almost on an equal position with the Central Committee of the Communist Party.

Mao Zedong thought that a small group of capitalist-roaders in the Party seized power from top to down. Something was going wrong within the Central Committee of the Party, within the Party committees of all provinces and cities, even within the army. So it was necessary to start a revolution to mobilize revolutionary masses to rebel, to seize the power back from the hands of capitalist-roaders and reactionaries.

Mao Zedong said in 1965 that "We should rebel if revisionism appears in the Central Committee of the Party".

In January 1967, the "Shanghai Workers' Revolutionary Rebellion Headquarters" led by Wang Hongwen seized power from the Shanghai Municipal Party Committee and set up "Shanghai Revolutionary Committee". Mao Zedong gave his approval for their action: "This is one class overthrowing another class. This is a great revolution." The Central Cultural Revolution Leading Group issued a notice to call on the whole country to learn from Shanghai. Thus a nationwide power struggle was launched vigorously.

Wang Hongwen won Mao Zedong's recognition for his successful rebellion and became vice chairman of the CPC Central Committee of China. Later, Wang Hongwen, Jiang Qing (Mao Zedong's last wife), Zhang Chunqiao and Yao Wenyuan formed the notorious Gang of Four.

The nationwide power seizure intensified the struggle between different factions. Factions emerged among the Red Guards, the worker rebels, the military and the government and Party organizations. The verbal struggle escalated to violent clashes and numerous people lost their lives in the mob violence.

The power struggle and violent clashes caused nationwide chaos. Leaders at all levels were brought down as "capitalist-roaders". Violent killings broke out between different rebel factions. Schools and factories were suspended and the government organizations were paralyzed. The whole country was in a state of anarchism. Life was difficult due to the lack of daily necessities.

Mao Zedong decided to let the army solve the problem. In March 1967, Mao Zedong decided to involve PLA into local Cultural Revolution, which was called "the three supports and the two militaries". The military was ordered to support the leftists, the workers and the peasants and to carry out military control and military training. Mao

Zedong asked the army to support the leftists and help "grasp revolution and promote production". Military control was to be carried out in some important areas, departments and work units. Military training was to be carried out in all schools.

The Revolutionary Committee was established in 29 provinces, municipalities and autonomous regions to replace the former Party and political organizations. The committee was composed of the representatives of revolutionary cadres, revolutionary mass and People's Liberation Army, which was called a Three-in-One Revolutionary Committee.

The Revolutionary Committee seized power from the Party and the government. Of the committee directors of the 29 provinces, municipalities and autonomous regions, 21 of them were military cadres.

The director of Guizhou Revolutionary Committee which was established in February 1967 was L who was then vice political commissar of Guizhou military region. After the military control was exercised, army forces were uncontrollably involved in the local factional struggle, which intensified the nationwide struggle between different factions.

Kaiyang Phosphate Mine was also under military control and a Three-in-One Revolutionary Committee was established. Uncle Zhang who lived next door to my family was head of the mine and was the revolutionary cadre representative in the committee.

The stories of different places had more similarities than differences. I will just tell you one of the stories which happened around me from which you will get the general situation of the country. What happened in other provinces or cities went even farther than Guizhou Province.

On 11 of April 1967, the Revolutionary Committee called a congress of Guizhou's Red Guard representatives who were elected by the pro-army Red Guard organizations. The Red Guards who were pushed out believed the election was unfair and couldn't represent the majority of the Red Guards. They attacked the meeting venue, held a large-scale demonstration and announced the establishment of Guizhou's Mao Zedong Thought Red Guard Four-One-One Fighting Team, publicly opposed to the Revolutionary Committee under the leadership of L. Four-One-One came from the date of the event on April 11.

The "Four-One-One" believed the Revolutionary Committee was going against Chairman Mao's revolutionary lines to crack down the Red Guards with different political views. Two highly factionalized Red Guard organizations emerged in Guizhou: the "Support the Red" and the "Four-One-One". The latter was against the red regime and was the disadvantaged side. They won the sympathy of the great masses and many workers and cadres joined them.

The two factions had their own fighting songs and military bands.

The Red Guards of the two factions were often engaged in battles of words. Many of the "Four-One-One" members were people with good knowledge. Many of those who sympathized with the "Four-One-One" belonged to the "Seven Black Categories" who were discriminated against during the Cultural Revolution. They were absorbed by the "Four-One-One". Therefore the Revolutionary Committee labeled the "Four-One-One" a reactionary hodgepodge organization.

What's funny was that when the two sides were engaged in a heated debate, quite often someone in the "Support the Red", conquered by the eloquence of his opponent, turned his coat and joined the "Four-One-One" on the front line. My friend Yang was one of them.

The "Support the Red" was the side with stronger power, while the "Four-One-One" was the disadvantaged side as what was said by Mao Zedong "Truth is always in the hands of the minority". The army which represented the red regime was involved in cracking down the "Four-One-One", which aroused the outrage and sympathy of many citizens and workers. Yang joined the "Four-One-One" on the battle line because she saw with her own eyes the Red Guards of the "Four-One-One" be beaten up, which she believed was not in line with the Mao

Zedong Thought because Chairman Mao told us to carry out "verbal struggle, not physical struggle".

We judged everything right or wrong based on Mao Zedong's words. But what he had said was quoted out of context. Every faction could find the basis of their argument from the *Quotations from Chairman Mao* or from his works or his words.

The Invincible Fighting Team of the mine belonged to the "Support the Red".

One evening, we heard that some workers were going to Guiyang to support the "Four-One-One". We stopped their truck on the road. Two childish boy workers refused to get off the truck. We yelled at them and tried to convince them that the "Four-One-One" was a reactionary organization and the "Support the Red" was the real revolutionary organization that defended Mao Zedong Thought. They kept silent with their heads lowered because they couldn't find anything to fight back to us, a group of teenage girls with glib tongues. Suddenly a low, deep and solemn voice came out of their throat:

I raise my head and see the Big Dipper,
I miss Chairman Mao in my heart.
I see the direction when I think of you in the dark,
I have courage when I think of you when I am lost.

This was a song the Red Army sang during the Long March when they were landed in great difficulties. During the Cultural Revolution, people would sing the song to encourage themselves when they were being persecuted.

"The Red Guards' congress, hey, is great. Ready, go!" I took a lead and the girls started to sing our fighting song. Our loud and clear voice split the night and covered the voice of the two boys. When we finished our last line, the two boys were still singing. Their sad voice was in a sharp contrast with our energetic voice full of fighting force and the crowd broke into laughter. We had a great sense of accomplishment because we defeated the "Four-One-One". Long after that day we were still immersed in the joy of our victory, talking about it over and over again.

The "Four-One-One" held demonstrations every day. The struggle between the two factions deteriorated and finally on July 29, 1967, a bloody battle broke out which was known as the "July 29th Incident".

On July 29 of 1967, 14 days after my 12th birthday, I didn't know what happened in Guiyang that day.

In 1971, Kaiyang Phosphate Mine recruited new workers. Many of them used to be Red Guards of the "Four-One-One" and later became my friends. Zhao Lina and Fan Mi'er were two of them and I heard from them a lot of stories which happened that day. The following story impressed me so much that I can't forget it all my life.

On July 29 of 1967, the "Four-One-One" was marching a demonstration in the street. The propaganda truck was driving ahead slowly in the city center followed by the parade. A girl's voice resounded in every street and alley through the loudspeaker on the truck, expressing their protest against persecution. The announcer was a 16-year-old beautiful girl who was called Morning Glory by her comrades.

The propaganda truck of the "Four-One-One" drove slowly with the loudspeaker playing their fighting song.

The brave "Four-One-One" blare the call to charge,
Brave wind and rain, fight heroically!
Form walls of bronze and the powerful current of the revolution.

The brave "Four-One-One" is the pride of the mountain city,
Brave wind and rain, fight heroically!
We prefer to be beheaded or shed blood than to discard Mao Zedong Thought.

The red flag of the "Four-One-One" will never fall down,

Brave wind and rain, fight heroically!
We will follow Chairman Mao and carry out the revolution to the last minute.

Slogans of Morning Glory's voice were shouted repeatedly through the loudspeaker to encourage the fighters to launch the attack. At that moment, the rifles and machine guns fired violently at the propaganda truck from a high building where L's troops stationed. Morning Glory had hardly jumped off the truck when she fell to the ground and said "I got hit". Fan Mi'er, who was then a 16-year-old boy, bravely rushed over to Morning Glory amidst the hail of bullets, carried her in his arms and ran to the hospital. In fact Morning Glory was already dead.

Two days later, Zhao Lina together with several Red Guard comrades-in-arms went to the hospital's mortuary to clean her body and change her clothes. The floor was covered with bodies of the Red Guards, workers and ordinary people who were killed in the mob violence. Zhao Lina was only 16 years old, but she didn't feel any fear.

There was a bullet hole in Morning Glory's left chest. When they turned her body over, they saw a bowl-sized wound on the back which indicated that the bullet went through her body from the front to the back.

It was hot in July and the swollen body was beginning to rot. When Zhao Lina and another young girl took the clothes off with great effort, they saw Morning Glory wearing a bra made from a handkerchief. At that time, there was no bra available in the market. People were very conservative. Young girls who just entered puberty were too shy to tell their mothers or sisters. They secretly sewed a bra using a piece of old cloth or a handkerchief.

They dressed Morning Glory in a military uniform with a military cap on her head and an armband around her left arm. They wanted her to leave this world in the image of a Red Guard.

One of the male Red Guards was in unrequited love with Morning Glory. He didn't hide his emotion anymore and cried his eyes out. He cut a hair from her head and put it in a notebook. He swore to her dead body that he would keep her in his heart forever.

Morning Glory's families were heartbroken and didn't know what to do. It was burning hot and the body must be buried as soon as possible. They couldn't find a coffin within a short period of time. They heard that one of the students had a coffin at his home which was prepared for his old aged grandmother. They went there but found no one at home. They decided to break into the house and carry the coffin away. The neighbors thought the grandmother of the family passed away and didn't stop them.

I didn't know Morning Glory nor had I met her. Since I heard the story, she, a blooming white-edged morning glory, has lived in my heart.

Like other places in the country, the Party Committee of Kaiyang Phosphate Mine, overthrown by the Red Guards and worker rebels, was replaced by a Revolutionary Committee. The former Party secretary and head of the mine were labeled capitalist-roaders.

The rhetorical clashes between the "Four-One-One" and the "Support the Red " also became actual battles at the mine.

There was a square at the center of the mine. During one battle, hundreds of people of the two factions were fighting bare handedly or with spears, iron or wooden sticks at the square. The Red Guard headquarters occupied the top floor platform of the hostel, where the propaganda team often had rehearsals, near the square. It was a commanding point. When I walked to the edge of the platform and looked down, I was shocked. What a magnificent fighting scene that could be only seen in movies!

We tore down the chimney and used the bricks as weapons to throw at the enemies. They organized invasion upstairs towards us. We blocked the stairs with furniture. Several times, the enemy nearly broke through our block. We were in imminent danger. We did all we could to resist. We were all teenage children, but we were not scared. We held on and didn't retreat until our aid came and repelled the enemy.

Wang Xiaolou, a capitalist-roader who was removed from power, had joined the War of Liberation fighting north and south in the late 1940s. He was detained in the building and could see the violent scene from the window of his cell. He exclaimed, "My God, this is another fighting north and south."

One day, we were giving a performance on the outdoor stage at the center square. Suddenly a hail of stone rain poured down. The enemy launched another attack. The audience dispersed in panic with hands holding their heads. Many were hit by the stone and blood was streaming down their heads. We were singing in a chorus on the stage. One girl standing beside me got hit on the forehead and blood was streaming down her face. We immediately sent her to the hospital. At that time, all the Red Guards lived in the auditorium. She slept on one of the broken beds. The doctor often came to check her wound and change medicine for her. The leaders of the Cultural Revolutionary Committee of the mine also came to visit her with fruit and food. She was obviously treated as a hero. I had only one thought: Why wasn't it me who got wounded?

Kaiyang Phosphate Mine was an inaccessible place surrounded by big mountains. About 30,000 workers and their families lived there. People knew each other. The clash was not that severe and the weapons used were wooden sticks or stones. There was no death, so we were lucky.

During that period of time, I changed my name from "Liu Heping" to "Liu Ping" to remind myself not to forget the class struggle. I wanted to make myself more bellicose since I was too soft according to the standards of the Red Guards. I could not see any sign of Heping (which means peace). I knew it was quite far-fetched because that "Ping" is also a very mild word which means even, smooth or flat. My parents didn't allow me to go too far to have a total new and strange name. "Heping" and "Ping" are quite mixed up in this book. Those who still call me Heping must be my family members, old acquaintances and childhood friends.

I find it almost impossible to bring the original face of that period of history to the readers. No one is in the position to judge who was right and who was wrong in the factional struggle during the Cultural Revolution. Only one thing was for sure: The victims were ordinary Chinese people.

In October of 1967, the Central Cultural Revolution Leading Group issued a notice to call on the students to return to school, making revolution while studying.

At that time, the "go to work in the countryside and mountain areas" movement was launched vigorously. The veteran Red Guards were to graduate from junior high or senior high schools. Mao Zedong called on them to go to the countryside to receive re-education from the poor and lower-middle peasants.

Unyielding Uncle Zhang

In about 1964, we moved into the newly-built No.13 Apartment Building. Our next door neighbor was the Zhang's family. Zhang was the general manager of the mine, and Julin and Juhua's father. We called him Uncle Zhang. Uncle Zhang was an old revolutionary. He was a high-ranking officer when the People's Republic of China was founded.

After he retired from the army, he was transferred to Grass River Mouth Pyrite Mine in Benxi County, Liaoning Province to work as head of the mine. My parents were among the batch of workers recruited from the countryside by Uncle Zhang. Later they followed him from the northeast to Jiangsu Province in eastern China, then from Jiangsu to Guizhou in southwest China.

There were seven children in Uncle Zhang's family and four children in my family. The two families were on good terms and both the children and parents were close friends. Uncle Zhang was my father's superior and his wife Aunt Song was my mother's good friend.

Uncle Zhang was a serious and kind person in my impression.

In the early days of the Cultural Revolution, Uncle Zhang was sent to the Daqing Oil Field, which was a model set up by Mao for the Chinese industry, to receive education. So he was not there when his eldest daughter Julin was leading the Red Guards breaking the old and fostering the new.

When Julin and Juhua returned from the "big link-ups", they found the situation of the revolution totally changed. The school was suspended and more than 10 Red Guard fighting teams which were spontaneously organized by the students emerged at the mine. The first Red Guard organization of the school was now labeled "royalist".

Some leaders of the Cultural Revolutionary Committee of the mine were labeled capitalist-roaders. Those who used to lead the Red Guards in rebellion were now rebelled against. This was quite common in the Cultural Revolution. Today you overthrew me and tomorrow I overthrew you. Julin, who was only a teenage girl, was also criticized because she was a member of the committee. The first Red Guard organization was disbanded. All the other Red Guard organizations shut their door on Julin. She became an unwanted person.

Not long after that, the Red Guards were divided into two factions: the "Support the Red" and the "Four-One-One". Julin was a "Four-One-One" fanatic. She threw herself again into the revolutionary battle and argued vehemently with the members of the "Support the Red", as if she was ready to shed her blood and lay down her life for defending Mao Zedong Thought.

One day, Uncle Zhang saw Julin in a heated debate with the "Support the Red", showing her eloquence and quoting from the works of Chairman Mao to prove her point. Her forceful arguments silenced her opponents.

At that time, the working class was completely involved in the Cultural Revolution. The situation of China became more complicated.

As an experienced Communist Party member and veteran revolutionary, Uncle Zhang had his doubts about the Cultural Revolution. He was secretly worried about his eldest daughter who was so simple-minded and naive. He told himself that he must get Julin out of this dangerous place. Otherwise who knew what big trouble she would get herself into?

It happened that a mining machinery factory in Sanmenxia City of Henan Province in central China was recruiting workers. Uncle Zhang resolutely sent Julin to Henan which was over 1,000 kilometers away to be a worker.

Not long after Julin left the mine, Uncle Zhang was labeled a capitalist-roader, renegade and scab, what Liu Shaoqi, then Head of State of China, was accused of.

It was a crazy and unreasonable period in China's history. Today you are revolutionary, tomorrow you may be counter-revolutionary. Today you are a capitalist-roader; tomorrow I may be the capitalist-roader. Today you are a leader of the Revolutionary Committee; tomorrow you may be kicked out of it. Today you are a guest of honor; tomorrow you may be a prisoner.

Many of the leaders were removed out of office and labeled capitalist-roaders. Most of them yielded to the rebels and admitted whatever charges that were wrongly put on them. Uncle Zhang was an upright man with moral integrity. He refused to admit what he hadn't done and suffered a lot in the public show-trial for not yielding to the rebels. Uncle Zhang got acute hepatitis. It was getting more and more serious because the Cultural Revolutionary Committee didn't allow him to see a doctor. They didn't even let him off when he was seriously ill.

Everywhere people were fighting, dividing into factions. There were factions in factories, schools, the army and the countryside. More and more people were killed. Nothing could be done to get the situation controlled. There was massive upheaval throughout the country. The Central Cultural Revolution Leading Group of the central government ordered all revolutionary committees at provincial and city levels to organize study workshops in Beijing and send capitalist-roaders there to receive reeducation. Kaiyang Phosphate Mine was subordinate to the H Ministry and the capitalist-roaders there attended the study workshops held by the Revolutionary Committee of the H Ministry.

The study workshop had little effect dealing with the nationwide chaos. Instead the rebels intensified their persecution against capitalist-roaders.

Uncle Zhang's illness worsened when he was in the study workshop. He was sent to 302 Military Hospital in Beijing.

When the study workshops were over, many of the capitalist-roaders who were sent to Beijing from all over the country were ill in hospital. The Central Cultural Revolution Leading Group made a decision that all sick capitalist-roaders should be sent back to local hospitals for treatment.

The Revolutionary Committee of Kaiyang Phosphate Mine was going to take all the capitalist-roaders back for another round of criticism. The doctors of 302 Military Hospital, out of professional ethics, suggested Uncle Zhang not be taken back to the mine but transferred to Guiyang Medical College for further treatment. After he arrived in Guiyang, Uncle Zhang was hospitalized in Guiyang Medical College under the arrangement of the Revolutionary Committee of Guizhou Province.

The rebels had prepared placards with words "Down with capitalist-roader so-and-so" on it. They got on trucks heading for Stalagmite Pass several kilometers away from the mine to intercept the capitalist-roaders and escort them to the center square of the mine for the public show-trial. The workers had already assembled at the square, waiting for the meeting to start.

The center square was near the No. 13 Apartment Building where we lived and we could see the outdoor stage at the square from the balcony shared by three families. Uncle Zhang's third daughter Juqiu, who was my good friend, was 14, the same age as me. She was standing on the balcony crying and kept looking at the direction of the outdoor stage. I ran to the center square trying to get some news about Uncle Zhang.

97

The capitalist-roaders were pushed onto the stage one by one, with placards hanging around their necks. I didn't see Uncle Zhang. I heard someone in the crowd say that Uncle Zhang was ill in hospital in Guiyang. I felt much relieved. The placards separately prepared by different departments or organizations of the mine for Uncle Zhang were hanging around some other capitalist-roaders' necks. The children of the Zhang family didn't dare to walk close to the center square. They saw from a distance several men behind placards with their father's name on it, but they didn't know which one was their father. I ran back to tell Juqiu that her father was not back yet.

When Uncle Zhang arrived in Guiyang, he secretly asked another capitalist-roader to bring a message and a parcel of dirty clothes to Aunt Song. He told Aunt Song in the message that he was ill in hospital in Guiyang and asked her to ask permission from the Revolutionary Committee to send him some money and clean clothes. He also told Aunt Song to tell the children not to touch his dirty clothes for fear of infection. After Julin left home, the second daughter Juhua who was then 17 years old became the mainstay of the family.

Juhua was going to Guiyang to see her father with some eggs, money and clean clothes. Guiyang was over 150 kilometers away from Kaiyang Phosphate Mine and it took about four hours to get there by driving because of the bumpy country road. There was no bus transportation from the mine to Guiyang. There happened to be an ambulance sending patients to Guiyang Medical College. A kind-hearted doctor sent a secret message to Juhua. Juhua went to the hospital of the mine to take a lift. Military control was exercised all over the mine and the hospital was no exception. The ambulance was guarded by two soldiers who were holding submachine guns in their hands. The moment Juhua stepped one foot on the ambulance, she was dragged out by one of the two soldiers. A doctor pushed her in and insisted the driver take Juhua with them. Awed by the doctor's sense of justice, the soldier gave in. Juhua felt some warmth in her heart in the hopeless situation.

When Uncle Zhang was in hospital, the rebels tried to take him away to Majiaqiao that was the station for the military control army of Kaiyang Phosphate Mine for a denunciation meeting. They were stopped by the hospital. Unwilling to return empty-handed, they took Uncle Ma with them.

Uncle Ma was the director of the worker's hospital of Kaiyang Phosphate Mine. He served in the Kuomintang army before liberation and was persecuted in the Cultural Revolution. He suffered from liver disease and it was very serious. Uncle Ma was taken away in the morning and was carried back in a stretcher in the evening. Down in spirits and taking to drinking to forget his sorrows, Uncle Ma died soon at the age of 42. Uncle Ma's wife, indignant at the maltreatment his husband suffered, went to the hospital where her husband worked and spread his ashes down from the roof of the hospital building.

Later the rebels used dirty tricks and trapped Uncle Zhang to return to the mine. Uncle Zhang's 16-year-old son Guolian went to Guiyang to pick up his father. They went back in a dark cargo wagon of train which was used to carry ores.

When they arrived at the mine, they found the rebels were already waiting on the platform of the railway station. They dragged Uncle Zhang directly to the waiting room for denouncement. Guolian helplessly watched his father being bullied and humiliated by the rebels. He could do nothing.

Uncle Zhang had a cousin who worked as a leader at Nangongshan railway locomotive depot which was not far away from Kaiyang Phosphate Mine. He helped Uncle Zhang's family a lot during the Cultural Revolution. To relieve the burden of the family and protect at least one child from being hurt, he managed to take Guolian along with him and found him a job as a railway worker.

When Uncle Zhang was released home, the rebels forced him to write self-criticism. Every day, there would be two rebels holding red-tassel spears watching over Uncle Zhang in his home, although he was seriously ill and even didn't have the strength to truss up a chicken. One early morning, the rebels came to Uncle Zhang's home to take him for a public denouncement meeting. Uncle Zhang hadn't had his breakfast and Aunt Song hurriedly slipped two steamed buns into his pocket. When he returned home in the evening, Juhua found the two steamed buns still in his pocket untouched. She refrained from tears and started to rub his father's swollen legs.

Once a mass meeting was held in the auditorium to criticize Uncle Zhang. Juhua was sitting under the stage and lowered her head from the beginning to the end. She didn't dare to look at her father on the stage. The people around her pointed at her and said, "Look, she is the daughter of the capitalist-roader." The 17-year-old Juhua was sad and guilty for not being able to protect her father. What's more, she herself had to suffer discrimination and humiliation.

The rebels forced Uncle Zhang to write self-criticism over and over again. They didn't allow him to see a doctor. Uncle Zhang was steadfast and didn't admit any charge they wrongly put on him. His self-criticism failed to pass repeatedly. His health condition worsened day by day.

One of the neighbors who lived in No.13 Apartment Building was a pediatrician. We called her Aunt Zhu. Aunt Zhu respected and sympathized with Uncle Zhang. She came to see Uncle Zhang secretly at night. Sometimes Aunt Song would secretly ask for a barefoot doctor in the countryside to come to see Uncle Zhang's illness.

Like thousands and thousands other Chinese people who were framed in the Cultural Revolution, Uncle Zhang, who made great contribution to the New China's chemical industry, suffered inhuman persecution.

Juhua became firm and indomitable tempered in the adversity. She went to the leader of the Revolutionary Committee and argued with him. She insisted that they send her father to see a doctor. They finally agreed and a doctor was sent to Uncle Zhang's home to check his illness. Uncle Zhang was critically ill and the doctor suggested he be sent to the hospital immediately.

After being hospitalized for two months in the hospital of the mine, Uncle Zhang didn't get any better. The committee agreed to send him to Zunyi Medical College for further treatment.

Uncle Zhang stayed there for a month. Juhua and her mother looked after him in the hospital. With no one at home to take care of the four younger children, they were sent to the home of Uncle Zhang's cousin at Nangongshan railway locomotive depot. The eldest among them was 15 and the youngest was only four.

Uncle Zhang was already at the serious stage of ascites due to cirrhosis. His belly became bloated and he was in great pain. The Revolutionary Committee kept inquiring into Uncle Zhang's political background even when he was in hospital, but they didn't find anything.

One day in October of 1972, Uncle Zhang caught a cold and his illness deteriorated. The hospital informed his family of his critical situation. Juhua dropped a telegram to her elder sister Julin 1,000 kilometers away, asking her to return home. Juhua reported his father's situation to the Cultural Revolutionary Committee and waited for their decision about how to prepare for his father's funeral.

The person who was in charge of the committee finally came to Zunyi Medical College to visit Uncle Zhang who was about to die. He said to Uncle Zhang, "Your problem is cleared now." The words finally came before Uncle Zhang breathed his last breath. "I am grateful to the Party, to the Cultural Revolutionary Committee of the mine, and to Chairman Mao!"

Uncle Zhang had a brother who worked in Sanmenxia of Henan Province some 1,000 kilometers away. He hurried to Zunyi as soon as he got the message. Uncle Zhang, knowing his younger brother was coming, hung on and did his utmost to keep the last light of his life. He did not want to give up before he saw his brother. He had something to tell him and he was worried about his old father who lived at his old home in Shandong Province. Traffic was inconvenient and it took at least two days to travel 1,000 kilometers by train. Uncle Zhang didn't make it to his brother's arrival. He said, "I cannot bear any more." Then he closed his eyes forever. Uncle Zhang died at the age of 47.

All of Uncle Zhang's family arrived for the funeral. The day before the cremation, Uncle Zhang's old colleagues out of good will arranged the children to see a North Korean movie *The Girl Who Sells Flowers*. But the movie was a very tragic story and the audience was all moved to tears. The Zhang's children, touched by the sad scene, thought of their father and choked with sobs.

Juhua described a detail during his father's cremation which left a deep impression on me. When Uncle Zhang's body was being pushed into the incinerator, his face was illuminated by the glow of the flame. The moment the tongue of flame touched his skin, the door of the incinerator closed. Being surrounded by a circle of red glow was the last image Uncle Zhang left for his family.

Uncle Zhang was going up to heaven, surrounded by the glow.

Uncle Zhang passed away on October 20, 1972. He was not completely rehabilitated until 1983. His bone ash was buried in the cemetery of Guiyang after it had been placed in the funeral parlor for 11 years.

Aunt Song suffered mental disorder after Uncle Zhang's death. She was basically recovered after many years' cure. She went to live with her eldest daughter Julin and didn't return to Guizhou since then. She died in 1993.

In 2008, the Zhang's children buried Uncle Zhang and Aunt Song together.

For decades of years, Uncle Zhang frequently appears in my dreams. His image is fixed at what he looked like when he was 47.

Uncle Zhang's full name is Zhang Fengchi and Aunt Song's full name is Song Caixia.

Uncle Zhang, we haven't forgotten you. You will always live in our heart. Wish you and Aunt Song live a happy life in heaven.

Friendship and Enmity of Two Generations

Where was my father when Uncle Zhang was being persecuted? Why didn't he stand out to defend Uncle Zhang?

After Uncle Zhang was labeled capitalist-roader, all his old colleagues and friends were detained in a study camp and were forced to expose Uncle Zhang and make a clean break with him. Those who have experienced the Cultural Revolution know that if they stood out to defend a capitalist-roader, they not only couldn't protect others but would involve themselves into the trouble and make things even worse.

The military representatives and rebels called meetings every day and put pressure on them. Everyone was forced to expose Uncle Zhang, otherwise he wouldn't be set free. My father considered Uncle Zhang a good leader and there was nothing to report about him.

They talked to my father every day and pressed him to examine himself and ask himself if he was going to cover up for a capitalist-roader. Other members in the study camp were released one by one. My father was the only one still detained. If he still kept his mouth shut, his charge would not be simply hiding up a capitalist-roader, but something much more serious.

My father racked his brains and tried to think of something that wouldn't bring big trouble to Uncle Zhang and at the same time helped him out. Finally he told them, "Zhang Fengchi's wife Song Caixia probably had a questionable family origin."

When my father was released, he had been detained in the study camp for about half a year. He was the last one to leave the study camp.

My father thought it was the only thing he could think of which might bring Uncle Zhang the least harm. After all, the Revolutionary Committee would inquire into Aunt Song's family background whether he told them about it or not.

When Uncle Zhang was labeled capitalist-roader, his eldest daughter Julin was busy running about for her father's rehabilitation. Every time she returned to the mine to visit her family, she would appeal to the relevant authorities of the mine, the district, the city and the province for help.

Not long before her father died, she went to the Revolutionary Committee to reason with them. The person in charge of the committee took out the minutes of talks and showed it to Julin. Julin saw my father's words about her mother's family origin.

Julin was enraged. She didn't expect that the man her father trusted most would drop stones on him who had fallen into a well. She ran to our home, pointed at my father's nose and condemned him bitterly, shaking with excitement. My younger sister Liu Hua still remembers the scene when Julin condemned our father. I was then busy all day long with my activities in the Mao Zedong Thought Propaganda Team and didn't know what happened in the family.

The two families used to be as close as one family. My mother and Aunt Song used to be close friends who kept no secrets from each other. One day, all of a sudden, the relations between the two families became strained. I didn't know why. But I often heard my parents talk and say that there was some misunderstanding between the two families and someone passed on the distorted message and made the problem more complicated.

I was aware that my father was trying his best to help Uncle Zhang's family. He wanted to do something to make up for what he had done and mend the relations between the two families. I noticed that Aunt Song and the Zhangs' children meaningly ignore my father's efforts and Aunt Song was cold to my mother too. The children of the two families also became estranged.

When Uncle Zhang was dying, his eldest daughter Julin kept him company beside his deathbed for the last eight days. Uncle Zhang kept telling Julin about the family history the last three days and nights, hoping that there would be a child in the family who knew about the family history and could wipe out his grievance after he left the world. The other children were too young, so Julin was his only hope.

Uncle Zhang particularly mentioned Aunt Song's family origin. He told Julin that her mother was born in a poor family. Her parents died when she was young and she had to leave home to earn money at a very young age to support her little sisters and brothers. Julin couldn't hold her anger when she heard these. She said, "Father, do you know who framed you up? It was your closest friend, the one you trust most." She said my father's name.

This is what happened 38 years ago.

To collect first-hand materials for my book and write down the history of my father's generation, I made a special visit to Guiyang to interview Uncle Zhang's second daughter Juhua. As she was telling me the stories, that period of history became clear in my mind like a movie going on.

I asked Juhua the question hidden in my heart for decades. What has caused the rift between the two families? Juhua gave me an implicit answer. I knew it was not the answer I wanted.

When I returned to Beijing, I felt I had not fully expressed my feelings in my conversation with Juhua. At the same time, I hoped I could meet Julin and understand that period of history from different points of views.

I invited both Julin and Juhua to come to Beijing. They met my parents who now live with me.

In front of my parents, Julin told us what she thought of my father at that time and the last conversation she had with her father. What my father cared most was Uncle Zhang's response. Julin said that Uncle Zhang hoped she could consider the problem in other person's shoes and understand that they did it because they had no choice.

I was not sure whether this was what exactly Uncle Zhang said. Maybe Julin said it to comfort my father. I didn't know if Uncle Zhang left the world with his hatred for father.

But there was one thing I was certain of: If Uncle Zhang hadn't got ill and survived, he would have understood his old colleagues and friends who did something against their conscience when they could hardly save their own lives.

I once asked myself: Could my parents do more for Uncle Zhang's family when they were not even able to defend themselves?

There is no turning back the clock. There are no if's.

During the crazy years when human nature was distorted, they did what they could.

I asked my father, "How do you know that Aunt Song probably had a questionable family origin?"

Julin had told us that Aunt Song's younger sister once worked with my father who was then the League branch secretary. When Aunt Song's sister joined the Communist Youth League, her family history was examined. This was how my father got to know about Aunt Song's family background. My father said there was indeed someone who raised doubts against Aunt Song at that time. In those years when right and wrong were confused, people's state of mind was also confused. My father was not sure the so-called truth he got was true. Political examination was extremely strict at that time. If any problem was found, the whole family would be involved.

I understand my father's explanation because I grew up in those years.

I am grateful to Julin who held my 80-year-old father's hands and said, "Please forgive me if I have offended you in the past."

I am gratified that my father could in his remaining years explain to Uncle Zhang's offspring his helpless situation at that time and untie the knot which had tormented him for decades.

Phoenix Nirvana

Before the Chinese New Year of 1965, a new family moved to Entrance 1 of No. 13 Apartment Building, father Yang Yuankun, mother Sun Guizhi and three children Yang Shaohua, Yang Shaofan and Yang Shaoqing. The first two children were girls and the youngest child was a boy.

My family lived in Entrance 2 of No. 13 Apartment Building. I met Yang Shaofan, the second child of the family by chance. One day, I saw a girl wearing pigtails walking by and I was immediately attracted by her temperament. She was not necessarily beautiful, but she was sunny and confident, making it hard for people to get their eyes off her. I followed her into Entrance 1 with my eyes and I realized she was my new neighbor.

I came with my parents to the big mountains of Kaiyang Phosphate Mine when I was only three and grew up in the backward and ill-informed environment. Every time a new family moved here, especially if they had a girl of my age, I would be very curious. If the girl happened to be nice and smart, I would be eager to make friends with her, to talk to her and to know about the outside world.

The girl was named Yang Shaofan and I called her given name Shaofan. She was three years senior to me and was in grade six in primary school. She was in the same class with Juhua. Juhua talked about her a lot, all words of praise, how good she was in her study, how smart she was, how eloquent she was and how much her teacher liked her.

Shaofan came here with her parents who were transferred from Dandong Mining Company in northeast China. The teachers were happy to have such an excellent student. The school even held an exhibition especially for her to encourage other students to learn from her, a good student who was both red and expert (be both politically sound and professionally competent).

I adored her so much that I wished I could be her friend. I didn't have much chance to talk to her because we were not in the same grade. So I tried my best to find a chance to talk to her and found excuses to go to her home to play with her. When we were having a conversation, most of the time, she was the speaker and I was the listener. She had so many stories and so much knowledge. I admired her from the bottom of my heart. I believed she would have a bright future. She would go to college, become a doctor or a scientist. Later she told me that at first she wanted to be an airwoman. When she was several years older, she had a new ideal to be a woman diplomat. I felt whatever dream she had, it would come true, since she was so extraordinary.

Shaofan's father was the chief engineer, a very high position only after the secretary of the Party committee and the general manager of the mine. Her mother was an accountant. Both her parents were in decisive positions at the mine.

Shaofan's father was a man of great learning. He had double degrees in mining and geology and could speak four foreign languages of English, Japanese, Russian and German, which was very rare in China at that time.

The Cultural Revolution began and misfortune befell Shaofan's family.

Shaofan's father was labeled a counter-revolutionary, secret agent and reactionary academic authority and was detained by rebels.

During the period of the puppet Manchuria regime, Shaofan's father was studying in Xinjing University of Technology (now Changchun University of Technology). As most of the Japanese didn't like to learn mining and geology, the puppet government spent money for Chinese students to learn the two majors.

The Red Guards came to ransack Yang's home. They searched out the photo in which Shaofan's father was dressed in Japanese style school uniform and asserted that her father was a Japanese spy because he was dressed like a Japanese soldier. They took away all the family photos, the diary and the autobiography manuscript of Shaofan's father and the gold rings and other love token of Shaofan's parents.

Both Shaofan's father and mother had received good education. They lived in the city and took a lot of photos when they were young. The father was either dressed in Japanese school uniform or Western style suit. The mother was dressed in school uniform or Chinese-style dress or Western style dress. The father was handsome and talented. The mother was beautiful and elegant. All these became proof of their guilt in the Cultural Revolution.

The education we received in our youth was that all those who were barefooted dressed in shabby patched clothes were poor or lower middle peasants or workers and they were good people. All those who were dressed in silk or fur coats, Western style clothes, uniforms, *qipao* (Chinese style dresses for women), leather shoes, wearing necklaces were land-lords or capitalists and were bad people. This was how movies, books and all the other works of art and literature portrayed good people and bad people. Judging from the photos, Shaofan's parents were apparently bad people.

In fact, Shaofan's parents joined the Communist Party soon after the founding of New China. They were, according to the Party Consti-tution, the working class's vanguard fighters with communist conscious-ness.

The rebels put up the photos on the big-character poster column for everyone to see and criticize. A large crowd gathered there to see the photos of Shaofan's family. I squeezed in and watched those photos and big-character posters. I was shocked. Counterrevolutionaries and spies were living among us, so close to us. I believed that Shaofan's father was a Japanese spy because he was dressed in Japanese uniform; Shaofan's mother was a bourgeois lady because she was dressed beautifully with pearl necklace around her neck. I was a small child and didn't know anything about the puppet Manchuria history. In fact, the northeast of China was under the enslaving education of Japan, and even my father who was in the countryside had learned some simple Japanese.

The rebels interrogated Shaofan's father and threatened him to admit that he was a Japanese spy, counterrevolutionary and reactionary academic authority. They tortured him cruelly. They frequently humiliated and punished him in public places. They bound him with coarse hemp rope, hung a heavy placard with his name on it around his neck and beat him hard with leather belt, electric wire or thick stick.

Shaofan was a stubborn girl. She often went to see the big-character posters directed against her father and attended the show-trial. She wanted to know what mistake her father had committed and whether he was a spy or counterrevolutionary or not. Whenever she appeared, people would turn to her to see her response watching her father being humiliated and beaten. Her father was tied up against a pole and was whipped with wire. Blood was streaming down his forehead and blurred his glasses. He was dragged down the stairs with his two knees covered in blood.

He kneeled on the ground and the rebels rolled him forwards over and over. Shaofan watched helplessly, tears rolling down her cheeks. What came into her mind were the scenes she read about in textbooks and watched in movies where revolutionaries were cruelly tortured in Zhazidong of Chongqing (a former concentration camp of Kuomintang to persecute revolutionaries in the late 1940s). Before her eyes was her father being treated brutally and inhumanly by the rebels.

Once Shaofan's father was sitting on the ground moaning with anguish and his eyes closed. He asked Shaofan to bring her youngest brother, who was born in the mine and only a baby, here for him to take a look. Shaofan realized that her father was going to commit suicide. She yelled at him, "If you die, people would say that you kill yourself from fear of punishment and your case will never get reversed. What about us? You cannot die. You should be responsible for us."

Shaofan's mother was removed from the post of accountant in the Financial Department and was sent to the quarry under reform through labor. There were three shifts and the intensity of labor was severely hard. Accidents were not uncommon. Once the stone hill caved in and a worker was hit to death on the spot right before Shaofan's mother's eyes.

When Shaofan's family came to Guizhou, the elder sister Shaohua was a second-year junior high school student. She learned Russian before, but there was no Russian class in the middle school of Kaiyang Phosphate Mine. So she went to Guiyang Girls' High School and lived in the school. She didn't see the tragic experiences of her family.

In 1968, Shaohua was among the first batch of educated youth to be sent to work in the countryside. She failed to pass the political examination because of her father's problem whenever someone came to recruit workers or enroll students. All her classmates were recruited one after another. Only she was left, lonely and helplessly, and stayed in the countryside for eight years. When the Cultural Revolution began, Shaofan's younger brother Shaoqun was seven years old and her youngest brother Shaojie was just born.

Father was imprisoned and mother was under reform through labor in the quarry. The three children were left at home. Fourteen-year-old Shaofan took on the responsibility of taking care of her home and two brothers.

The rebels said that Shaofan's father was a Japanese spy, but they had no evidence. They searched their home over and over again in the hope of finding the nonexistent certificate of appointment issued by the Japanese.

Shaofan's first brother Shaoqun was born in 1959 and had bad health since childhood due to the three-year difficult period of famine. The rebels frequently ransacking the house, parents being cruelly persecuted, all these happened before a little child's eyes. Shaoqun was badly scared and got epilepsy.

Shaoqun had frequent recurrences of his illness. When he was playing outside, he might suddenly fall onto the ground, twitching and white foam oozing out of his mouth. A large crowd of people surrounded and watched him but no one helped him. He had to try to get up himself after he regained his consciousness. The Cultural Revolution distorted people's soul. When they saw Shaoqun suffer, not only they showed no sympathy but also said that he deserved it because he was a bastard of a counterrevolutionary. Many times, Shaoqun fell and had cerebral concussion with his head covered with bumps and bruises and mouthful of teeth broken. He had intermittent loss of sight. Shaofan was often seen carrying her younger brother on her back to the hospital with her youngest brother in her arms.

The kindergarten at the mine refused to admit her youngest brother because he was the child of a counterrevolutionary and Japanese spy. Shaofan wanted to find a baby-sitter to look after her youngest brother, but nobody dared accept the job. She had to look after her two younger brothers, do the cooking and laundry and go to visit her father in the house of detention and prepare food and clothes for him.

Her father's salary as a chief engineer was 150 yuan a month and the mother's salary as an accountant was 80 yuan a month, which were very high at that time. Life used to be very comfortable for the family. When the Cultural Revolution began, the father's salary was reduced to 18 yuan. When he was discharged from employment and expelled from the Party in 1970, he had no income at all. All the deposit was frozen. Eighty yuan of the mother's salary was all the family had to keep themselves from starvation and they also had to support Shaofan's two grandmothers who lived in the hometown in northeast China.

When Shaofan's father was discharged from public employment, the rebels didn't allow them to live in the apartment and forced them to move out. They forced into the house and moved the furniture out. Shaofan tried to stop them by leaning against the door from inside but in vain. They broke in and threw all the furniture and articles out of the window.

The family was forced to move into a shabby house made of asphalt felt, which was formerly used as a pigsty, by the Yang Water River. All the domestic and industrial sewage was dumped into the river which was dirty and stinking. The house was only six square meters. Shaofan put a double bed and a double-layered bed and there was hardly any space left for a person to stand. It often rains in Guizhou. Whenever it rained, rain drops came in through the leaking roof and big or small pots and pans were placed everywhere on the ground to hold the rain. In stormy days, the entire roof would be blown off the house. During the summer, the Yang Water River easily got flooded and their house was washed away a couple of times. The asphalt felt was combustible and fire risk was common. Shaofan's mother was under reform and couldn't take care of the family. Shaofan, with her two younger brothers, was living in an abyss of suffering with no one to turn to.

The family lived in the asphalt felt house for 10 years. Shaofan put up a small kitchen and a small house on the open space outside the house. Tempered in adversity, Shaofan became strong and resolute at a young age.

Shaoqun didn't receive proper treatment for his illness and was getting worse and worse. Shaofan couldn't be around him all the time. She bought him a fishing rod and let him sit in front of the bed and stretch the fishing rod out of the window to the river to fish. She tied her brother to a chair so that he wouldn't fall. Sometimes he had a recurrence and suddenly fell onto the ground. If nobody else was home, he would wet his trousers with urine and shit.

In 1971, the mine began to recruit workers. Most of the students who graduated from high schools were admitted. Shaofan went to the recruitment office and asked for a job. She was refused bluntly, "You bastard of a spy. There is no way for you to get a job."

A young workers' platoon (military words were widely used at that time) was formed at the mine which accepted the children of bad family origins or those who were defined as reformable for odd jobs. Shaofan joined the platoon and did all kinds of dirty and tiring jobs such as working underground, building road, loading or unloading the wagons, etc. She spared no effort in whatever she did and was even more able than a man.

Shaofan was a courageous girl. Whenever there was an opportunity to go to work or get higher education, she would fight for it even if she knew there was little hope. Every time her hope was shattered, she would run to the house where her father was detained and reproached him crying bitterly, "What on earth have you done? My future is ruined because of you!"

Shaofan's teacher was concerned about her and hated to see such a talented student being wasted. During the Cultural Revolution, many youth broke off relations with their parents to prove their loyalty to Chairman Mao. One of the teachers suggested that Shaofan break off with her family to save her future. There were many examples of those who abandoned their families and were set as models and recommended to universities. Shaofan didn't take the teacher's advice.

Shaofan met Luo when she was 19 years old in 1972. Luo was a worker recruited from some other place. He was very sympathetic with Shaofan. After Shaofan's father was dismissed from office and expelled from the Party, Shaofan and her mother started to run about for her father's case. They went to all the relevant higher authorities and asked them to investigate her father's case. Luo went with them. When Shaofan was in the darkest period of her life, Luo walked into her life.

Shaofan wouldn't have come to Luo if it was not for the Cultural Revolution. Luo was a worker who didn't receive much education. But he was brave and had a sense of justice. He opened his warm heart to Shaofan when everybody else avoided the family like plague. He gave her a sense of security that she had someone to rely on. I fully understand the emotion between the two of them. What the family experienced was too much for a girl. It was unbearable pain.

Once on her way to appeal to the higher authorities for help, Shaofan fell ill and got a fever. She fell off the train and was paralyzed. She was bed-stricken for half a year. During that time, Luo was by her side taking care of her. He carried her on his back to the hospital, cleaned her body, and changed sanitary napkins for her when she had her period. He did everything for her. When she recovered, Shaofan decided to spend the rest of her life with this man.

Shaofan took Luo to visit her father in the prison. Her father asked, "Are you a Communist Party member? Do you have a college degree?" When he knew that Luo was neither a Party member nor a college graduate, he didn't approve of their date. Shaofan had a big quarrel with her father, took Luo's hand and left.

In order to get her father's case reversed, Shaofan repeatedly went to the relevant authorities to ask them to investigate into her father's case and clarify the facts. What she didn't expect was that not only was her father's case unreversed, she got herself into trouble as well. She would be sent to the countryside to receive reform through labor as a negative example of the untransformable children. She had no way out and couldn't stay at the mine.

Luo said to her, "Come to my home. I grew up there and have many friends who can take good care of you together with my mother."

Shaofan married Luo. She left her parents and two younger brothers and came to Luo's hometown Anshun County which was about 200 kilometers away from Kaiyang Phosphate Mine. Luo found Shaofan a job as a substitute teacher in a local primary school. Shaofan lived with Luo's mother in a shabby plank house with walls pasted with used homework paper. Luo stayed at the mine alone.

The monthly pay for substitute teachers was 29 yuan. Substitute teachers in China were not on the permanent staff and there was a big difference between their salary and benefits and those of regular teachers. But Shaofan was satisfied. Although life was difficult, she could finally live with dignity. The local people, who knew nothing about her family background, were friendly to her and treated her with respect.

Shaofan cherished her job very much and worked conscientiously. She did well in teaching and was popular among the students and their parents. She was chosen as the Excellent Teacher and Excellent Young Pioneers Counselor. She became a famous person known to every household in Anshun County.

Shaofan got married in 1974 and gave birth to a son in 1975 when she was 23 years old. Life was more difficult with one more mouth to feed. Her husband was also low-paid. He got 31.5 yuan a month, kept 10 yuan as his living expenses and sent the rest of the money back to his family.

When Mao Zedong passed away in 1976, Shaofan sobbed her heart out. She thought that her father's case would never be overturned after Chairman Mao's death.

At the same time, Shaofan's father was deprived of the right to mourn over Chairman Mao's death. In the later stage of the Cultural Revolution, although he was not imprisoned, he was put under house arrest. A memorial meeting was held at the mine. Shaofan's father pinned a small white flower on his chest, put a black armband around his left arm and went to the meeting venue. He stood at the back of the crowd mourning for Chairman Mao. The organizer of the meeting noticed him and immediately drove him away.

Luo dared speak boldly in defense of justice and was loyal to his friends, so he made a lot of friends. His friends were also workers with little education. They usually gathered together, eating, drinking and playing cards. Sometimes they gambled with small notes when playing cards.

In 1977, a campaign to crack down on crime was launched across the country. One of Luo's friends got caught in gambling and exposed Luo. Luo was caught and sentenced to eight years in prison.

Although the Cultural Revolution ended in 1976, its influence could be found everywhere. Luo was arrested, no interrogation before the court, no defense, no arrest warrant. No legal procedure at all. Nobody knew where he was kept. Shaofan hadn't seen her husband or heard from him for two years.

Shaofan cried out about her husband's grievances. With no money to take a bus, she carried her two-year-old son on her back and walked tens of kilometers to Kaiyang County Court to appeal for intervention. She walked round the house where her husband might be detained; singing revolutionary songs which she wished her husband could hear.

Shaofan had a talent for speaking. She was knowledgeable and educated. What she said was reasonable and convincing. She left a very good impression on the president of the court. Through her relentless efforts, the court changed the original sentence to four years.

Shaofan kept her loyalty to her imprisoned husband. Shaofan's father pressed her to divorce Luo. Shaofan wouldn't listen to her father and was determined to wait for Luo.

With only one small pay, the family fell into bitter poverty. They couldn't even afford articles of everyday use such as toothpaste and had to brush teeth with salt for years. Meat was not to be seen on the table and they could only buy some pig's offal for the Chinese New Year. They couldn't afford a doctor. When the child was ill, he was never sent to see a doctor but took some pills Shaofan bought from the pharmacy.

Shaofan hadn't been allowed to see her husband after he was taken away until 1979. Luo was ill in the hospital of the prison. Shaofan came to see him with their son. Luo threw himself on his wife's knees and cried bitterly for half an hour. The doctor and nurse standing nearby were moved to tears. Shaofan didn't shed a tear and kept consoling her husband.

The president of the court was deeply touched by Shaofan's strong will. He said to Luo, "You must be good to Shaofan in the future. You wouldn't have today if it were not for her love." He later became a friend of the couple.

Shaofan's father was not rehabilitated until the end of 1979. On December 31, the last day of 1979, Shaofan's mother came to Anshun to tell Shaofan that her father got rehabilitated. Shaofan burst into tears and cried loudly.

According to the state policy, Shaofan could return to Kaiyang Phosphate Mine and be assigned a job. She and her younger brother Shaoqun got a job at the same time in 1980.

Fourteen years had passed since the beginning of the Cultural Revolution in 1966, Shaofan, who had been tortured in the sea of bitterness for 14 years, finally saw the sun.

In 1983, 31-year-old Shaofan got the opportunity to study in Guiyang Accounting Technical Secondary School for two and a half years, where she gave full play to her intelligence and ingenuity.

Shaofan believed it was the Chinese Communist Party that gave her a second life. She joined the Party at school. Shaofan and her father, though persecuted in the Cultural Revolution, still maintained their belief in communism and their loyalty to the Communist Party, which was a true portrayal of quite a lot of Chinese people.

After graduation from the school, Shaofan did financial jobs and became a professional backbone acknowledged at the mine. Though she has gone through all kinds of hardships, she remains optimistic and has an ardent love for life.

In mythology, when a phoenix dies, it burns itself in raging flames, rises from the ashes and gains a second life with even stronger vitality. It is called "phoenix nirvana". Shaofan is such a phoenix born of fire.

Shaofan retired in 2008. Having survived the crucifixion of the Cultural Revolution, Shaofan's parents who are both nearly 90 years old are still in good health, which is a blessing given by Heaven. Shaofan always says that God is fair after all.

Her eldest sister Shaohua is also retired and lives in the same city. She takes her parents to her home and looks after them with her husband.

Shaofan and Luo have grown old together. There is still difference between the two of them, but it doesn't influence their love for each other.

Younger brother Shaoqun's illness got treated properly and is getting much better. He has started his own family, living a simple but happy life.

Youngest brother Shaojie, a medical university graduate, runs a private hospital in Ningbo. He has achieved a great success and is the pride of the family.

Shaofan's biggest comfort is that her son graduated from college, has a successful career and a happy marriage with a lovely child. Shaofan and Luo enjoy being grandparents and are blessed with a happy family.

Propaganda Team of the People's Liberation Army

When the general atmosphere of chaos and violence prevailed in China, Mao Zedong sent troops to intervene in the local Cultural Revolution which were called "Mao Zedong Thought Propaganda Team of the People's Liberation Army" or "PLA Propaganda Team" for short. Individuals were called "PLA Representatives".

When the PLA Propaganda Team came to Kaiyang Phosphate Mine, the physical struggle was over and the PLA didn't get involved in the violence. So the impression they left on me was basically good.

Hundreds of soldiers stationed at our mine. There were PLA Representatives in every work unit who exercised joint leadership with the local leaders. We started to return to school and continued with the revolution there. We learned nothing but *Quotations from Chairman Mao* and Chairman Mao's works at school.

Most of the PLA Representatives came from poor villages and didn't have enough education. But we had to listen to them. Our admiration and respect for them were from the bottom of our heart. We young children went to see them drill every day. The boys all tried to make friends with them. The PLA was strict in discipline and the soldiers were not allowed to go out with girls, not even talk with them alone.

The headquarters of the PLA Propaganda Team was located in the building opposite to our apartment, which was formerly the head-quarters of the Red Guards. Some PLA officers lived there. When they first came, they brought with them a Communication Squad that was busy installing telephones and transmitter-receivers. There was a young soldier in the Communication Squad who was about 15 to 16 years old and looked extremely handsome. The Communication Squad also lived in the headquarters. Our balcony and the young soldier's room window faced each other across a distance of about 50 meters. When I went to the balcony, I often noticed the young soldier looking through a window towards my direction.

One of my girl classmates met the young soldier once and could never get him out of her mind. She often came to my home and watched the soldier at our balcony and said plaintively, "If only I lived here."

The young soldier made friends with a neighbor boy of mine named Hong Xi. Hong Xi's family lived on the same floor of No. 13 Apartment Building with my family and Uncle Zhang's family. My female schoolmates often came to Hong Xi to ask about the young soldier.

Not long after that, the installation of the telephones and transmitter-receivers was finished and the young soldier was leaving.

The day before their departure, I saw the young soldier again from our balcony. He was standing still by the window staring at the direction of our balcony. I was confused and scared. I walked to and fro between the room and the balcony, wondering how long he was going to stand there. My neighbor Juqiu and the sister-in-law of Hong Xi also noticed it and came to look on. The young soldier stood for about two hours and disappeared. I suddenly felt a loss in my heart.

The next day, I went to see them off with my classmates as a student representative. The soldiers of the Communication Squad, so cute in military uniform, stood in a queue, listening to the command of the squad leader. The young soldier stared blankly ahead at the squad leader, though he knew that we were looking at him by his side. They got on a military truck. The moment before the truck started, he took a glance at me, his eyes glistened with tears.

The young soldier wrote a letter to Hong Xi: "You, Heping and I are all young, only 15 or 16 years old. We are the successors of the revolution. We must work hard to learn Mao Zedong Thought and devote ourselves to the cause of communism."

I hadn't expected that the young soldier would mention me in his letter. We never talked. I was aware that he liked me. Decades of years have passed since then. Whenever I think of the young soldier, I would still feel sweet and happy.

I often gave performances to the PLA soldiers and many of them knew about me.

I had no stage fright. Every time on the stage, I was filled with enthusiasm and the performance was well received by the audience. I began to have some reputation at the mine and among the PLA Representatives.

I was only a little girl and some of the middle-aged officers didn't have to avoid me. They always expressed their affections for me when they met me. I felt happy. It was a great honor to be liked by the PLA. My younger sister was only seven or eight years old then. She often received sweets from those PLA soldiers. She said they treated her well because of me.

I felt warm and happy when the PLA soldiers were around us.

I had dry skin and my hands and feet were heavily chapped in cold weather with some cuts as big as baby's mouth. The station troop had a doctor. He would apply Vaseline to my fingers and heels, and then bind them up with cotton gauze.

The local people spoke their own dialect and few of them could speak Putonghua (standard Chinese pronunciation). I was good at it, which was a big advantage for me. I was the announcer in the propaganda team.

The headquarters of the station troop was tens of kilometers away. They also had a Mao Zedong Thought Propaganda Team which often came to our mine to give performances. We also went there to give performances. We didn't talk with each other. They had no women soldiers. All the propaganda team members were male and most of them were art soldiers recruited specially from Guiyang, the capital city of the province.

They were very talented in performing, but none of them did better than me in speaking Putonghua. Therefore they were very curious about me. The director of the propaganda team was an officer in his thirties. He was fond of me very much. Every time they came to give a performance, he would place a small wooden stool near one side of the stage so I could watch the performance clearly. The team members would often try to find an opportunity to talk to me when it was not their turn to go to the stage. I felt I was the happiest person in the world.

We also had a PLA Representative in the propaganda team of our mine. He had a very pleasant name "Tian Miao" (meaning seedlings of cereal crops in the field) and we called him Representative Tian. He was responsible for the political and ideological work. He was very kind and amiable. We liked him very much and we turned to him for help when we had something on our mind. Many of the members were recruited by him personally. I practised my performing skill very hard and was often praised by him. Once he said to me, "Keep up the good work. I will recommend you to join the Communist Youth League ." I was much excited. The Communist Youth League is a political organization for the young people. It was replaced by the Red Guards during the Cultural Revolution. It was widely said that the Communist Youth League would soon be restored. To be a member of the Youth League had to be recommended by a Communist Party member or a Youth League member.

Representative Tian was a platoon leader. Military officers were allowed to find girlfriends. We young girls introduced him to a big sister in the propaganda team. I volunteered to be the matchmaker. To our disappointment, the sister took no fancy to him. Representative Tian had to leave when the troop was withdrawn from the mine. We cried so hard as if we were melting into tears the moment we saw him off.

There was another officer who was a battalion commander. I forgot what his surname was. He would greet me warmly whenever he met me. He was dispatched to a factory in Guiyang to support the Left there. He said a lot to me when we went to see him off. The general idea was I should study hard and practice my skill of dancing hard and I would have a bright future.

Soon afterwards, a grievous news came. He died. He was on an inspection visit to a factory that was making weapons for faction fights. An accident happened when the workers were testing the grenades. He was killed in the explosion and more than 40 shell fragments were found in his body.

I went to Guiyang to attend his funeral. I felt as if I were in a dream when I saw his face which changed beyond recognition.

Revolutionary Ballet

It was a great advantage if you could sing and dance well during the Cultural Revolution. At that time, a single propaganda team of a school, a factory, a commune or a military area alone could put on a model play.

Jiang Qing, the last wife of Mao Zedong, selected two ballets and six Beijing operas to form eight revolutionary model plays. They were the only plays performed at that time because they were regarded the only ones in line with Chairman Mao's revolutionary literature and art route. All Mao Zedong Thought Propaganda Teams, professional or amateur, were staging the eight model plays. I played many roles in the eight model plays.

The eight revolutionary model plays were made into films. Whenever a film was to be shown in the open air at the mine, it must be one of the eight model plays. We had watched them so many times that we could remember all the music and lines.

The propaganda team decided to rehearse the prelude and the first scene of a revolutionary ballet drama *The White-haired Girl*. I was to play the female leading role Xi'er.

Growing up in the mountainous area in Guizhou, I had never come into contact with ballet, let alone any basic skill in ballet. The film *The White-haired Girl* was specially dispatched by the Revolutionary Committee of the mine from the capital city of Guiyang for us to imitate. Later we went to Guiyang to learn from a propaganda team of the army.

People were courageous and daring at that time. We were armed with the Mao Zedong Thought and there was no difficulty that could beat us.

Young people would learn playing the musical instruments or singing or dancing whenever they had the chance. Within a short time, large numbers of art talents sprang up. Chinese people were indeed extraordinary. Nothing was impossible as long as we set our mind to it. There would be a string band or brass band or orchestra in each of the propaganda teams. Almost all of the players were amateur and learned to play an instrument within a very short time through intensive learning and training.

There were many munitions factories in Guizhou. Many munitions factories were moved to the mountains of Guizhou for strategic consideration. It was a pride to be able to work in a munitions factory. Many of my friends were recruited by the munitions factories when they were 16 or 17 years old. Some of them who I thought had no talent at all became backbone of the propaganda team in the factory and gave a full performance of the revolutionary ballet *The Red Detachment of Women*. When they came back to visit their families, they came to my home carrying their ballet shoes and showed me their performance. To my surprise, they were quite good.

I would never miss any chance to learn and improve my ballet skill.

The propaganda team of Guiyang Bearing Factory came to the mine to put on a performance of *The White-haired Girl*. The girl who played the role of Xi'er was particularly good and I admired her very much. The propaganda team arranged her to instruct me. She was very proud and looked down upon me as a country bumpkin. The more she was impatient, the more I got nervous and constantly failed to do as she taught. It was the first time I heard that I had to stretch the hipbone as a ballet dancer. We had never received any professional training. How could I possibly do it? I was worried to tears. I looked very unprofessional when I was dancing ballet at the beginning.

I worked very hard and spent more than 10 hours practicing and rehearsing every day. I would never miss any chance of learning. Gradually I felt more confident and was doing better and better.

The mine recruited "art workers" from the educated youth in the countryside who had been sent there for reeducation. The first choice of those educated youth who had talent in singing and dancing was to be "art soldiers" in the army. If they couldn't join the army, they would still be envied when they became "art workers".

One day, two big boys came to our propaganda team. One of them was named Xu Meilin and the other was named Fu Yang. Xu Meilin used to play the role of Dachun, Xi'er's fiancé, in the propaganda team of Guiyang No. Six Middle School. Fu Yang used to do stage art there.

125

They failed to pass the political examination due to their family origin whenever there was recruitment. This was why they were still left in the countryside. Someone recommended them to the PLA Representative who agreed to let them help us rehearse *The White-haired Girl*.

The two boys were very talented and I was fond of them. I hoped the PLA Representative and the leaders of the mine would keep them. I was touched and felt sorry for them when I noticed that they were eager to stay and spared no efforts to show the best of them.

That year, I was 15 years old and they were just a little over 20. Tempered in the hard life in the countryside, they looked more mature.

Xu Meilin could play all the roles in *The White-haired Girl*. With his help, we finished the rehearsal of the prelude and the first scene. I was born with the instep which was not suitable for ballet dancing. I practiced and practiced until my toes were bleeding and my toenails came off. My painstaking efforts paid off. Finally I could dance standing on the tip of my toes.

Fu Yang did the setting. Our first performance was a great success. When I was dancing on the stage, I heard a girl sitting in the first row exclaiming loudly, "Aiya, Heping performs as well as the player in the film."

I particularly enjoyed the process of playing the role of Xi'er. I felt I were Xi'er and forgot myself when I was on the stage.

The synopsis of the story:

Prelude: Flames of Fury

Before liberation, at the gate of landlord Huang Shiren's mansion. The oppressed peasants walked past the gate, being whipped. Singing: How many hired hands are being enslaved; how many girls like Xi'er are being persecuted. Our grievances are endless and converge into surging rivers and seas.

Scene One: Deep Hatred

A Chinese New Year's Eve during the War of Resistance Against Japanese Aggression, Yang Bailao's home, Yangge Village, Hebei Province.

Xi'er is happily preparing for the New Year. Her father Yang Bailao just arrives home after staying away to avoid creditors. Despotic landlord Huang Shiren and his henchman Mu Renzhi break into Yang Bailao's home and force him to bring Xi'er to Huang Shiren as payment for his debt. Yang Bailao resolutely resists and is beaten to death. Dachun (Xi'er's fiancé) and the villagers come to stop them. Huang Shiren fires shots and carries Xi'er away.

Dachun is going to risk his life fighting with them and is dissuaded by Uncle Zhao who is an underground communist. He advises them to join the Eighth Route Army and the revolution.

When Xi'er was lifted by the hatchet men of the Huang family and carried off the stage, my part of the play was over. Then I would squat at a corner of the curtain, hold my knees and watch the group dancing to the end of the play. Every time I finished my dancing, I would be exhausted dripping with sweat. But I felt happy and contented in my heart. That kind of fatigue filled me with a sense of accomplishment.

At that time, it was improper for men and women to touch each other's hand in passing objects. Dachun and Xi'er never held each other's hand as required by the script during the rehearsal. They only did so in the formal performance.

Xu Meilin was the director and normally didn't play any role. There was only one time he played Dachun. When the prelude ended, the cast did the ending pose. Xi'er stood on the tip of toes of her right foot, her right hand put lightly on the shoulder of Dachun with her left leg raised high to the back. Then the curtain slowly fell. The young girl who was assigned to draw the curtain was enchanted by Xu Meilin's dancing and completely forgot her job. I couldn't hold the position any longer and reminded her in whisper "Draw the curtain". This was heard by the audience sitting in the front. When the play was over, we two were criticized by the PLA Representative.

I was exhilarated that I could dance on the same stage with Xu Meilin. More over, what we played were two romantic roles.

127

Xu Meilin and Fu Yang didn't stay very long because they could not pass the political examination. I wept when they left.

Many people may not believe that I once played Xi'er so well in a revolutionary ballet. It is a pity that I haven't kept any stage photo. For many years that followed, I relived those moments when I danced *The North Wind Blows* in my dreams. It is the theme song of *The White-haired Girl*, also the first solo dance of Xi'er in the first scene.

The Cultural Revolution is a disaster for Chinese people. However, those days when I danced in the propaganda team left me with some sweet feelings and tender thoughts for the years.

Personality Cult of Chairman Mao

"Three Loyalties and Four Boundlessnesses" was the product of the Cultural Revolution and extreme expression of the personality cult. "Three Loyalties" called for loyalty to Chairman Mao, loyalty to Mao Zedong Thought and loyalty to Chairman Mao's revolutionary line. "Four Boundlessnesses" meant boundless love for, boundless belief in, boundless cult and boundless loyalty to Chairman Mao, Mao Zedong Thought and Chairman Mao's revolutionary line. There was also the "Four Greats", with which we termed Chairman Mao as the great teacher, the great leader, the great commander, and the great helmsman.

"Read every day" called upon us to read Chairman Mao's Little Red Book every day. After the Cultural Revolution began, almost every Chinese had a red-covered *Quotations from Chairman Mao* in hand. Every day, people could be seen reading aloud the Little Red Book in the school, in the workshop, in the barracks and in the field.

When I started to work at the age of 15 in 1971, we had to work in the daytime and take part in the political study in the evening, learning

Quotations from Chairman Mao and *Selected Works of Mao Zedong,* reading newspapers or having meetings for criticism and self-criticism. An old worker surnamed Huang, who was illiterate, couldn't recite the Little Red Book. We forced him to read the Quotations every day during the political study session and criticized him for being disloyal to Chairman Mao if he couldn't recite it. The old worker happened to be one of my neighbors in No. 13 Apartment Building. Every time I met him, I would ask, "Have you memorized the first paragraph of the first page of the *Quotations from Chairman Mao?*"

Many people could recite all the pages of the Little Red Book fluently from memory. Schools or factories often checked up on whether the students or workers could recite *Quotations from Chairman Mao* or not.

When we were in a meeting or political study, the first thing to do was to recite some parts of *Quotations from Chairman Mao.* The leader of the meeting would say "Please turn to the first paragraph of the first page. Our great leader Chairman Mao teaches us", then all the people recited in chorus "The force at the core leading our cause forward is the Chinese Communist Party. The theoretical basis guiding our thinking is Marxism-Leninism."

"Request instructions in the morning and report in the evening" was a political ceremony which had to be done every day. The first thing one had to do after he got up or before he started the day's work or study was to "request instructions from our great leader Chairman Mao"; after a day's work or before going to bed, one had to "report to our great leader Chairman Mao". If one made some mistake or did something wrong during the day, he or she had to stand before Chairman Mao's portrait and make self-criticism. There was a piece of wall with Chairman Mao's portrait and the Chinese character 忠 (loyalty) put up on it in every household. The political ceremony had to be repeated when one reached the school or the work place.

I had a loud and clear voice and was often chosen to lead the "Request instructions in the morning and report in the evening".

Everybody stood facing the portrait of Chairman Mao, holding the Little Red Book to their chest. I started loudly, "First, let's wish the reddest sun in our heart, our great leader Chairman Mao", all people cheered in chorus lifting their right hands and waving the Little Red Books, "Long long life! Long long life! Long long life!" Then I continued, "Let's wish Chairman Mao's close comrade-in-arms Vice Chairman Lin", "Good health! Good health! Good health!" Then I would lead everybody reading some paragraphs from the Little Red Book according to that day's situation. If we were to do a tiring physical labor, we would usually read "Be resolute, fear no sacrifice and surmount every difficulty to win victory". If we were to denounce somebody in a show-trial, we would read "Everything reactionary is the same; if you do not hit it, it will not fall", or "A revolution is not a dinner party or writing an essay, or painting a picture, or doing embroidery; it cannot be so refined, so leisurely and gentle, so temperate, kind, courteous, restrained and magnanimous". I was always devotional when I did this kind of ceremonies.

Another reflection of the cult was that everyone wore a Chairman Mao badge on their chest. Many factories began to produce Chairman Mao badges. Kaiyang Phosphate Mine also made Chairman Mao badges and Red Guards were involved in it. I remember I injected red liquid pigment to the roughcast of Chairman Mao badges. The badges came in different patterns and sizes. Some of the badges were as big as a plate and would block the entire chest. Someone pinned dozens of Chairman Mao badges on the chest to show his love for Chairman Mao. I once saw an old man pin dozens of badges on his skin and the wounds got inflamed and festered.

The cult was promoted to its zenith by the loyalty dance which was a group dance to fanatically express people's devotion and loyalty to Chairman Mao. Every morning everywhere men, women, old people and children could be seen dancing together in large streets and small lanes. The students had to do the loyalty dance before class began; the workers had to dance before they started to work; the government officials had to dance before they started their daily work. In the countryside, commune members had to do the loyalty dance in the fields during breaks.

In some places the loyalty dance even went to extremes. The Red Guards set sentries at every crossroad, intercepted passers-by and asked them to dance a section of the loyalty dance. If they didn't know how to dance it, they were forced to learn on the spot and were not allowed to pass the sentry until they could dance it. The same thing also happened at the railway station. The passengers were not allowed to get on the train until they could dance.

The scene of the loyalty dance was very spectacular and the atmosphere touching. Tens of thousands of people, men, women, the aged, the young, workers, peasants, businessmen, students and soldiers, everyone was singing and dancing, holding a Little Red Book in their hands, "Beloved leader Chairman Mao, the red sun in our hearts; Beloved leader Chairman Mao, the red sun in our hearts. We have so many intimate words we want to tell you and we have so many loving songs we want to sing you. Ten million red hearts facing Beijing and 10 million smiling faces welcoming the red sun. We wish our beloved leader a long long life, we wish our beloved leader a long long life."

My younger sister and I were both experts in the loyalty dance. We taught people to dance wherever we went. My sister was only four or five years old then and she went to father's work place to teach the workers there to dance. My father continued to practice the dance when he returned home from work.

The extremely crazy personality cult of Chairman Mao lasted for four years from the spring of 1967.

Go and Work in the Countryside

There are two most popular explanations as to why Chairman Mao decided to send large groups of young people in the cities to the countryside. The first is that Chairman Mao decided to bring the Red Guard movement under control. According to the second, the unemployment pressure in the cities was the basic driving force behind the movement.

By 1968, the Red Guard movement had lasted for more than two years. Although the central government called upon the students to return to school to continue with the revolution, disorder and chaos were still out of control. Since May 1966 when the Cultural Revolution began, colleges and universities had been closed and factories had stopped recruiting workers and more than four million middle and high school students who graduated in 1966, 1967 and 1968 had nothing to do in the cities, which became a social problem to be solved urgently.

Whatever the reason, the fact was many youths actively responded to the call of Chairman Mao to go to the mountains and the countryside to temper their heart and will.

Chairman Mao waved his hand and we would march forward.

My good friend Yang was a typical example of tens of thousands of educated youths.

One day in September of 1968, when Yang was riding a bicycle in the street of Guiyang to see big-character posters, she ran into a parade beating gongs and drums to celebrate the announcement of the latest instruction from Chairman Mao which called on "educated youth to go to the countryside to receive reeducation from the poor and lower-middle peasants".

132

The new instruction was closely related to the destiny of Yang and other tens of thousands of middle and high school graduates. Yang joined the parade at once.

Yang thought it over for three days and decided to respond to Chairman Mao's call to go to the countryside.

Yang would never hesitate a second to respond to Chairman Mao's call. The reason why she thought it over for three days was that going to work in the mountains and the countryside was a very important mission which one should set up one's mind to stay there for the whole life. She also had another apprehension that being the child of the "Seven Black Categories", she didn't know whether the honor of being the first batch of educated youths to go to the countryside would fall on her.

Yang's father used to be the president of Guizhou Agriculture College and was denounced as counter-revolutionary revisionist and capitalist-roader. Yang's mother was a revolutionary cadre and was severely wounded in the Liberation War for New China. She was labeled traitor of the revolution and was imprisoned in an illegal prison by the rebels.

Yang returned home and told his father, "I have decided to respond to Chairman Mao's call to go to the countryside to receive reeducation."

"You should consider it carefully. If you have made up your mind, you should go ahead and never change your mind," her father said.

Yang went to see her mother in the illegal prison and told her about her decision.

Her mother said, "Good. Go ahead. You don't have to worry about your father and me. I am not a traitor and I will stand the test of the Party and will be cleaned soon. Compared with many of our comrades, we are lucky. We are still alive. We haven't been seized by the enemy or been tortured. We have nothing to complain about."

With parents' support, Yang didn't have any hesitation.

Yang submitted her application to the school. Her school hadn't started to mobilize the students to go to the countryside and Yang was the first one to apply for it.

The person who was in charge said, "Why are you in such a hurry? You child of the Seven Black Categories! You just want to clutch the straw of the revolution." The expression "to clutch the straw of the revolution" was quite often used to satire those who took the advantage of the revolution.

"I am responding to the call of Chairman Mao. If you say no, you are a stumbling block in the movement," replied Yang.

They still didn't approve of Yang's application asserting that she was trying to clutch the straw of the revolution.

Yang went to the Educated Youth Office of Guiyang and expressed her determination to go to the countryside. They told her that all she needed was a certificate issued by her school which proved her to be a student of her school. Yang went back to school and persuaded the director of the Cultural Revolutionary Committee to issue her the certificate. When she got to the recruitment office, the day's work was already over and the staff were about to leave. She got enrolled at the last minute and became one among the first batch of students to go to the countryside as she wished.

Yang clearly remembers that she departed Guiyang on October 5, 1968. A grand farewell ceremony was held in the city of Guiyang. The trucks carrying the first batch of 169 graduated middle school students started off slowly from the downtown area and tens of thousands of citizens walked following the trucks for over one hour. Yang's elder sister, small uncle and a good friend were among them. The trucks speeded up and drove to different directions. The 169 young students were assigned to different parts of the countryside, all places with the harshest living conditions.

Yang and other more than 20 students were assigned to Kezhai Village of Kapu Town, Pingtang County in southern part of Guizhou. Kapu Town is where the Maonan minority ethnic group live in compact community, about 200 kilometers away from Guiyang City. The road transportation was terrible at that time and after one and a half days' travel, they arrived at the town. The staff workers of the Educated Youth Office handed the students over to several villagers who were there to meet the students and left.

A group of students, the youngest 14 and the oldest 19 years old, carrying an infantry pack on the back and a string bag which contained a washbasin, soap, towels, toothpaste and brushes, etc. in the hand, followed the villagers and walked one and a half hours crossing two mountains and finally arrived at Kezhai Village.

Yang stayed here for five years as a peasant.

Since then, the "go to work in the mountains and the countryside" movement was launched in full swing. All the middle and high school students supposed to graduate in 1966, 1967 and 1968 but stuck in the school because of the revolution were sent to the countryside in the year of 1968. The total number of educated youth who were sent to the countryside during the Cultural Revolution reached over 16 million, with one tenth of the country's population swarming from cities into the countryside, which was a great migration rare in the history of mankind.

Later, factories and mines began to recruit workers. I had my first job two years later in 1971 and became a member of the working class.

My Dream to Be a Soldier

During the Cultural Revolution, there were three main options for young people: to be a soldier, to be a worker or to be a peasant. To join the army would be everyone's first choice.

We learned it since childhood that it was a great honor to be a soldier. If there was a soldier in the family, the whole family would feel proud and a red horizontal board with the inscription "Family of Honor" would be sent by the government amidst beating of gongs and drums. When people saw the red board, they knew that this family had someone in the army and would soon cast a respectful and envious glance.

The prestige of the People's Liberation Army was promoted to an unprecedented height during the Cultural Revolution when Chairman Mao always received the Red Guards in his green-olive military uniform.

When I was 12 years old, the Red Guards of the mine were going to Guiyang to attend the parade to celebrate the inauguration of Chairman Mao's statue at the Spring Thunder Square. The Red Guards were to perform a formation at the square. Dressed in military uniforms with leather belts and caps, we felt like we were soldiers.

We got on the trucks at midnight and arrived in Guiyang the next dawn. It had been raining heavily all the way and we got wet like drowned rats.

Many PLA soldiers came to the celebration too. Whenever I saw a soldier, I would stand attention and gave him a military salute. Many of the soldiers were puzzled and the people in the street were amused to see a little girl who was drenched through with rain wearing a drooping fake military cap and saluted seriously to every solider she met. Then I saw an officer coming over. I stepped forward and greeted him with a military salute. He returned me with a salute. I can still remember his looks though many years have passed.

At that time, military uniform, cap and leather belt were what most young people dreamed of. Some of them would even turn to theft and violence in order to get a real military uniform, leather belt and cap. Once before I went to Guiyang for a performance, I borrowed a leather belt from an officer who came to our mine to recruit soldiers. The leather belt got stolen. When I came back, I went to apologize to the officer crying bitterly. He said it didn't matter, but he was cold to me since then even though he had liked me very much before. I was attacked by a bunch of Red Guard boys who accused me of losing a PLA officer's leather belt.

When military control was exercised, hundreds of soldiers stationed in the small valley of the mine where we lived. We admired them from the bottom of our heart.

What a great honor if I could be one of them.

Who we admired most were those art soldiers of the military Mao Zedong Thought Propaganda Team. The young boys and girls looked extremely handsome and smart in military uniform.

I had a good friend whose name was Hua. She had a very good voice. Her elder brother was recruited by Guizhou Art School to learn vocal music. Hua also liked singing. She could sing very well with her brother's help and instruction.

Hua and I were both in the Mao Zedong Thought Propaganda Team of the mine. I admired her and followed her everywhere. We became close friends.

Hua was missing one day. Her family told me she had gone to Guiyang to see a doctor.

Several days later, she showed up and told me excitedly that she went to Guiyang to take the examination for art soldiers.

She told me that the army would send some officers here to give her an audition and then she would introduce me to them.

When the day came, I was out with the propaganda team to give a performance at a construction site. It was raining and we walked to and fro dozens of kilometers in the rain. When we got back, everyone was soaked through with muddy water all over and a tree branch in hand as a walking stick.

When we walked past the hostel where the Red Guard headquarters was once based, I heard a girl's voice shouting my name loudly "Heping! Heping!" When I looked up, I saw Hua and two officers standing on the flat roof of the hostel. The two officers were staring at me. I was so embarrassed for my lousy appearance.

Apparently I left no good impression on the two officers. They didn't even give me a chance for a test.

Hua got recruited by the two officers. Her brother also became an art soldier.

I took the examination several times but failed every time.

The last time I tried, I felt quite good about myself and the officer who auditioned me also told me that I was hopeful of success. I waited for a long time. There was still no result. I totally gave it up.

One day, an officer made a special visit to the mine to tell me that I was recruited by the propaganda team of the army and the admission notice would be sent in a few days. He told me not to lose heart and wait patiently.

The news quickly spread at the mine. Some of my classmates came to visit me and they said downstairs, "Maybe Heping is already dressed in her military uniform now!"

Ironically, I didn't get recruited. I failed the political examination because of my Big Uncle.

It was an overwhelming blow to me.

Many of the people who I knew got enlisted in the army and their stories were quite legendary.

I had a PE teacher who was two meters high and graduated from the Department of Physical Education of East China Normal University in Shanghai. He was recruited by the army to play basketball.

Another teacher who was good at painting was also recruited because the mine's huge oil painting of Chairman Mao was painted by him.

A friend of mine is now a high-ranking official in the Chinese government. He could play the cello and was one of the educated youths sent to the countryside. One day, a military Russian brand car drove directly to the field and took him away.

Another friend who now is a professor of Peking University was also recruited because he could play the clarinet.

I always dreamed that I was dressed in military uniform and became a PLA soldier. My heart was filled with happiness and pride. I wished I would never wake up.

After Hua joined the army, the first time I met her was in a military hospital in Guiyang. She had something wrong with her vocal cords and was hospitalized for a surgery. I tried to hold my tears during the several hours when I was with her.

When Hua came back home to visit her family, I went with her parents to meet her at the railway station. When Hua saw her father, she gave him a smart military salute. A smile of happiness and pride was on her father's face. I felt I was suffocated with envy.

On the way to her home, all the people in the street were looking at her and praised her with clicking of their tongues. A group of small children gathered at the door of Hua's house to see Hua who was the only woman soldier from the mine.

Later I went to college and gradually we became estranged from each other.

I completely gave up the idea of becoming a soldier. But I still admired soldiers. This was why I found a soldier as my boyfriend not long after I graduated from the university. He was my first boyfriend. I married my ex-husband also because he was a soldier. His father was a doctor in the army. There was a universal phenomenon that if the family was related with or had strong contacts in the army, it would be much easier for the children to join the army from the "back door". Both of my ex-husband and his younger brother joined the army. His younger brother was only 14 years old when he was enlisted.

Many among the first batch of Red Guards in Beijing joined the army because of their parents' contacts.

Receive Reeducation from the Working Class

I was only 13 years old when Chairman Mao called upon educated youth to go to work in the countryside. I also wanted to work as a peasant because Chairman Mao told us to and it must be right. But my parents pulled a long face when I told them that I wanted to go to work in the countryside.

We were offspring of the workers at the mine, so we didn't have to go to the countryside.

I was to graduate from middle school in July of 1971. In May of 1971, the mine started to recruit workers, so I became a worker before finishing my education in the junior high school, like many of my classmates. I was only 15 years old then.

It was in the middle stage of the Cultural Revolution. The school was restarted, though the content of learning was still revolutionary. I was getting older and started to realize the importance of learning to my future and I wanted to continue my study. Finally I changed my mind and decided to take a job to support the family. My parents also wished I could get a job. A couple of my classmates continued to study in the senior high school and I envied them very much.

Hundreds of us young children, aged between 15 and 20, were recruited. Military control was still exercised and we new workers had to spend one year in the young workers' company to temper ourselves through physical labor.

We did heavy physical jobs during the day such as building roads, carrying logs, loading and unloading railway wagons with rocks. In the evening, we had political activities to study Chairman Mao's works and newspapers or to criticize capitalist-roaders.

There was a veteran worker named Tao Dechen who was a model worker with high prestige at the mine. He taught us new workers how to carry and pile up logs which were pitprops used down the mine. I always carried logs with Tao Dechen. A log weighed at least 50 kilograms. I carried the lighter end and he carried the heavier end and the two of us worked in harmony with each other. He always spoke highly of me in front of people that I didn't spare effort when doing my work. I was anxious to outdo others though I was thin and weak. I could get a monthly pay of 18 yuan for eight hours' hard physical labor every day.

We dug one side of a hill with pickaxe and used the earth and stone to build the road. We shoveled earth and stones into the cart and loaded each cart with about one cubic meter of earth and stones. Then three of us pushed the cart to the section of the road which was under construction and paved the road with earth and stones.

I didn't spare strength and worked nonstop with my pickaxe. Every time I lifted up my head, I could see someone staring at me in astonishment. They couldn't believe their eyes. When they met me before, I was either performing on the stage singing and dancing or walking in the street with my head high up and looking steadily forward. I impressed people of my age as being a proud and finicky girl who saw nobody in her eyes. But to their surprise, I worked hard as if I was crazy when doing physical labor.

Later I always thought that if I hadn't used my strength so excessively at that time, I would have grown taller.

Although I did strenuous physical labor during the year in the young workers' company, I was happy and contented. No matter what happened around me, I wouldn't be influenced. I remained optimistic and I enjoyed the atmosphere in the communist big family.

Maybe I was too young to know what pain was. More importantly, I cherished lofty ideals and a great longing for a bright future.

Once we three girls pushed a heavy cart full of earth with all our strength. We couldn't catch up with it when going downgrade and had to let go of it. The cart tumbled downhill and fell down the trench. We laughed heartily at the interesting scene.

Suddenly we heard a roar, "What are you laughing at?"

It was the head of the young workers' company, an old worker. We rushed down the trench to get the cart back. One of the girls was a little bit plump and she ran hastily down the hill like a penguin, which made me and another girl burst into laughter again. Our head got exasperated and yelled at us, "You dare laugh again! Are you so happy to see the state property falling down the trench? What is your stand now?"

There was a dispute between two girls that day. A girl took off her sweater to cool off and put it aside. When she went to get her sweater after she finished her job, she found out that a beautiful glass button on her sweater was missing. She suspected a girl took it. The two of them started to quarrel and had a fight.

That evening, a meeting was held to criticize us three girls who didn't feel sorry but laughed heartily to see the state property being damaged. Everyone was encouraged to speak at the meeting. A girl said, "You laughed when you saw the country suffering property loss because you have bourgeois ideas deep in your heart. If you don't pull back before it is too late, or remold your ideology, you will turn traitor if a war breaks out in the future."

We all did self-criticism, expressing that we had realized our mistakes and felt deeply sorry for it. But deep inside, we were not convinced that we were wrong.

The next day, a big-character poster was put up on the wall. The subject was "Deep thinking brought about by a button and a cart". A detailed analysis was given: A button is worth only several cents. But it is private property and the loser kicked up a row and even had a fight with other people. A cart is worth several hundred yuan and is state property. When the three girls saw the cart fall down the trench, they not only didn't feel sorry, but also broke into laughter. If such kind of ideas was allowed to continue, revisionism would be restored in China and the red flag would fall down when the satellite flies to the sky, which means if people only cared about the development of science but not the ideological remoulding, China would change from socialism to captalism.

We were criticized for several days in succession.

After we received one year's remolding in the young workers' company, we were assigned to different work units to work as apprentice electricians, bench workers, lathemen, planers and drivers.

Several girls and I were assigned to the explosive magazine to make explosives. It was a job that required high labor intensity but low technical skill. The magazine was located in a deep mountain valley several kilometers away from the mining area. We worked in three shifts. I was the leader of one of the shifts. Every day, I drove a hand tractor to a warehouse to load ammonium nitrate, and then drove back to the explosive making workshop. I had to do the loading and unloading myself. Each bag of ammonium nitrate weighed 50 kilograms.

I spent only two hours learning how to drive a hand tractor and dared drive it on the precipitous mountain road with a deep trench on one side. I can hardly understand how I could be so bold at that time.

The workers mixed the ammonium nitrate, sawdust and diesel oil proportionately on a big aluminum plate and sent it to the high-temperature shop to dry. The indoor temperature was over 50 degrees Celsius with even higher temperature of the bed-style drier. The workers had to go in there every 10 minutes to turn the explosive over. After the explosive was dried, we would dip the paper in wax, put the explosive on the paper and rolled it into tube-shaped explosive. Now and then, we had to take the explosive and detonator and find an open space to test the explosive performance of our product.

Our appliances for labor protection were working clothes, caps, rubber shoes and face masks. We also got a high-temperature work allowance of seven yuan every month. There was a public bathhouse near the workshop and it was great to be able to take a shower every day. We didn't realize how bad the work environment was or if it did us harm to make explosives. Almost all the girls had blood in their stool. The blood made the whole latrine pit red.

I worked in three shifts. After a day's hard work, all I wanted was to go to bed and have a good sleep. I had no appetite at all. My mother bought eggs with my high-temperature allowance. What I usually had for three meals a day were nine poached eggs because I didn't feel like eating anything else. What I dreaded most was the night shift. When I was sound asleep at late night, my mother would wake me up. Sometimes I went to the work place with fellow workers and sometimes alone. It was pitch-dark and quiet. All I could hear was my footsteps and heartbeat. Sometimes I was scared to death by the wildfire that glimmered above the burial ground on the mountain slope.

My dream was to be an art soldier, but there was no hope that my dream would come true. I felt I was on the verge of collapse. But I still had dreams in my heart. I wrote a poem "I am a worker as well as a soldier" to encourage myself.

> *With a pair of shining eyes and a blue cap on head,*
> *She reminds people as if she is a soldier on duty safeguarding the frontier of the motherland.*
> *The shovel in her hands for turning the explosive materials looks like a sub machinegun of a soldier.*
> *She is thrilled and feels bolder and braver when everyone says that she looks like a soldier.*
> *Yes, I am a worker as well as a soldier and at any time ready to go fighting.*

After half a year's work in the explosive magazine, I was transferred to a mining area and became an apprentice electrician. It was the best type of work at the mine and few girls could be an electrician, especially the electrician working underground. I was the first woman underground electrician in the history of Kaiyang Phosphate Mine. I liked to do something unusual, so I cherished the opportunity very much.

I was put in an awkward position on the first day I registered at the electrician team. The team leader designated an electrician who was in his thirties and named Zhu Zhide to be my master. He refused to accept the job. He had a quarrel with the team leader and left with a slam of the door. The reason why he was unwilling to be my master was that I used to sing and dance in the Mao Zedong Thought Propaganda Team. He thought all the girls who made public appearances singing and dancing were not decent girls and he didn't want to be the master of an indecent girl. Finally the team leader had to be my master himself.

I loved my job very much. I arrived at the workshop early every morning, cleaning, making a fire in the stove and boiling water. I worked hard learning maths, physics and principles of electrical engineering and practiced winding coils, cutting steel wire and climbing up poles. I had nimble legs and feet because of dancing. My best record of climbing up the pole was one minute up and down a ten-meter pole.

Zhu Zhide was touched by my enthusiasm at work and became my master tacitly. Once, I was working high above the ground on the pole. Suddenly it began to rain heavily. All the workers ran away to shelter from the rain except him. He stood under the pole to keep me company. He didn't leave until I finished my work and came down the pole.

As an underground electrician, I had to work down the pit often. A mine was scrapped and all my fellow electricians had to go down the pit to recycle the cable. The lighting had been removed and we had to carry the coal miner's lamps with us. The six of us carried a several-hundred-meter long cable on our shoulders dragging it towards the exit. I was thin and weak and was almost pushed forward by the force of inertia. I stumbled along, knocking into the wall on the left and the right. We worked like this continuously for a week and retrieved all the cable. The sulphuric acid in the storage battery of the lamps burnt a lot of holes in my work clothes.

The days when I worked as an underground electrician were the happiest time besides the propaganda team. I enjoyed my job because there were so many things to learn every day. I felt I could be an underground electrician the rest of my life.

Weird Relations between Male and Female

During the Cultural Revolution, no romantic scenes could be found in any movies, books or other works of literature and art.

Sexual relations were dirty things in our mind. If a boy courted a girl, the girl would call him a stinking hoodlum to his face or in a letter written to him. Loving couples made their dating such secrecy as if they were engaged in covert evildoing.

A boy and a girl in the propaganda team fell in love with each other. The boy Lin Xiang was recruited to our mine from other places. He was about 20 years old and was a versatile boy. He was the director and leading player of the propaganda team. The girl Yueji was about 18 years old and her father was my father's colleague.

When the propaganda team went to Guiyang for a performance, the two of them secretly went on a date. They came out of the guest house one on the heels of the other to avoid being seen by others. It happened to be spotted by me and several other girls who were going out for shopping. We followed them for quite a while to see when they would come together.

The relationship between them became a popular topic of our conversations.

Lin Xiang and Yueji had sex in the single dorm.

It was an extremely serious matter to have sex before one got married and only reckless people would do such a thing. People at that time could overcome various human emotions and desires for the cause of revolution.

Lin Xiang and Yueji were caught by the worker rebels in the act when they were making love. They took Lin Xiang back to his factory and Yueji to her school. Yueji had already finished the junior high school, but was stuck in the school because of the Cultural Revolution like all of her classmates who were still under the supervision of the school.

When Yueji's younger brother saw his sister locked up in a classroom, he ran home in tears to tell his parents.

Yueji's father hastily went to the school to take her daughter back home. To protect his daughter, he pressed her to tell people that it was Lin Xiang who forced her to do so. In fact, we all knew that it was Yueji who was fond of Lin Xiang and kept pestering him. In our mind, Yueji was not good enough for Lin Xiang.

Lin Xiang went to Yueji's home. He kneeled down before Yueji's parents, begging them to marry their daughter to him. Yueji's parents resolutely disagreed. If Yueji got married, she could no longer find a job. Only single young people were recruited at that time.

When Kaiyang Phosphate Mine started to recruit workers, all the students in the propaganda team were recruited except Yueji who was disqualified because of her depraved style of life.

People thought Yueji was dirty. Whenever we met Yueji, we would feel sorry for her. Her life was ruined. Her parents and her brothers were disgraced and found it hard to raise their head. Later Yueji was sent to her hometown by her parents.

The story of my friend Weiwei was even ridiculous and laughable.

A boy whose name was Jiahua wrote a letter to Weiwei inviting her to a date with him at the railway.

The railway was under construction and the spacious roadbed became an ideal place for young couples to date. If we said we met who and who strolling at the railway, we referred to something shameful.

Jiahua was a handsome boy of great stature. He was a troublesome boy who had no interest in study. He was a bad child in our eyes.

Weiwei handed the letter to the PLA Representative of the school who came up with a stupid idea. He asked Weiwei to meet Jiahua as scheduled and arranged some soldiers and students to lie in ambush near the roadbed. When Jiahua showed up and walked close to Weiwei, they would catch him and take him back to the school for an interrogation under the charge of dating a girl. In the following period of time, Weiwei was under the protection of the PLA Representatives and her classmates who feared Jiahua would retaliate against her.

My friend Shanshan found a boyfriend who was a worker recruited from the countryside. They went through the marriage registration but held no wedding ceremony, so they couldn't live together.

The girl had a change of her heart and began to coquet with other men. The boy noticed it and was enraged. The boy was always in night shifts and had a room in the dormitory in the workshop. One day when the workers were at work, the boy deluded the girl into coming to his dormitory and coerced her into having sex with him. The girl resisted desperately, screaming and crying for help. The workers crowded at the door, listening in high spirits the noise inside the room. After a while, the boy came out holding a sheet in his hand which had a clear blood-stain on it. The girl's family went to the police station to accuse the boy of rape. The policeman said what the boy did was a lawful act.

The girl's father had died long ago. The mother found it hard to stand the disgrace the girl brought to the family and broke off the mother-daughter relationship with her for many years. The girl married the boy in the end. At that time, if a girl was not a virgin, she would be discriminated against and no man would want her.

In the workshop where I worked, a girl slept with her master worker who was a married man. When we found it out, we held meetings every night to criticize them indignantly. The girl was a youth league member and the Youth League organization held meetings to discuss how to punish her. Several young workers including me firmly insisted that she be expelled from the Youth League. The League branch secretary talked with us and asked us to give her a chance to correct her errors and make a fresh start. Although we gave in, we felt indignant deep in our heart.

Several years later, she married my senior fellow apprentice, the boy who once criticized her most severely.

She was a tall and beautiful girl while my senior fellow apprentice was a very short man with homely face. If the girl had no such a stigma, she wouldn't have married him. I was told that he had married her for the purpose of improving the stature of the next generation because all of his family members were unusually short.

Go to College

All the universities were closed between 1966 and 1972. When the universities restarted to enroll students in 1972, only workers, soldiers, and educated youths who had worked in the factories, the countryside or served in the army for over two years were qualified to be recommended. They didn't admit newly graduated high school students. Only those who worked hard and were politically qualified could be recommended by the workers, peasants or soldiers.

By the summer of 1973, I had worked for two years. My master worker encouraged me to apply for the college entrance examination.

I told him that my educational level was too low and I wanted to prepare for another two years before I took the examination. I wanted to learn mechanics and electronics in the university.

When Uncle Weiping who was responsible for the college admission at the mine came across my father, he said, "Tell Heping to enter her name for the college. There is a vacancy in the English major."

"I am afraid she wouldn't be admitted. Her educational level is too low."

"Heping is good at speaking Putonghua, so it wouldn't be difficult for her to learn a foreign language."

When my father came home, he told me that Uncle Weiping hoped that I could take the examination for college.

But I didn't like English. I wanted to learn mechanics and electronics.

My father asked some people who were recognized as being learned men at the mine to persuade me that to go to college, the younger the better.

One had to first pass the appraisal and recommendation of the working class to go to college. My work performance was there for all to see. I was highly appraised by the workers and was recommended to enter for the college entrance examination.

I had come round to the idea that I might as well learn English.

When Richard Nixon visited China in 1972, I watched it in the documentary, the ping-pong diplomacy and Nixon and his wife watching the revolutionary ballet *The Red Detachment of Women*. I was greatly impressed by the Chinese diplomats, especially the two women diplomats Wang Hairong and Tang Wensheng who followed Chairman Mao for all the events as his interpreters. I thought it was good to be a diplomat and they could also make contributions to the revolution.

The college entrance examination was very simple then. The major I applied for was English and I had to take two examinations in Chinese and English. For the Chinese examination, the candidates were asked to write a critical essay. As to whom we were asked to criticize, I cannot recall it.

The examination was held in a classroom in the high school of the mine. A teacher named Liu Jianhua, who taught Chinese in the high school, was our invigilator. When I was buried in writing my essay, Liu Jianhua came over and stopped by my side, looking at me. I got nervous and suddenly my mind went blank. He was aware of my nervousness and walked away. After the examination, someone told me that teacher Liu Jianhua said my essay was beautifully written.

Actually I only got over 70 points in the Chinese examination, while the full score was 100 points. But it was not bad for me who had only received three years' education in the primary school.

I never learned English before. I had no time to prepare for the written examination. I turned to the English teacher of the high school for help. I asked him to teach me some simple sentences in English to deal with the oral examination.

The English teacher surnamed Li used to be a translator for the Kuomintang at the Sino-American Cooperation Organization in Chongqing. He was persecuted during the Cultural Revolution and suffered a lot for it.

Teacher Li wrote down some daily expressions on pieces of paper and taught me to read them. I annotated every sentence with Chinese characters to memorize their pronunciation. I had to memorize them mechanically. When I was having a dialogue in English with teacher Li, many students were standing outside the window to watch us. They didn't know that I was parroting without understanding the meaning of the words. Most of the students were not interested in study, especially English. They admired me a lot when they saw that I could have a dialogue with the teacher in English.

Teacher Li's son was also teaching English at the school. Teacher Li said to her son that I was apt for learning English.

I got goose egg for the written examination. I remember one of the questions was to translate a sentence into English which was "I will do whatever the Party has told me to do". Like many of other candidates, I wrote on the back of the examination paper a guarantee saying that if I was lucky to get admitted, I would learn hard and win honor for the school and so on.

During the oral examination, none of the sentences I prepared beforehand came into use. I told the teacher that I had never learned English before. Maybe he had seen it a lot before, so he was not surprised. He asked me to imitate his pronunciation. I stared carefully at his mouth and read after him. I thought he was a little exaggerated with the way he made the pronunciation. I imitated carefully even though I knew I looked ugly with my mouth opened like that. The teacher's remarks for me were that I had clear enunciation, correct pronunciation and quick response and was apt for learning a foreign language.

There were some workers at our mine who were educated youths recruited from the countryside. They used to live in the cities like Shanghai and had received better education before the Cultural Revolution began. If candidates were admitted to universities solely based on the examination results, I couldn't compete with them. But in terms of one's performance and sense of responsibility in one's work, they were no match for me. The most important condition for a person to go to college was to be positively appraised and recommended by the working class. Besides that, I had another advantage which was my young age.

After the examination, I was anxiously waiting for the admission notice of the university. Many candidates received their notices and left for school one after another. I didn't get any notice. We thought there was no hope. My mother took my 10-year-old sister to our hometown in northeast China to visit my grandparents. My father had gone to Guiyang to study in the Party school, which had rotational courses for the communist cadres.

When I was about to give up, the notice came. I was admitted by the English Department of Guizhou University. Later I knew that when they were checking my political background, they found out my Big Uncle's historical problem. But when they saw the workers' high appraisal of me, they considered it for a long time and finally decided to recruit me. This was why the admission notice came late.

My parents were out. Only my two younger brothers and I were left at home. I had to pack myself. The family was poor and I couldn't even find a decent suitcase. I found a canvas case which had been used for at least 20 years and a broken mosquito curtain which had dozens of big and small holes in it. I tried to clean the case with water. Out of my expectation, the hard lining inside the case was made of paper and the case totally sagged when it was soaked. It didn't look like a case any more even if it was dried. I found some odd bits of cloth to mend the mosquito curtain. There were so many holes in the curtain that I didn't finish mending it until the day before my departure.

I remember that the day before I left home was the traditional Mid-Autumn Festival. It was the occasion for the whole family to get together eating moon cakes and enjoying the moon. Mother was not at home and there was no one to help me prepare my luggage. It was raining and the moon was nowhere to be seen. I had mixed feelings of longing and melancholy.

Father hurriedly came back home specially to send me to school.

The next day, I carried the canvas case bundled up with rope and got on a truck heading for Guizhou University. That day was the first turning point in my life.

Worker-Peasant-Soldier College Students

One had to pass simple examinations to go to college in 1972 and 1973. But from 1974 to 1976, no examination was even required as long as one was politically qualified.

Chairman Mao said educational system should be shortened and students should be educated in a revolutionary way. So the schooling of all the universities was reduced from four years to three years.

We were called worker-peasant-soldier college students because we were recommended to college by the workers, the peasants and the soldiers.

All the students of the English Department came from factories or the countryside. The eldest student was 28 and I was 18, the youngest one in our department.

The parents of many of the students who came from the countryside were commune cadres. It was difficult for children of the ordinary peasants to go to college. The parents of many educated youths and the students who came from factories were also local personages. So many people believed that the college entrollment system based on the recommendation of the workers, the peasants and the soldiers could give rise to black case work and provided easy access to backdoor deals. It was true.

There were two reasons why I could go to college. The first reason was that I did well in my job and the working class was satisfied with me. The second reason was that there was a rule which stipulated that those who had worked for five years could go to college with salary. Many of the fellow workers of my age in the mine wanted to go to college with salary and preferred to wait till they had worked in the mine for five years, so I had few competitors.

We worker-peasant-soldier college students went to college with the mission to "attend the school, control the school, and reform the school with Marxism-Leninism and Mao Zedong Thought".

I was in grade three in primary school when the Cultural Revolution began. So I jumped from grade three directly to college.

The first semester went on normally. We started to learn English from ABC. I found everything difficult. I always wrote critical essays when making revolution in the mine. Although I copied most of them from the newspapers, I could always win praise for my essays. But here in the college, I was taught for the first time that there is a subject, a predicate and an object in a sentence. Once the teacher who taught us literature gave me the following remarks after he reviewed my essay: The essay doesn't read smoothly and is full of wrongly written characters.

154

I had never received such kind of criticism. It was the first time my pride was badly struck and I cried bitterly.

I made up my mind to work hard to change the situation. I got up at five every morning, did jogging and went to the small forest behind the classroom to read English. I read aloud and the whole school knew that there was an extraordinarily hardworking girl in the English Department.

I didn't know how hardworking I was until one day it began to snow in the midnight and I found that the first row of footprint on the snow was stepped by me. I knew that I was the one who got up earliest in the school. Two girl students in the English Department swore to get up earlier than me. But they never managed to do it.

When the first semester was over, we lagged behind our teaching plan. The reason was that study had to give way to the political movement. There was political movement one after another and we had to suspend classes from time to time to learn Marxism-Leninism and Mao Zedong Thought and to take part in the political movement. It was not important if we didn't do well in study, but our thoughts must be revolutionary. Our slogan was "We prefer socialist weeds to capitalist seedlings. We will never be sheep-like students". Sheep-like students referred to those bookworms who were obedient and had no rebellious spirit. We were also encouraged to become college students who were both red and expert. If we were not red but expert, we would cause the severe consequence of restoration of capitalism and China would be taken down the road of revisionism like the Soviet Union.

At the end of the first semester, the whole class was sitting around in a circle and having dialogues in English as the final examination. First one had to introduce himself and his family in English, and then the teacher and the classmates would ask questions. When it was my turn, there were many questions.

"What is your name?"

"My name is Liu Ping."

"Are you a teacher?"

"No, I am not. I am a student."

"How old are you? "

"I am 18."

"Do you have any brothers and sisters?"

"Yes, I do. I have two brothers and one sister."

...

"Is your father a cadre?"

"Yes, he is."

"What is your mother?"

"My mother is a cadre, too."

I answered all the questions fluently and the teacher gave me a very high mark.

From the above dialog you can tell how basic our English was.

During the winter vacation, I studied at home every day. I prepared all the lessons we didn't finish in the first semester beforehand. When everyone was going out visiting relatives and friends in the Chinese New Year, I was at home absorbed in my studies. The people who came to visit my family could see me holding a book reading carefully. Soon I became known as a hardworking student at the mine and many parents set me as a model to teach their children.

By the beginning of the second semester, I had made substantial progress in my English and study was getting easier for me. I became one of the good students in the class.

Our spoken English and listening were particularly poor. When we were having listening classes, we didn't catch what was said in the tape recorder and looked at each other helplessly. During one class, the teacher asked us to listen to one sentence. It was repeated several times, but none of us knew what was said. The teacher called my name. I stood up and answered hesitantly, "A short visit." "Right!" the teacher shouted excitedly. Finally there was one student who got it. It was really not easy for the teachers to teach students like us.

At the beginning of the second semester, we went to the country-side in response to the "open-door schooling" policy. College students were required to receive reeducation from the working class and poor and lower-middle peasants and to work on farms, in factories or on military bases.

We came to a poverty-stricken village of Bouyei ethnic minority for our open-door schooling.

We worked with the peasants on the field during the day. We did all kinds of work such as planting crops, vegetables, carrying water and feeding pigs. I worked very hard and the villagers said that I could make a living by myself if I lived in the countryside. I considered it as the highest evaluation from the poor and lower-middle peasants and I felt very proud of myself.

Several of my classmates and I lived in a poor peasant Aunty Wang's home. She was blind and remained single all her life. We helped her carry water and do other housework. Soon, she could recognize us by listening to our footsteps. In the evening, she would tell us ghost stories. There was no electricity in the village. We had our classes or political studies under the kerosene lamp after dark.

We rehearsed programs to give performances for the peasants on the day of a fair. The peasants there had no cultural life. When we were giving a performance at the town, the local people and many more that came from neighboring villages crowded around the simple outdoor stage so tightly that one couldn't even move. Some villagers even climbed on the roof of a house under construction for a better view. When my classmate Gong and I were performing a theatrical dialogue of "learn from the poor and lower-middle peasants" on the stage, we were extremely nervous to see a dense crowd of people under the stage. Suddenly, we heard a bang. The house collapsed and the spectators who stood on the roof all fell to the ground. A small child died. Although many years have passed, I feel sad whenever I think of the child who lost his life for watching our performance.

We stayed in the countryside for two months. Not long after we returned to school, the movement to criticize Lin Biao and Confucius began.

The teacher asked me to write an essay in English to criticize Lin Biao and Confucius and to attend the denunciation meeting held by the Heavy Machinery Plant of Guizhou Province. I copied an article from the English version of *Beijing Review*. At that time, all the publications including the English versions were about politics, so it was easy for the students to copy well translated articles on politics from *Beijing Review*.

We college students and the workers sat around in the workshop to criticize Lin Biao and Confucius in English. I remember that several workers and the student representatives read aloud their critical essays with strong emotions and were constantly interrupted by the shouting of slogans. A girl student who was one grade higher led us shouting at the top of her sharp voice, "Down with Lin Biao! Down with Confucius!"

Worker-peasant-soldier students varied a lot in terms of their educational level. I especially admired and liked the schoolmates who were junior and senior high school graduates of 1966 to1968. When the Cultural Revolution began, most of them had at least finished their junior high school and had comparatively solid foundation in learning. They were good at study and had higher comprehensive quality.

Those who came after them were students like me who had weak basis but was young and hardworking and had some advantages such as spoken English. My favorite class work was to paraphrase English texts and retell them with my own words. Every time I wished the teacher would call my name and ask me to do the paraphrase.

There was also a kind of students who had received little school education. Some of them were no better than illiterates.

The teacher had to take all the students into consideration, so the teaching plan had practically no function.

Worker-peasant-soldier students came from different places of the country with different backgrounds. All kinds of stories happened among them.

A girl student of Miao ethnic minority of the Department of Chinese Language and Literature was expelled from school because she made love with a male classmate on the football ground, which was absolutely unforgivable for unmarried college students at that time. I couldn't understand why the male student was not dismissed, but he was certainly punished by the school. The reason why the girl was expelled was that she got pregnant. She had too bad an influence, especially as a minority student.

Two of my classmates fell in love with each other. Both of them were middle school teachers before they went to college. They were good at study, especially the girl, who ranked first academically in the class. They each had a sweetheart back home. It was considered immoral if one shifted one's love to another person.

They often went out on a date secretly. Sometimes they stayed outside all night long. All the classmates understood what was happening but kept silence. The girl was a good friend of mine and she always told me that she stayed with her old classmate who was in the Department of Physics. I believed it. One day, I met her classmate and we had a small chat. To my surprise, she told me that the girl had never stayed overnight at her place. I noticed that every time she went out, she would bring a large piece of plastic cloth with her. There was a period of time when she was low-spirited and absent-minded in class. I also heard that she had her period for a whole month. I could tell that something had happened to her, but there was no proof. I could feel that both of them were very depressed.

Later, I heard that after graduation from college, they returned to their native places and married their former girlfriend or boyfriend respectively.

There was a girl classmate who came from the countryside. Her mother gave birth to a boy when she was 21 years old. Her mother with the newly-born baby came to live in the school for a long time with her daughter who shared a dormitory room with us five girls. The school didn't dare to drive them away because her mother was a poor peasant and the school had to stand on the side of the poor peasants. I could often see the three of them sitting in the sun on the bench in front of the dormitory building. Her mother held her baby brother in her arms and breastfed him as if there was no one else present. The baby brother was so weak as if he would die at any minute.

Those who attracted most attention on the campus were soldier students who looked extremely handsome in military uniform. Most of them majored in politics, Chinese, philosophy and history.

When I first came to the university, I came across a soldier student whom I thought I had met before. I was surprised and happy when I recognized him who used to be one of the PLA Representatives stationed at the mine. I went to his dormitory for a chat with him for a couple of times. Later a rumor spread that I was associating with the soldier student. Since then, I kept a distance from him.

There were two computers in the Department of Mathematics which were the treasures of the school. The students of the department took turns to watch the computers every night and lived in the same room with the computers. One weekend, two girl students were on duty. They didn't attend the class the next Monday. Later they were found dead in their room, stabbed to death with more than 100 cuts on each of their bodies. Classes were suspended for three days for the police to solve the case. But it is said the case hasn't been solved to this day.

During the three years in the university, we went to work twice in the countryside and twice in the factory, having meals, living together and working with the workers and peasants. The time which was really spent on study was no more than half a year and the rest of the time was devoted to the revolution. We hardly had any examination during the three years, so we didn't care if we did well or not in our study.

A Person Who Has Influenced My Life

On the day of the university's registration, I met a girl at the outdoor registration place. She was dressed in military uniform wearing two pigtails. She was beautiful and graceful and had a special temperament which caught my eyes immediately. She was Yang of whom the stories were told in the previous chapters. She was also a student of the English Department. She was the first person I met in the university.

We didn't know each other at the beginning because we were not in the same class. She was four years older than me and was born in a revolutionary cadre's family. She had worked in the countryside as an educated youth for five years before she went to the university. She was commissary in charge of the Department's arts and sports activities. She was particularly good at sports and was once champion of the youth breaststroke competition in Guizhou Province. We often rehearsed and gave performances on the campus which were all revolutionary songs and dances related to the political movement at that time. She was strong in sports and I was strong in artistic performance. Whenever she came to me for help, I was more than willing to help and did my job conscientiously. She was touched by my dedication to work and was grateful to me.

We soon gained popularity in the school. The performance given by our department was always the best. The whole school knew that there was a girl in the English Department who was good at dancing. Some of them even thought I was better than some of the professionals. While Yang's reputation was not only for her excellence in sports, but for her all-round development.

We always worked together for the recreational and sports activities of our department, so we became good friends. I didn't expect that making friends with her would mean heavy fetters for me. Nor did I expect that 16 years after our graduation, she would change the track of my life's journey and led me into the tourism industry where I realized the highest value of my life.

Since I was a child, I was eager to make friends with someone who was better than me.

Since I became a good friend of hers, I had felt pressure all the time, which never happened before. She was too excellent. I had to try hard to be as good as she in every aspect. But I never made it.

Besides classes of the English Department, she sometimes attended the lectures of the Philosophy Department. During the Cultural Revolution, we were required to learn the philosophical thinking and works of Marx, Engels, Lenin and Mao Zedong. She really learned them out of interest. But I attended the philosophy lectures only because she was there and I never really understood what I had learned.

She was good at writing essays. I tried to be as good as she, but what I produced after I racked my brains was still an unreadable essay with no clear main idea. Our literature teacher spoke highly of her, but I never got praised.

She had a very good handwriting. But no matter how hard I practiced, my handwriting still looked childish.

I learned how to swim, how to ride a bicycle and how to play volleyball in the university only because she could do them.

She was a breaststroke champion, which was an unattainable goal for me. She could ride a bicycle with great ease. But I had hardly seen a bicycle in the valley at the mine. When I learned to ride a bicycle in the university, I often lost control of the brakes and once even drove myself into a bush, hurting my head badly.

There was another important reason for me to learn bicycle riding and swimming. I always thought that if a war broke out in the future, I should devote myself to the war and both bicycle riding and swimming were necessary skills a soldier should possess.

She was the leading player of the volleyball team. I began to practice my volleyball skills because of her. I worked hard and was finally recruited by the volleyball team and became one of the leading players. But I was still not as good as she. During the second provincial university games for the worker-peasant-soldier students, when we were struggling for second place with another team, she served 15 balls at one stretch which our rival missed all. So we easily won the first game. The second game was very dramatic. At its beginning, Yang aced seven services. When the eighth ball flew over, they surprisingly caught it while we all stood there relaxed and watched the ball dropping on the ground. That year, we came second in the university games.

Her beauty and charm were something I could never have. I had a sense of inferiority when I was with her. When we went out together, she would always be the one who attracted people's eyes, especially the male students. If I introduced her to my friends, they would shift their interest to her. My friends endlessly discussed in front of me how good she was. I felt more inferior to her.

She was liked by everyone except those who were jealous of her or didn't know her.

She influenced me substantially. Growing up in a small valley, I didn't see much of the world or meet anyone who was as extraordinary as she was. There was a huge distance between the two of us in every aspect, but I wished I could be someone like her. If a sparrow aspires to fly as high as an eagle, how tired the sparrow must be. I was that sparrow.

She was my idol and I always followed her. She said that she wanted to go to Tibet after graduation. She wrote an application, so did I. When Chairman Mao passed away, she said she wanted to go to Beijing. She didn't go, but I went.

She was passionate and always participated in all kinds of activities. She was nicknamed Old Revolutionary. I always followed her and was nicknamed Little Revolutionary.

Fortunately we didn't have examinations in the university. Otherwise I would be too ashamed to live in the world if she outdid me in every examination.

After graduation, I returned to the phosphate mine to be a high school teacher. She was assigned a job in the foreign affairs department of Guizhou Province. The distance between us became wider and wider. I could no longer compete with her.

The time when I felt most disappointed about myself was when I was giving birth to my son, while she was going to work in the United States. I felt a great sense of loss when I thought that I might be a housewife for the rest of my life, while she would have a bright future in the US.

During a long time after I graduated from college, whenever I came up against some difficulty, I would first think what Yang would do if she were in the same situation.

Later when she became head of the Guizhou Tourist Administration, I worked in the foreign affairs department of the H Ministry.

A few years later, I joined China's largest tourist enterprise thanks to her recommendation. My talent was given full play and I achieved unprecedented success in my career.

Now many people consider me as a successful woman. The reason why I have succeeded is that I entered the tourism industry and Yang is my benefactor who led me the way.

Yang didn't stay in the United States. She returned and continued to work as a government officer, while I became an entrepreneur.

I Want to Join the Communist Party

Not long after I entered college, I delivered the application for the Communist Party membership. It was the biggest wish of almost every Chinese to join the Chinese Communist Party. My motive was simple. I believed that only if I joined the Party could I have more opportunities to listen to the instructions of the Party, better serve the Party and make greater contributions for the cause of communism. Only excellent people were qualified to join the Party. The status of a Communist Party member could prove the person's political reliability.

We received the education from the Party since childhood and we knew that it was the Party that liberated China and enabled the toiling masses to live a happy life. The Communist Party was the vanguard and the Communist Party members were the first to endure hardships and the last to enjoy comforts. Almost all the heroes in the movies or in the textbooks were Communist Party members or posthumously admitted as members of the Communist Party.

Communist Party members had priority going to college, joining the army or being promoted. If a university only recruited one student from an unit, the one who was a Communist Party member would be given preference even if the other was as good as he or she in other aspects. If two universities recruited students at the same time, the one who was a Communist Party member would be more likely to go to the better university. There were some people who wrote the application for innumerable times and wouldn't give up hope even if they were in declining years. There were some people whose last wish was to join the Chinese Communist Party before they closed their eyes.

I too was eager to join the Chinese Communist Party. I was once told by a fortune-teller that I would join the Party at the age of 25. Good heavens! What a terrible thing to join the Party so late at the age of 25?

The fact is that I had never been accepted by the Communist Party and I finally joined one of the non-Communist parties in China when I was 45.

The English Department of Guizhou University totally enrolled 100 students in the year 1973, only three of them were Communist Party members. During the three years, most of the students applied for the Party membership. In some other departments of the school, many students successfully joined the Party before graduation. But in our department, no one was admitted to the Party except three of my male classmates who applied for working in Tibet were accepted by the Party branch of the department at the last moment before graduation. A girl named J among the three Party members was the chief culprit for creating obstacles for her classmates to join the Party. She was six years older than me and had rich social experience.

She had an eccentric character and was jealous of anyone who was better than she. She couldn't stop others from surpassing her in other aspects, but she could use her power as Party branch committee member to stop anyone from joining the Party.

I handed in the Party membership application and it was one of her jobs to have talks with me to help me improve my ideological level and understanding of the Party. The trick she played during our talks was to give me a stunning blow when I was high-spirited. For example, if our performance won a prize, she would remind me that someone told her I was conceited. When she saw me work hard, she would ask me if I was going to be a sheep-like student. When she was learning English, she would cover her English textbook with newspaper, pretended she was reading the political articles in the newspaper when someone was looking at her. When I was highly praised for my dancing, she turned to

Yang and analyzed to her why I always designed a solo dance in the performance was that I wanted to show off myself.

I could forget it if I couldn't join the Communist Party. But why was Yang not qualified for it? I really couldn't understand it. She was a perfect student in every way. She had applied for the Party membership several years before she entered college. But upon graduation, she was still not a Party member. In fact, it was J who was too jealous of her to let her join the Party.

What I couldn't understand was that how she alone could stand in the way of the Party's organizational development?

Upon our graduation, three of our classmates joined the Party all of a sudden. Their applications to go to work in Tibet were approved and the Party committee decided to accept them as Party members. This time, J could do nothing to stop it. There were only three students who would go to Tibet in the whole school. They all came from the countryside. The reason why they chose to go to Tibet was that they didn't want to return to the countryside to be a teacher. The policy at that time was that the majority of the students would be assigned to work at their native places after graduation.

Many years later, things had a dramatic change. When I no longer wanted to join the Communist Party, the Party organization repeatedly had talks with me and hoped I could join the Party.

Yang joined the Communist Party not long after graduation. I joined Jiu San Society, one of the non-Communist parties that have accepted the leadership of the Chinese Communist Party. J and her husband lived in the capitalist Europe for many years and didn't return home until her husband obtained his Ph.D. degree.

All of the three Party members were assigned with good jobs when majority of the students were sent to their native places and became middle school teachers in the villages, towns, counties, factories or mines. J became a government officer in the capital city Guiyang and the other two stayed in the school and became university teachers.

The One Who Survives a Disaster Is
Destined to Good Fortune in the Future

When we were sophomores, we were assigned a task by the university. Our country imported 13 big chemical fertilizer projects from the United States and one of them was the Chishui Natural Gas Chemical Plant which was under construction. Personnel of foreign languages were in great demand to translate large quantities of English materials and manuals of the equipment and technology. So the relevant authority turned to the universities which had English majors for help. Reference books were needed to do the translation, but the school was extremely short of specialized English dictionaries. The students were encouraged to borrow the reference books by themselves. There was a library at the phosphate mine and there might be some useful reference books. So I decided to go back to the mine to borrow the dictionaries.

I got on a bus heading for the city proper of Guiyang which was about 15 kilometers away. Kaiyang Phosphate Mine had an office in the city and there were trucks which transported goods back to the mine every day. In the late afternoon, I got on a "Liberation" brand truck. Before we were leaving, I met a middle school classmate who was studying in Guizhou University of Technology. He asked me to carry for him a full cylindrical backpack of five kilograms of cutlass fish to his home. There were three people including the driver sitting in the driver's cab. I put the backpack at my feet and for some unknown reason I tied the belt of the backpack around my wrist.

Kaiyang Phosphate Mine was over 150 kilometers away from the city of Guiyang. Most of the way was bumpy mountain road. About 30 kilometers away from the mine, there was a place called the Gate

168

of Hell where the road passed through two high cliffs. There was a winding mountain road past the Gate of Hell. Down the winding mountain road to the foot of the mountain was my home—Yang Water River Valley.

When we were close to the Gate of Hell, it was dark outside and was drizzling. Everything on the mountain path was blurred in the mist. The driver who was talking cheerfully a moment ago now kept quiet, opened his eyes wide and drove carefully. Suddenly, he said to me, "Heping, wind down the window to see if there was any obstacle out there." Anxious and flurried, I got the wrong handle and opened the door. I hurriedly slammed the door.

We reached a mining area after we passed the Gate of Hell. Two miners who were on the night shift were walking in the rain. What a hard job for these miners! I thought to myself and was wondering where the two miners were going on such a dark night. All of a sudden, the door opened and I was flung outside from the driver's cab. The moment I fell to the ground, I saw the back wheel rolling towards me and I hurriedly turned over and stood up just in front of the two miners, with five kilograms of cutlass fish hanging on my wrist.

The two miners, who were walking in the dead hours of the night, were given a good start by me, an alien dropping from the sky in front of them. The driver was too concentrated to notice there was one person missing in the cab. The other hitchhiker was scared to death and began to yell, "Heping fell off the truck!" The truck was already over 200 meters away when it jerked to a halt. The hitchhiker jumped off the truck and ran wildly towards me. He was astonished to see me standing there safe and sound. The driver didn't get off the truck. He was scared stiff and couldn't move his legs. When I sat back in the driver's cab, I was covered in mud all over with muddy water dripping along my hair.

The driver didn't start the truck. He buried his head on the steering wheel for at least 20 minutes and then slowly raised his head and looked at me with red eyes. He said, "Several similar accidents happened before.

Those people either died or became permanently disabled. You survived the disaster today not only because your parents are good people, your family for generations are all good people. With their blessing, you made a narrow escape. You are destined to good fortune in the future."

When I arrived at home and stood by the door, my parents stared at me as if they didn't recognize me. I said, "Don't be afraid. I am Heping."

When I was having a bath, I found many bruises on my body and there was a small hole at the ankle which kept bleeding. The next day, I went to the library and luckily I got some useful reference books. The third day, I went back to Guiyang carrying a full backpack of reference books on my back. The shuttle bus to Huaxi where Guizhou University was located was suspended. At that time, politics was given absolute priority and if there was a political meeting or campaign, production or classes could be suspended.

I decided to go back to school on foot.

The backpack was getting heavier and heavier. I waved my hand all the way in the hope of getting a lift, but no truck stopped. I gave up the idea of hitchhiking and marched forward with big strides, singing "the Red Army fears not the trials of the Long March". When I was about five kilometers away from the school, a truck stopped by my side and the driver stretched his head out from the driver's cab, "Get on the truck." When I was sitting in the cab, I asked him why he was so kind to stop. The driver said, "It is hard not to be attracted by a small girl who is spiritedly marching in goose step carrying a backpack on her back. I was wondering what she was doing."

To express my thanks to him and to satisfy his curiosity, I narrated the story of how I fell off the truck to him. He exclaimed, "The one who survives a disaster is destined to good fortune in the future."

Death of Premier Zhou Enlai

It was rumored that in 1976 somewhere in northeast China, three big and numerous small meteorites dropped from the sky. The three big meteorites symbolized the deaths of the three great men Zhou Enlai, Zhu De and Mao Zedong, who died on January 8, July 6 and September 9, respectively, and the small ones symbolized the 242,706 people who lost their lives in the Tangshan earthquake on July 28, all in the same year of 1976.

The first strike of the year to the Chinese people was the death of Premier Zhou Enlai. The whole country was in extreme grief. During that period, I was almost soaked in tears every day. Zhou Enlai was a perfect person in my mind.

I grew up in the inaccessible mountains of Guizhou and my political sensibility was far behind that of my peers in Beijing. But I was still aware that severe struggle was under way in the central government. For a long period of time, the pictures of Chairman Mao and Premier Zhou couldn't be seen at the same time in the newspapers. I suspected that someone in the central government was sowing discord between Mao Zedong and Zhou Enlai. I was disappointed. I didn't know it was the Gang of Four that was pushing out Zhou Enlai. I always believed that only Zhou Enlai was Mao Zedong's best partner. I didn't dare to admit that in my mind the image of Zhou Enlai was even greater than that of Mao Zedong. When we saw Premier Zhou in documentary films, he was either visiting impoverished people or dealing with some important diplomatic events. When we saw Chairman Mao, there was always a boundless red ocean as the background.

We watched the memorial meeting of Premier Zhou in the school's black-and-white TV. Everyone was sobbing. When Jiang Qing appeared on TV, I was astonished. She didn't take off her hat during the whole process of the memorial meeting even when paying respects to Premier Zhou's remains. Mao Zedong didn't attend the memorial meeting and Jiang Qing didn't take off her hat. What's wrong with the central government?

I got to know later Mao was seriously ill at that time.

Later I came to know that Zhou Enlai was the big obstacle to the Gang of Four's scheme to usurp Party and state powers. They were afraid that people would mourn over Zhou Enlai's death, so they held down the memorial activities. This was why the memorial meeting was very low-key.

I was deeply grieved over Zhou Enlai's death. Every night in that period, when I was lying in bed, tears would stream uncontrollably from the corners of my eyes and wet the pillow.

People mourned over Premier Zhou's death in their own ways when they were not allowed to express their sorrows publicly. The poetry in memory of Premier Zhou was widely spread in all universities across the country. We exchanged the poems which we got by various means.

The following poem was the most widely-spread one at that time.

I am in grief over Premier Zhou's death,
When I hear the ghosts screaming.
I am weeping,
When the jackals and wolves are laughing.
I shed my tears to mourn the hero,
I hold my head high and draw my sword from the scabbard.

The poem gives expression to Chinese people's grief over Premier Zhou's death and determination to root out the Gang of Four.

The school began to investigate who made copies of the poems. Out of my expectation, I was exposed by my classmate and good friend.

Our class monitor secretly informed me and I immediately destroyed the notebook which was full of the poems I copied. When I was inquired about it, I denied categorically. With no evidence, they finally let the matter drop.

On January 8, 1977, the first anniversary of Zhou Enlai's death, we finally got the opportunity to express how we loved and missed him.

At that time, I already had a job doing translation on the construction site of Chishui Natural Gas Chemical Plant.

I made with my own hands paper flowers for a flower basket in memory of Zhou Enlai. My eyes were brimming with tears while I was making the basket. Every flower I made was filled with my emotion.

On the day of December 26, 1976, it was the birthday of Mao Zedong, and a picture in which Mao Zedong and Zhou Enlai were together appeared in the headline news on the front page of the *People's Daily*, which aroused my boundless feelings.

I wrote a poem titled "A Precious Photo" to memorize Premier Zhou and was chosen to attend the poem recitation contest in memory of Zhou Enlai.

When I was reciting the poem filled with my heartfelt emotion, tears were streaming down my cheeks. The audience was also moved to tears.

Here is part of the poem.

On the day of December 26 of 1976,
The People's Daily published a precious photo,
It was on a meeting of the Party Central Committee,
Chairman Mao and Premier Zhou were talking cordially.
My hands are trembling as I hold the photo,
Tears are brimming in my eyes as I stare at the leaders,
How kind, how amiable,
How I miss them...
...

A thousand thoughts come to my mind,
When I hold the photo in my hands…
At the moment of victory,
How can I not think of the founding fathers of our country?
Our great leader Chairman Mao,
Respected and loved Premier Zhou,
To be alive forever with heaven and earth,
And shine forever like the sun and the moon.
They live forever in our heart.

A precious photo,
I will treasure it forever.
The lofty image will guide me to go ahead,
Never stop on the road of the revolution,
And devote myself to
Realizing communism—a bright future!

The next day, the recording of my recitation of the poem was played on the construction site through the loudspeaker.

I had to admit that the image of Zhou Enlai in my mind was not unchanged. When I was mature enough to see things objectively, I realized that Zhou Enlai was a man, not a god.

Go to Beijing for Chairman Mao's Funeral

On the afternoon of September 9, 1976, a classmate and I took a walk in the Huaxi Park near the campus. We were chatting while walking with a bunch of yam bean in our hand. At 4:00 pm, the Central People's Broadcasting Station delivered to the country and the world the news of the death of Chinese people's great leader Chairman Mao. We were stunned by the news from the loud-speaker in the park.

Ah, we exclaimed. It was too sudden to be accepted. We threw the yam bean into the river and ran back to the school. When we were children, we believed that Chairman Mao would never die. Later we knew that such matters as birth, death, illness and old age happened to everyone. But we heard some children say that Chairman Mao would live 300 years because the Soviet doctors said so after they gave Chairman Mao a physical check. The first idea that came into my mind when I heard the news was what would become of China?

To tell the truth, I was not heartbroken over Mao Zedong's death. I felt guilty when I realized that my heart was not broken over Mao's death. To be exact, I was sad over Zhou Enlai's death, but I felt heavy at Mao Zedong's death.

Our graduation was postponed because of Mao's death. The general atmosphere was tense and the whole country was in the state of first-degree combat readiness. I remember that when Yang's younger brother returned home to visit his family for the first time after he joined the army, the next day came the news of Chairman Mao's death. He was immediately recalled. On the night before his departure, the family cooked many good dishes and I was invited. The atmosphere was heavy. On the one hand, the whole country was mourning over Chairman Mao's death, on the other hand, Yang's younger brother returned home for the first time after he joined the army three years ago, but he was ordered to go back to the army the next day. The family had mixed feelings of grief and joy. A little drinking was taken, quietly of course. All recreational activities were suspended throughout the country after Chairman Mao's death.

Yang told me that she wanted to go to Beijing. I said I wanted to go with her. I had a classmate who came from Beijing. She was thinking to take this opportunity to go home and always tickled me to go with her. I had only one idea in my mind. Since I hadn't seen Mao Zedong when he

175

was alive, I should never miss the chance to see him when he was dead. When I was about eight years old, I wrote a letter to him to express my love to him. I told him in the letter that I would study hard and make progress every day to be a qualified successor to the proletarian revolution. I also told him how much I missed him and how much I wanted to see him. The address I wrote on the envelope was Tian'anmen Rostrum of Beijing and the addressee was Chairman Mao.

As a poor student, I couldn't afford even a hard seat ticket to Beijing. I came up with an idea that I could buy a ticket to the nearest place and get on the train first. If the train attendant found it out, I would say that I was going to Beijing to see Chairman Mao. Who dared stop me from going to see Chairman Mao?

It was a journey of two days and two nights. The train attendant checked tickets for several times and let me off every time. He said that it was ok with him as long as I could get out of the Beijing station. I began to curry favor with him in the hope that he would take me out with him when the train reached Beijing. I helped him sweep the floor, collect rubbish and serve boiled water to the passengers. When we reached Beijing, he really helped me out of the station.

I had planned that I would go to Tian'anmen Square to attend Chairman Mao's memorial meeting. But when I arrived in Beijing, I was to find that the Chang'an Avenue was under martial law and it was impossible to walk near to Tian'anmen Square.

I stayed at my classmate's home for a week and was very frustrated. Every day, I would walk to the place nearest to the Tian'anmen Square and looked to the direction of the Tian'anmen Square.

I wrote down my emotions in my diary those days.

September 13, 1976

I have spent one day and two nights on the train. It is my first long-distance travel. The train just passed the Yangtze River. Although it was dark outside, I could still feel the surge of the river. Ten years ago, Chairman Mao, our great leader, was swimming in the river. But now, he has left us forever.

People go forward in the strong wind and big waves and grow stronger.

I will keep Chairman Mao's instructions in mind. I will temper myself in the great storms of the revolution and prepare myself to meet difficulties head-on.

September 15, 1976

Today is the third day since I came to Beijing.

My wish couldn't come true at all.

The Great Hall of the People was guarded by the worker militia and PLA soldiers. One was even not allowed to walk near the Tian'anmen Square. All I could do was standing far away, and look at the direction of the Great Hall of the People, filled with great sorrow and boundless respect...

The deceased Chairman Mao, our great leader and mentor who is loved by people of all nationalities, is now lying quietly in the Great Hall of the People. I have traveled a long distance and come to Beijing, so near to our beloved great leader and mentor Chairman Mao, but my wish to see Chairman Mao couldn't come true. My feeling at this moment is beyond expression.

September 17, 1976

At three o'clock tomorrow afternoon, the Memorial Meeting of Chairman Mao Zedong — Our Great Leader and Mentor — will be held at the Tian'anmen Square. To my great regret, I couldn't attend it although I am here in Beijing.

I got on a bus which would go past the Tian'anmen Square in the evening. The bus was running on the broad Chang'an Avenue. It apparently slowed down when it was near the Tian'anmen Square. I stared at the grand Tian'anmen Square, the place I dreamed of every night. I missed Chairman Mao even more. The color portrait of Chairman Mao was changed into a black-and-white one framed with black silk. Chairman Mao has passed away and left us forever. My heart is broken.

Respected great leader Chairman Mao, I will always be your loyal revolutionary fighter. I will defend your revolutionary lines forever and devote myself to the great cause of the proletarian revolution to the end of my life.

September 20, 1976

I came to the grand Tian'anmen Square this morning. Everything was the same as the day of the memorial meeting.

There is a solemn atmosphere in the square. The banner which hang on the Tian'anmen Rostrum has the words in black and white "Memorial Meeting of Chairman Mao Zedong — Our Great Leader and Mentor". A seven-meter high portrait of Chairman Mao is put up in the middle of the red wall of the rostrum. On the newly-built red high platform in front of the rostrum are placed rows of green pine and cypress and light yellow chrysanthemum, and wreaths presented by the Party and state leaders.

I have a picture taken at the Tian'anmen Square which would be my life-long memory. I don't regret coming to Beijing, although I am worried deep in my heart.

We wore the mourning band for a month after the great leader's death. Elegiac couplets and black silk could be seen everywhere. People in the streets were all dressed in dark blue, grey or olive green, wearing black armbands, looking sad or with no expression on their faces. On the day of the memorial meeting, I listened to the live broadcast of it at my classmate's home.

The curfew was lifted when the memorial meeting was over. My classmate took me for a tour around the city of Beijing and took photos of me. I looked serious and depressed in all of the photos.

I didn't want to stay any longer, not even one day. I wanted to go back to the school and see what we were going to do after the death of Mao Zedong. My classmate's mother hoped she could stay home a few days more, but I was anxious to return school as soon as possible. I hadn't been in Beijing before, but I had no interest at all in sight-seeing. I was here to see Chairman Mao. Besides, the Forbidden City, the Temple of Heaven and the Summer Palace and all the other historic sites were not open to the public. My classmate's mother cried on the day of our departure. I knew she was loath to part with her daughter. I felt sad too.

I bought a ticket for half of the journey. When the train arrived in

Guiyang, the classmate who came to meet us bought two more platform tickets and we managed to get out with the platform tickets.

My parents thought that I went to Beijing with many of my class-mates. When they got to know that I went there alone, they were so mad at me, shut me in and gave me a good tongue-lashing. They scolded me for being too crazy, too fanatic and too simple-minded, "Everybody loves Chairman Mao. Why must you go to Beijing to see him while everybody else didn't?"

When I think back, I believe it was passion hidden behind my fanaticism and simplicity. Fanaticism and simplicity have disappeared with the increase of my age, but my passion has never faded, which leads to my success today.

Tangshan Earthquake

The Tangshan earthquake which happened on July 28 of 1976 before the death of Mao Zedong caused 242,706 deaths and 164,851 serious injuries.

My keenly felt pain about the earthquake came from one of my classmates. Her father was head of a county in Guizhou Province. When he was leading a group of leaders at the three levels of the county, the town and the commune to visit Dazhai of Shanxi Province and Shashiyu of Hebei Province, the two models for agriculture, they came across the big earthquake when they passed through Tangshan. Of the total 267 people, 232 died. Almost all the leaders of the county died in the earthquake including my classmate's father.

When I was coming back from Beijing, I met a Tangshan man on the train. He said that after the earthquake, the Party and Chairman Mao cared much for the people in Tangshan and people all over the country were trying their best to help them. He said full of emotion, "Do you know how considerate the government was? Even the toilet paper was distributed."

When we asked about his family, he said peacefully as if he was telling the story of somebody else, "My daughter and my father died in the earthquake."

The people who survived the earthquake were strong.

Another impression the earthquake left on me was that more than 4,000 children were orphaned by the earthquake. When I heard my parents' discussion about their intention to adopt an earthquake orphan, I strongly wished that it would come true. But the government had unified arrangement for the orphans and not everyone could adopt an orphan just as he wanted. I always thought that if an orphan had come to my home, he or she would be happy because the whole family would treat him or her very well.

After the earthquake, the United Nations and many countries expressed their intention of support to the Chinese government, but they were all declined.

The *People's Daily* carried an editorial which clearly stated that "The disaster relief relying on our own efforts has demonstrated that the people who are equipped with Marxism-Leninism and Mao Zedong Thought and have endured the trial of the Great Proletarian Cultural Revolution are invincible and that the socialism under the proletarian dictatorship of our country has great superiority."

I felt so proud of my country.

Thirty two years later when the Sichuan Wenchuan earthquake happened, China accepted international aid at the first place.

Go to Tibet

According to the job assignment policy, worker-peasant-soldier students were to return to where they came from upon graduation. If one didn't want to return home, he could ask to go to some place where the conditions were even worse. This would not only be easily approved but also bring the opportunity of being promoted as a model.

I had to go back to Kaiyang Phosphate Mine and would be assigned a job there. But I didn't want to go back to the remote mountainous area and work at my parents' side. I yearned for the outside world and I wanted to have a successful career in the future.

Although what I learned in the university was very limited, I had developed a great interest in English. I wished I could be engaged in diplomacy or foreign affairs after graduation when I repeatedly watched the Ping-Pong diplomacy and Nixon's visit to China in the documentary.

Before graduation, the Party committee of the school held a meeting to call on the graduates to go to work in the countryside or the border area. It was quite a fashion to work in areas inhabited by ethnic minorities at that time. One of my childhood friends whom I admired very much went to Tibet after he graduated from the Tsinghua University. The newspapers, broadcasting stations and the magazines propagated every day the college students who went to work in the countryside and the border area, calling on us to learn from them. I decided to follow them and submitted my application to the Party committee.

Respected Party Committee,
I have been tussling with myself ever since I had the thought of going to sup-

port the border areas. After listening to the pep-talk of the Party committee of the university and thinking it over, I have realized that I should have the attitude as a successor to the proletarian revolution and the attitude the Party and the people expect from us worker-peasant-soldier students. Like the thousands of worker-peasant-soldier students who have gone to support the countryside and border areas, I am also one of the youths of the times educated by the Party and the people. If they can do it, why can't I? They have the courage to break with the obsolete traditional ideas thoroughly and have taken measures to restrict the bourgeois rights in practice; why can't I? Now, the Party committee has called upon us to support the countryside and the border areas. I have made up my mind to actively respond to the call of the Party and devote my life to the revolution in Tibet and the construction of Tibet.

When we look back to the history of struggle of our Party, when we look at today's Soviet Union and imagine the destiny of our country, don't we clearly know the important task of our generation? Don't we know how we should take over the responsibility?

The happy life we have today was won by our revolutionary predecessors who sacrificed their lives. The struggle is not over yet! Revisionism is still the main danger at present and the bourgeoisie is hiding in the Party. There are still capitalist-roaders and the capitalist restoration may happen at any minute. If we are not aware of it and just sit idle and enjoy the fruit of the revolution, if we only think about personal comfort, the lesson of Soviet Union will repeat itself in China and we will lose the socialist state power under the proletarian dictatorship after having obtained it.

We should never let it happen in our country! We should remould ourselves according to the requirements of the Party and the need of the revolution. We should consciously make a clean break with revisionism and all obsolete traditional ideas. We should respond to the call of the Party and the people and go to work in the places with the harshest conditions where we are needed most and fight all our life to consolidate the proletarian dictatorship.

I know it clearly that it is only the first step to make the decision to go to work in Tibet. It is easy to make the first step, but it is not easy to carry on to the end of the journey. I firmly believe it won't be wrong if we walk unswervingly along the path directed by Chairman Mao. We should win honor by fighting with our whole life for Chairman Mao and for the proletariat with our own actions and give a forceful counterattack to the clamor that "worker-peasant-soldier students are of poor quality" and to the restoration scheme of the capitalist-roaders.

I earnestly wish the Party committee would approve my application. At the same time, I would prepare myself to achieve the goal. If my application was refused, I would still accept the job the Party has assigned me. No matter where I work in the future, I would study hard and work hard, persist in the philosophy of struggle and devote myself to the great communist cause.

I had another reason for going to Tibet. I wanted to work in the foreign affairs department of the Tibet Autonomous Region. If I returned to Kaiyang Phosphate Mine, my only alternative was to be a middle school teacher.

My application was not approved. Guizhou itself was one of the places with the harshest conditions. Besides, the number of students to be assigned to Tibet was small. Only three applications were approved in our university. They were all my classmates and came from very poor rural areas. If they didn't go to Tibet, they would probably have to go back to the countryside to teach English.

They were publicized as heroes in the school.

They entered politics after they went to Tibet and neglected their major of English. Two of them were transferred back to the hinterland after more than 10 years in Tibet and only one of them is still there. Very few university students from the hinterland would stay in Tibet for the whole life.

Unforgettable First Love

Not long after I returned to school after the winter vacation in 1976, we, the students in the last school term were asked to go to the factories for the "open-door schooling" and to receive reeducation from the workers.

We were assigned to different munition works all over the province. Several classmates and I came to a machine works some kilometers away from Guiyang. We were assigned to various workshops to work with the worker masters. My master was called Jianguo and I was learning lathe skills from him. We were also asked to learn politics together with the workers. The League members were under the leadership of the Youth League Committee of the factory and joined them in the political study and other activities. Besides, we had another important task which was to teach the workers English.

When I went to the office of the Youth League Committee to talk about the Youth League affairs, secretary Weihong asked me, "When will you start to teach the workers English? Hongtao can't wait to learn English from you." Only at this moment did I notice that there was another person who was standing by my side. He was a tall and handsome boy with broad eyes like limpid pools. He was staring at me. I could feel my heart go thump-thump-thump. It was the first time in my life that I palpitated with excitement at the sight of a boy. What made me more interested about him was that I didn't expect in such a remote area there was a worker who was so eager to learn English.

The English class began. I became the teacher of Hongtao and other dozens of workers. The English class every night became my happiest moment. Most of the workers studied English on the spur of

184

the moment and their enthusiasm only lasted for a while. In the end, I had only three students, Hongtao, my master Jianguo and Caixia, a girl whose name meant Sunglow.

The more I knew about Hongtao, the more I liked him. At that time, besides Mao's works, we had to study the works of Marx, Engels, Lenin and Stalin that referred to Marxism-Leninism in general. To tell the truth, their books were totally beyond my understanding, which I was ashamed of. Once I asked Hongtao if he had a book by Engels. He said yes and he could lend me the book. When I went to his dormitory to get the book, he opened a big trunk. To my great surprise, it was full of books of Marxism-Leninism. I was amazed and admired him from the bottom of my heart. I had never met someone like him, not among my classmates or friends. At that time, people were judged good or bad by whether they read the books of those communist leaders or whether they worked hard and lived in a plain way. Hongtao had all of these merits and was no doubt a good person.

My three students persisted with their English study. Sunglow and I became good friends and we kept no secrets from each other. Although Sunglow and Hongtao were colleagues, they had few dealings with each other. They began to know each other because of the English class. They had something in common. Both of them came from big cities and their families had military background. Hongtao once told me the sad story of his family. Hongtao's father who had been an officer in the army was severely persecuted in the Cultural Revolution and committed suicide in the Yuhuatai Martyr Memorial Park in Nanjing. Hongtao wanted to join the army, but was not recruited because of his father's case. His uncle who was also a military officer found him a job in the machine factory which was subordinate to the army. I was shocked by the story of Hongtao's father. It was so moving and tragic and my heart was broken when I heard it.

I had moments alone with Hongtao. When we were together, we talked about nothing but our dreams and aspirations. He talked of his mother full of his admiration for her. I had never heard about any son who admired his mother so much. I couldn't help thinking over and over again what kind of a woman his mother was to be admired by her son so much and to bring up such an excellent son. He also told me about his younger sister who was a worker-peasant-soldier student of Shanghai Textile Institute. I admired his sister for having such a good brother. He also mentioned his youngest sister in a soft tone that she was spoiled and had bourgeois ideas. I was envious of every one of them because they were linked to Hongtao by flesh and blood.

Sunglow's father was an officer in the General Logistics Department of People's Liberation Army. He was a PLA Representative in the machine works during the Cultural Revolution. Sunglow and Hongtao had the same family background, and they would have had to go to work in the countryside as peasants if they hadn't come to the machine works.

I was aware that Sunglow too admired Hongtao very much. She didn't hide her good opinions of Hongtao when she was talking of him. Sunglow was a very proud and picky Beijing girl who seemed to see nobody in her eyes. I always wondered what kind of husband she would find in the future because few men could live up to her expectations. My prediction was right. Sunglow who is one year older than me has remained single to this day.

A month later, I was summoned back to the university by the volleyball team to attend the college students' sports meeting in Guizhou Province. When I returned to school and talked about Hongtao in a chat with my good friend Yang, she said I was terribly in love.

During the competition, I couldn't stop thinking of Hongtao. In the past, if someone talked about love or marriage, I would not even listen to it because it was too far away and was not something a youth who had high aspirations like me should consider. But now, I totally changed my mind. If Hongtao asked me to marry him, I would say yes without any hesitation. I would do whatever I was asked to do for him. That year, I was 20.

I hid my feelings for Hongtao in my heart and I didn't know what he thought of me. Sometimes, I felt he had the same feelings for me; sometimes I felt that he had such a pure mind that he wouldn't have thought of such a thing. Many people said that Hongtao wouldn't stay long in Guizhou. He would certainly return back to Shanghai some day in the future and wouldn't find a girlfriend in Guizhou.

Gradually, my affections for Hongtao were no longer a secret. I had a sense of inferiority in my relations with Hongtao. Someone told me that Hongtao also liked me, but I considered it only a guess and dared not take it seriously. The factory appointed a woman worker to be our political instructor who was called Master Wang. She said that we would be a good couple if we came together.

I did not realize that Hongtao and I were actually on closer terms than I had remembered until I read my diary again recently. It just faded from my memory.

June 13, 1976

I had a long conversation with Hongtao this morning, and I found it very rewarding.

"Have you ever thought what kind of person you would like to be in the future?" Hongtao asked me. How can I not? This is the very question I consider a lot in my mind. I said, "I want to be an honest person. I am determined to devote my life to the cause and ideal of communism. I will work hard for it."

But how could we do better to realize the goal? In my opinion, the most important task for us at present is study. Hongtao thinks so too.

For me, the purpose of study is to prepare ourselves for the battle in the future and to master the weapons to be used in the battle. We are very sensitive to erroneous things, but we cannot analyze them theoretically. So we know it is wrong, but we don't know why and how to deal with it. Moreover, the class struggle is getting more and more complicated, if we don't learn Marxism-Leninism by heart, we won't be able to tell the true Marxism from the false Marxism, to tell the right lines from the wrong lines, and would probably end up serving as cannon fodder in the future

187

struggle. We should be aware that all those who attempt to restore revisionism and capitalism deck themselves out as defenders of Marxism-Leninism. They could deliberately distort Marxism-Leninism. Therefore, we are required by the situation of the struggle to grasp the real Marxism-Leninism.

"The focus of the class struggle won't be in Tibet." Hongtao's words set me thinking (I told Hongtao that I would go to work in Tibet after graduation).

Further consideration is truly needed (Referring to going to Tibet).

I have come to know more about Hongtao through our conversation. I have put my trust in him and I believe he also trusts me. He is even better than I have expected and he is a good comrade. What would it be if I could live with him the rest of my life?

Although I liked Hongtao very much, I felt we were not destined to come together. There were too many scruples and obstacles, especially under the political atmosphere and social system at that time. Tears would roll down my cheeks whenever I thought I wouldn't be able to be with Hongtao in the future. Hongtao didn't know it because I had never told him how I felt for him. Sometimes I even wished that Hongtao were a girl and we could spend time together without so many worries.

After graduation, I returned to Kaiyang Phosphate Mine and became a middle school teacher. My affections and yearning for Hongtao grew stronger with each passing day. Finally I picked up my courage and wrote him a letter. The letter was addressed to his home in Shanghai where he spent the Chinese New Year with his family. I told him in the letter how I felt for him. The letter was written with such difficulty that a thick pack of letter paper was used up when I finished it. After I mailed the letter, I thought it over again and again if I had said anything inappropriate in the letter or if there were any wrongly written words. What would Hongtao's mother think of me if she read the letter? Hongtao wrote back to me and in the letter he severely criticized me for having such thoughts.

On the occasion of the first anniversary of Premier Zhou's death, I wrote a poem and mailed it to Hongtao. He wrote me a letter in reply which was full of enthusiasm with a poem written by him to memorize Premier Zhou. I began to cherish hope again.

After the college entrance examination was resumed in 1977, Hongtao was admitted to the English Department of Guizhou University, my alma mater. I didn't know if the English I had taught him was helpful for him to pass the examination. But deep down, I hoped so. I always thought how popular Hongtao must be among his female classmates.

I met a professor of my university later when I came to work in Beijing and told him about the story of Hongtao. The old professor who was in his seventies offered to help me. He found Hongtao after he returned to the university. I didn't know what he said to Hongtao. He told me in a letter that he believed Hongtao and I would come together sooner or later and said "All shall be well, Jack shall have Jill". Soon, I got a letter from Hongtao who seemed very frustrated and criticized me with even more harsh words.

I went to Guizhou University to visit Hongtao once. We had a long walk in the Huaxi Park near the campus. We talked a lot, anything but our emotions. I was in a passive position during the talk and constantly made mistakes, giving the wrong idioms or the wrong pronunciations. Hongtao pointed them out directly. I felt awkward and embarrassed. Hongtao must look down upon me. We neglected our studies in the Cultural Revolution. Hongtao spent his childhood in Shanghai with much better education conditions. Hongtao's families were better educated, especially his mother, who had a college education in English. Hongtao had a more solid cultural foundation than me.

After that meeting, I felt I would be very tired if I lived with Hongtao for the rest of my life. I would be tortured by a sense of inferiority because the gap between us was too huge. Before that, I had never given up my affections for him. His attitude to me always made me feel there was a gleam of hope for us. It was not his problem, it was mine. I liked him, so it was not easy for me to give it up.

Many years later, I heard that he returned to Shanghai, got married and had a daughter. He was working in a travel agent and sometimes traveled as a national guide. I was also transferred to China's largest travel service at that time and I thought maybe we had a chance to meet each other. Later I heard that he had gone to the United States for advanced study.

During the first few years, Hongtao would frequently appear in my dreams. All my dreams were pure with revolutionary romanticism. I can still meet Hongtao from time to time in my dreams and the story is set against the 1970s. If a man makes me dream about him for decades of years, how much I must have loved him.

When I look back upon the experience now, I am undisturbed. It is only a memory of those years in my youth with no heart-touching emotion any more.

Jianguo and Sunglow were transferred to Beijing one after another. We often talk about Hongtao when we get together. One Chinese New Year, we sent our wishes to Hongtao on the phone.

Three years ago, I went to America for a business trip and the city happened to be where Hongtao lived. I contacted him. Hongtao and his wife drove to the hotel to pick me and my colleague Yanxiang to his home. Time has made little change to Hongtao. He was still impressively handsome, more mature but not old. Yanxiang had heard about the story from me, so he was very curious about Hongtao. After we left Hongtao's house, he told me he agreed that Hongtao was an outstanding man and he could understand why I fell in love with him.

Hongtao has a happy family. His wife is also outstanding and his daughter is pretty and intelligent, studying in a famous university in the United States. Hongtao has obtained his doctor's degree during the 10 years in America and has never returned to his country.

I told Hongtao's wife that I once secretly loved Hongtao when I was young. But she didn't believe it. Yanxiang was there and proved that I had told him the story. I emphasized that Hongtao didn't know about it and it was only my unrequited love.

After I met Hongtao's wife, I could feel the love and understanding they had for each other. She was the right woman for Hongtao. I had imagined her appearance in my mind again and again. What an extraordinary girl she must be to make a good match for Hongtao!

I kept in touch with Hongtao's wife through e-mail after we met last time. Not long after that, we lost contact. I got no reply for the e-mail I sent them. Hongtao and his wife shared the same e-mail address. Later my computer had a breakdown and all the e-mails were deleted. I lost their e-mail address.

I still have the phone number, but I have never called them since then.

The First Step of a Ten-thousand-*li* Long March

I felt suffocated whenever I thought I had to go back to the phosphate mine after graduation. Three years ago when I entered college, I felt I was ready to spread my wings to fly high. I hadn't expected that I would return to where I started three years later. At the same time, I was ashamed at having such thought which was not in line with the spirit of "I will do whatever the Party has told me to do". Therefore I did self-criticism and wrote it in the following diary.

It is the people who have recommended me to the university and I should study for the people.

I should realize it through my action.

Job assignment on graduation is a challenge for me. Although I know it is not determined by my will where I shall go to work after graduation, I hope I can go somewhere better than the phosphate mine where I can give better play to my advantages in English. But is it true that I cannot use English if I return to the phosphate mine? I have to admit that I have selfish ideas and personal considerations. The middle school of the mine is in short of English teachers and the English classes of the second and third year students have been suspended. I have made up my mind to follow the Party's instructions and go where the Party needs me to go. But why do I have conflicting ideas? It turns out that I am not a person who can stand the test of time; I am not a revolutionary youth who has high aspirations; I am not one of the worker-peasant-soldier students whom the Party and the people expect. I should be ashamed of myself.

We usually referred to it as the first step of a ten-thousand-*li* long march when we started to do something. It was not only because the first step was particularly important, but we also used it to remind ourselves that there was still a long way to go. The first job after graduation was the first step of my ten-thousand-*li* long march.

In October of 1976, I returned to Kaiyang Phosphate Mine and became an English teacher in the local middle school.

The first English sentence I taught the students was "Eternal glory to our great leader Chairman Mao".

The Cultural Revolution had just finished and the students were not yet ready for serious study. Most of them were not interested in study, especially not in English. English was not even required in the college entrance examination when universities restarted to enroll students directly from middle schools in the winter of 1977.

I didn't like my job at all. But I had no choice. I had to accept my assigned job. The interests of the revolution overrode anything else and I would do whatever the Party told me to do. The Party needed me to be a middle school teacher. I would do it well no matter I liked it or not.

I wrote the poem "Take an Oath" to encourage myself.

I stand solemnly in front of the portrait of Chairman Mao,
Emotions and thoughts are surging like ocean tide…
A worker-peasant-soldier student of yesterday,
A teacher of the people of today,
At this moment,
What do I have on my mind?

The future of the country, the ideal of the mankind,
The trust of the class, the expectation of the Party,
How should I take the first step of the ten-thousand-li March?
How should I walk on the journey?

…

Filled with strong revolutionary enthusiasm, I started the first job after graduation from college, no matter I liked it or not.

I was asked to sit in on Jin Que's class on the first day I started my job in the school. Jin Que came from Shanghai who responded to Chairman Mao's call for reeducation in the countryside of Guizhou. She was recruited to be an English teacher. Although she hadn't been in college, her English might be better than mine. Jin Que was several years older than I and had laid a solid foundation in study before the Cultural Revolution. She had the pride the girls born in big cities had.

When I was on Jin Que's class, the majority of the students were not willing to learn and she was obviously impatient to the students. I thought it was the teacher's responsibility who didn't teach in the right way if the students had no interest in study. I was too young to know about the ways of the world. When the class was over, I told Jin Que to leave first and that I had something to say to a student in her class who I had known before. She gave me a confused look and left the classroom. Then I began to give tutoring to the students whom Jin Que showed impatience to in the class. Actually, I was violating a taboo by doing this. They were not my students after all. Jin Que must feel offended if she

193

found it out.

I was unusually patient to the students at the beginning. On the weekend, I asked the two slow students to my home and helped them with their English lessons. I even prepared sweets and peanuts for them which they apparently enjoyed better than the English words I taught them.

The students' lack of interest in study was not the biggest headache. What made me feel most uncomfortable was the factional struggle between the teachers who were divided into two irreconcilable factions. The Cultural Revolution was over, but not its influence.

The headmaster was a worker surnamed Wang who had received little education. It was not uncommon at that time for a layman to lead the experts. He was in support of one faction against the other. When I first arrived at the school, he was particularly kind to me. He read my files with my Party membership application and the highly favorable comments transferred from the university. He said he would let me join the Party within a month. I was wild with joy. I had worked hard for so long and was still not admitted by the Party. Now I could be a Party member I had long dreamed of in a month! I didn't expect I would offend Wang without myself knowing it. Once during a meeting, a verbal fight broke out between the two factions. Beyond the limit of my patience, I stood up and said, "Why cannot the leaders of the school be fair? The leaders are supposed to be neutral. If they are involved in the factional struggle, how can they effectively manage the school?" My sharp words totally offended Wang who from then on put me on a hot spot whenever he got the chance and took revenge on me. His promise to recommend me to the Party came to nothing naturally.

Later the following story happened.

The place where my family lived was a valley surrounded by big mountains with Yang Water River running through. Although a two-meter river embankment was built on each side of the river, they had no use on ordinary days. During the dry season, the river became very narrow and the riverbed covered with cobbles became children's play-ground. But the small river would give us a hazardous trial every rainy season. Several times the floods burst the river embankment, inundated the first floor of the apartment buildings and workshops on both banks of the river and devoured tens of lives.

That day, I was ill and stayed at home. It had rained heavily for two days and the river kept rising. I was sick with anxiety. Suddenly, I heard someone calling me downstairs. I looked out of the window. It was teacher Cai, secretary of the school's Communist Youth League branch. He was wearing a raincoat and shouted at me, "The mountain torrents came down and washed away the mine timbers piled on the river banks. Now the students have gone to the upper and lower reaches of the Yang Water River to save the timbers. Will you come with us?"

The timbers were used in holding tunnels and shafts underground in the mine. Growing up in the mine, I knew how valuable they were.

I was a teacher. Certainly I would go.

I ran wildly towards the lower reaches of the river. There, hundreds of my teenage students were fighting against the natural disaster.

"Teacher Liu Ping, there is someone struggling in the river. It's a child." I looked up towards the upper reaches of the river. A head and two waving hands emerged in the torrents. One couldn't tell if it was a man or a woman, an adult or a child. Tears welled up in my eyes. I had students too in the upper reaches fighting against the flood.

In an instant, the roaring torrents brought the person to the lower reaches, bumped him or her against the pier of the bridge and rushed the body towards where we stood.

I was the only teacher there. When I looked around, everyone cast a glance at me. I had no alternative. I ordered the students to stay there and jumped into the river. I swam to the drowning person and caught one of the legs. At that moment, two male teachers swam over and the three of us pulled and dragged the person ashore. Learning swimming was a right thing I did in the university.

It was the only heroic deed in my life. But we failed to save the person's life.

The drowned was a middle-aged woman. The body was damaged by the water and became unrecognizable. Later I saw Haizi, my classmate at primary school, standing by the side of the body, crying bitterly. Then I realized it was Haizi's mother, one of the neighbors who lived in the apartment building next to ours.

Haizi's mother worked in the water pump house near the riverside. She had a light green woolen sweater which was envied by every woman at that time when everyone was dressed in dark blue or grey. When the flood came, she had been evacuated to a safe place. But the woolen sweater was left in the water pump house. She went back to get her woolen sweater and…

After the flood receded, the phosphate mine held a rally to commend those individuals that had displayed extraordinary courage in fighting the flood. I believed I would be awarded for my brave deed to jump into the river to save a drowning person. But nobody informed me on the day of the rally. When I went to the school, I saw the students and teachers were lined up and walking out of the school gate. I asked them where they were going; the students told me that they were going to attend the rally and they were surprised why I was not going. Later I knew that my brave deed was placed on another female teacher. The only reason was that Wang didn't want me to be praised.

No matter how hard I worked, I couldn't win Wang's favor because I refused to stand on his side. I was not in support of any side, I just held to the opinions which I thought were true.

I was not accepted by the Party just because I had offended Wang, the Party secretary of the Party branch.

"Fuck Your Mother!"

I was 21 when I graduated from university and looked like a middle school student with two pigtails on my head. The eldest student was only two years younger than me. Of all the English teachers in the school, only I had the English major in university. So I was assigned many classes.

One day, when I was giving a lesson to a class, a student kept talking with others and didn't listen to me. I warned him several times, but he just ignored my existence. I had just come to the school and didn't know some of the students' names. I asked him his name, but he gave me no reply. One of the other students answered, "His name is Wang Xitang."

"Wang Xitang, stand up!" I yelled at him. The students broke out into a secret laughter. He still ignored me.

I raised my voice, "Wang Xitang, stand up!"

"Fuck your mother!" He suddenly shouted at me.

I was stunned. I quickly picked up my textbook and left the classroom sobbing. Later I came to know that the student was named Wang Ye and Wang Xitang was actually his father's name. To call the father's name of someone in public was something quite insulting.

The teacher in charge of the class led the two students to my office and asked them to apologize to me.

Wang Ye was a handsome boy. He was spoiled because he was the only son of the family. He was bad at his study as many of the other students. He was a little bit embarrassed whenever he met me after the unpleasant thing happened. Actually, he was a lovely boy.

Wang Ye became a tram driver under the pit after he graduated from middle school. Once when he was driving a tram, he stretched his head out of the driver's cab and bumped his head heavily against the wall when it was making a turn. He became severely disabled after the accident. I had already come to work in Beijing at that time. Whenever I returned home to visit my family, I could see him walking difficultly in the street supported by someone. He could recognize me when he saw me and greeted me smilingly.

Several years later, he died, only in his twenties.

There are some enjoyable memories too. I was the leader of the girls' basketball team. During the time of training, I lived on the campus with the students and trained them every day. Sometimes I mingled with the students and played the game. Nobody found out I was a teacher.

I was younger than 11 when the Cultural Revolution started in May of 1966. I did hardly get any school education since then until I went to university in 1973.

Julin (left), the neighbor girl of my family, was the head of the first Red Guard Fighting Team in Kaiyang Phosphate Mine. Yang (right), who was a city girl of the capital city of Guizhou Province, was my close friend in the university and has been a life-time friend since then.

北京天安门留影 1966

My friend He Ruixue (left) with her fellow Red Guards took this photo just after they were received by Chairman Mao.

Zhao Lina (middle) with her fellow Red Guards after being received by Chairman Mao. Zhao Lina was the comrade-in-arm of Morning Glory, a 16-year-old girl who died in the fight between two Red Guard factions in 1967.

Juhua, one of my neighbor sisters, was one of the luckiest children of the mine, who has met Chairman Mao.

Red Guard Long March Team of Kaiyang Phosphate Mine.

My sister (middle) was a member of Mao Zedong Thought Performing Arts Propaganda Team of the Little Red Guard.

I am the one splitting.

Popular revolutionary poses.

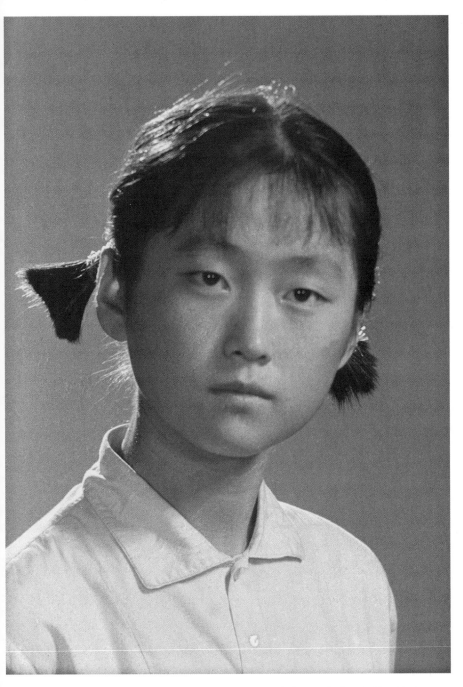

The photo was taken when I was 15, dancing revolutionary ballet in Mao Zedong Thought Performing Arts Propaganda Team. I didn't have any stage photos taken at that time.

My friend Yang Shaofan, who badly suffered during the Cultural Revolution, is a legendary woman.

Shaofan's parents during the period of Manchurian puppet government. Her mother was labeled Ms. Bourgeois because of her elegant dress and her father was labeled Japanese spy for his Japanese style school uniform.

Uncle Zhang, labeled a capitalist-roader of the mine, died miserably during the Cultural Revolution.

Family of Uncle Zhang before the Cultural Revolution with the biggest daughter Julin missing from the photo.

After Uncle Zhang was labeled a capitalist-roader, all his old colleagues and friends were detained in a study camp and were forced to expose Uncle Zhang and make a clean break with him. The PLA Representatives and rebels called meetings every day and put pressure on them. Everyone was required to say something about Uncle Zhang, otherwise he wouldn't be set free. My father (second left, third row) was detained for six months and was the last one to leave the study camp. The picture shows all people in the study camp with PLA Representatives.

The Revolutionary Committee with workers, carders and PLA Representatives of a factory in Yunnan, a neighboring province of Guizhou. I bought this picture for 300 yuan in a small village in Yunnan Province in 2008.

My friend Yang (second from left, front row) answered the call of Chairman Mao and went to the countryside for re-education from the poor and lower-middle peasants. She stayed there for five years.

My friend became an art soldier of Mao Zedong Thought Performing Arts Propaganda Team and I became a physical laborer when I was 15, working underground and making explosives.

With my fellow workers when I was an explosive maker.

As I could not be recruited as a soldier myself, I dated a soldier who played the violin in the Mao Zedong Thought Performing Arts Propaganda Team in the army.

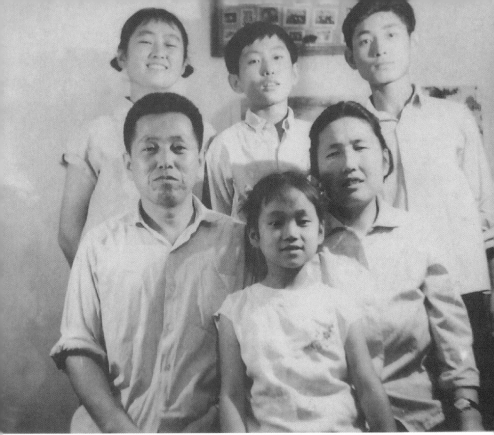

My family in the late stage of the Cultural Revolution.

With my classmates outside the gate of Guizhou University.

Yang often wears her Red Guard uniform covered with patches in the university.

The image of the Worker-Peasant-Soldier College Students. I am the one in uniform (right).

My classmates are listening to the radio for a bulletin to criticize the Right Deviation. The slogan on the wall reads "Firmly counterattack the Right Deviationist trend to reverse verdicts". Lily Yang (second left) and Yan Shengjian (first right) are my good friends, now living in the Unite States.

The photo was taken before the evening performance party of the university. The students of English Department performed a dance "The Song of Worker-Peasant-Soldier Students" at the party.

The women's volleyball team of Guizhou University, taken in 1976.

My university graduation photo.

My friends say that I look like a revolutionary bravely facing execution.

Reunited with my middle school classmates after the first semester in the university. I was the only one in this photo who went to university. The house on the right is the No.13 Apartment Building.

There was a solemn atmosphere in the square. The banner on the Tian'anmen Rostrum showed the words in black and white Memorial Meeting of Chairman Mao Zedong—Our Great Leader and Mentor. A seven-meter high portrait of Chairman Mao was put up in the middle of the red wall of the rostrum. On the newly-built red high platform in front of the rostrum were placed rows of green pine and cypress and light yellow chrysanthemum, and wreaths presented by the Party and state leaders.

-From my diary of Sep. 20,1976

北京天安门留影 1976.9

I am reciting a poem written by myself at the ceremony in memory of Premier Zhou Enlai on Jan. 9, 1977, one year after he passed away.

Yang (right), Lily (left) and I in Chishui Natural Gas Chemical Plant in 1977; I was an English interpreter trainee then.

The construction site of Chishui Natural Gas Chemical Plant. The two women walking on the muddy road are my classmate Lily Yang (left) and her colleague. We are very excited to work for the foreign experts despite hard life.

Foreign experts and their interpreters in Chishui Natural Gas Chemical Plant in 1977. I always wonder how much they would be shocked to see the changes if they come back to China today.

The girls' sport team of the middle school of Kaiyang Phosphate Mine where I taught English for two years.

Chapter Four

Be Ready

On October 6, 1976, the Gang of Four was crushed and the Cultural Revolution was over. I had a presentiment that my destiny would change from then on, so I grasped every opportunity of learning to prepare myself for the change in the near future.

My major was English. Since I did not learn much in the university, I felt like a fool when I graduated. I had never seen a foreigner, let alone speaking English with them. I was not satisfied with myself.

I started to learn English like mad after graduation. Few English books could be found at that time, so I studied the English version of *Selected Works of Mao Zedong*. No reference books on English were available in the bookstore, and then I copied a grammar book of several hundred pages from A to Z. I worked much harder than my students.

The Chishui Natural Gas Chemical Plant was under construction and scores of foreign experts were working there. Some of my classmates who had been assigned to the foreign affairs department of Guizhou Province were sent there to work as interpreters for the foreign experts. Yang was one of them. I admired those classmates who could work with foreigners.

Chishui Natural Gas Chemical Plant

Both Kaiyang Phosphate Mine where I worked and Chishui Natural Gas Chemical Plant were subordinate to the Chemical Industry Department under the provincial government of Guizhou. My father went to his old friend who worked in the Chemical Industry Department and asked him to help me get the opportunity to work in the chemical plant as a trainee during school vacations.

Chishui County was well-known throughout the country for two things. The first was the mobile war the Red Army fought with the Kuomintang army at the Chishui River during the Long March of the Agrarian Revolutionary War in the 1930s. Secondly, the town which was famous in the world for producing the liquor of Maotai was located by the Chishui River. Chishui River was a tributary of the Yangtze River. It originates from Yunnan Province and is running through Guizhou and Sichuan. It is also the boundary river between Guizhou and Sichuan provinces.

When the winter vacation began, I started on my journey alone.

Although Kaiyang Phosphate Mine and Chishui Natural Gas Chemical Plant were in the same province, due to the poor transportation, I had to go to Sichuan first and then transfer back to Chishui County in Guizhou.

I rode on the cargo wagon of the train from the mine to Xiaozhaiba station where I got on the train to Chongqing City located at the downstream of the Yangtz River. After a night's journey, I arrived in Chongqing and took another train to a place called Zhuyangxi where I changed to a ship which took me to Hejiang County of Sichuan Province. It was already dark. I stayed overnight in the county. The next day I took another ship for several hours before I finally reached the construction site of the Chishui Natural Gas Chemical Plant.

It was the first time I went on a long journey after graduation. My luggage was extremely heavy with all the clothes and books. Although I was ill and had a high fever on the day of the departure, I was not held back.

It was stifling hot in Chongqing in the summer and the city was nicknamed a heating stove for its hot weather. I thought it would be warm too in the winter, so I took off my sweater and only wore a shirt and a thin coat before I left home. In fact, the winter in Chongqing was as wet and cold as that in Guizhou. It was freezing cold all the way from Xiaozhaiba to Chongqing and my illness worsened because of the cold. Most of the passengers on the train from Chongqing to Zhuyangxi were country folks. The carriage was old and shabby and crowded. The air was foul because of poor ventilation. I felt I was dying when the train arrived at Zhuyangxi.

After I got off the train, I heard the steam whistle and saw a steam-ship anchoring at the dock which was about 200 meters away. It was the ship which would take me to Hejiang County. But my legs were as heavy as laden with lead. I could hardly move a step forward carrying the luggage full of bedding on one hand and a canvas bag on the other, filled with all the books I bought when I was in the university. The ship was sailing soon and I was worried to tears. I begged a young man who was walking by to help me carry the baggage. It was heavy even for the two of us. We each carried one end of the rope which was used to tighten up the baggage and the rope cut into the flesh. At last, I managed to get on the ship.

The deck was crowded with passengers. I sat on my bag and looked at the billowing river water, feeling relaxed. A few minutes later, I began to feel a fever and my head was splitting. An old man who was sitting beside asked me if I was ill. I told him that I had a headache. He groped for something in his pockets for a while and then handed me two white pills. I swallowed the pills without even asking what they were.

We got off the ship in Hejiang County when it was getting dark. The old grandpa carried a basket on his back and helped me carrying my bag with one of his hands. We walked in the streets to find a hotel where we could stay overnight. The meeting for cadres of three levels of county, town and commune was being held in the county and all the hotels were filled to capacity. We still couldn't find a place to stay after walking in the streets for a long time. The grandpa had accompanied me finding the hotel all the way and helped me carrying my baggage. I felt sorry for having caused him so much trouble. I bought two towels and two soaps from a street vendor and wrapped some salted duck eggs I brought from home and secretly put them in his basket as my heartfelt gratitude for him. After two hours' walking and searching, we finally got me a makeshift bed on the floor of the lobby of a hotel. I slept without taking off my clothes after I said goodbye to the grandpa.

It was drizzling at five or six o'clock the next morning. I hurried to the dock to catch the ship heading for Chishui Natural Gas Chemical Plant. At about two or three o'clock in the afternoon, I finally reached my destination.

Graduate of English Major Could Not Speak English

There was a two-story building on the construction site of Chishui Natural Gas Chemical Plant. The first floor was the translators' office and the second floor was the office for the foreign experts. Chinese were not allowed to stay alone with foreigners according to the rules for foreign affairs. All the foreign experts were under the management of the foreign affairs department of the province and each of them had two translators to help with their work.

They would come to the first floor to ask the translators to go with them if they were going to the construction site.

I was here on a short-term training, so I was not assigned to any expert at the beginning. I held a textbook all day long and practiced my oral English. I read so hard that I always got my lips numb. Touched by my diligence, the leader of the foreign affairs department arranged me to work following a translator who was a teacher of Guizhou University of Technology.

Most of the translators working in the chemical plant graduated from my old school Guizhou University and many of them could only speak or understand very limited English. Only a few of them could communicate with foreigners relatively well. Therefore, everyone would hold a book and learn English as soon as he or she was free.

A translator was assigned to do the interpretation at a dinner party. She was so nervous that she started to prepare for it many days before-hand. When the day of the dinner party came, her voice became hoarse due to too much reading and she couldn't utter even one word. In the end, an engineer who knew just a little English helped do the interpreta-tion.

I spent a winter vacation and a summer vacation in Chishui Natu-ral Gas Chemical Plant. Most of the time, I was learning and following someone else. I couldn't do the translation or interpretation on my own.

There was a young American man among the foreign experts who was very energetic and enthusiastic. Sometimes he would come to the translators' office to learn Chinese. Once a translator taught him "lai de ji" and "lai bu ji" which he couldn't understand. The translator explained them to him in English: If it takes you one hour to get to the airport, but you have only 40 minutes, then there is not enough time for you to get there which is "lai bu ji". If you have one and half an hour, you will make it which is "lai de ji". I was standing beside and listening to them. I exclaimed to myself, "Wow! How can he speak such complicated English!"

At that time, foreigners were rare in China. Translators who worked with foreigners and could speak fluent foreign languages were envied by everyone. The college graduates who were assigned to Chishui Natural Gas Chemical Plant were considered the elite.

When the new term began, the school urged me to come back to teaching. But I dreaded having to go back to teach those students who had no interest at all in study. During the time I worked in the chemical plant as a trainee, I had foreseen my future. I realized that my career development in the future would be closely related to the language of English. I had made up my mind to escape from the out-of-the-way valley where I had lived for 20 years.

Every Westerner Might Be a Spy

We had to observe strict disciplines working with foreigners. The translators were not allowed to talk with foreigners except at work or in the office. Nobody was allowed to have a chat with foreigners even if he could speak English, unless he was a translator or foreign affairs officers. Every day after work, we had to keep a daily record of what we did with and said to the foreign experts during the day's work and reported it to our superior.

One day, a foreigner asked me where I came from. I replied that I came from Kaiyang Phosphate Mine. A middle-aged woman translator who was together with us immediately gave me an angry stare and said, "How can you disclose a state secret?" I was frightened. I didn't know if it was a state secret or not or how grave the consequences would be for leakage of a state secret. She was a college English teacher and could speak fluent English. She felt quite good about herself and was critical to others. I spent the whole afternoon writing my report and making self-criticism for having disclosed the state secret.

Besides the foreign affairs department of Guizhou Province, the Ministry of State Security also had staff that was stationed on the construction site. The foreigners were not encouraged to go to the street at will after work or on the weekend. The foreign experts lived in the guest house for foreign guests. The translators, foreign affairs officers and security officers lived in a residential building which was not far from the guest house. The whole building had been commandeered. The foreigners had to walk past the building if they went out to somewhere. One weekend, I was chatting with Xiaoqun in her dormitory who worked for the Ministry of State Security. We looked out of the window and happened to see an American passing by. Xiaoqun stood up in no time and took out a pistol from one of the drawers. She smartly and elegantly loaded the gun and ran out to follow the American. It turned out the American was going to the county town several kilometers away to do some shopping. Xiaoqun returned back after she followed him there. Certainly nothing happened. I thought Xiaoqun was a heroine who dared to tail a foreign "ghost" all by herself. Chinese people called Westerners "ghosts" for they look so different with blue eyes and pointed noses.

I had only been to the foreigners' guest house once during the several months I worked in the chemical plant. Whatever happened in the foreigners' guest house was mysterious to us. If some foreigner's spouse or children came for a visit, we would get together and talk about with great relish what they were dressed in, what they said or what they did.

It was on the Chinese New Year's Eve in 1977 that I went to the foreigners' guest house the first time. The foreign affairs department asked us to prepare some performances for the get-together party with the foreign guests. I was appointed to be in charge of the rehearsing. The performances included several revolutionary dances, a clapper talk performed by a boy and my solo dance *The North Wind Blows*, a selected passage of the ballet *The White-haired Girl*. We also made flower bouquets and wreaths with colored paper as the stage prop. The foreigners' enthusiasm was aroused and they all watched the performance in high spirits. It was a rare opportunity for them to get together with so many Chinese. The boy who performed the clapper talk was so nervous that he always forgot his lines. I had to stand nearby to prompt him all the time and my voice was sometimes even louder than his. A foreigner who was sitting in the front kept encouraging me to get on the stage myself because he didn't understand what I was doing. Two translators sang an Australian song "Click Go the Shears" which an Australian expert enjoyed so much and made him laugh loudly. When we finished our performance, the foreign guests sang two songs. At about 8:00 p.m., the organizer of the event from the foreign affairs department declared the end of the party. Not having enjoyed themselves to the full, the foreigners couldn't understand why the party was over so early. We were having a good time and felt it a pity too. But it was the discipline. Our contact with foreigners was restricted to work and the activities arranged by the foreign affairs department.

An American expert specially came over to me and praised me for my dance, "You are a perfect dancer." I was very glad but I didn't dare to chat with him. I just replied with typical Chinese modesty, "It was not good at all."

There was a chef in the foreigners' guest house who could speak a little English. One day he could no longer refrain himself and spoke a few sentences with a foreigner. It was absolutely against the foreign affairs discipline. He was criticized and sent back to his former work unit.

In our opinion, every foreigner might be a spy.

Personally, I liked those foreigners. The Australian man who was an expert on electric welding was particularly fond of me. I worked with him for several days. Once he said to a male translator that Liu Ping was a charming girl. The translator conveyed his words to me, wearing a weird smile on his face. I asked him, "What does charming mean?" He explained it to me. The Australian expert was standing by and looking at me smilingly. I stared at him angrily and thought "How can you be so shameless". People at that time couldn't even accept words of praise like this. But now even if a foreigner lauds me to the skies, I can accept it without my face turning red or my heart beating any faster. Nowadays, Chinese girls can be seen everywhere going in pairs with foreigners. What a change!

One day, I went to the construction site with the Australian expert. When we reached there, he suddenly took me by the hand and started to run. I didn't know what was happening and just ran as fast as I could with him. When he stopped, he bawled angrily at the Chinese engineers. Later he explained to me that he saw the X-ray detector was on, inspecting the welding seam of the piping, when we reached the construction site. The X-ray detector was highly radioactive which had great harm to human body, especially to females which might cause them sterility. According to regulations, a security line should be set up outside the safe distance as a sign of warning when the X-ray inspection was carried out. But there was no warning at all. This was why he took me by the hand and started to run as soon as he noticed it with no time to warn the male translator and the engineers.

I thought this Australian man couldn't be a spy.

Boyfriend with No Hand Touch

When I was 22 years old, a big brother who lived in the neighborhood introduced me to a boy who became my first boyfriend. The big brother was the art soldier who I mentioned previously and had a younger sister who was also an art soldier. The boy he introduced to me was his comrade-in-arms who played the violin in the propaganda team in the army.

The name of my boyfriend was Jianshe. During the one year when we were dating, I only met him three times and the time we spent together amounted to only two weeks. He served in the army in Henan Province which was over 1,000 kilometers away from Guizhou and we kept in touch through letters. From our first date to when we broke up, we had never held each other by hands, not even once.

His father was deputy director of Guiyang Aluminium Factory, a state-owned enterprise, and was a high-ranking official in the province.

Jianshe was extremely handsome although both his parents were plain-looking. His outstanding appearance made me feel unworthy of his company. I knew I was no match for him in appearance. When we were walking together in the street, almost all the girls would be attracted by him. When he took me to his comrade's home to visit his old mother, I clearly read the old lady's doubt in her eyes "How come Jianshe has selected such a plain-looking girl". I was grateful to Jianshe that he had chosen me. He liked me for who I was not for my appearance.

I cared for him very much. I always liked men in military uniform. Besides, he was my first boyfriend.

Jianshe told me that all the technology and equipment in Guiyang Aluminium Factory were introduced from Japan. He encouraged me to learn Japanese so that I might be able to work as a translator in the factory. Although I knew it was unrealistic, I still listened to him and started to learn Japanese. There was an engineer in Kaiyang Phosphate Mine who had studied in Japan. He was in his seventies. I took him as my teacher and learned Japanese from him. During the summer before we broke up, Jianshe took me to his home to see his parents. I lived in his home for a week. I could feel his parents were not satisfied with me, especially his mother.

Jianshe had a younger brother and a younger sister. His brother had a girlfriend who was very fashionable and pretty. I was thrown into the shade by her. The brother's girlfriend and parents came to see me after I arrived. I could tell that the parents felt so confident about and proud of their daughter when they saw me.

Jianshe's sister was in high school. Out of occupational habit, I got up very early every morning and dragged her outside to read English without asking her whether she liked it or not. I studied every day. I was thinking of pursuing my study to a master's degree. I knew I was deficient in knowledge and I could foresee China would soon enter a new era of knowledge explosion. I must be prepared at all times.

I understood Jianshe's mother perfectly. I was by no means ugly, but I was not good enough for her son. What's worse, I always held a book and was absorbed in my studies as if I didn't belong to this world. Jianshe was her pride and was the dream boyfriend of all girls. It shouldn't be a girl like me.

After we left his home, I could feel the change in his attitude towards me. I could tell he was under great pressure from his family. I was waiting for him to say the word to me, but he didn't. His brother supported him in terms of our relationship, and I was thankful to him for it.

Later, the big brother passed on a message to me which made me realize that the relationship between me and Jianshe would come to nothing. He said that Jianshe's parents thought there was little possibility for me to be transferred from the mountainous area to the city, so they wouldn't give their consent to us. I knew it was only an excuse. It was not something difficult for his father who was in such a high position to transfer me to the city of Guiyang. But I understood them. I just wanted to hear it from Jianshe.

I decided not to make it difficult for him. I decided to give him up.

After Jianshe returned to the army the last time we met each other, I wrote big brother a letter in which I said that I would break up with Jianshe. Jianshe wrote a long letter to my father telling him that he wouldn't break up with me and he wished I would give him some time to persuade his parents. He knew that my father liked him very much. The letter was intercepted by me. I wrote another letter to big brother and firmly expressed my attitude.

I was heartbroken to break up with him. I made the decision on an evening. There was a film on in the open air. I sat there in the crowd, tears rolling down my cheeks uncontrollably. I was more resolved to go out of the big mountains after I broke up with Jianshe. Not long after that, I left Kaiyang Phosphate Mine.

In 1979, Jianshe joined the China-Vietnam Counterattack in Self-defense. I said to one of my friends that I would come to him if Jianshe was wounded or became disabled in the war. My friend thought I was out of my mind.

The fruitless love is still sweet in my memory. I always think, of all the people in the world, why it is me who met him and became his girl-friend for one year. It is predestined affinity we Chinese people believe in.

Chapter Five

Economic Reform and Opening-up to the Outside World

I lived in an out-of-the-way valley which was surrounded by big mountains. I could see the thatched houses on the high mountains in distance with smoke curling up to the sky. Many times I wanted to climb high to see how people over there lived and to see what it was like on the other side of the mountains. In winter, there were white frost flowers on the top of the mountain and I would wonder how they went down the mountain and contacted with the outside world.

When I was a child, I always dreamed I climbed to the top of the mountain and saw a lot of skyscrapers like mirage at the horizon of the sky. One day, I finally climbed to the top of the mountain, but what I saw was still endless mountains.

I would always stare at the graves on the mountain slope, my heart filled with melancholy, "Would I be buried here too after I die?"

I was depressed and unhappy. I had only one wish. I wished I could go out of the mountains and see the outside world. But I was in despair. It was by no means easy to go out of the mountains.

Out of the Mountains

When the summer of 1977 was over, I had to go back to teach in the high school of Kaiyang Phosphate Mine. I was sad and frustrated. When I saw my classmates who would have a bright future working in Chishui Natural Gas Chemical Plant, and thought of myself who had to wait for who knew how long the opportunity to speak English and work with foreigners, I sank into despair. My dream was to go to the world, but now I couldn't even go out of the big mountains.

From the autumn of 1977 to the spring of 1979, I worked in obscurity as a teacher in the middle school. Most of the students were still not interested in study. In 1977, universities started to enroll students directly from middle school graduates. Those who were enrolled from the society also needed to pass the examination to go to college. During that period, the only thing that cheered me up was several of my students who worked extremely hard got admitted to university.

At that time, China gradually opened itself to the outside world. Many large-scale state-owned enterprises began to introduce technology and equipment blindly from abroad. Kaiyang Phosphate Mine also launched its plan to refurbish the mine by introducing advanced technology and equipment. A chief engineers' office was set up and I was temporarily transferred there to do the translation. By that time, the construction of Chishui Natural Gas Chemical Plant had been finished and several of my classmates who had worked there were transferred to the mine to do paper translation first and would work as interpreters when foreign experts, technology and equipment were introduced. Later we were sent for training in a higher leading body — the Chemical

Mining Bureau of the H Ministry which was located in a county named Z County in Hebei Province about 70 kilometers away from Beijing.

I owed my thanks to a man who helped me get the opportunity to work in the chief engineers' office and to be trained in the Chemical Mining Bureau. His name was K who was director general of the bureau.

During the Cultural Revolution, K was head of Kaiyang Phosphate Mine. After he was labeled a capitalist-roader, he was publicly denounced and was forced to accept reform through labor and work under the pit. All the workers and their families tried to avoid him, while I still greeted him warmly and called him uncle whenever I met him. He had very good impression on me.

I got on the train heading for the north on the Chinese New Year's Eve. The trains in China were usually overcrowded and it had long been a torture for Chinese people to travel by train. The Chinese New Year's Eve was the most important occasion of the year for the family to gather together. So the train was virtually empty. There were three other soldiers in the carriage. I was reading English all the way, harboring my longing for a bright future. The rumbling of the train covered the sound of my reading. When the train pulled in at a station, the carriage became quiet and resounded with the sound of my reading.

Every cell of my body was filled with joy. I had escaped from the big mountains finally. I knew it was only the first step of my ten-thousand-*li* journey to go to the world. I had made the first step, after all. It was the spring of 1979 and I was 23.

An important thing happened in China in that year. Deng Xiaoping made an inspection trip to the city of Shenzhen and decided to develop it into a special economic zone. Shenzhen Special Economic Zone became the first window of China's reform and opening-up to the outside world. Later Deng Xiaoping's trip was written into a song *A Story in Spring* and the song has spread to every corner of China.

In the spring of 1979,
A senior comes to the South Sea of China and made a great decision.
New towns are erected like mythos,
Golden mountains are built up like miracles.
The spring thunder awaked the people by the two sides of the Great Wall,
The bright spring warmed the lands at both banks of Yangtze River.
Ah, China, China,
You make a new step with power and grandeur,
Strike forward to the spring with everything fresh and new...

This man was Deng Xiaoping, the chief designer of China's reform and opening-up policy. The spring of 1979 had significant meaning to both the Chinese nation and me personally. The reform and opening-up has changed the destiny of our generation.

Personnel System with Chinese Characteristics

I was trained and worked for a year in the mining bureau. I actually did not get too much training, but worked as a willing cheap labor. There was an Import Office which was responsible for the examination, approval and implementation of the technology and equipment imported by the country's chemical mines. At the beginning we helped translate a lot of paper materials. Later we took part in all kinds of negotiations as trainees and sometimes worked as interpreters for the foreign engineers or experts who went to chemical mines and factories for inspection.

A year later, the import fever was beginning to cool down. Great financial losses were caused due to blind investment in importing technology and equipment. So the central government began to reinforce the management and supervision. The import plan of Kaiyang

214

Phosphate Mine was cancelled. K, director general of the mining bureau, asked my father if he wanted me to stay and work in the mining bureau. The leader of the Import Office also told me that they were short of hands and he wanted me to stay.

At that time, all the jobs were arranged by the government and we could not change jobs as we liked.

Although they said I could stay, there was no formal job transferring procedures. I was too young and innocent. I thought I could stay as long as I worked hard to improve my ability. I didn't realize that personal relations worked much better than ability and I needed to maintain the old relations and built up new ones. Most of my colleagues who came for training in the mining bureau also wanted to stay. They waited for some time, seeing no hope of being transferred, left one after another. Stubbornly, I stayed.

As stupid as I was, I did not spend any time and energy to maintain and build up any necessary relations, but just gave myself wholly to my work and study. Another year had passed and there was no sign that I would be transferred to the bureau. I finally plucked up to meet director general K and asked him to speed up my job mobility from the mine. K said he would write a personal note to the director of Chemical Industry Department of Guizhou Province and asked him to approve my job transfer and give me my personal files. I was confused and asked him if a transfer order issued by the Division of Personnel was needed. He said no. According to the regular procedures of a job transfer, the mining bureau should first send a transfer order to Kaiyang Phosphate Mine. If Kaiyang Phosphate Mine approved my job transfer, it would send a consent letter to the Chemical Industry Department of the province where my personal files were kept. When the Chemical Industry Department approved my job transfer, it would post my personal files by mail to the mining bureau. It was against the rules to get one's files out with some leader's note. But at that time in China, all one needed was a word or a note by the person in charge to get something done. It was a very common phenomenon. Since K had given his order, there should have been no problem. But something unexpected happened.

There was a woman in the mining bureau named Xiu who was transferred from Kaiyang Phosphate Mine by K. It was widely rumored that K had an affair with Xiu who was rather good-looking. I had seen how Xiu coquetted with K and I could tell by intuition the relationship between the two of them was by no means normal. Xiu was a shrew, but she was timid and lovable as a little bird in front of K with rosy cheeks and soft looks. It was easy to imagine the fatal attraction such a woman had to an old cadre. K's wife was an ordinary housewife with ordinary looks. Xiu came in and went out of K's home as if she was also a family member. When I heard people talking about the relationship between K and Xiu, I felt very sorry for K's wife.

Xiu was chief of the Division of Labor and Salary. The personnel department in government agencies and enterprises was divided into two parts: the Division of Personnel and the Division of Labor and Salary. The former was in charge of the cadres and intellectuals, and the latter was for physical labors.

Xiu was my mother's colleague when she was in Kaiyang Phosphate Mine. Before I was transferred to the mining bureau, many people suggested that I ask her, who liked to be treated as a savior for everyone, for help. But I didn't. My job transfer was not the business of the Division of Labor and Salary. I might have offended her for it when so many people were obsequious to her while I ignored her.

Relying on her relationship with K, Xiu acted tyrannically and made many enemies. The chief of the Division of Personnel was a demobilized army man called W. W hated Xiu who put on disgusting airs and always had a hand in the affairs of his division. W and Xiu became enemies. It was only natural that Xiu would speak ill of W at K's ears and K certainly wouldn't like W.

Without having gone through the normal procedures, I went directly to the Division of Personnel holding my own files. W was annoyed and refused to deal with my job transfer. I felt much embarrassed. It was not my fault, but I had to take the consequence. I thought K was the director general after all and he would solve the problem sooner or later. I might just have to wait for some time.

I went to work in the Import Office every day and worked harder than anyone else. I had no salary because I was not officially received by the mining bureau. Faith moves mountains. I believed as long as I worked hard, W would come to know me and therefore accept me. Then a new problem cropped up unexpectedly.

A basketball competition was held in the mining bureau. Xiu and I were in the same team. We all took it as a recreational activity and didn't take it to heart whether we won or lost. But Xiu was an exception. She was arrogant, easily got angry and always quarreled with the judge. When the game was over, the players of the other team came over to me and said, "Please tell Xiu that we think she is unreasonably arrogant." With the intention to ease their anger and reconcile the two parties, I said, "This is typical Xiu. She didn't mean what she said. She was also like this when she was in Kaiyang Phosphate Mine. It is not necessary to be mad at her." I didn't like her from the bottom of my heart and maybe I revealed it subconsciously when I said it.

Walls had ears. What I said that day soon came to Xiu's ears. She found me and made a scene and threatened that she would teach me a lesson.

Xiu started to retaliate against me. She said evil things in front of director general K and made him hate me. K believed whatever Xiu had told him. After the thing happened, K not only didn't help me, he wanted to kick me out. He asked the head of Yunfu Pyrite Mine in Guangdong Province to transfer me to his pyrite mine which was a day's bus ride from Guangzhou City that is about 2,000 kilometers away from Beijing.

It was widely spread that I was transferred to the mining bureau through the back door. K was a man of boldness of vision and he wouldn't care for others' opinions if he really wanted to help me. But now he was anxious to get rid of me, who was the enemy of his woman. Someone suggested that I should find K and explain it to him. I was too young and didn't have the courage to measure my strength with K's mistress.

W changed his attitude to me and even showed me his sympathy. The mining bureau was divided into two factions with one faction in support of director general K and the other against him. Many people harbored bitter hatred for Xiu and wished I would go to find her trouble. I knew they wanted to use me to attack Xiu. Although I lacked social experience, I was not the kind of person who liked telling tales. So I kept silent from beginning to end in the struggle between the two factions.

I worked very hard and never caused trouble. I was easy to get along with and everybody spoke highly of me. But my personal files were laid aside in the Division of Personnel and nobody touched it as if it were a hot potato. Nobody would handle my job transfer procedures because no one dared offend Xiu. I was in a dilemma.

I still went to work on time. Every day, I got up early in the morning and read English in the corridor of the office building. When everyone else came to the office, I had already read English for two hours. When everyone else left after a day's work, I still stayed in the office studying English and didn't leave until it was very late. I was widely recognized as a hard-working girl in the mining bureau and many people set me as an example to educate their children. I had no pay for 10 months. Many people praised me for my strong will, "Nobody could persevere as long as Liu Ping," they said.

The headquarters of the mining bureau was located in Z County of Hebei Province. It also had an office in Beijing which was responsible for foreign affairs and liaison with the relations up and down. I started to shuttle between Z County and Beijing when I was able to do some interpretation. Gradually I had the opportunity to work with Westerners

218

and communicate with them in English. I was absolutely ecstatic. I made up my mind to improve my English. I had realized English would be the tool I needed to use all my life and it would be closely related to my future.

My English was getting better and better. I was a second-class citizen in the office because I had not yet been transferred here officially for my files were suspended. I was only considered when there was no one else to do the translation or nobody wanted to do it, for example going to a mine with harsh conditions to work as the interpreter of a foreign expert for a month. I would do whatever was assigned to me. I knew I must be prepared at any minute. I wouldn't forgive myself if I let the chance slip away because of my own incompetence. I also knew that I must make good use of every minute working with Westerners if I wanted to improve my English. I worked and studied hard as if I had endless energy.

Seeing that worker-peasant-soldier students were on various levels of education, the government made a decision to hold an examination among all the worker-peasant-soldier college graduates who worked as translators and matched the title of assistant translator with their examination results. We were given three months to prepare for the examination.

At that time after my personal files were suspended for 10 months, the Division of Personnel notified me that they had decided to transfer me to L High School which was a subordinate unit to the mining bureau. The school was located in a village in Z County and all the students were children of the staff members of the mining bureau and subordinate units. The reason why I wanted to come to work in the mining bureau was that I could be a translator. If I wanted to be successful and go to see the world in the future, I had to work in the front line of the reform and opening-up. But I was helpless. On the one hand, I was faced with Xiu's retaliation; on the other hand, there came another translator whose husband worked in the higher body as a translator for the leaders of the chemical industry. There were four translators in the Import Office including me and there was not enough work for all of us. The Division of Personal asked me to report for duty at L High School after the examination.

I worked extremely hard during the three months' preparation. I read through all the reference books and did all the TOEFL (Test of English as a Foreign Language) examination papers I could get. I also kept on reading *China Daily* every day. When I was doing an examination paper to test my English level, I would finish it within the time limit and calculate the mark to see my scores. I took the examination as a critical battle which would determine my future and destiny.

I had turned to deputy director general Mu of the mining bureau for help for my job. Mu was disgusted with K and Xiu and was sympathetic with me. As a deputy director general, Mu could help me if he wanted. But he didn't. It wasn't worthwhile offending his superior for a callow girl like me. He just said indignantly to me repeatedly, "How ridiculous is that a government department refuses to handle the job transfer procedures of a staff member who has worked here for 10 months and got no payment? Liu Ping, this examination is a critical opportunity for you. If you do well in the examination, you prove to others that you have been transferred here through your own efforts; otherwise, you have no way out."

I was under overwhelming mental pressure. How could I ensure that I would be successful in the examination?

There were dozens of worker-peasant-soldier students in the H Ministry who were preparing for the English examination. We all attended classes in T University. Everyone was full of confidence and didn't work as hard as me. Most of them graduated from key universities. Two of my colleagues who worked in the same office graduated respectively from S Foreign Languages Institute and G Foreign Studies University. I was the only one who graduated from Guizhou University which was in the most underdeveloped province in southwest China. I didn't feel inferior myself, but my two colleagues would use it to discourage me from time to time and I was beginning to lose heart in myself. Sometimes we did examination papers in class and the teacher asked us to calculate our own marks. Everybody looked happy and relaxed as if they had got high marks. I felt I could barely pass it after I added up my marks. I was convinced I was the worst one among them. I had no alternative but try my best.

When I was reviewing my lessons in the office, the two colleagues were busy chatting with other colleagues. Then someone would say, "Look at Liu Ping! How hardworking she is. What you do all day is chatting." I would explain at once, "I have too weak a foundation in English. So I have to study harder."

Once I translated an article from Chinese to English as exercise and asked the colleague who graduated from G Foreign Studies University to read it and appraise it for me. After she read it, she told everyone behind my back that she hadn't expected my English was so poor. I believed what she said was true. It was another blow to my confidence. I was embarrassed in front of my colleagues because they all knew my English was poor. The reason why I had worked so hard was that I wanted to prove I was a talent and it would be a right decision for the mining bureau to recruit me. But things didn't happen as I wished.

I was 25 that year and what had happened was beyond my psychological endurance. I had no relative or friend to pour out my bitterness. I couldn't say what was on my mind to any of my colleagues to avoid trouble. I had to endure it myself silently. I was on the verge of collapse and I had to find someone to unburden myself of all my grievances. I turned to a translator who worked in the construction corporation under the H Ministry and I got to know her in the classes in the T University. I didn't know which apartment building she lived in and finally I found her place after a lot of inquiry. I was sitting in front of her and her husband and let tears run down my cheeks. I had no handkerchief and had to constantly wipe my tears with my hands. They listened so attentively to me that they completely forgot to give me a towel to wipe tears. In the end I asked, "Could you please give me a towel?" We didn't have tissue in China at that time.

Three months passed quickly. The night before the examination, I went to see a movie to relax myself, while the colleagues who chatted all day long were making last-minute preparation that would prove too late.

When the examination was over the next day, we gathered together to check our answers and those who had been arrogant looked frustrated. When the result came out, I turned out to rank first among the examinees in the mining bureau and its subordinate institutes and second in the H Ministry.

When the examination was finished, I went to work in L high school.

Not long after that, I was conferred the professional title of "assistant translator" according to my examination result and then "translator". Several years later I became "associate translation editor" which was equivalent to associate professor in China's personnel system.

Xiu's coming to no good end convinced me that evil would be rewarded with evil.

Xiu was jealous of a woman of her age named Lan who worked in the Division of Personnel. Lan's husband was a military officer. Xiu sent an anonymous letter to Lan's husband and spread rumors against her, which caused alienation between the couple. When the couple turned to the police for help, the rumormonger turned out to be Xiu who wrote the letter and asked her son who was just a pupil to copy it. She was dismissed from office and expelled from the Party. Later I heard that she went to S City to make a living with the help of director general K.

The mining bureau became much quieter after that.

Opportunities Always Favor Those Who Are Prepared

When I was teaching English in L High School, I didn't give up the hope of becoming a translator and studied hard in my spare time.

With the professional title of assistant translator, I was looking for a chance to return to the Import Office. When the school holiday began, I would go to work in the Import Office as a volunteer. I would offer to do the work, no matter how hard or tiring it was.

With the reform and opening-up deepening, the foreign affairs tasks also increased. The Import Office became short of translators, and the task of doing on site translation at the mine or construction site was relatively more demanding which not everyone wanted to do. I would offer to do the task and seize the opportunity to enhance my ability and boost my courage. I was determined to stand my ground in the Import Office and become the chief translator.

In the summer of 1983, Guangdong Yunfu Pyrite Mine started a company in Shenzhen and set up a quarry there. The equipment was imported from Japan. Translators were needed when the Japanese engineers came to Shenzhen to test the new equipment. No translators of Japanese were avalable, so they asked me and another translator to work for the Japanese engineers. It became my opportunity to leave L High School.

Shenzhen at that time was by no means what it is today. The city was under construction and the whole city was like a big construction site. Living conditions were rather tough.

I worked in Shenzhen for several months and the National Day was approaching. At this time in Beijing, the autumn sky was clear and the air was crisp. The streets were all decorated with lanterns and festoons and the whole city was in a festival atmosphere. But in Shenzhen, there was no festivity at all. When I was walking in the street, I heard someone with the accent of northerners curse "Fuck, it seems that Shenzhen is not part of China".

I missed Beijing very much, not only for the festival atmosphere, but also for her distinct four seasons. It was awfully hot in Shenzhen. We lived in a simple building with no air-conditioning and worked at the construction site under the scorching sun. We had to wait for several hours in the post office to connect with our families. When we were finally put through, the sound was so low that we had to shout to be heard. What's more annoying, disconnection was usual and we had to wait for a long time to be put through again. Every weekend, we would accompany the two Japanese engineers to the post office to call their families and give a call to our families by the way. It was common to wait for three or four hours to get a phone call connected.

When the day to return to Beijing finally came, the Import Office sent us a telegram asking us to do the translation for a training program of Yunfu Pyrite Mine which would last for a month in the same province with Shenzhen. The translator who worked with me in Shenzhen insisted on going back to Beijing. So I went to the pyrite mine alone. I took the task as another opportunity and worked there for a month. It was almost winter when I got back to Beijing.

Guangdong Yunfu Pyrite Mine purchased 100 30-ton dump trucks from an American company. There was something that needed to be adjusted with the generators of the trucks. The American company constantly sent engineers to rebuild the generators and to train the local mechanics and drivers. I went to work at the pyrite mine a couple of times and stayed from half a month to a month every time. No one fought with me for the opportunity to work in the mine in the remote mountain area with arduous conditions. So I made remarkable progress in my English.

We lived in the humble guest house of the pyrite mine. The rooms for the foreign guests had been renovated with indoor toilets and bathrooms. We translators lived with those strangers who came to the mine on business. Four persons shared a room and used the public toilet and the public bathhouse.

Growing up in the mine area myself, I was used to the tough conditions. But the Americans who were used to a comfortable life found it hard to endure.

An American who was called Roger Brown came to the pyrite mine twice and stayed for about a month each time. Those days were really an ordeal for him. I enjoyed talking with Roger. I wanted to improve my oral English. Besides, I was eager to know about the outside world and American people. There would always be someone else or another translator present when we were chatting. It was the foreign affairs discipline. I wished I could have more time to speak with Roger to improve my English. At the same time, I could help him relieve his boredom. But there was always someone else there, so we couldn't talk as much as we liked. If the person wanted to go, I would finish my conversation with Roger as soon as possible. Occasionally I would chat with Roger in the evening alone, but I didn't dare to stay too late.

Roger told me that one day seemed like a year for him in China. He was not used to the food, the room and the boring life without entertainments at the mine. When he was working at another mine with another American, the two of them would shout hysterically at the big mountains for a while when the loneliness became unbearable. Some Westerners who worked in China on a long term would go to Hong Kong almost every weekend or holiday.

Translators were given special treatment in Yunfu Pyrite Mine and we could have meals with Roger in the canteen every day. Roger asked us to tell the cook to put less ginger in the dishes. Neither of us knew what ginger was until we looked it up in the dictionary.

Roger would bring with him a lot of things to eat whenever he came to China, canned food, instant food or something like that. The first fruit juice I had was the American brand instant juice TANG Roger brought from home. I did not know there had been such a delicious beverage in the world!

Roger told me that the small spoon put beside the coffee cup was used to stir the coffee. When he first saw us drinking coffee with the small spoon, he couldn't help laughing at us. I was sensitive and kept in mind that I should not drink coffee with the spoon since that day. My colleague was forgetful and still drank coffee with the spoon. Roger and I would laugh at her secretly.

We developed a friendship with the foreigners after working with them for some time and it was natural and normal that we were reluctant to part from them.

Once I accompanied an American engineer, who would leave China the next day, to Guangzhou from the pyrite mine, and we stayed in the best hotel in the city. When I was in my room, I got a call from the American who asked me if it was proper for me to go to his room to have a chat. It was the only way we could chat alone. At that time we were not allowed to accept the foreigner's invitation to eat or drink. Considering that this engineer was as old as my father, I said I would like to go to his room. During our conversation, he intentionally kept the door opened.

Now, I often have foreign friends to come to see me or live at my home for a few days. We talk of everything cheerfully and are close as families. My staff members or friends go to pubs and bars, drinking, dancing or even dating with foreigners. The tour guides in my company always hug the foreign guests, crying and kissing good-bye to each other at the airport. All these changes just have happened in a short time of over 20 years.

I worked hard and volunteered to work in those places with harsh conditions. My efforts paid off and my oral English and translation ability were improving rapidly.

My chance came. An old translator left the mining bureau. I seized the opportunity and officially came back to the Import Office and became the chief translator not long after.

"You Cannot Walk with Foreigners Shoulder to Shoulder"

At that time, foreign affairs rights were all concentrated in the central ministries. The mining bureau had no direct external rights and all the negotiations with foreigners were arranged by the Foreign Affairs Department of the H Ministry or by the Construction Corporation (hereinafter referred to as HCC) which had the rights in foreign affairs. There must always be some officials from the ministry or HCC to participate in the projects with foreign affairs of the mining bureau. There was an official surnamed Wang from HCC responsible for the foreign affairs of the mining bureau. He often participated in the negotiations or went to the mines and factories with us. But he didn't care much about the effect and the progress of the project negotiation or inspection, but kept close watch on the Chinese staff to supervise them. I felt an eye was on me no matter what I did or what I said. I was eager to communicate with foreigners, but I had to guard the supervision of others. When I was doing interpretation for the foreign guests or walking with them, there would always be someone who pulled me by the sleeve reminding me of what I should not say or standing too close to the foreign guests. I knew it was Wang even if I did not see him. One day when I was seeing off some foreign guests outside the office building of HCC, Wang pulled me again. I didn't know what he meant, so I looked back at him, puzzled. He said, "Do not walk side by side with the foreign guests". I didn't know which foreign affairs discipline stipulated this.

At that time, the civil aviation capacity between cities was limited and we often went to the mines or factories with foreign guests by train. One of the advantages of doing foreign affairs jobs was that we could enjoy the four-bed soft sleeper with foreign guests. I was not allowed to be in the same compartment with the male foreign guests I accompanied. My superior would rather let me share a compartment with three male Russian strangers than allow me to stay in the compartment with our own foreign guests.

Gifts Given by Foreign Guests Should Be Turned In

At that time, materials were very scanty in China. Any gifts presented by foreign guests were especially rare to us. It was stipulated by the foreign affairs discipline that we shouldn't accept gifts from foreign guests. If they insisted on presenting the gifts, we must turn them in. By the end of the year, the Foreign Affairs Department would draw lots to distribute the gifts to the whole staff.

Foreign guests were sincere when giving us the gifts. I thought it was impolite to hand in the gifts given by foreigners. Normally I would firmly refuse to accept their gifts. There was only once I couldn't resist the temptation and accepted the gift when an American gave me a small alarm clock which I liked very much. He also gave me a big pack of good quality tissue, which was not available in China then. I turned in the tissue and kept the alarm clock. Later, I found that many people did the same thing, secretly keeping the favorite gifts and handing over the gifts they didn't like or less valuable.

Once I worked for some foreigners from a Swiss chemical company and accompanied them to inspect some factories. When we were chatting in the car, I pointed at an oil stain on my trousers and asked them, "Can the products produced in your factory get rid of such oil stains?" They all leaned over to study the oil stain on my trousers and then discussed which products could remove such oil stain.

Soon after that, I received a large package which was mailed from Switzerland. In it was a wide variety of washing powder and detergents. My leader asked me, "Why did the foreigners send you so many things?" I replied that I didn't know they would send me all those things. The leader gave me a doubtful look and raised his voice, "You don't know? Why did they mail the things to you if you haven't asked them to do so?" I felt much wronged but didn't want to argue with him. I just silently distributed all the things among the colleagues.

The Leader Said I Was Skittish

When I was working for foreigners, I was eager to improve my oral English and would communicate with them as long as I had the opportunity. Sometimes we enjoyed our conversation so much that we would break into laughter. Actually many foreigners liked me for my personality.

One day, we went to DYK Phosphate Mine in H Province on an inspection trip. The phosphate mine held a warm reception dinner and then entertained the American engineer with the movies *Nezha Conquers the Dragon King* and *Look at This Family*. The American got a little drunk and was very excited. *Nezha Conquers the Dragon King* was an interesting cartoon. I made it even funnier by my exaggerated translation. The American laughed heartily from time to time which could be heard by all the audience. His laughter infected me and I broke into laughter myself.

Soon after I came back to Beijing, the leader of the Import Office entrusted an old colleague to talk to me. He said it very implicitly and did not make himself clear for a long time. I got impatient and pointed it out, "Do you mean that I am skittish when working with the foreigners?" He replied, "Yes, that is exactly what I mean. You should pay more attention to it in the future and be serious when working with foreigners." He also told me that it was Wang who asked my leader to talk to me and that he would not allow me to work in foreign affairs if I continued to be like this.

Interestingly, I am regarded as a successful person in the industry today. One of the important reasons for my success is that I am good at communicating with foreigners and I have a sincere and passionate personality.

Foreign Ghosts Entering the Village

Since the early 1980s, I had opportunities to accompany Westerners on business trips in China. At that time, there were not so many Westerners coming to our country. Therefore, the local people would crowd round and stare at the foreigners whenever there was an opportunity.

We went to investigate mining resources in remote mountainous areas. There was no one around when we first arrived. But after a while, the villagers dressed in rags came one after another, men and women, old and young, pointing at the Westerners and talking joyfully around us. The villagers were amused by every move of the Westerners and burst into laughter from time to time. Wherever I went, they would call me "translator officer", the address they got to know from the role of a Japanese interpreter in a movie set in the backdrop of anti-Japanese war. When the Westerners talked with them in English and I interpreted it into the local dialect, they would click their tongues in admiration and highly praise me. The villagers were all very kind and hospitable and invited the Westerners to have *shangwu* (lunch) at their homes. Some even invited the Westerners to "stay for a night". Only the earthy farmers could be so personal and they knew nothing about the discipline of foreign affairs. Some Westerner was modest and unassuming and would take the tobacco pipe handed over by a villager and smoke it for a while. I liked this kind of Westerners from the bottom of my heart.

Although there was no means of communication, the villagers could always get the news and came to see the foreigners crossing over the mountains. Once, I saw rows of trees far away on the top of the mountain, but after a while I found the trees were all moving. Looking hard, I found they were not trees but the villagers who came from far away to see the foreigners.

The Westerners I received always enjoyed grand reception wherever they went. They would be called foreign guests by us Chinese and it was a privilege to join in receiving them. Wherever the foreign guests went, almost all the local leaders would receive them in person. When entertaining two or three foreign guests, there would be dozens of or even some 100 Chinese accompanying them, ranging from the provincial leaders, prefecture leaders, county leaders, district leaders, to the commune leaders, even the public security officers were included. In most cases the major leaders would accompany the foreign guests having meal in a single room, while several to a dozen tables would be set in the outside dining hall or next door.

This was also true with the on site inspection. Several foreign guests would be escorted by a large crowd of Chinese. The team would be dragged very long. The Westerners felt baffled and always asked me, "Do these people have no work to do? Why do they always follow us?"

Most of the time we went to the mines. The foreign guests stayed in the guest house. Prior to their arrival, the guest house had been renovated and equipped with bathtubes and flushing toilets in the rooms. Hot water for bath, which was boiled by a boiler, was carried by the waitresses and waiters to the foreign guests' rooms in buckets and poured into the bathtubs. I was treated equally as the foreign guests. Although the work conditions were tough, I could enjoy hot water bath wherever we went, which was better than at home. At that time, ordinary Chinese people all took a bath in the public bathhouse.

There was usually no washing machine in the guest house. All the foreign guests' clothes were hand washed by the waitresses and waiters. After we came back from the inspection site, we could see a lot of underwear, socks, shirts and jeans hanging on the rope in the courtyard like the flags of various countries fluttering in the wind. Foreign guests joked with each other guessing whose underwear, whose shorts, whose socks and whose shirts. Occasionally there would be a female foreign guest coming to visit the mine. The local people would be very curious about her silk panty hose hanging on the rope and discuss about it with great interest.

Power failure was common decades ago, so the rooms were all equipped with flashlights and candles.

When I accompanied the foreign guests to visit Kaiyang Phosphate Mine, we went down to the underground by a tramcar. The seats were all covered with new and shining golden threaded velvet. The foreign guests asked me smilingly, "Are these seats covered with golden threaded velvet every day?"

Once we went to visit a newly-built mine. There was a bed prepared specially for the mine manager to have a nap in his office. The bed was covered with a brand new bed sheet, an embroidered pillow and a satin quilt as if it were a bridal chamber. Obviously all these things were prepared before the foreign guests came. The foreign guests looked at the bed curiously with a puzzled look on their faces.

Chinese people always treated foreigners as distinguished guests. The result was that when we went to the United States on a business trip later, we felt somewhat disappointed when we were not treated as we did for foreigners.

Foreign Exchange Certificate

Foreign exchange certificate came into existence in 1980 and was out of circulation in 1995.

In the early phase of China's reform and opening-up, with the development of the tourism industry and the increase of economic and cultural exchanges, more and more foreigners came to visit China and a growing number of overseas Chinese, Hong Kong, Macao and Taiwan compatriots came back to China as well. Many hotels, shops and other organizations which specially served them came into being. At that time, the circulation of foreign currency was prohibited in the country. In order to facilitate their shopping in these places and also distinguish them from domestic residents, on April 1, 1980, the State Council authorized the Bank of China to issue the foreign exchange certificate or FEC. Foreigners should first convert the foreign currency into foreign exchange certificates in Bank of China or other designated foreign exchange sites, and then use them in a specified range of places.

FEC was equivalent to RMB. In the time of material scarcity, owning FEC meant owning those "fancy goods" such as color TV, refrigerator and the like which couldn't be bought with RMB.

The most typical consumption channel of FEC was the Friendship Store. Many friendship stores were set up in some larger cities. In the 1980s when China's commodity economy was still underdeveloped and per capita wage was only 40 yuan, friendship stores became the shopping place specially for the dealings settled in FEC. Up-market commodity such as Swiss watches over 1,000 yuan and Venus brand color TV sets, and goods in short supply such as soap, washing powder and Dacron cloth were all available there. All of a sudden, FEC became a symbol of status.

Most of the Chinese residents owning FEC had relatives overseas who sent them foreign currency. They converted it into FEC in designated banks, and then strutted into the friendship store filled with a great sense of satisfaction and happiness.

Ordinary people couldn't enter the Friendship Store randomly. You had to have a passport or some certification before you got admitted. The first time I entered the Beijing Friendship Store was in 1985 when I had my first passport. I went there not for shopping, but to satisfy my curiosity and vanity.

At that time, there were few international marriages in China. A Westerner, even if a poor student, was a rich person in the eyes of Chinese people. Even the poorest Westerner was richer than a Chinese. Some very brave Chinese girls who had foreign boyfriends would go in and out of the Friendship Store like a proud princess. They were generally pretty and tall, wearing delicate makeup on the face and dressed in fashionable clothes. They walked in and out with their foreign boyfriends arm in arm. I was like a country bumpkin in contrast when they passed by me. Few Chinese girls wore makeup at that time. I was always in simple clothes with a plain face. Once a Western young man who had a Chinese girlfriend asked me why I did not wear makeup. I said, "There is a beauty in simplicity" which I just learned from a book.

Foreign guests needed to pay FEC in the designated shops. But it was much more flexible in other shops which also accepted RMB as well. I often had opportunities to accompany foreign guests to travel to remote areas, where FEC was not accepted or FEC and RMB were both accepted. FEC was not a currency in circulation and couldn't be used directly in the market. Some foreign affairs workers took advantage of their work and exchanged RMB for FEC with foreign guests to buy the goods in short supply or to sell the FEC 20 percent higher than the face value in the black market. They would have a net gain of 20 percent which was a great lure to the poor Chinese people. The overpass in front of Beijing Friendship Store was once a black market for transactions in foreign exchange.

Although I could also take advantage of my job to make money, I never did it. Poor as I was, I had self-esteem and would never do something which was illegal. I had a simple idea that I should never lose Chinese people's face in front of the foreigners. I had a colleague called T, who was one of those becoming rich through illegal foreign exchange transaction. Every time he received foreign guests, his first consideration was how to get FEC from the foreign guests' hands. He would bring a lot of cash with him to facilitate the exchange whenever there was a foreign affairs task. When he asked to exchange for FEC with foreigners, I could see doubt, reluctance and contempt on their faces. He would pay the bills first for the foreigners in RMB when they were shopping or checking out and then ask them to pay him back in FEC. Sometimes he would make a mistake. When he accompanied some foreign guests to travel on business in some remote areas or cities, he thought FEC wouldn't be used all the way and exchanged all their FEC even before departure. Out of his expectation, some store or hotel only accepted FEC and he had to quickly take out FEC to pay the foreigners' bills in the presence of a large crowd. I felt embarrassed and uncomfortable as his colleague, but T himself was composed and at ease as if nothing had happened. There were many discussions about T among the leaders and other colleagues who all expressed their contempt for him while asking him to help them get FEC. Although he was not liked or trusted by the leaders because of his poor professional competence, he was still very popular because he could get FEC. Everyone was gossiping about him behind his back, but at the same time asking him for help. T's home was always the most stylish with all the home appliances which were in short supply in the market. People would talk on and on about the luxurious life of his family with mixed feelings of jealousy and contempt.

The foreign guests who often came to China learned that one could make money through speculative reselling of FEC. They offered to help me but were refused by me politely. Although I didn't become rich, I gained friendship and trust which couldn't be bought with money.

I stuck to my principles. I was poor but with lofty ideals.

With the deepening of reform and opening-up, the development of the market economy greatly increased the quantity and variety of commodities. Foreign exchange certificate, as a product at the time of commodity shortage, withdrew from the stage of history in 1995.

Today, I have achieved what I want through my hard work and enjoy a peace of mind.

First Time Abroad

In April 1985, I got the chance to go abroad for the first time at the age of 29. A delegation of the H Ministry went to visit Finland and I went with them as the interpreter.

The seven of us, five from the Ministry, one from HCC and I from the mining bureau, flew to Moscow and stayed for one night. The next day we arrived in Helsinki.

The Red Square was the first place I wanted to visit when we arrived in Moscow. I had seen in movies the military parade at the Red Square for numerous times. When we were small children, we thought that the Soviet Union was the symbol of communism and the best place in the world.

At that time, few people spoke English in Russia. No one could understand us when we asked the way to the Red Square. We tried to strike up a conversation with them by mentioning the name of Lenin and Stalin. But they still shook their heads probably because of our wrong pronunciation. Finally a person understood us when we mentioned Kremlin. In fact, we were already close to the Red Square. It soon appeared in front of us after we bypassed a building.

Standing at the center of the Red Square, I felt my heart rising and falling like waves. I couldn't believe a child who grew up in the mountains of Guizhou would some day stand at the place which all revolutionaries of the world had yearned for. At the same time, I felt somewhat disappointed because the Red Square was much smaller than I had imagined and was different from what I had seen in the movie.

We went to the grave of Lenin to pay respect to his remains, which was so vivid as if it were unreal. It was hard to believe the man lying in the crystal coffin was comrade Lenin who was respected by and familiar to all Chinese people through the films *Lenin in 1918*, *Lenin in October* and *In the Name of Revolution*. During the Cultural Revolution, the movies that could be shown were limited to some Soviet and North Korean movies besides the eight model plays. We had seen *Lenin in 1918*, and *Lenin in October* so many times that we could recite almost all the lines.

We met a middle-aged Russian man who could speak English. I chatted with him. An old comrade in the delegation came to remind me, "You had better stop chatting with him. Be careful he might be a KGB."

We spent the night in a big state-run hotel not far from the Moscow airport. The living conditions were simple and there was not much choice on food besides some bread. The waitresses paid little attention to the customers and gathered in small groups chatting with each other. Seeing us, they made gestures pointing at their chest and said, "Mao". Later we figured it out. They were asking us why we did not wear badges of Chairman Mao. China was still at the stage of the Cultural Revolution in their impression.

There was no one to meet us when we arrived in Helsinki. Foreign affairs official Mr. Li from HCC gave a call to the Chinese Embassy and then an embassy official came to send us to the President Hotel arranged by the Finnish government. Our Finish host was surprised to learn that we had arrived in Helsinki one day earlier. At that time, there were few flights to Europe. We arrived there a day in advance based on the flight table, but we didn't inform the Finnish host. We thought it was no big deal, but the Finnish host found us incredible and asked us as soon as they met us, "How did you arrive ahead of time?"

President Hotel was a five-star hotel. The host arranged a single room for each of us, but we insisted on two sharing a room. According to the foreign affairs discipline, one could not participate in any foreign affairs activity alone. Now we were abroad, we certainly couldn't live alone. There were seven people. Naturally one of us had to live alone. The delegation leader Mr. Yan was arranged to stay in the single room. We were on the same floor, but his room was some distance away from ours. He was not willing to stay by himself in a single room, but he had no other choice.

We followed an overall rationing system of our expenses that were kept by the foreign affairs official Mr. Li. And the money left would be distributed to individuals in the end. At that time, Chinese people were poor, so going abroad on business was also taken as an opportunity to earn money. We all tried to save money as much as we could and spent little money on meals. Sometimes we just bought some bread and sausages. One of us kept the sausage in the suitcase. The sausage fermented and exploded in the case, which made a mess in his suitcase and the whole room stink. I was the one who could endure hardships the least in the delegation. Hunger was unbearable to me, and I often asked Mr. Li for my money to buy chicken legs. I had the least money left by the end of the journey.

We were all ill at ease when invited to dinner by our Finnish host. Before dinner, the host asked us what we would like to drink; we all replied politely in the typical Chinese courtesy "No, thank you." Actually, we expected the host to ask us again. But they didn't and drank themselves. We were too embarrassed to ask for drinks by ourselves since we had already said no. This was a cultural difference between the Chinese and Westerners. We were suffering excruciatingly from trying hard to save face as the Chinese old saying described.

Later on, when someone invited us to dinner, we knew what we should do. When the host asked me what other people in the delegation would like to drink, they would not say "No" but "Anything will be fine". I said, "You can't say like that because the host will not be able to serve you." They complained that my attitude was too stiff. I was actually just straightforward.

Before going abroad, we received training on foreign affairs discipline and some common knowledge, among which was not making any sound while eating. Once someone made a slight sound, others reminded him, "Don't make the noise!" Then the one who was reminded lost the appetite immediately.

During the entire visit, I was in a state of semi-starvation.

One day, many foreigners suddenly appeared in the hotel. There were originally few people on the same floor we stayed. We felt very unsafe to see so many people walking to and fro in the corridor and glancing around stealthily.

Mr. Bai and Mr. Zhang shared one room. One day, when Mr. Zhang was taking a shower, Mr. Bai went out to chat with other members. When Mr. Zhang came out of the bathroom, he found the door slightly open. He was scared and his first reaction was to search the pocket of his suit hanging in the wardrobe, only to find his money, passport and air ticket all gone. He rushed out wrapped in the bath towel to tell us. We immediately reported it to the Chinese Embassy to Finland who reported it to the police.

Mr. Zhang had a quarrel with Mr. Bai complaining that it was Bai's fault who didn't lock the door.

The police came but they didn't find out anything.

Mr. Zhang got a new passport from the embassy and a return ticket from Air China. But the money was gone which was about 280 US dollars, a large sum at that time.

The Finnish host told me that insurances were bought for all the members of the delegation, including theft insurance. We could get about 80 percent of cash compensation from the insurance company. When I told the good news to the delegation leader and the official from the embassy, they did not cheer up, but immediately held a meeting to discuss whether they should get the compensation from the insurance company. Is it the foreign host's trick to corrupt us? The embassy official was also very cautious. The Cultural Revolution had been over for eight years, but Chinese people were still alert to the "class struggle".

Several meetings were held to discuss this matter. In the last discussion, all including the embassy official reached a consensus not to take the money except Mr. Zhang and I. Mr. Zhang had no say on this matter. I knew he was anxiously waiting for the final decision and hoped we would agree to allow him to accept the compensation from the insurance company.

I always believed it was unnecessary for the Finnish host to woo and corrupt us on this matter. I thought it was "gauging the heart of a gentleman with one's own mean measure". But I hesitated whether I should speak it out or not. I didn't want others to think that I was on the foreigners' side.

Finally, I cast aside my scruples and stood up, "I think we should accept the compensation from the insurance company. I believe the Finnish host indeed has bought insurance for us. I think there is no need for them to corrupt us."

What I said played a decisive role, and everybody agreed that Mr. Zhang should accept the compensation from the insurance company under the condition that the host could prove the money was from the insurance company. At that time, there was virtually no insurance business in China and we knew very little about insurance.

Seeing us slow in making a decision and speaking so vaguely, the Finnish host began to show some coldness in their attitude to us. The person responsible for the reception was a lady of my age. She was warm-hearted and contacted the insurance company many times after the theft happened. She also comforted us that the insurance company would undoubtedly compensate for our loss. But by the time her work was almost done, we were hesitant and didn't give her a clear reply. She got some clue of what we were thinking and no longer took the trouble.

At the beginning, we were told that the Finnish host would pay the accommodation for the delegation. But they no longer mentioned it after the insurance accident. It was impossible for a Chinese delegation to afford the accommodation of a five-star hotel. Finally they said to our delegation leader that they would fill the gap after we paid first. I felt it was too humiliating.

Mr. Zhang was uplifted after receiving his compensation of about 250 US dollars. He said to me, "Come to my home to eat dumplings when we return to Beijing." Twenty-six years has passed, and I still haven't had the dumplings.

There was another funny thing. The hotel where we lived was very close to the train station and we often went there to buy food. Outside the station was a multi-screen mobile advertisement poster. In one of the advertisements several girls in bikini were taking a sauna. Every time our foreign affairs official Mr. Li walked by the poster, he would stop to wait for the one with bikini girls appearing. He wouldn't move his steps until he appreciated enough of those sexy girls. There were no such a kind of ads in China.

We spent the International Labor Day in Finland. The Finnish also celebrated the May Day which was not only the Labor Day, but also a holiday for the graduates and for the coming of spring. The streets were full of young people wearing white hats in revelry. They greeted us warmly and asked, "Japanese?" "No, we are Chinese." Then we heard their surprised whisper "Chinese!" At that time, few Chinese had the chance to go abroad, but groups of Japanese tourists could be seen everywhere. Westerners would take people with black hair and yellow skin all as Japanese.

Dream of Learning Abroad

Class struggle lasted for decades since the founding of the People's Republic of China in 1949. China was closed to the outside world for decades except the several years of opening to the socialist countries in Eastern Europe in the 1950s. When the reform and opening-up began, Chinese people could study abroad, which became the biggest dream of the intellectuals.

I passed my primary, secondary and university years during the 10 years of the Cultural Revolution. I learned little because we were drawn into class struggle all these years. So studying abroad became my biggest dream.

In the 1980s, I heard a lot of my college classmates had gone to study abroad. I didn't have much contact with them, but my heart was with them all the time. I always pictured in my mind that they walked in a hurry with books under their arms on the campus, they studied hard in the spacious and bright classroom and they talked freely with Westerners. I envied them.

In the early 1980s, China began to re-send students abroad and tried to walk out of the isolated situation caused by the Cultural Revolution. Those who were sponsored by the government to study abroad were generally politically reliable backbones of universities and research institutes. They were sent to European or North American countries as visiting scholars or students in advanced studies. China had just started its reform and opening-up and there were still serious confrontations between China and the West, so most of the people sent to study abroad were chosen after a rigorous selection. Many of them had reached their middle ages. Their prime years were wasted in the class struggle, so they cherished the hard-won learning opportunity all the more.

In the beginning, the English test for going abroad was very easy, but later TOEFL was required. In 1985, the system of qualification approval to study abroad at one's own expenses was abolished, followed by a boom in studying abroad at one's own expenses. To study abroad, one had to have someone abroad to provide guarantee. Many people used every means to go abroad. Some young people, especially girls, often went to five-star hotels to get to know Westerners, especially Americans and then went to study abroad through their relationship. A friend of mine went to the United States in this way. She couldn't speak English. I wondered how she got to know the American in the hotel.

My friend Lily was nearly 50 when she was sent to the United States as a visiting scholar. She went there alone and never came back. I have never heard anything about her since she left 20 years ago. She is in her 70s now.

Her story is somewhat tragic.

Before the Cultural Revolution, Lily was a talented girl in the High School Affiliated to Beijing Normal University. Although her examination result was good enough for her to be admitted to Tsinghua University or Peking University, she was not admitted because of family background. She was assigned to a university in Inner Mongolia to major in mining.

Lily was a beautiful girl and was admired by all the male classmates. In order to change her political background, Lily chose a classmate who was 10 years her senior and was politically reliable as her boyfriend. He had work experience before going to college and was the monitor of the class. Lily didn't have much feeling for the monitor but just took the advantage of him when she did not have any choices. But the monitor loved Lily very much. All the male classmates were jealous of the monitor.

After graduation, Lily and the monitor were assigned to a mine in H Province as mining engineers. They got married there. As a woman engineer working at a mine, she suffered a lot. After the reform and

243

opening-up, they were transferred to a research institute in J Province. Although Lily didn't love her husband, she fulfilled her responsibility as a wife and gave birth to two children. Lily's mother-in-law also lived with them. Lily was very kind to her. The monitor was a good man acknowledged by all, but Lily just didn't love him. Lily felt quite guilty when speaking of him. But love was not something that could be forced. At that time, divorce was regarded as a shame and would affect one's career.

Lily went to Beijing to attend a foreign language training course. There was a male classmate who was very outstanding. Lily and he admired and loved each other. However, they both had a family. Lily said to me, "The temptation is too much." I could understand her. She was so excellent and so beautiful, but she couldn't love as she wanted.

In the mid 1980s, Lily got an opportunity to go to the United States as a visiting scholar. We often met when she was waiting for the visa in Beijing. Lily was 20 years older than me. Although we talked a lot, I still felt she had some reservations. My instinct told me that Lily would not return to China. At that time, visiting scholars were government-sponsored and they must return when the study was finished. If people in charge knew her intention to stay abroad, they certainly wouldn't let her go.

Many years' unfair treatment made Lily a very cautious person. I often felt that she was eager to confide in others but at the same time kept alert against others. She was kind to everyone, but she wouldn't open her heart to anyone. One day she told me, "I am not going to come back." I was very moved because I knew how much she trusted me.

More than 20 years has passed since Lily left and few people have heard of her. Later, she got her daughter and her son to the United States, leaving her husband alone in China. In fact, I was very sympathetic with her husband. Both Lily and he suffered a lot of hardships. I always hope I can find Lily because I miss her very much, and I want to know about her life and feelings after so many years' living abroad. If we met now, we could talk freely without any reservations.

In 1986, I was sent to work in a small town called Lakeland in Florida of the United States for six months. I often went jogging around a lake where there was a local college. I often sneaked into the college, watching the students come and go on the beautiful campus, envious of them. I peeped through the window into the students' lounge, carpeted, with a comfortable sofa and a color TV. I thought how fantastic it would be to study here. At that time, many Chinese families didn't have a TV, let alone a color TV.

I also met some Americans who offered to provide guarantee for me to study there. I couldn't make up my mind. I was already married. If I abandoned the family to study in the United States, I couldn't have a child in the next few years. My parents-in-law were looking forward to a grandson. I was already 31 then. If I chose to study abroad, I didn't know when I could return home and I felt it was unfair to my husband's family. But deep down I felt grieved. I didn't love my husband but had to give up my ideals for him and his family. No one forced me to do so, but I was a traditional Chinese woman deep in my heart.

On the plane back home from the States, a professor from Tsinghua University sat beside me. I chatted with him, a stranger, about my dream to study abroad and my marital status. He said, "You should go to study in America. Your marriage is hopeless and is not worth sacrificing your future."

But I still gave birth to a child and became a mother one year later after I returned home.

When my child reached about the age of two in 1989, I got an opportunity to take an examination to study for one year in the UK. At that time, the British government sponsored 100 Chinese civil servants to study in the UK for one year annually. The H Ministry had some quota every year. In 1989, one was reserved for the mining bureau and I signed up for the examination.

It's heart-wrenching to make this decision. If I succeeded, I had to be away from my child for one year. I was not sure if I could bear such a pain.

After giving birth to my child, I stayed at home for one and a half years taking care of him. According to the family planning policy, if a woman who had late childbirth gave up the only-child allowance, she could have the maternity leave for one and a half years. My English was neglected for such a long time, and the examination wouldn't be easy to me.

I began to study hard again. On the day of the examination, I traveled by train from Z County, Hebei Province to Beijing. The examination site was in the University of International Business and Economics. Most of the questions were like TOEFL. The last question was: Why do you want to study in the UK?

I was not ambitious. I just wanted to be a better translator in English.

I passed the examination, but I was not admitted. Some people pointed it out to me: How could you say that your purpose was to be a better translator? Why does the British government spend money training a translator? What they need are government officials and management personnel. When these people come to power in the future, their attachment to the UK would be conducive to the development of bilateral relations and trade cooperation between the two countries.

I didn't know whether it was for this reason, but my dream of studying abroad was shattered. I didn't regret much this time because of my child.

If I went to study abroad then, I must have a completely different life now.

I didn't go abroad, but have experienced the whole period of the 30 years of China's reform and opening-up. Otherwise, I probably would have stayed overseas. Looking back, I don't regret it at all. I even feel lucky that I have stayed. What I learned during the 30 years of reform and opening-up is something one couldn't gain from any university. The experiences of those 30 years have become my precious treasure. I had many opportunities to have contact and cooperate with Westerners due to the nature of my work. Reform and opening-up has brought me a lot of opportunities and enabled me to travel around the world. Such experiences have become my advantage. I not only know China but know the world as well, which helps me become more competitive in the industry I am engaged in.

I envied my classmates who studied abroad then and now they are envious of me as well.

Making Up for the Time Wasted by the Gang of Four

People of our generation began to learn crazily when China started its reform and opening-up in 1978. Our slogan was: Make up for the time wasted by the Gang of Four.

Our generation may be the most diligent generation in the Chinese history. Every day the young and middle-aged could be seen reading in the park, on the bus, on the train or on the platform.

I was one of the most hardworking people of my generation. So far, I haven't seen anyone around who studies harder than me. I listened to English on the phonograph while washing clothes and listened to English on the radio while cooking.

In the 1980s, the import and export trades were all controlled by three major companies (China National Machinery Import and Export Corporation, China National Instruments Import and Export Corporation, and China National Technical Import & Export Corporation). All these three headquartered in a building in Erligou in Beijing. And that building was called the "Negotiation Building" because all negotiations

in foreign affairs were done there at the beginning of the economic reform and opening-up. At that time, there was a fever of introduction of
foreign technology and equipment, and there were endless negotiations
in the "Negotiation Building" every day. As a result, foreign language
talents were in great demand.

The mining bureau had no foreign affairs rights and all the
negotiations with foreign counterparts were arranged by the Department
of Foreign Affairs of the H Ministry or HCC. I was only assigned
to the foreign affairs tasks left over by the interpreters of the senior
departments who had the priority to choose their favors first. It was
all right with me as long as I could communicate with foreigners. At
the beginning, I was arranged to take part in the negotiations with
experienced translators. Their English was at different levels, mostly not
good. I studied very hard and tried my best to memorize new words. I
would volunteer to do the interpretation as long as I had the chance.

No one would believe that I was actually a very shy person. But I
really was, and still am. I kept telling myself: Now that I have chosen to
be a translator, I must keep on going. I can't retreat. I must make it! I
must overcome myself!

As long as there was a chance, I would say to the veteran translator:
Can you let me have a try? If I cannot cope with it, then you take it over,
please.

The reason why I have succeeded and surpassed those in the same
trade from the same starting line is that I have the courage and the spirit
of constantly seeking self-improvement. Most people at my English
level at that time would retreat. But I did not choose to retreat though I
was also nervous and afraid of losing face.

In February 1984, I got married at the age of 28. At that time, my
English had improved, but by no means outstanding. I still didn't gain
recognition from my colleagues and leaders. I decided not to have a
child before becoming an excellent translator.

But I got pregnant accidentally. When I was accompanying the experts from World Bank to investigate mines in Yunnan and Guangdong, I had strong pregnancy reaction. The World Bank financial expert brought his wife with him. My main task was to accompany his wife who was also three months pregnant.

After the inspection tour, I decided to have an abortion that was common and acceptable in China. Chinese had prejudice for married women if they were not capable in their profession. I would lose a lot of opportunities if I had a child then. So I decided not to have a child until my competence was generally acknowledged.

I had an abortion. My parents-in-law were obviously unhappy.

Not long after the abortion, I got my first chance to go abroad to visit Finland.

The World Bank decided to give loans to several mines for pre-feasibility study projects and needed to send a technical delegation to Florida to work with the engineers of an American company named Jacobs Engineering.

Before the project was confirmed, the World Bank and Jacobs Engineering who won the bid of the projects came to China for inspection and negotiation many times. Once I made full preparations for an important negotiation. But the head of the Import Office of the mining bureau was not sure about my translation ability for such a big and important meeting and still asked an experienced senior translator from HCC to do the interpretation. I was fully confident that I could do the task well. So I said to the old translator before the negotiation started: Would you please let me translate today under your supervision?

I interpreted the whole morning, and it turned out to be very good. The technical experts said that I was better than the old translator and my interpretation was terse and precise. The old translator disappeared that afternoon and never showed up in the next days' negotiations.

This was another major turning point in my career. That year, I was 30.

I heard that HCC would send the old translator to work in the United States with the delegation that would work with Jacobs Engineering for the pre-feasibility study of the project. The old translator also wanted to go very much. At that time, one could earn foreign currency to buy expensive items such as TV, washing machines, tape recorders, etc., which were not available in the market. Although the old translator often went abroad, the opportunity to stay abroad for several months was rare. The longer you stayed abroad, the more foreign currency you could earn and the more chances you could buy expensive items. I had done a lot of work for this project. It was me who accompanied the foreign experts to the remote mines, and it was me who translated hundreds of pages of paper documents. I would not give up the chance this time. I didn't care much about buying expensive items. I just wanted to distinguish myself in professional competence.

I found the top leader of the mining bureau and said, "Do you think this is fair? The work is done by me but someone else is assigned abroad. The several-hundred-page pre-feasibility study report of this project needs to be translated into Chinese in the future and the American engineers also need to inspect the mines in the future. Will the old translator do all these too?"

Several opportunities of mine had been given to others before. I wouldn't give up my chance this time because I was already a good professional translator in the chemical mining field.

The leader thought what I had said made sense, so he went to HCC to put in a word for me. In fact, the old translator felt himself in the wrong. He specially came to me and said, "I have got you another chance to go abroad." The implication was that I should give this chance to him.

In June 1986, I went with the technical delegation of the mining bureau to the United States and worked in Florida for five months. Within less than a month after I returned, I went again with another technical delegation to the United States and worked there for another month. Going abroad twice successively, I felt the importance of myself and had a great sense of accomplishment. I had become the best translator for this project. It had to be me if the quality of the work was to be guaranteed.

Not long after I returned from the United States, I decided to have a child because my professional ability had already been recognized.

When I was three months pregnant, some experts from the World Bank came to visit China again. My leader gingerly asked me if I could accompany the delegation on the inspection tour. I was pleased because it was a happy thing to be recognized and trusted. It indicated that no one could replace me. I agreed to do the interpretation for the World Bank delegation.

Many people couldn't understand me. The conditions at the mines were very tough and the road was very bumpy. Ordinary people could hardly endure it, not to mention a pregnant woman. I could perfectly say no. But I just wanted to do it.

The World Bank delegation brought a Chinese American with them as their interpreter, but it was too difficult for her to translate for the chemical mining industry. So it was me who virtually did the interpretation from the beginning to the end. And I enjoyed being needed.

It was indeed a tough trip. The road conditions were very bad especially from Wuhan to one of the mines. It was terribly bumpy all the way. During the bus ride of more than 10 hours, I was covering my belly with my hands. I feared that I would lose the unborn baby. The World Bank experts and the Chinese leaders also began to worry about it. But everything turned out to be fine.

This was my last travel with foreigners before the childbirth.

The World Bank financial expert's wife gave birth to a lovely girl. In the first few years, she would send me a Christmas card every year with a family photo, but we lost contact later.

I often think of the first child sacrificed for my career. What would he look like if he had been born? My heart aches at the thought of it.

I was already 32 when my son Zheng Han was born.

Six Months and the Whole Life

I would begin to feel homesick when staying abroad for more than a week. I miss my family; I wish I would return to my motherland soon.

When I am taking a rest in the airport's business lounge, tasting good wine in the business class cabin of different airlines, enjoying a room with the sea view of a five-star hotel in Abu Dhabi, paying the bill with credit card when I invite my American friends to eat in the best restaurant in the Chinatown of New York, I can't help asking myself, "Why me? Why is it my life? Why God has chosen me?"

Twenty years ago things were totally different. I enjoyed such great pleasure that I almost forgot to return home when I was staying in the Western countries. I didn't want to come back and always felt that the time was too short. It was between the end of June and late December of 1986 when I worked twice in Florida for six months in total. When living the moments of enjoyment, I felt depressed at the same time. My heart would sink whenever I thought that six months later I had to return to my former life where I was controlled, supervised and had no freedom, that I had to return to the tatty house and suffer the unhappy marriage. I always thought that I had enjoyed all the happiness in my whole life during the six months and there would be none in the future. The practice of democracy at that time in China could not compare with what we have today; people who did foreign affairs jobs were subject to many restrictions. My mood was getting worse with the day of my departure approaching.

I visited many states from the east coast to the west in the United States. The project I worked for was the pre-feasibility study of the phosphate concentration process. So, most of the mines, factories,

252

research institutes and exhibitions that I visited were located in the mountainous areas or deserts. Besides, I also had been to many cities, such as San Francisco, Los Angeles, Las Vegas and Salt Lake City and so on. As a Chinese, from my point of view, I found little difference between the cities and the countryside. Not until I had watched many Hollywood movies did I realize that they Americans also had the concepts of townspeople and bumpkins. However, I didn't see the difference over 20 years ago. The interstate highways extended in all directions, and with a car you could go to any corner of the country. Sometimes you were driving and couldn't find any trace of a human being; suddenly, a small village or a town, which was quite modern, came into view when you made a turn. Along the trip, flush toilet and toilet paper were available in every gas station or small restaurant. Usually we stayed in motels where the conditions were more than good enough for us Chinese at that time.

What I liked better was the level of civilization and legal awareness of Americans. Over two decades ago, Chinese people had to queue to buy many things due to the shortage of goods. It was common to see a large crowd of people making a panic purchase of something or someone jumping the queue. I felt good when staying in the United States where people queued orderly no matter how long the queue was. You wouldn't feel panic or worried in that situation. Americans would clean up everything, even the degradable fruit peel after a picnic in the wild.

When we were in Lakeland of Florida, we always went to a restaurant run by a Taiwanese who was very hospitable and always told us a lot of his experiences in the United States. He said, "In America, if a student is found cheating in the test, it will be written in his or her personal file which will influence the rest of his or her life, so American students care much about their reputation since childhood. The teachers in primary schools will ask the pupils to keep their textbooks in good condition, so the books can be passed on to the lower grade. In this way, the books can be used for more than 10 years and a large quantity of paper and printing expenses can be saved. Certainly, the quality of the textbooks is quite good." He also told us that Americans cared for children very much. Once, when his son was crossing a road, suddenly all the textbooks and notebooks he held in his arms dropped and scattered on the ground. The traffic policeman stopped all the cars and didn't let go of them until the boy collected all his books and walked to a safe place. No one complained about it and all waited with patience. Basic codes of ethics like these often touched the bottom of my heart.

I also like Americans for their high work efficiency. I wrote in my diary, "The work efficiency of Americans is amazing. Yesterday morning, I went to the office of our American partner the first time. Some relevant counterparts came to see us and finished the meeting within several minutes, no superfluous words; no unnecessary greetings; and then they went back to their work."

When we went to visit an exhibition of mining machinery in the city of Phoenix, we passed through Las Vegas and spent a night there. The American host gave each of us 20 dollars to play the slot machine. We didn't have extra money, even if we had, we would never spend it on gambling. Before 10:00 p.m., we were asked by the delegation leader to go back to sleep. The American colleagues who accompanied us had been to China several times and knew something about our foreign affairs discipline. They regretted that I could not enjoy and get to know the city of Las Vegas, but they didn't press me because they knew I had to obey the rules. I came back to my room and went to bed early. However, I couldn't fall asleep. The neon lights were glimmering all night long and even the curtains couldn't cover the light. A sleepless night! The next day, the American colleagues said jokingly, "Only Chinese people would stay in the room and waste the time on sleeping when they come to Las Vegas." Of course, they only dared joke to me.

I came across an acquaintance in the mining machinery exhibition in Phoenix. When I was looking around, suddenly a man came over to me, stared at my badge and called out, "Ping". Then, I recognized he was the mining engineer who visited China several years ago. I had accompanied him to several provinces to inspect the phosphate mines there. He was the first American to visit my home, Kaiyang Phosphate Mine. He was the one to get me criticized by my boss for my "imprudence" because I laughed with him when watching a Chinese cartoon movie.

He and his wife came to visit the exhibition. We were both overjoyed to meet each other. They lived in Lakeland. What a small world! They insisted that I should go to see them and have dinner after I went back to Lakeland. But I couldn't meet foreigners alone according to the foreign affairs discipline. So, I had to take one of my colleagues to come with me. I had to interpret for my colleague and I couldn't enjoy myself to full. Before the dinner, the engineer showed me the film he made when he was in China, in which I was still a baby in his words. It's a pity that I cannot remember the name of the engineer.

When in the United States, I enjoyed the treatment of "ladies first". It was nothing special for American women; but most of the Chinese women had never had the experience before. For Chinese women, they were familiar with "men and women are the same", "seniors first", "husbands first" and most importantly the "leaders first". At the beginning, I was not used to "ladies first". Gradually I got used to it and began to enjoy the privilege as a lady. Most of the time, I was the only female in the delegation. The unsophisticated Americans didn't know much about the Chinese culture. They followed the rule of "ladies first" even when I was with my leaders. They let me enter the lift first, helped me take off or put on the coat first and helped me take my seat first, all of which annoyed the Chinese delegation leader and put me in an awkward situation.

I also admired their equal and mutually respectful relationships between superiors and subordinates. I liked the way Americans call each other by names directly regardless the position or status. The superiors and subordinates played jokes with each other, and went to watch a baseball game or had a picnic together, which were all unimaginable in China. Once, I went with a Chinese delegation to visit a chemical plant. The workshop was a multi-storey building. When we were going upstairs, the workers on the top floor were doing cleaning and swept the dust down the stairs. All of a sudden, our faces were covered with dust. The Americans burst into laughter, so did I. The delegation leader and some other members got angry and said seriously in Chinese that it was too rude and too impolite. I didn't interpret it when I found the Americans, who were also covered with dust on their hair and face, were not aware that the Chinese guests were angry.

I liked the ecological environment of the United States, which I talked about a lot when I returned home. Near the office building of Jacobs Engineering, there was a pond which seemed like a natural swale. Clusters of green plants grew luxuriantly at the lakeside and white cranes flew about from time to time. I always thought what a lofty realm of thought the people who lived here had attained, if such a small pond could attract the white cranes. There was another lake not far from our apartment. I named it "Swan Lake". Whenever I had time, I would go jogging around the lake, about four and a half miles a round. There were many kinds of birds and a lot of people jogging or walking around the lake, coexisting in peace and harmony. White and black swans were swimming leisurely in the lake. In the thick grass at the lakeside there were swan eggs that people could reach easily. But no one would disturb the swans' lives. When jogging along the lake, I couldn't help thinking if it was in China, both the birds and the eggs would not escape from the human hands. When visiting the Kennedy Space Center, I was touched by the scene when tourists were sitting in the battery car and there were crocodiles lying in the ditch at the roadside. Man and beast didn't disturb each other and lived in peace.

I bought a pair of white sneakers which I liked very much. The shoes were still clean and white after I wore them for several months. If it were in China, they would be dirty in no more than one day. During the six months, my fingernails were always clean no matter how long they got. I often told my friends when I returned to China, "Even the dry nasal mucus is transparent when in the United States."

I was the only one who could communicate in English in the delegation. I was active, cheerful and sincere, and was popular among the Americans. One of my American colleagues told me that his son was collecting currency of different countries. I kept it in mind and collected a whole set of currency of RMB when I went back to China. He was deeply moved when I brought it to him during my second visit to the United States. A whole set of RMB currency was a big sum of money for me at that time. He invited me to visit his son's school and watch the soccer game in which his daughter played. After visiting the classroom, the playground and the swimming pool in the primary school, I exclaimed that how lucky American children were. When would China catch up with the living standards of the United States?

Our expenditure abroad was limited and we had to live in the relatively low-cost apartment in Lakeland, which was good enough for us. Everyone had an individual bedroom with a washroom and a shower room. There was a modern kitchen and an open-air swimming pool in front of the apartment. Where I lived in China was a tube-shaped apartment with a public toilet and a public kitchen shared by several families and I had to go to use the public bathroom only once or twice at most a week.

We cooked ourselves and often went to the supermarket to buy food stuff. The dazzling supermarket had everything that one expected to find and shopping was very convenient. At that time, there were no supermarkets in China yet.

At that time, there was a world of difference between the United States and China. When enjoying the modern and comfortable life in the United States, I became more and more depressed. This was the life I pursued, but it was so short. I couldn't predict what China would be like and what I would be like in 20 years.

Maywood Chesson, an American colleague, invited all the members of the delegation to his home and showed us around his luxurious villa. He had visited China many times and we were good friends. He was acquainted with the poor living conditions in China. So he emphasized time and again that he was not showing off his comfortable life, he just wanted us to know more about American people's life. I assured him, "Don't worry. I am envious of your life, but I don't feel inferior because of my poor life."

A blog friend told me the following story. In the 1980s, one of his friends worked as an interpreter for a delegation of six to seven people during a visit to the United States. Everyone wanted to stay, but no one dared speak it out first. They got together soon after they came back and talked about their secret, they blamed one another, "If one of us said that he or she wanted to stay, the rest of the others would unanimously respond to it and defect."

I readily believed the story was true. However, I knew it perfectly that my stay abroad was paid by the government, and I didn't have to worry about the living expenses. The relationship between the American colleagues and me was that of business partner, and I didn't need to depend on someone for a living. If I defected, life would be very hard for me without money and the political status. If I stayed in America in this way, if I was no longer their colleague, would they still help me and treat me as they used to do? I had no other skills except English. If I left China, I would be nothing. Unlike the author of *Mao's Last Dancer* who was an outstanding ballet dancer and could lead a decent life in America, I would have to work in a restaurant washing dishes to earn my tuition fees and living expenses like thousands of overseas students who studied abroad at their own expenses. I would have to start all from the beginning. So, I must go back. I must experience every step on the journey of struggle from having nothing to having everything, from rags to riches and from weak to strong.

Purgatory — Who Should Decide My Life?

In the spring of 1987 I finished the translation work for the pre-feasibility study project financed by the World Bank. I was 31 years old and my working ability was widely acknowledged. I thought it was time to fulfill my responsibility to play an important role in my life — to be a mother.

At that time I lived in Z County, a place in Hebei about 70 kilometers away from Beijing, where the Mining Bureau of the H Ministry was located.

The pregnancy went through the whole summer when it was extremely hot. I had no house of my own. The first three floors of the office building of the mining bureau were offices while the top floor was dormitories for unmarried staff. I lived in one of the dormitories and used the public kitchen and toilet. It was sweltering hot in the room after the ceiling was scorched by the sun all day long. There was no air conditioner. Only a ceiling fan swirling day and night, gave out endless noise. Life was so hard!

After I returned home from the United States, I couldn't help comparing my real life with that of the United States, which made me feel even bitterer and more depressed. I had a good time working with the American colleagues and established friendship with them. I made my last trip with the foreign experts from the World Bank to the mines when I was three months pregnant. After that I was not allowed to take part in any foreign affairs activities. When the American colleagues came to China and didn't see me, they inquired of others about me. The foreign affairs discipline was strict. Generally, we were not allowed to contact with foreigners except at work. When I was eight months pregnant, an American engineer wrote me a letter saying that he hadn't seen me for a long time and didn't know what had happened to me and he and his colleagues all missed me. He said he finally got to know I was pregnant. He asked me in the letter why I didn't want to meet them and said that pregnant women were most beautiful. But the fact was that I was not allowed to see them personally. All the meetings with foreigners were arranged by the mining bureau.

My husband was still on service in the army at that time. I lived alone most of the time when I was pregnant. His encampment was not far from home. Even if he came home, he didn't help me with the housework and I had to cook for him. So it didn't make any difference if I had a husband or not!

I didn't take any pregnancy check-up except the physical examination for all employees of the mining bureau when I was five months pregnant. Although my parents-in-law were both medical staff members, none of them had the awareness of sound child bearing.

My mother was retired that year. She came from Kaiyang Phosphate Mine to Z County to look after me when I was about to give birth.

At about 2:00 a.m. on October 6, 1987, the labor pains came with blood. It was a week later than the expected date of confinement. I got up and prepared all the necessities, and then left for the First People's Hospital of Z County accompanied by my mother and husband. It was lunar August 14 and the moon was round, beautiful and charming.

I walked into a four-bed ward. There was an empty dirty bed with only a bloodstained mattress. My mother-in-law, who worked in this hospital, hurried in and put clean sheets she brought from home over the bed.

I went to the hospital at about 2:00 a.m. on October 6, but I could not give birth to the baby until 5:30 p.m. of October 8. I was pushed into the delivery room and pushed out several times. In the afternoon of

October 7, I was again pushed into the delivery room. I was lying on the obstetric table. My conditions were not mature for the childbirth, so I was just left there without being taken care of. It was getting cold. There was no mattress or quilt to keep myself warm. The door was open and anyone could peep in. My colleagues came to see me and talked with me standing at the door. I didn't want them to see me in such an awkward situation. I was undergoing the unprecedented challenge physically and mentally.

Next to my obstetric table was lying a pregnant woman who was 10 years younger than me. I was there when she was giving birth. Everything went well and it lasted no more than half an hour which greatly encouraged me. I said to myself "I can make it". The doctor came to check on me and sent me back to my ward again.

On the morning of October 8, I couldn't stand the pains and asked the doctor to give me the caesarean birth. Since my mother-in-law was a doctor in the hospital and the gynecologist was a good friend of hers, she had to consult my mother-in-law who suggested that I should give a natural childbirth. The pain was unbearable and I cried loudly. Dozens of hours had passed. When the doctor came to check the heartbeat of the fetus, she found it was becoming weak and warned me, "Do not waste your physical strength. The heartbeat of the fetus is becoming weak and it might die." Her last few words were very effective and I immediately stopped screaming.

At about 4:00 p.m., the doctor decided to make me deliver the baby naturally and forceps delivery would be used if necessary. I was pushed into the delivery room again. I tried my best to cooperate with the doctor, but no matter how hard I used my strength, the baby wouldn't come out. I heard the doctor say, "I can see the head! I can see the head!" Suddenly, she asked me to stop trying and decided to do the caesarean birth. Later, I heard that the doctor shed tears when she made the decision. I was pushed into the operating room. On my way to the operating room, I found my mother, my mother-in-law and my husband were all wiping away their tears. At the door of the operating room, a male nurse rudely took off the quilt on me and I was pushed into the room naked. I felt humiliated even in such great physical pain. I was extremely angry at his rudeness. I felt helpless, and had no dignity at all.

The doctor decided to use local anesthesia. When my abdominal cavity was cut open, I heard her say hurriedly "general anesthesia". Suddenly, I felt everything was spinning round, and I was floating in the universe with whirlpools around me and I kept sinking. I felt no pain. For a while, I felt that my body was hollowed empty and I faintly heard the cry of a baby.

When I woke up, the operation was finished. I was pushed back to the dirty ward.

My mother-in-law was there from the beginning to the end of my childbirth. I didn't want her to be there because she was not a gynecologist. However, it was not up to me. There were many times when my life was at risk, but she didn't tell me. I knew she didn't do it on purpose. She just dealt with it in the way of thinking of her generation. Nobody cared about my will or my feelings. It was not me who decided my life!

The doctor told me the following story.

When I was putting in all my energy to give birth, the doctor found that the baby's elbow was pushing against my belly which became thin and somewhat transparent. If she still insisted on the natural childbirth, my life would be in danger in case of a hemorrhage if the uterus was broken by the pressure of the elbow. So the doctor decided to give me the caesarean birth at the last minute. She cried when she made the decision. Local anaesthesia was used first. When the doctor found the uterus was covered with intestine which increased the difficulty for the operation, she decided to use general anaesthesia.

When I took the first look of my baby, I saw a bump on his head. It was caused by the pressure when I tried to give natural childbirth. I understood why the doctor cried. I had tried my best. After all the pains, I still had to endure the operation in the end.

I lost a lot of blood in the course of childbirth, which my mother-in-law tried to conceal from me. No matter what her reason was, I hated to be deprived of my right to decide my own life. It happened 23 years ago. I am still filled with anger when I am writing about it.

My Hgb dropped from 13 grams to five grams because of excessive loss of blood. The doctor suggested that I take a blood transfusion. I didn't understand why the Hgb would drop so low. My mother-in-law could first get the result of the test. It was up to her what to tell me and what to conceal from me.

Although it was in 1987, I was aware of the safety problem of the blood transfusion in China. I refused to receive a blood transfusion. I ate pork liver, chicken broth and millet congee with red dates as much as I could in the hope of getting some blood back as all the Chinese women do after childbirth.

After the second test, the doctor insisted that I receive a blood transfusion. I still refused to accept it. Then my mother-in-law said, "I don't want to tell you. But now I had better tell you that your Hgb has dropped to 4.8 grams."

I was enraged, "How can you not tell me? Who gives you the right to conceal it from me?"

Certainly I just said it in my heart. Maybe my mother-in-law still doesn't know why I "hate" her.

The doctor told me that the haemopoiesis function would be affected if I insisted on not receiving a blood transfusion. As a result, my health would be damaged and I might be weak the rest of life. I had no choice but to receive a blood transfusion. I said I wouldn't accept the blood from the blood bank. I thought if I was infected with AIDS because of the blood transfusion, it was impossible for me to find the person responsible for it. If it was the blood from the donors on the spot, I could trace the root of the problem. I had these ideas deep in my mind not because I was afraid of AIDS, but because I wanted to protect myself from any possible harm by my husband in case that something unexpected happened. My husband had never trusted me partly because I had worked with foreigners.

There was a team of compensable peasant blood-donors in a village not far from Z County and the hospital contacted them. I raised my doubts: What if they are infected with AIDS? At that time, most of the hospitals had no means to test AIDS or it was not required. But I was sneered at by the doctor and my parents-in-law for my unnecessary worry. "AIDS is the rich men's disease. These peasants have difficulty making a living. How can they get AIDS." I had no choice.

My work unit sent a car to bring the two blood donors from the village to the hospital. The story of my difficult labor was widely spread and everybody thought I was dying. So they would satisfy whatever requirement I put forward.

I turned my face not to look at the blood bag during the whole process of blood transfusion. My mother-in-law came over and said that she had seen the two blood donors, a man and a woman, both young with ruddy cheeks and it looked like they had good health.

Looked like healthy? Was it what a doctor should say?

Two days after the blood transfusion, my mother-in-law came to take my blood sample for the liver function test. I was shocked. The two blood donors were not tested for the liver function before the blood transfusion! I was driven crazy. At that time, there was no daily liver function test in the county-level hospital. It happened to be the physical examination for annual soldier recruitment, and temporary liver function test was set up in the hospital those two days.

When my son was one month old, a nurse came to see me and told me that I lost a lot of blood in the operation. She was the first one to tell me the truth.

When I was suffering the pains, I didn't think of my parents, my husband or my colleagues. What constantly came to my mind was that if my American friends knew that I gave birth to a child in such conditions, how sorry they would feel for me. When I was working with them,

I was a young, lovely, capable and ambitious Chinese girl. They wouldn't associate me with that miserable scene. They often came to work in or visit the remote mountainous areas, they knew China and wouldn't be surprised if my story happened to a rural woman.

I was mentally hurt in the childbirth. When my sister who was eight years younger than me gave birth at 32, I strongly advised her to take the caesarean birth. She took the caesarean birth on the expected day of confinement, no suffering at all. Her daughter was born in Beijing Fuxing Hospital where the conditions were much better. Thank God!

Twenty years later, my godson "Bao'er" was born in a private hospital in Beijing with conditions as good as that of the hospitals in the Western countries.

Today the medical conditions are still poor in some areas in China. Many rural women might not even get the medical treatment what I received over 20 years ago. This is the true situation in today's China, a society where advanced development and backwardness coexist.

I wish all the Chinese women could finish their mission of childbirth in a comfortable hospital with dignity.

However, for China, there is still a long way to go!

Screw and Go to Sea

There were very few private enterprises in China 20 years ago. All the people were regarded as the government's people except peasants. People had no freedom to choose their jobs. Your whole life was arranged by the government. Once you were assigned a job, you had to stick to it all your life whether you liked it or not. It was required by the revolutionary cause. We were all a screw of the revolution machine. We would stay wherever the Party put us and give light and heat there. Your promotion or job transfer was determined by your work unit. You were not supposed to ask for it from the leader. You should do whatever was assigned to you, and whatever the Party told you to do.

The work unit was once very important for the Chinese people. Once you had a work unit, you had a lifelong guarantee for birth, old age, sickness and death, and the wedding and funeral. The work unit was a place where you worked — a school, a factory or a government agency.

If you were ill, you would be sent to hospital by your work unit who would also reimburse most part or all your medical expenses.

If you wanted to get married, first you needed a letter of introduction from your work unit before going to the marriage registration office, otherwise you couldn't get married.

If you had a fight with your wife, the work unit would reconcile between you.

If you had an extra-marital affair, your wife would ask for help from the leaders of your work unit who would criticize you, help you, even punish you till you repented and made a new start.

When you retired or died, your work unit would provide for you in your old age or take care of your funeral.

Everyone belonged to a work unit except peasants. If you lost your work unit, you lost everything, your job, your income and your political status.

For about three decades starting from the mid 1950s, the rationing system was adopted in China. Without a work unit, you couldn't get the cloth coupon, food coupon, cooking oil coupon or sugar coupon, etc. If you had no coupon, you couldn't buy anything even if you had money.

My parents had job transfer twice their life, both arranged by the government. Since they were transferred to Kaiyang Phosphate Mine in 1958, they had worked there till retirement. They were the screw of the revolution machine and made contribution at the spot where they were twisted in and had never chosen their jobs.

Another common phenomenon was the long-term separation of couples. If the husband was transferred to the remote mountainous area, more than often his wife would choose to stay in the city. It would be almost impossible for him to be transferred back to the city. So they couldn't have a reunion unless the wife was willing to go to the mountainous area to share the joys and sorrows with her husband. A colleague of my father, named Chen Shoubin, worked in Kaiyang Phosphate Mine. His wife and children stayed in Tianjin, a distance of more than 2,000 kilometers. He could only stay with his family for one month a year, which lasted more than 10 years. He was not transferred to Tianjin and reunited with his family until after the reform and opening-up.

In Kaiyang Phosphate Mine, there were a large number of peasant workers who were recruited from the countryside. They could go back to help plant or harvest crops during the busy season. Their wives were peasants who were not allowed to stay at the mine for a long time. Occasionally, someone's wife would come to visit her husband, which would stir unrest among other peasant workers. The next day, the husband would blush and be teased by others who made jokes of his sexual life.

In the early 1980s after the country adopted the policy of economic reform and opening-up to the outside world, many people chose suspension from duty without pay and "went to sea" to do business. "Going to sea" means running the risk of going into business by giving up everything arranged by the government and making a living on one's own, which is just like jumping into sea at the risk of one's life. The job was retained, but the salary was suspended. From then on, Chinese people had the freedom to choose their jobs. The first group of business people in China was courageous. They had to give up all the guaranteed things. If they succeeded, they would be the group who got rich first; if they failed, they would lose everything. Fortunately they still could go back to their work unit. However, with more and more people "going to sea", many work units cancelled the policy of suspension from duty

267

without pay. You had to completely break away from your work unit if you chose to "go to sea".

My younger sister Liu Hua was one of the earliest to "go to sea".

She graduated from Guizhou University of Finance and Economics in 1986 and was assigned to be an assistant to the director of Guizhou Yongjiang Instrument and Meters Factory. It was a job envied by lots of people. She resigned in 1987 and started to do business herself. I felt she became rich overnight. She earned 70 yuan a month in the factory, but she could earn 1,000 yuan a month after she started her own business as a vendor, which she had to work in the factory for a year to earn. Like most of the businessmen at that time, she did all kinds of business. She had sold meters, clothes, tobacco and liquor, even gold. She was a rich person in my eyes. I earned about 200 yuan a month and life was more difficult with the birth of my son. But my sister was wearing three gold rings on her fingers. Rich people at that time liked showing off by wearing gold things from the neck to the ankle. I had many fashionable clothes, all given by my sister.

One of my childhood friends was assigned to be secretary of the vice mayor of Haikou City of Hainan Island after graduation. He also resigned and began to do business in real estate. He made a great success and asked his brothers, sisters and friends to follow him. One year, he came back to Kaiyang Phosphate Mine with his wife, child, brothers and sisters for the Chinese New Year, driving three Audis all the way from Haikou City over 1,000 kilometers away.

In the early 1980s, many people across the country abandoned their jobs and went to make a fortune in Shenzhen which was the frontier of China's reform and opening-up.

In the mid 1980s, more and more people "went to sea" to do business. Most of them established a bogus company, and made profits by reselling. Some company only had two staff members, the general manager and the vice general manager. A joke went like this, "A brick dropped from the top of a building and hit three people, two of them were general managers and the third one was a vice general manager."

Few of them were really successful. What most of them did were speculative ventures. Few of the bogus companies have sustained to this day. The bosses I was acquainted with then have all disappeared.

The biggest change in China's personnel system is the free flow of talents. Nowadays, college graduates find jobs by themselves. They can go to work anywhere as long as employers accept them.

However, I still gave others quite a shock when I resigned from a large state-owned enterprise by the end of 2001.

Household Registration

Many stories that happened later were related to *hukou*, the household registration.

The movement of population was restricted before the reform and opening-up.

Once your residence was registered in a place, it was very difficult to transfer it to other places. An unbridgeable gap was built between city dwellers and rural people by *hukou*. The household registration system divided people into different social ranks.

No private enterprise existed in China between 1958 and 1978. All the people who worked in state-owned enterprises had urban *hukou*. People with rural *hukou* were all peasants. All those who had urban *hukou* were paid for their work by the government.

My parents became permanent urban residents in 1950 when they became workers from peasants. Since then they have had a totally different life.

For a long time, the government called on the cadres and intellectuals to go to work in the rural areas and border areas. So it was easier to transfer *hukou* from big cities or more developed areas to small cities, rural areas, border areas or other places with harsh conditions. To move in opposite direction was as difficult as to touch the sky.

Some college graduates were assigned to Kaiyang Phosphate Mine and settled down there. If their boyfriends or girlfriends were still in the city, normally the relationship wouldn't last long. It was impossible for them to be transferred to the cities, which meant that they had to live separately all their life except the one-month reunion every year if they got married. Few people would sacrifice the comfortable urban life for love. Married couples would prefer to be long separated. With one settling down in the city, the other at least could have visions of being transferred to the city some day.

The love of Chinese people lost its romance because of the household registration. Most people could only get married with the locals. If you fell in love with someone from other places, you had to give up your love because of all the inconvenience caused by the household registration after you got married. If the girl came from a small place while the boy came from a metropolis, the parents of the boy would make every attempt to sabotage their relationship. There was a rule which stipulated that the child's residence should be registered with the mother. The rule was amended in 1998, which allowed parents to register their child's residence according to their will.

What would happen if people stayed in a place without household registration? All the food, cloth and daily necessities were rationed. One could only get the coupons with the household registration locally. If a couple with household registration in two difference places insisted on living together, it would mean one person's ration shared by two and both of them didn't have enough to eat or to wear, not to say if they had children.

More importantly, people with no *hukou* would be labeled "black people", which might become factors responsible for social instability. It was an era when class struggle was rooted in everyone's mind as Mao

Zedong had said "We must remind ourselves of class struggle every year, every month and every day." The public security bureau, local police station and the residential district committee knew clearly how many people were there in every household. If there was someone in the household whose name was not in the residence booklet, it would soon be noticed and someone would come for an investigation.

There was no identity card at that time. If you went somewhere on a business trip or returned home to visit your family, you needed to take a letter of introduction issued by your work unit or local police station with you to buy the train or bus ticket and to get accommodation. You could not travel without household registration.

According to relevant regulations, people could only live where their residence was registered. "Black people" couldn't find a job. Their children were also "black people" with no *hukou* and would not be accepted by schools.

Chinese people had no freedom to choose their jobs before 1978. High school, middle school and college graduates were all assigned jobs by the government. They settled down with their *hukou* where they worked. My parents were transferred from Lianyungang of Jiangsu to Kaiyang Phosphate Mine in Guizhou in 1958 and their *hukou* is still in Guizhou today though they have already lived with me for over 20 years. People today can move freely without *hukou*.

Living in the Single Dorm with My Son

In 1989, Mr. Lu, chief interpreter of the Foreign Affairs Department of the H Ministry, was going to study in Europe and he recommended me to take over his place. So I was temporarily transferred to the Foreign Affairs Department of the H Ministry from the mining bureau.

"Temporary transfer" was a specific phenomenon with Chinese characteristic. Usually, the higher unit would borrow someone from the subordinate to work there temporarily when they were short of hands. "Temporary transfer" meant you had a chance to be transferred upward officially, so most people would like to be temporarily transferred. They were also called "borrowed staff".

For me, "temporary transfer" meant I might be transferred to work in the capital city of Beijing from a county town in Hebei Province.

I had no house in Beijing, so I had to leave my two-year-old son in Z County. At first, my husband was happy about my "temporary transfer" because it might help the whole family be transferred to Beijing and he asked his mother to take care of our son. I went to Beijing alone.

I shared a dormitory with two other girls in the residential building for the employees of the H Ministry and we called the community C Courtyard. We used the public toilet and public washroom. I would go home by train to see my son on the weekend if there was no foreign affairs task. We worked six days a week at that time. I got on the train bound for Z County on Saturday night, and it was already past 10 when I got home. I would spend the whole Sunday doing housework to make up for my self-reproach for not being able to take care of my son for a week. The next morning I would catch the early train for Beijing. I was heartbroken every time I had to leave my son, especially when he kept a distance from me and didn't want me to hug him. My husband also blamed me for it. My heart ached!

After one year's hard work, I became one of the chief interpreters of the Foreign Affairs Department. For a long period of time, I was the one who did the interpretation for all the important foreign affairs events. I had also worked on many important occasions, which greatly broadened my horizons.

I had no advantageous background. It was difficult for people with no background like me to be transferred to Beijing. I was devoted to my work and study. My interpretation proficiency was improving rapidly. I enjoyed every bit of my progress every day and I loved my job, especially when I was encouraged by the foreign experts who trusted me. They had met many unqualified interpreters in China. They showed me respect when they found that I could well interpret the meetings in the field of a certain industry.

I made up my mind to be transferred to Beijing through my own efforts.

Although my husband supported me at the very beginning, he began to complain a year later when he found out that I had no chance of being transferred and couldn't take care of the child. I had to shuttle between two places and was very tired. Once we had a quarrel, and he said sarcastically, "Who knows what you are doing in Beijing!"

I resolutely took my son to Beijing to live with me in the dormitory. We slept on a single bed. We shared the room with a pregnant woman, whose husband worked in another city, and her mother. So, the four of us lived in a room of about 20 square meters. The pregnant woman was unhappy and grumbled, "How can four people live in such a small room?" But she could do nothing more. "If your mother can live here, why cannot my son?" I wouldn't live here with my son if I had an alternative.

I sent my son to the kindergarten during the day and we stayed outside as late as we could. I repeatedly told my son not to make any noise and not to disturb the aunt and grandma. But how could you expect a three-year-old boy to behave well all the time? I had to constantly smile to them apologetically.

There was a reception room on the first floor responsible for dormitory supervision and receiving letters and newspapers. An old lady and an old man were on duty in turn in day shift and night shift separately.

I often chatted with the old man after I came back from work, and he treated me well.

When the Asian Games was approaching in 1990, the government started the population control and all the rural migrant workers, peddlers, even borrowed government staff whose *hukou* was not in Beijing were cleared out.

The old lady knew that I was not a local resident and warned me to leave Beijing as soon as she met me.

The personnel system was freaky at that time. I was a borrowed interpreter who worked in a ministry-level department. On the one hand, I was the backbone who did the most important foreign affairs interpretations, on the other hand, I was not a Beijing resident and enjoyed no social security.

The old lady and old man changed shifts at 6:30 every morning and evening. The old man was a warm-hearted person and he didn't drive me away. But the old lady pressed on me to leave whenever she saw me. She showed no sympathy even when she saw me carrying my young child. In order to avoid her, we went out before 6:30 in the morning and didn't come back until 7:00 in the evening. It was too early in the morning and the kindergarten was not open, then I would take my son for a walk around. I didn't dare to come back before 7:00 in case the old lady was still there who would scold me to my face and lock us out.

At that time, housing reform had not started yet and all the housing was distributed among the employees by the work unit. Borrowed staff members were excluded.

With my son in arms, I often strolled in the streets of Beijing, staring at a myriad twinkling lights of the city and thought to myself, "When would I have a small room of my own?"

Pain of Being Borrowed

Temporary transfer usually happened in state-owned enterprises and government departments.

The person still belonged to and was paid by the original work unit. For example, I was transferred to the Foreign Affairs Department from the mining bureau. I worked in the Foreign Affairs Department, but my personal file was in the mining bureau and I was paid by the mining bureau.

There were several different situations for temporary transfer.

Firstly, the higher level unit was short of hands and temporarily transferred someone from the subordinate unit to complete the task; secondly, there was no qualified person to do the task although the work unit was overstaffed; thirdly, someone with "background" was temporarily transferred first, then waited for the opportunity to be officially transferred in the future.

My situation was the first kind, but was also related to the second one.

Temporary transfer existed in China for a long time. Most of my time between the age of 24 and 36 was in the situation of temporary transfer during which I suffered a lot. But I was lucky. Having gone through all sorts of ordeal, I finally succeeded because of my perseverance.

No one knew exactly how large the temporary transfer group was. They were considered as a special group in China and they had their joys and sorrows during this period of life.

There were more opportunities working in the higher level unit, so most people wanted to be transferred temporarily.

For most people, there was a long way to go from temporary transfer to official transfer, in several years or even tens of years, yet still remaining a borrowed staff member in the end.

Borrowed personnel were the backbone of the government agency and at the same time the disadvantaged group.

They were the backbone because they were competent and did the most important tasks. They were the disadvantaged group because they were not treated equally as the regular staff members. They had no chance of getting promoted. If there was an opportunity to study abroad or receive advanced training, the regular staff would be considered first. It was a common practice in China to promote the staff by seniority. What's worse, the borrowed staff wouldn't be considered either, by their original work unit if there was an opportunity to be promoted, to go abroad or to receive training. As a result, the borrowed group had to sacrifice their opportunities on both sides.

The borrowed personnel were more capable and took more jobs. In order to be transferred officially soon, they would work hard without complaint. They would devote themselves to work wholeheartedly to be recognized by their leaders and colleagues. However, some regular staff would take advantage of it and throw the tasks they didn't want to do to the borrowed people.

As a girl from the remote mountainous area without any background, I had to work extremely hard to climb upward through the springboard of temporary transfer, although every step was long and difficult.

It was my biggest dream to be able to work in a department directly under the leadership of the H Ministry. I had to seize the opportunity, though I could foresee how hard the road ahead would be. In fact, the road ahead was more difficult than I had expected.

After I was borrowed to Beijing, I worked desperately and studied hard like a student even if I was already 34. My dream was to be chief interpreter for the ministers of the Ministry.

The department director, surnamed W, was a lecher. I found him disgusting deep in my heart, but I treated him with respect as a subordinate to the superior. He would find every chance to harass me with his words or even hands no matter what the occasion was.

I dared not offend him. My hope of being transferred to Beijing would turn out to be a bubble if I did that, and my career would be ruined. He constantly lured me that he would soon report my official transfer to the personnel department and hinted that I should repay him for it first.

It was determined by my personality that I would never pander to him. I fought him with wisdom, though it was very very difficult.

During the office hours, he asked me to come home with him to give English lessons to his daughter. He had a lovely daughter though he was ugly both in appearance and character. I felt sorry for the girl. Why did Heaven give her such a father?

"The drinker's heart is not in the cup"— he had some ulterior motive. After we finished the lessons, he asked his daughter to go back to her room and I was left alone with him. He began to take liberties with me again.

I was wearing a green fluffy sweater. When he tried to press his body on me, I said, "The floss comes off easily. If you stand too close, your coat would be covered with the green floss and people in the office would figure out what you do with me when they see I am wearing a sweater with the same color." "Why do you wear such a sweater?" W was frustrated. Thank God! His daughter was right in the next room. How shameless he was!

There were quotas for the employer recruitment of the government. Every year the central government had some quotas to be distributed to its ministries and their subjected departments and bureaus.

Once he told me that the Foreign Affairs Department got a quota of recruitment and he would apply to the ministry to transfer me over in a few days. He also asked me to wait for him at home and he would come over at 8:00 that evening. I had moved to a single room, which was more private, with my son in the other entrance of the dormitory.

I didn't know what to do and told it to a friend. "If you really want to be transferred to Beijing, you had better pander to your leader. I can help you take care of your child and you can stay with him tonight." I was scared by her attitude!

After work, I went to pick up my son, and then strolled in the street and didn't come back home until midnight. My neighbor told me that a man had come to look for me and kept knocking at the door for half an hour.

Nobody knew my pain in the Foreign Affairs Department. I couldn't tell anybody. It would only cause me more trouble if I did so. I didn't want others to know about it because it would hurt his wife and daughter. Certainly it would ruin my future which was in the hands of W. No one could help me! I didn't expect that someone would offend his or her immediate superior for me.

I was going to give up. I felt depressed each time I thought I couldn't continue with my favorite job. My heart ached as if stabbed by a dagger.

I enjoyed doing interpretation. Every day, I could feel I was making progress with my spoken English and I particularly enjoyed the process.

When W found that I wouldn't submit to him, he got impatient. Two years had passed and I still didn't give him any hope. He felt my stay in the Foreign Affairs Department was an evidence against him and would put him in a dangerous situation. So he began to find fault with me and tried to kick me out.

All the colleagues in the Foreign Affairs Department believed that I would be transferred some day through my own efforts, but no one knew the truth. I was the backbone of the department and often interpreted for the minister. They thought I must be on good terms with the minister. In fact, I had no personal contact with the minister except at work. The network of connections in the governmental departments was unbreakable. It was impossible for me who had no background to get in.

Yao was transferred to the Foreign Affairs Department after me. Her mother-in-law was head of the department of human resources in a large company subordinate to the H Ministry. She couldn't speak any foreign language. If she had no such strong background, it was impossible for her to be transferred to the department which mainly dealt with foreign affairs. Before she came, I was the only one temporarily transferred here. After she came, I realized I had less hope.

Yao was no match for me in terms of work ability. I was the interpreter for the minister and the department needed me. However, she had a powerful mother-in-law and I didn't. Not surprisingly, Yao was transferred officially to the Foreign Affairs Department. I was still waiting desperately in an abyss of darkness.

I was still happy for her. Yao originally worked in some other place as I did and her husband worked in Beijing. It was a good thing that the couple could reunite. But Yao divorced her husband not long after she was transferred to Beijing.

I got along well with most of my colleagues who gave me a lot of help. But it was beyond their power when it came to the job transfer. I did very well in my work and W couldn't find any excuse to fire me, so he stealthily tried to make things difficult for me. No one knew what had happened except me.

Finally, W found a fault of me. When Christmas came, he gave me a pile of greeting cards sent to the minister from abroad and asked me to reply to them. I replied the Christmas cards selectively and put those from which I could not find the identity of the senders aside.

W found it out and took the opportunity to get rid of me. A deputy director had a talk with me, "You are in big trouble now." I knew I couldn't stay in the Foreign Affairs Department any more. Population flow was restricted at that time. No government department or state-owned enterprise in Beijing would recruit a person who was not a local resident, which meant if I left the Foreign Affairs Department, I had to return to Z County.

When I was at the end of my rope, Yang, my best friend and a famous person in the domestic tourism circle, recommended me to work in the tourism industry. Finally, after experiencing some twists and turns, I got a job in a large state-owned travel company in China.

"I quit!" I told W when I got the transfer order. I felt relieved and relaxed. I was finally free from W's hands. It was indeed a miracle that I could be accepted by a large state-owned enterprise. All my colleagues in the Foreign Affairs Department couldn't believe it.

Before leaving the Foreign Affairs Department, I told one of my colleagues who was also my friend about W's ugliness. He sighed with emotions and repeated, "It was too hard for you! It was too hard for you!"

"If I told you in the beginning, could you help me?" I asked.

"I am afraid I couldn't..." he said. He admitted it was a tough problem and he didn't expect that I would keep it inside for such a long time.

I was about to give up a thousand times when working in the Foreign Affairs Department. If I had given up, I wouldn't have achieved what I have today.

In January 1992, I left the chemical industry. In 1999, government organs were streamlined, and the H Ministry was dismissed.

By the way, "temporary transfer system" has existed for decades, and still exists today.

Interpreter for the Ministers of the People's Republic

Working for the ministers of the H Ministry was the peak of my career as an interpreter. A child who came from the big mountains of the Yunnan-Guizhou Plateau could be an interpreter for the ministers of the People's Republic; it was blue smoke rising from one's ancestral grave in the Chinese old saying.

But I didn't achieve the highest level I should have achieved. If it was not for director W's retaliation, I would have stayed in the H Ministry and become one of the best professional interpreters in China.

I enjoyed the challenge of being an interpreter. There was so much to learn that I felt I could be an interpreter in the field of chemical industry all my life.

I was already 35 when I worked as an interpreter for the minister. People at my age should be stable in their professional level, but I was still climbing up the mountain from half way. I started late and became good at English basically through self-study. If I stopped climbing and relaxed in my efforts, I would slip downward and retrogress.

Lian was the first female minister of the H Ministry. She was amiable and eloquent and expressed her ideas with good logic and clarity, so I had no pressure and felt relaxed when doing interpretation for her. What she talked most when receiving foreign guests was the macro situation and policy in the chemical industry. It wouldn't be difficult to follow her as long as the interpreter loved to learn and paid close attention to the current affairs. I could give full play to my English when doing the interpretation for her and every time was a great success. I remember the first time I interpreted for minister Lian was on the banquet for the guests from CG, UK. A British Chinese engineer of the company said to his colleagues that I was the best interpreter he had met in China.

When I was working in the ministry, I read *China Daily* every day. I was the one among my colleagues who knew the most new vocabulary. *China Daily* was not necessarily the best English newspaper, but surely the most practical. If my colleagues didn't know some word, someone would say, "Ask Liu Ping, she must know it." One day, there was a meeting in the Foreign Affairs Department. Suddenly, a colleague rushed into my office and asked, "Liu Ping, what's Fei Mao Tui Dao Dan (scud missile) in English? The interpreter is waiting for the answer."

Minister Lian was amiable and easy of approach. She would have a small chat with me after the meeting, for instance a word of praise for my dress. She always encouraged me to pursue the fashion. I believe I would develop a profound friendship with her if I hadn't left the H Ministry.

I was the chief interpreter of the ministry and I undertook all the interpretation for minister Lian. Later a new interpreter was transferred to be deputy director of the Foreign Affairs Department. He gradually replaced me. Therefore, I had less opportunity to see minister Lian. There were two reasons for it. First, the deputy director was an excellent interpreter; second, director W was trying to kick me out and didn't want me to have any more contact with minister Lian. He was afraid I would expose his true colors to the minister some day. I hadn't seen her for a long time before I left.

Although I didn't work long for minister Lian, the ideas I have learned from her still benefit me today. It was in the early 1990s when China's reform and opening-up was relatively reserved and the foreign affairs discipline was strict. Minister Lian said, "When working with foreigners, we should first make friends with them and develop friendship and mutual trust so that we can better cooperate with them." Although what she said was not likely to be put into practice, it was refreshing and enlightening to me like a spring breeze.

Bayer Group's chief representative in Beijing invited me to have dinner with his family after a meeting. He could speak fluent Chinese and we often met during the work. His invitation was sincere. I asked a deputy director for his permit. He asked me to refuse it politely. The reason was that I was invited alone. I declined the invitation although I felt it was very impolite. I had to observe the discipline. So I was inspired with enthusiasm when I heard the minister say we should make friends with foreigners.

Ironically, the deputy director who restricted me with strict discipline was arrested for leaking state secrets not long after his retirement.

I also did interpretation for vice ministers Sheng and Cai.

It was most demanding to interpret for vice minister Sheng. He was an engineer himself and knew technology and some English. When I was interpreting, he always interrupted me pointing out my mistakes. Sometimes, he was right. But most of the time, he didn't hear me clearly and got me wrong. Sometimes when I was half way interpreting, he would interrupt to correct me. I would lose my train of thought and didn't know how to continue with it.

To tell the truth, it was not easy for me to do the interpretation in the field of this certain industry. I had never learned the subject and had no knowledge in the industry. There were many subdivisions in the field of this certain industry and it was impossible to be proficient in all aspects no matter how hard I studied. My performance would fluctuate with the subjects of the interpretation.

I could interpret with facility when working for vice minister Cai. He was in charge of chemical mines. Interpretation in chemical mining and deep processing was my strength. I was always taken for a professional in the field.

Usually on important occasions, the ministers would not talk about professional issues in details and their speeches were prepared beforehand. If it was an improvisation, it would require the interpreter to have a quick response and adaptability to changes. I liked the challenge.

Once I attended a banquet held in the Diaoyutai State Guesthouse with vice minister Cai. I was told at first that the vice minister was not going to give a speech that night and I wouldn't be asked to do any interpretation. I was there just in case. There were several hundred people attending the banquet, all from different ministries and commissions and research institutes. Vice minister Cai was seated at the head table accompanied by a Chinese from the foreign side. I was asked to do the interpretation for a table. There were dozens tables with one interpreter for each table. Some were my colleagues and others were interpreters from other ministries and commissions. The atmosphere was relaxing, and the hosts and the guests were talking cheerfully and humorously.

Everything went on smoothly. I was listening to the host making his speech and finding fault with the interpreter in a relaxed and joyful mood. Suddenly, the director of the Foreign Affairs Department came hurriedly over to me, "Liu Ping, vice minister Cai decided to give a speech just now and you will do the interpretation."

It was the practice that government officials only used their own interpreters on formal occasions.

Standing by the microphone and looking at the hundreds of domestic and foreign guests, I felt it was really something. I was doing interpretation in the Diaoyutai State Guesthouse! It was where President Nixon stayed when he visited China in 1972. His visit aroused my interest in English and about 20 years later I was standing here interpreting for the minister of the People's Republic. What great honor!

Vice minister Cai began his improvised speech. I did a good job and perfectly rendered his words, his tone and his humor. The atmosphere was good and the audience broke into laughter from time to time. When vice minister Cai looked at me appreciatively, I felt very happy. When I returned to my seat, the people at my table all stood up and warmly applauded me.

I couldn't enjoy my job more. When faced with the challenge, I was also immersed in the joy of progress and success, enjoying the respect and admiration from my colleagues, leaders and the foreign guests.

I wouldn't have left the Foreign Affairs Department of the H Ministry if I could stay. I enjoyed being an interpreter.

After I left the ministry, my vocabulary began to shrink dramatically. Many words I learned in practice faded from my memory due to being neglected for a long time, which could be counted as one of the biggest regrets in my life.

I had psychological barrier when getting along with leaders. I had never developed close personal relationship with any of my superiors, let alone the superior at such a high level. Many friends said that I wasted a lot of resources.

I often think of my old chiefs in the H Ministry and follow their news on the internet. Vice minister Sheng and vice minister Cai are already in their eighties and there is still reporting about them taking part in social activities.

I once wrote a letter to Lian who was then president of a national federation and told her about my work in the letter. She called me back and said, "Liu Ping, why don't you come to see me?" I was moved.

She is nearly 76 now.

I have seen her many times on TV. Recently, I attended a party and saw her far away. I had a sudden impulse to go over and greet her. I haven't talked with her face to face for nearly 20 years. I resisted my impulse. It was a grand occasion and she was busy greeting all the leaders from all circles. I didn't want to behave myself improperly.

It has been a great honor in my life to have worked as an interpreter for the ministers of the People's Republic. The experience is a spiritual wealth I will cherish all my life.

My Benefactor Ms. Flying Swallow

Flying Swallow is my benefactor. I wouldn't have achieved what I have today without her. I have two benefactors in my life. One is Yang and the other is Flying Swallow. Yang, my friend at university, was the director-general of Guizhou Tourism Administration and Flying Swallow was the president of the Head Office of an international travel company (hereinafter referred to HO).

Unable to bear the harassment and retaliation of W, chief of the Foreign Affairs Department of the H Ministry any longer, I poured out my trouble to my good friend Yang. Yang said her good friend Flying Swallow had once asked her to recommend some talented people because the HO needed qualified middle managers. She asked me if I would like to work there.

The HO was a well-known large enterprise and was a dream place for many job seekers. It was very difficult to get in there even if one's permanent residence was in Beijing. Since I had no Beijing *hukou*, I didn't have any extravagant hope that I could get in there. I had no way out anyway, so I decided to give it a try.

Yang made a phone call to Flying Swallow and praised me excessively.

Flying Swallow was a decisive and farsighted woman leader. Although I was already 36 with a four-year-old son, had no Beijing *hukou* or experience in tourism, she accepted me resolutely. I had never seen any leader so daring and decisive before. I joined the HO in February, 1992.

Flying Swallow was one of the few leaders who refused to be restricted by the rigid personnel system. Before I came, she selected more than 20 talented people and transferred them to Beijing and solved their *hukou* problem. I came later, so I missed the timing to get my Beijing *hukou*. Unfortunately, few of them lived up to Flying Swallow's expectations, which exposed her weakness of being credulous and appointing people by favoritism.

About three years later, Flying Swallow was given a life sentence for corruption. She should be still serving her sentence now. Someone said she has been released on bail for medical service. I couldn't get exact news of her. I don't know if there would be anyone else who would say openly that Flying Swallow is his or her benefactor, although she did help many people in the past. I miss her and have mentioned many times to my old colleagues in the HO that I would like to visit her in the prison, but I was dissuaded by them every time. All those who licked the feet of her then are nowhere to be found now.

Flying Swallow was once a successful person. She was once an excellent teacher, president of Women's Federation in a municipality and director general of the tourism administration of the city. She was an overseas Chinese returning from Southeast Asia. Her glorious deeds had been reported in many newspapers and magazines. What impressed

In the early 1980s, I took some Westerners to my home at Kaiyang Phosphate Mine for the first time. The British young man Stone who had studied Chinese in Beijing, was an interpreter working for an American company. The two miners used to be my fellow workers.

I accompanied the two Westerners to visit the underground work area where I worked as an electrician.

Life was still quite hard in the early 1980s. The rural children were very curious to see foreigners for the first time.

We usually stayed in this kind of guesthouses when we visited the mines. I was always happy to travel with Westerners to the remote area where I was very much needed. I am the one standing by the tree in the middle, interpreting for the people around me. The local people had a thorough cleaning before we came.

The places we visited were all open mines or underground mines. There were always a lot of local people following us wherever we went.

In 1983, I went to Yunfu Pyrite Mine several times to interpret for the training sessions by WABCO who sold the mine 100 dump trucks. The guy in the photo on the right is Mr. Rodger O. Brown. We worked together for about one month. We talked a lot and exchanged many personal stories with each other. Rodger was a very funny guy who made life easier in the desolate area. He tried to contact me after he went back to the States but could never reach me. I got to know this from a letter he sent me three or four years after I became a mother. The American engineer in the photo on the left is as old as my father. I had a hard time to say good-bye to him when he left the mine.

When Debbie Larroque traveled with her husband Pierre Larroque, financial expert of the World Bank, to China in 1984, I accompanied them to southwest China. Both Debbie and I were pregnant. She gave birth to a baby girl who is sitting on her leg, but I took an abortion after the trip. Debbie sent me Christmas cards for several years before we lost contact with each other.

With the worker trainees at Yunfu Pyrite Mine in Guangdong Province.

In April 1985, I went abroad for the first time with a delegation from the H Ministry to Finland. We stopped over in Moscow. The first thing we wanted to do was to visit the Red Square and Vladimir Ilyich Lenin's Memorial Hall.

In 1986, I visited USA twice and stayed there for about six months. I built up deep friendship with my American colleagues in Jacobs Engineering especially with Mr. Maywood Chesson (third left, back row, left picture above). He was the one who shared a tobacco pipe with a local farmer. He was thirty-three years older than me, but I never felt the generation gab between us.

I visited a lot of chemical mines and factories in the States. In the photo on the left, I am interpreting for Mr. Xin Bingquan, director-general of the mining bureau who insisted that I should be the one to come to the States with the delegation. He passed away a couple of years ago.

We also made friends with the families of our American colleagues. Maywood Chesson (back row, middle) invited us to his community club where we swam and played volleyball with his family and neighbors.

I had my 31st birthday in the States. Mr. Zellas in charge of the cooperative project presented me a gift, a doll like a real baby. He died of heart attack when jogging in the morning not long after my birthday. I cried my heart out. I had traveled with him several times when he came to China. He was very handsome and a lot of Chinese believed that he was a Hollywood star.

Maywood Chesson's two grandchildren. One weekend the boy came to our apartment to see me and gave me a big hug. I was very touched. His grandfather apologized to me when he saw me the next day for his grandson's "abruptness". I told him I was really happy for his grandson's visit and we Chinese did not make an appointment either when we went to see somebody.

Helen, a Philippine American in yellow blouse, took good care of us during our stay in Jacobs Engineering based in Lakeland, Florida.

The photo was taken in front of the launch pad of the Challenger in Kennedy Space Center in Florida in the fall of 1986. When the disaster of the Challenger occurred on January 28, 1986, I was traveling by train in China with Maywood Chesson and his colleagues all from Lakeland of Florida. I was shocked when I heard the tragedy from the loudspeaker on the train. I was the first one to tell the American engineers about the bad news.

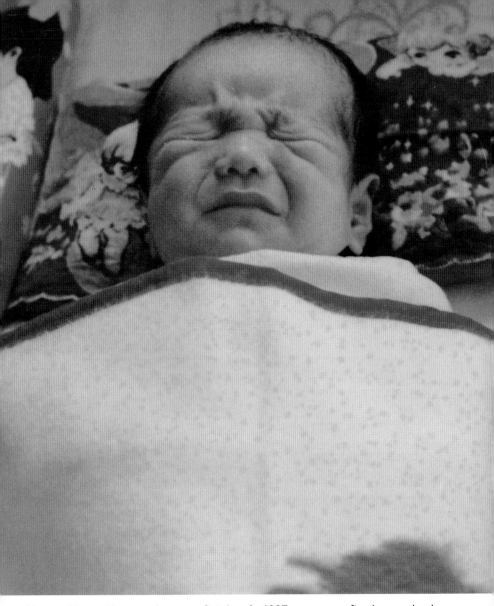

My son Zheng Han was born on October 8, 1987 one year after I came back from the United States. I had been very much depressed since I came back because I always compared my life in China with that of the six months in the States. I was suffering serious postpartum psychosis and was always nervous and worried about my son. People around me knew nothing about melancholia and my family could not understand me. I was fastidious about cleanliness and didn't like anyone to kiss or touch my son. There were very few psychologists in China. I read in a magazine about a psychologist in Beijing who cured a lot of patients. I went to see her, but came back disappointed. Because of my personal experience, I always feel sorry for those who suffer mental problems and try my best to help them.

This photo was taken when my son was one hundred days old. The Chinese people have the tradition of taking a one-hundred-day photo.

Not long after my son's two-year-old birthday, I was borrowed by the Foreign Affairs Department of the H Ministry and had to leave my son to his grandmother for one year.

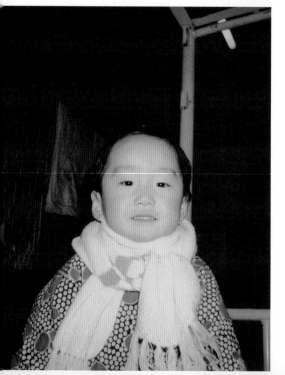

I always feel guilty because I did not take good care of my son when he was a little boy. He got parotitis with swollen cheeks in this photo. I still remember that morning he said to me: "Mom, my cheeks are painful." I took him to see the doctor. He was happy that he did not have to go to the kindergarten.

One day after I picked him home from the boarding kindergarten at the weekend, I found he was snuffling. Later, he sneezed out a cotton ball from his nose. His nose was bleeding and his teacher filled in his nose a cotton ball and forgot about it. When I found it, it was already three days later.

I was an interpreter in the Foreign Affairs Department of the H Ministry during the period of 1989-1992.

In 1991, visiting Bayer Head Office with a chemical industry delegation led by a vice minister.

In 1991, at the site of the remaining Berlin Wall.

me most was an article under the title of "A Swallow Flying High". She took good care of her husband who was confined to bed by paralysis for more than a dozen years.

She was an elegant and attractive woman with refined manners and good taste in clothes. She was always surrounded by a crowd of people who curried favor with her. I liked listening to her when she was making a speech which was full of passion and inspiring.

In the early 1990s, the HO held a grand celebration in the Great Hall of the People for its 40th founding anniversary. It's said over a million yuan was spent on it. The big cake made by a hotel of an international brand alone cost 80,000 yuan. Hundreds of overseas clients were invited to attend the celebration. I felt proud to be a member of such a big and powerful enterprise.

When the celebration began, Flying Swallow walked in the hall with a vice premier of the State Council. She was dressed in a satin *qipao* with a Chinese style cape over it. She was graceful and attractive with a brilliant smile on her face. When seated on the rostrum, she took off her cape and her fair-skinned arms caught everybody's eyes. I liked her easy manner and way of doing things. I appreciated those women who paid attention to their appearances. I was proud of working for such a woman leader.

Everybody in the HO thought I got the job because of my personal connection with Flying Swallow. They talked about me behind my back and embarrassed me to my face that I got in by the back door. In order not to cause trouble for Flying Swallow, I never cottoned up to her. I worked hard as I usually did and at the same time to win credit for Flying Swallow. I thought the best way to repay her for her help was to support her with my hard work and to make achievements. But I was wrong. Flying Swallow liked to be followed, surrounded and flattered. She said to Yang, "I don't know what's wrong with Liu Ping. She keeps me at a distance and avoids me."

To clear up her misunderstanding, I specially went to her office and explained why I kept a distance from her. I told her I wanted to make some achievements through my own efforts and to prove to others that she recruited me for my ability not for some other private reason. My explanation worked. Flying Swallow understood me further. She used to be an overseas Chinese and returned home from Southeast Ascia after New China was founded in 1949. So she had paid special attention to the Southeast Asian market. She wanted me to be in charge of the market development in this area. I said it would be better not to give me the promotion until I made some achievements. Actually, I didn't want to give up the Dutch market to which I had devoted a great deal of time and energy.

When China transformed from a planned economy to a market economy, many people failed to resist the lure of money. Due to the defect in the legislative and supervision mechanism, many government officials and leading cadres of the Party sank to the abyss of corruption. Flying Swallow was one of them.

The leading position of the HO in the domestic tourism industry and its lion's share in the inbound market established Flying Swallow's incomparable influence and standing in the industry. She changed to another person, arrogant, dictatorial, extravagant, going in for ostentation and extravagance and abusing her power to seek personal gains for her relatives and friends.

One friend told me the following story. The National Tourism Administration held a national conference for the leaders of the tourism industry in Zhongshan of Guangdong Province. All participants were required to live in the official hotel. But Flying Swallow made an exception of herself. She came from Guangzhou in a limousine and showed up high profile at the conference, dressed in a white leather jacket. Yang was also there and felt sorry for the change of her friend. She said: "Flying Swallow is so full of selfish desire now!"

A Hong Kong businessman opened a restaurant in Wangfujing Street at the center of Beijing. The HO made it a rule that all the tourist groups should have the Beijing roast duck in the restaurant and the tour guides should lead the guests into the restaurant by first passing the shop of the restaurant. Many operation managers were reluctant to follow the rule. Why go to have Beijing roast duck in a Hong Kong restaurant instead of in a real Beijing duck restaurant? Flying Swallow was angry with the employees who were disobedient. She said at a staff meeting, "We cooperate with the Hong Kong restaurant in the spirit of mutual benefit. Our tourist groups have roast duck there and the restaurant provides our canteen with duck bone for free, so our staff members can have duck bone soup every day." She also punished a guide who didn't take the group to the shop of the restaurant. The Hong Kong businessman, with Flying Swallow as his strong backing, was arrogant and less cooperative. When I think of what Flying Swallow did, I feel it is ridiculous and hard to believe. Tour guides today are not allowed to lead groups to go shopping without approval by the clients. But the HO then required the tour guides to lead the groups to the designated shops!

One year, the HO invited the first three prize winners of Miss Hong Kong to come to visit the company and to take photos with Flying Swallow. That year's wall calendars of the company were all the photos of Lu Fengyan with the Hong Kong beauties.

Flying Swallow was a successful career woman, but at the same time she was a typical woman with women's weaknesses, credulous, vain and susceptible to flattery. Some people took advantage of her weaknesses and trapped her into doing investment projects in which she lost every cent invested. She was fooled by a Hong Kong swindler who in the end vanished with all the money.

Flying Swallow had a friend named L who was former vice mayor of X City and got a suspended death sentence for bribery in April of 2001. When he was studying in the Party School of the CPC during the first half of the year 1999, he went to Hong Kong for gambling and lost 3.5 million Hong Kong dollars over one day and one night. It's said he had some connection with the HO because of Flying Swallow.

I don't remember on what charge Flying Swallow was sentenced to a life imprisonment. All I know is the HO suffered a heavy loss because of it.

Flying Swallow certainly deserves her punishment, but I still think the society and the administrative system then provided the environment and condition for her corruption. What's more, the HO as a state-owned enterprise had a collective leadership. How did she make all the decisions alone? How did the decisions get passed? Where was the supervision mechanism?

Flying Swallow was Flying Swallow. She admitted her guilt without shirking responsibility and shifting the blame onto others. Though she is guilty, I admire her for being bold enough to face up to her mistakes and take the consequences. I despise those who used her, those who avoided her like rats deserting the sinking ship and those who hit her when she was already down.

No matter what she did, I owe her a debt of gratitude for her appreciation and recognition of my talents. Someone said that the most meaningful thing Flying Swallow did was leading me into tourism and producing an outstanding talent for China's tourism industry.

If it was not for Flying Swallow's help, I wouldn't have entered tourism. I don't know what my life would be like or if I would be as successful as I am today.

Flying Swallow has received her punishment. To me, she is my benefactor.

The two benefactors in my life have come to completely different results. Flying Swallow became a prisoner for corruption, while Yang remained a clean and honest official all her life and now is in the United States as a visiting professor. This is a true portrayal of polarization of cadres of the Party.

Flying Swallow is approaching 70 years of age. It's said her husband died many years ago. I wish she will spend her remaining years in comfort.

Stepping into the Tourism Industry

I entered into tourism at the age of 36. I was assigned to the Italian division of European Department One. I started by doing odd jobs for everyone in the office.

European Department One consisted of cruise division, English division, French division, Italian division, logistics division and accounting division. I started my job after the Chinese New Year of 1992. Everyone worked in a rush. I felt guilty for not being able to help. I didn't understand why people working in a travel company were so busy. The office was always in a mess. I did everything I could, such as sweeping, fetching the boiled water for making tea and some other odd jobs. Sometimes I would buy breakfast on my way to the office for some colleagues who came to work without having breakfast. Most of the colleagues in the Italian division learnt Italian in the university. The division chief was named M and was an English major. He played a decisive role in the development of my career. I can say I wouldn't have achieved today's success without his "help".

Rumors that I got in through the back door circulated in the department. I could see disdain in their eyes. I worked hard silently. Most of the time, I did odds and ends for an operation manager named T.

The logistics division was providing logistic support for the operation managers, making restaurant, train and air ticket reservations. The person who was responsible for the logistic work of the Italian division was called X. I always went to the logistics division to file the documents for T. Each group had a file. Computers were not well used yet in the office and the logistics office was always in a mess with all

291

the files. Sometimes one had to spend a lot of time finding the file one needed. Being a newcomer, I had to ask X for help sometimes. She was very impatient. She and her colleagues were always chatting, joking and sometimes said spicy jokes. I didn't understand why she was impatient since she was not busy with her work. But I said nothing.

Not long after I came, the department head asked me to take charge of the Dutch market. There was another male colleague called H who was in charge of the Dutch market. He had worked in the department for two years when I came. He was going to the Netherlands to receive training by a Dutch client and was waiting for his visa. During the two years, he might also spend most of the time doing odd jobs and the one who had been really in charge of the Dutch market was division chief M of the Italian division. The Dutch market share was too small to set up an independent division. Later, M was promoted head of the North American Department. I didn't know why he picked me to take over his Dutch market. I was still a new hand.

M briefed me on the job within one hour and handed over all the files to me. From then on, I fell into the abyss of sufferings. I had no work experience in tourism before and knew nothing about how to operate a tourist group. There was nobody to help me. I was supposed to learn from H. To my surprise, he knew little about the group operation though he had worked there for two years. Later, I came to know clients meant everything in a travel company in China. Those who had clients in their hands did everything possible to stop others from getting involved and would rather be exhausted to death than to ask someone else to share the job. This was the reason why there was no team spirit in China's travel services. The function of a sales manager was mixed up with that of an operation manager. There was no one purely involved in marketing. Every sales manager held their own clients and was busy with details of operation.

M took office in the North American Department. Faced with a large pile of documents, I didn't know where to start. Fortunately, there was H to help me. I prayed every day that H would be denied by the Dutch Embassy for the visa. H got his visa and left soon. I started work at seven in the morning and didn't return home until nine at earliest in the evening, up to my neck with work, day in and day out. I was helpless.

M came to my office from time to time, turned my documents and dropped a sentence, "You should do *zhuanjian* to this group." I had no idea what it was, when and how to do it.

Zhuanjian was to make the official and final schedule for a group or individuals confirmed by the client and then mailed the paper schedule down to the relevant local travel agents who were in charge of the land service in the local cities including the arrangement of transportation, accommodation, shopping and entertainment and so on. If *zhuanjian* was not done in time, there would be serious consequences such as there would be no tour guide to pick up the guests at the airport or there would be no hotel rooms reserved and so forth.

I had received no training for my job. It was always at the last minute that I realized I hadn't done *zhuanjian*.

As a result, I received numerous phone calls from the local agents and tourists. The local agent said the tourists found them, but they didn't receive any schedule from the HO, so they made no arrangements for the tourists. The tourists complained that there was no guide to meet them at the airport or the railway station. The foreign tour leaders who traveled with the groups also complained the arrangements of the local agent were not in line with those in the schedule we had confirmed. I turned over the original documents anxiously to find out the problem and to check if the client's requirement was in accordance with the content of our offer. All the phone calls were urgent and the tourists or tour leaders were waiting for my answer. I felt my heart was torn with anxiety and it was a torture for me who had such a strong sense of responsibility and self-respect. During that time, I would become excessively nervous whenever I heard the telephone ringing.

A professional delegation of over 100 doctors was confirmed by M one year ago before I joined the HO. I took over the file from him and made reservation based on the itinerary Beijing-Xi'an-Guilin-Shanghai. One week before the arrival of the delegation, the client sent me a fax to confirm the itinerary for the last time. It was only then that I found the itinerary was changed half a year ago and the delegation would enter in Shanghai instead of Beijing. I looked over all the documents and finally found a crinkled fax with illegible words which proved the client did change the itinerary half a year ago. For such a big and important incentive group, there was no one to remind me and teach me how to handle it. You can easily imagine how worried and anxious I was at that moment. I had to cancel all the reservations of hotels and air companies and to renew all the reservations within one week.

Quotation was the most difficult part. If M spent a little more time explaining it to me in detail, it wouldn't have been so difficult. The HO would quote contract prices of the tourist groups in series and the individual tourists to the clients at a fixed time of the year. Whenever there was a request, for groups in series, there was a confirmed price; for individual tourists, most of the time the operation manager just needed to do some addition and deduction according to the contract price. But nobody told me that. The logistic person put all the fax and telex from the Netherlands on my desk every day. I studied them carefully one piece after another and calculated the price according to the requirements. I didn't know there was a contract price for the whole year. Whenever I got a new request, I made a new calculation. The efficiency was terribly low and I couldn't finish my work until nine o'clock in the evening. Quite often, it was already midnight when I got home.

The next day when I received reply from the client, it was usually a complaint. I explained to them that I was a newcomer and asked them to forgive me. Sometimes, the client was impatient. I felt my self-esteem was hurt. At the same time, I was gnawed with a sense of guilt and blamed myself for not being able to do my job well.

The Dutch market is known for its large number of individual tourists. Dutch people are very experienced tourists. They are fond of hunting for novelty and adventures. The itinerary they demand is unusual and long. If you see backpackers, tall and big with long legs, marching on the remote country road in the Yunnan-Guizhou Plateau, Tibet or Xinjiang or the like, mostly they are Dutch. What they are interested in is not leisure tour. The places they want to go are usually less accessible with harsh conditions. So it takes you a lot of time to design the itinerary for them, to find the suitable transportation and accommodation and to find ways to reduce the cost.

Later, I asked B, head of the department, why he dared put me, a newcomer, in charge of the Dutch market. He said that nobody was willing to take over the Dutch market, so they decided to take the risk to let me have a try. They were prepared for the worst. Even if I lost the whole market, it was only 3,000 people at most a year. The HO still cornered the inbound market at that time and losing a market of 3,000 people was no big deal for them. It also indicated how challenging it was to do the Dutch market.

I didn't know how I survived those days between February and December of 1992. I feel as if I were still in a nightmare when I think of it today. I didn't know what to do and there was nobody to help me. I was lonely and helpless. I was the first to come and the last to go. When colleagues around me finished their work easily and began to relax themselves chatting and joking, I couldn't help thinking how could I be so stupid and so disappointing.

Someone told me: M does more than 3,000 Dutch tourists a year. If you can keep his record, you will gain a foothold in the HO. If the number drops, you will be in trouble.

Finally, I collapsed. One day, I quoted an itinerary of over 20 days to a Dutch client. The route was particularly unusual and I didn't finish the quotation in a few days. The client was very unsatisfied. I returned home very late, exhausted and despaired. I couldn't sleep and started to cry. I didn't stop crying until four in the morning. It was in the summer and the day broke early. I left home at four. The city was quiet with no traffic and I reached the office before five and started another day's work. When I finished the day, I couldn't hold out any longer. I came to one of my few good friends in Beijing and burst into loud sobs. She escorted me home and kept me company the whole night. I cried another night.

One day, I couldn't restrain myself and sobbed in the office which attracted the leader's attention. He appointed a veteran colleague who would retire soon to help me with the Dutch market. I gave her the request for the long itinerary that I hadn't finished. She looked at the deadline and said to me, "You haven't quoted it after so many days. I must finish the quotation today; otherwise we would lose the client because of you." I was so ashamed that I wished I could find a hole to hide myself.

Three days later, when I found the veteran who had worked in tourism all her life didn't finish the quotation, I felt much better.

I still worked hard every day and began to win people's favorable opinions. When you are weak, you will find people around are kind to you.

One day, when I was sending a fax in the logistic office shared by all the divisions, a colleague from the French division said indignantly, without looking at me, "M is so mean to throw up all his work to a newcomer without detailed explanation. He did it intentionally. He just wanted to see you make mistakes and didn't want you to do better than him." I was not on close terms with the colleague. I just listened and didn't make any comment. Deep inside, I agreed with the colleague. But I didn't dare to speak it out.

I was driven to the brink of desperation. I didn't like my job at all. I had no Beijing *hukou* and I had no place to go if I left here. I missed my four-year-old son who was temporarily looked after by his grandmother after I was transferred to the HO. If I continued to work like this, how long would I have to wait before I could live with my son? A chill ran down my back when I thought I had to work like this all my life and had no time to take care of my son.

I was on the verge of collapse. One night, when I walked past the public toilet of Zhongshan Park by the side of Tian'anmen Rostrum, I saw the doorkeeper sitting there smoking leisurely. The idea flashed into my mind: I would rather change jobs with him.

Before 1992, all the schedules were written by hand and then sent to the typewriter room. The typewritten schedules would be printed and posted to the local agents and hotels concerned. In 1992, a computer center was set up in the company and every sales manager or operation manager was equipped with a terminal. It was required that all the schedules should be done by computer. Most of the staff members were beginners in computer. All the scenic spots, restaurants and hotels were represented by codes and we were all required to memorize the letter codes. It took a long time to finish a schedule. I had many schedules to do every day. I was not skillful with the computer and couldn't remember the codes. One day, I couldn't find the code for the Great Wall at Mutianyu. I asked H what to do. He told me to replace it with the code for the Great Wall at Badaling. I looked at him, doubtfully, "Are you sure?" "Sure." He said. When the group arrived in Beijing, the Dutch tour leader called the office and asked why it was the Great Wall at Badaling. Mistakes of this kind were very common at that time though they seem stupid now.

During the 10 years between February of 1992 and December of 2001, I expanded the Dutch market from 3,000 people to 4,000, 5,000 and eventually more than 10,000. I succeeded. M said I wouldn't have made such great progress if he did not treat me like that at the beginning. I always told people I was thrown into the ocean when I could not swim and had to struggle desperately to survive. Maybe it was true that without the pressure from M I could not learn so fast, but I would never treat a newcomer as he treated me. Only unkind people would do that. Up to now I still bitterly hate those people who don't treat new employees well.

Westerners' Arrogance

In the summer of 1993, the HO did an incentive program in cooperation with a travel company in the Netherlands. The 37 members of the delegation were all male employees of a Dutch company AN. The Dutch travel company repeatedly emphasized the importance of the group and asked me to be the guide personally. I had worked in the HO for only one and a half years and had never been a tour guide. Although I had no experience, I was willing to serve the people with my heart and soul and had a responsible attitude towards my work. This was probably why they chose me to take care of the group. Given the importance of the group, the Dutch travel company appointed its senior manager Agnes to be the tour leader. I had a lot of contact with Agnes at work and knew her well. I believed we would be good partners.

Incentive travel is an important part of modern tourism. The purpose is to reward the employees for good performance with a travel at public expense to increase their sense of honor and to strengthen the team spirit. Incentive travel is not limited to sightseeing or leisure tour. The company would find a professional travel service to design and organize a theme party, a cocktail party or a special event to give their employees a surprise. It is a good opportunity for the company to develop the corporate culture and to express its gratitude to and care for the employees or distributors. The travel enables every participant to enjoy being a VIP and have a lifetime experience. Companies encourage and motivate their employees to create more value by incentive travel.

AN was one of the leading industrial enterprises in the world and was the biggest paint producer ranking first in the field of decorative

298

paint and functional paint. It was also the main global provider of chemical products. It was an important client of the Dutch travel company.

Although incentive travel had been popular in European and North American countries for many years, it was a new concept in China. Most of the travel services in China didn't know how to do an incentive travel. There were no professionals for incentive travel, not to mention the professional training on it. For a long time, domestic travel services preferred to handle groups of leisure tours. The programs of each group were the same and all they needed to do was copy. If there was an incentive group, it was also operated as a common tourist group. Although the overseas incentive travel companies were dissatisfied with the service from their Chinese partners, they had no better choice.

The quotation and itinerary of the AN group were done by my colleague H. I took it over later.

The delegation leader of the AN incentive group was Hens, public relations manager of the company. The group stayed in China World Hotel, then the best hotel in Beijing.

Hens was not satisfied with our service from the very first moment and found fault with everything. I perfectly understood him. The quality of the service of domestic travel companies was by no means up to the standard and requirement of an incentive group. Actually I was also learning in practice. I tried my best to cooperate with Hens and to meet his demand.

Hens often went to the Western countries for his company's incentive travel. He was bound to be disappointed when he compared China with the Western countries and felt the difference. No matter how rude or arrogant he was, I could understand him. He was not nice to Agnes either. I was grateful to Agnes for her support and willingness to share my trouble. If the two leaders joined hands to condemn me, I would be dead.

No matter how hard I worked, Hens was still unhappy. I felt

wronged but still served the group members attentively with smile on my face. Actually the group members enjoyed themselves, which was more or less some comfort for me.

The itinerary included Beijing and Shanghai. When we left for the airport from the hotel, after the group members were all seated and I counted the number, I asked the driver to start off. Then something unexpected happened.

Hens pulled a long face and said to me, "What are you doing here? Get off the bus."

I was stunned, "I am the national guide. I am going to Shanghai with you. How can I get to the airport if I don't take the bus?"

"Find yourself a place in the baggage van and look after the baggage."

"There will be a baggage clerk to take care of the baggage. We have only one group air ticket and the national guide must stay together with the group and board the plane with the group."

Hens fell into silence, his face pulled even longer.

I felt embarrassed and humiliated at that moment. I didn't expect Hens to be so unreasonable. I no longer expected to please the arrogant Dutch man. I would treat him as courtesy required.

However, what happened later made Hens look at me with new eyes.

After we checked in, we went to wait in the airport lounge. The flight was delayed due to the weather. It was the old terminal building with bad conditions and service. Many flights were delayed, but the counters were still handling boarding procedures. More and more passengers crowded in the lounge hall. All we knew was the flight was delayed and nobody told us the exact news. The announcement was only made in Chinese. The foreign travel groups with no national guides and individual tourists couldn't understand it and were anxiously walking around. Only my guests were sitting there leisurely chatting and joking. I made inquiries everywhere and kept my guests informed of the situation.

300

We arrived at the airport around 12 o'clock and didn't get any news after having waited for several hours. It was announced that every passenger would be compensated with a little cash for their loss. I got the money and bought bottled mineral water and chocolate bars for my group. Few foreigners went to receive the money because they couldn't understand it. I continued with my inquiry and at the same time kept my guests informed of the latest news. They were waiting patiently and showed no anxiety. They had a sense of superiority when they saw other foreign tourists running about to make inquiries themselves. Hens could do nothing and sat there quietly. He softened his tone when speaking to me and smile appeared on his face.

Flights took off one after another. The foreign passengers couldn't understand the boarding announcement except Shanghai, Xi'an or other city names. There were many flights to cities like Shanghai or Xi'an, so they didn't know which their flights were. A large crowd surrounded the information desk in the middle of the waiting hall and there was absolute chaos. I tried my best to help the foreign passengers. But there were too many of them and I couldn't help all. My guests were sitting there looking at the confusion and thought they were lucky to have a national guide.

More and more airliners took off on time. The delayed flights were not given priority. The Chinese passengers of a flight held a demonstration in the waiting hall holding a sign with the flight number on it, circling around the information desk and chanting slogans rhythmically. I had never seen such a scene before, let alone the foreigners. My guests all took out their cameras to take pictures.

It was five in the afternoon and there was still no indication that our flight would take off. I called the China World Hotel to make reservation for the night and informed the hotel in Shanghai that we might cancel the reservation for one night there. I also informed the driver to drive the bus to the airport on standby. I asked the airport if I could take my guests out for dinner. They agreed and said they would inform me of the news of the flight. I reserved tables in the Mexico restaurant of Lido Holiday Inn.

The group was really lucky to have me as their national guide. Normally, hotels and restaurants wouldn't accept direct reservations from tour guides. Only sales managers had the right to change the schedule. I was a sales manager myself, so there was no problem. Professional guides had limited rights. They needed the permit from the sales managers to change the schedule. That day was a weekend and it would be troublesome for the tour guide to contact the sales manager. It was in the early 1990s and most of the sales managers had no mobile phones or telephones at home.

When we arrived at the Mexico restaurant of Lido Holiday Inn, the guests were very excited. What they had had before were all Chinese meals. Hens was happy too. He admired me for my work ability that I could solve the problem within such a short time and make the guests happy. I was informed that our flight was delayed to the next day. When we returned to the hotel, the rooms were ready.

The next day, we got to the airport at the same time. The flight was still late. Agnes and I had established absolute prestige in the group. Nobody complained and all were waiting patiently at the gate of our flight. The flight didn't take off until very late in the evening. When the plane was flying at the height where the safety signal was removed, it happened to be midnight. The 37 members began to sing the Dutch birthday song in chorus. It was one member's birthday. What an unforgettable day! Who could celebrate his birthday in the air at the beginning of a day?

There were many problems with the program in Shanghai. Hens was still unhappy, but he was not directed against me. Agnes and I actively helped him solve the problem. The three of us went to every restaurant for a pre-check. Hens was not satisfied with the arrangement of the tables, he guided us to make the setup personally. Although Hens still looked serious, he showed his care and support for me. When I was busy attending to the guests during the meal, he asked me to enjoy my food and not to bother about others. A guest said his suitcase was broken and I promised to go with him to buy a new one. Hens said to the guest, "Don't trouble Ping. You can do it yourself."

On the way to the airport, Hens said some words of gratitude and praise for me which won the warm applause of the whole group. Hens took out a thick envelope and said, "Thank you for your excellent service. Here is your gratuity." I did a thing that made me proud all my life. I said, "Thank you, but I can't accept your gratuity." "Are you sure?" "Yes, I am sure. But I have a request. I hope you will still choose our company in the future. We will do much better then." "We certainly will." Hens said.

It was bad luck that our flight was delayed. But it helped me. It made Hens understand me and the important role of a national guide.

Agnes didn't go back with them to the Netherlands. She stayed to inspect hotels. After we sent off the guests, the grievances and tiredness of those days surged through our mind and we cried. Agnes said even if AN wouldn't cooperate with her company in the future, they would continue to cooperate with me. I forgot my purse in the car when we took a taxi to the hotel. I suffered a great loss because I refused the gratuity and lost my purse. Agnes and I kept guessing how much the gratuity would be. Our conclusion was it wouldn't be a small sum. The envelope was thick and the foreigners still used the foreign exchange certificate at that time.

Although Hens was rude to me, sometimes even insulting, I never hated him. I learnt a lot from the experience, which enlightened me for entering the incentive travel industry in the future.

How Westerners should cooperate with Chinese people is something worth serious consideration. They should keep learning and making progress as we Chinese do. They shouldn't just copy their previous experience with other countries when in China. If the national guide was not someone like me who could swallow humiliation for the sake of overall interests, he would have a row with the delegation leader, which would bring a disastrous result for the delegation.

In fact, there are still some Westerners who have no idea how to cooperate with Chinese people or Chinese companies. They are making things more complicated with their attitude or way of doing things. If they work together with the Chinese partners in an unpleasant atmosphere, they are not likely to provide the guests with the best service. As a travel company in China, we are not in the position to teach our foreign counterparts. We should first do our job well. If the quality of our service is good, leaving no room for criticism, our relationship with the foreign counterparts can be simple. Now we have made rapid progress in both the hardware and software for developing the incentive travel industry. It is unlikely that our clients are still not satisfied with our service.

Night of the Mid-Autumn Festival

It was the Mid-Autumn Festival on September 20, 1994. I was having dinner and enjoying CCTV special program for the festival with my son and the *ayi* (working as a babysitter and housekeeper, usually a rural young girl living with the host family). Suddenly the telephone rang. A Dutch tourist had a heart attack and died in Peking Union Medical College Hospital. My colleague H, who came back from the Netherlands after six-month training, was in charge of the group, but he had gone to his girlfriend's home to have the family reunion dinner. The person on duty at the HO couldn't reach him, so they called me.

Mid-Autumn Festival was a traditional Chinese festival for the whole family to get together. Since I began working in the HO, I was busy all year round and to have a peaceful family dinner became an extravagant wish.

I hurried to the hospital and thought on the way what I should say to console the poor widow.

The old couple was Indonesian Dutch and came with a travel group. On the day the husband was sent to the hospital, their group left Beijing for the next destination.

The heartbroken wife was sitting on the bench outside the emergency room, with a blank look in her eyes. I squatted by her side, held her hands and said in a gentle tone, "Don't worry. I will be here to help you."

But the old lady couldn't speak English. She could only speak Dutch and Indonesian. We couldn't communicate with each other. I was worried and didn't know what to do. Fortunately, a Chinese Indonesian who came to visit a patient helped me with the translation.

The next important thing was to deal with the remains. Should we cremate it or deliver it back to the Netherlands? The old lady said she needed to discuss it with her family before she made the decision.

The doctor said to me, "Now we are going to move the remains to the mortuary. Usually we need the help of the family to deal with it. Since the dead has no other family except the old lady here, we have to ask you for help."

I was ready to help!

The corridor to the mortuary seemed endless. I walked on with one hand resting lightly on the wheeled stretcher and holding the old lady with the other hand. I tried to pass my warmth to her. I understood how heartbroken it was to lose a family member in a foreign country.

Rows of freezer cupboards were standing in the mortuary with the name and number on each cupboard. The hospital staff member pulled out an empty cupboard and said, "I carry the head and you carry the feet. Let's put it into the cupboard."

I had no hesitation. I believed it was the arrangement of some god in the unseen world to let me see off the old man whom I didn't know.

It was already 11:00 in the evening. The next thing to do was to find a place for the old lady. The doctor said there had to be someone to accompany the old lady during the night.

The old lady was already dependent on me and held me tightly by the hand wherever we went.

I arranged a hotel for her and helped her get through to her family. I called my son and told him that I wouldn't be able to come home that night. I had to accompany the grandma from the Netherlands because the grandpa passed away.

The next day, I handed over the remaining problems to H. H felt very guilty and said, "I am terribly sorry to have given you so much trouble. I promise I will go to carry the dead body myself the next time."

The next time? I wished there would never be "the next time".

Behind the Success

I succeeded. In 1999, I was awarded "Excellent Individual" of the Capital Zijin Cup which was the highest honor in Beijing's tourism industry.

An article under the title of "Bitter Cold Adds Keen Fragrance to Plum Blossom" was published in the corporate newspaper to publicize my meritorious deeds. The article started with the following introduction to me:

The year 1999 is the eighth year since Liu Ping joined our company. During the eight years, she has developed from a layman to the best employee, from an ordinary sales person to deputy general manager of European Department Three. The number of tourists and business volume of the market under her charge have been on an increase for eight years successively. The Dutch-Greek Division created a gross profit of RMB 10.49 million under her leadership in the year of 1998. European Department Three was set up as required by the market development at the end of

1999 and Liu Ping was appointed deputy general manager. At the time when the market suffered a series of crisis such as the economic crisis in Russia, the Kosovo War and NATO's bomb attack against Chinese Embassy in Yugoslavia, the department overfulfilled the business volume quota and created a gross profit of RMB 15.41 million.

Since I joined the HO in 1992, I was given four promotions during the seven years, from a grass-root employee to a division deputy director, division director, executive deputy general manager and finally general manager of a department. My promotion was proportional to the volume of business and profit I had created for the company.

European Department Three was set up at the end of 1999 for the development and sales of the travel market in northern Europe, eastern Europe, the Netherlands, Greece and Russia. I was appointed deputy general manager of the department with no general manager above me and was allocated a car by the company. When the key of a brand new Santana 2000 was handed to me, I didn't know what to do with it. I felt a pie fell from the sky and just dropped into my mouth. Besides, I couldn't drive.

Everyone thought I was lucky. But those who knew me well knew all the ups and downs behind my success. I had no ambition since the very beginning. I just wanted to do my job well. Those who were bent on getting promoted couldn't realize their dreams no matter how hard they tried. A watched flower never blooms, but an untended willow grows.

No pains, no gains. During the 10 years in the HO, I spent countless weekends and holidays working in the office.

I was on duty in the office every Chinese New Year that is the most important occasion of a year for Chinese people who will have at least one week off. But our business partners abroad still work during our holiday. E-mail was not in popular use then. In order to keep contact with the clients and to deal with emergencies, there was always someone available in the office during the festival.

I worked hard and left home early and returned late every day. During the winter, I went to work before dawn and when I came home, the moon was up.

My son came back to me from his grandmother after I had worked in the HO for a year. I sent him to a boarding kindergarten and picked him back every weekend. Parents could take their children home for the night every Wednesday, but it was not compulsory. I was too busy and never took my son home on Wednesday. The teachers were quite displeased with it. If all the children were taken home, they could have a rest that night. I had to smile to the teachers apologetically.

Every Wednesday, most of the children were picked by their parents and only few kids were left. They were hurt when they saw other children going home with their parents. My son hated staying in the kindergarten for the whole week and it was a torture for me to send him there. Every Wednesday afternoon, the teacher would seat the children who would be picked home on a row of small stools near the door waiting for their parents, and asked the children who wouldn't go back home to play in the courtyard. My son always told the teacher that I would come to pick him up and went to sit on one stool waiting for me though he knew I wouldn't come. When all the other children left, he would still be sitting there alone hoping I would suddenly show up.

I was always absent for the parents' meeting in the kindergarten. Once I couldn't attend it again because of an urgent meeting. I went to the kindergarten to ask for leave. When I was leaving, my son started to cry and wouldn't let me go. He cried silently, tears rolling down his cheeks.

When my son was at school age, no school accepted him because he had no Beijing *hukou*. I used all my connections, looked to friends for help and sent gifts, and finally got a place for my son in Sanlitun Third Primary School. I had to pay extra school fees every semester. I worked extremely hard. I must gain a strong foothold in Beijing and create a good living environment for my son.

Every day, I got up at six in the morning and cooked breakfast for my son. I left home at seven and sent my son to his school by bicycle. Then I rode to the subway station and went to work by tube. The *ayi* picked my son in the afternoon and took him home by bus. I always worked overtime and had no time to help my son with his study. When I worked late in the office, I kept thinking about my son. When I got home and found my son's homework was in a mess, I was racked with anxiety, but there was nothing I could do. Many parents sent their children to extra-curricular clubs to learn an instrument or a sport. But I had no time for that.

I wanted to use the vacation to send my son to learn something or to help him make up for his study. But my husband required that our son stay with him during the winter or summer vacation. It was natural that a father wanted to spend more time with the son. But my husband just left our son to his employees or his mother. He was the general manager of a resort where my son stayed the whole vacation. He was indulged by the employees and was free to do what he pleased. His grandma was able to take care of him, but she couldn't supervise his study. When my son returned home, his homework was either not finished or in a mess. I had to urge him to finish his homework one or two days before the school started.

My son was an active boy. The teacher in charge of his class was a young girl. She didn't like my son and my son was also resentful to her. I would usually send her a small gift or a ticket for some performance.

Once before the New Year, I prepared several exquisite calendars for the teacher. I wrapped them in colored paper and asked my son to take them to the teacher. His classmates were curious at the gifts, so my son opened them for his classmates to take a look. Everyone had a touch and made the calendars dirty. My son wrapped the calendars carelessly and gave them to the teacher. Seeing the dirty gift, the teacher was angry and thought the parent was unreasonable. I didn't know about it until I had a conversation with the teacher long after that.

A Dutch client once came to Beijing with his wife and son. His wife was a teacher. I asked the headmaster of my son's school if I could show my client and his family around my son's class. The headmaster agreed. I gave the class 300 yuan as the reception fee. They prepared sweets and beverage, decorated the classroom and prepared performances. The client and his family were received warmly. My son's classmates gave a lot of performances. My son didn't take part in the performance. He and several other naughty boys were seated at one corner of the classroom in case they would make trouble.

The most difficult time for me was when my son got ill. He got polyp of sinus and had surgeries three times. I was always sobbing silently the night before each of the surgeries. But I wouldn't shed tears in presence of my family. The mixed feelings of anger, guilt and worry were torturing me.

I was under overwhelming work pressure and there was no one to share with me the responsibility of bringing up my son. I felt exhausted physically and mentally.

Things were getting more difficult in winter, especially on snowy days. My son was growing heavier and heavier. It was extremely difficult for me to ride on in the snow carrying him.

We lived in an apartment of 40 square meters with a bedroom and a living-room. The *ayi* slept in the living-room. My son and I shared a double bed. My son was big and tall and it was very uncomfortable for the two of us to share the same bed. We had no air-conditioning in the room. When summer came, it was as hot as in the oven with the ceiling scorched by the sun during the day. When lying in bed, we were drenched in sweat and neither of us could have a good sleep. Housing was allocated by the state. State-owned enterprises allocated houses by seniority. I didn't work there long, so I couldn't get a bigger house even if I created a lot of wealth for the enterprise.

When my son reached the high school age, I resolutely sent him to a private boarding school. I pushed the responsibility of his education to the school so I could have a chance to catch my breath. I was guilty for not being able to take care of him and educate him.

Once I was talking to my son over the telephone in the office and was heard by a colleague. He was quite moved. In his impression, I was always in a hurry busy with my work. He was surprised I would speak to my son so patiently and gently. Whenever I told my son that I couldn't come back home early, I felt as if a knife were piercing my heart. Although I had a husband, we had in fact separated since my son was born. If there had been someone to share my pressure, life would have been much easier.

Seeing I was always the first to come and the last to go, the gate-keepers were touched by my hard work and were particularly kind and warm to me. Sometimes I would stop at the gate and had a small chat with them. It was a great consolation to me when I was helpless and depressed.

When I was promoted general manager of the European Department Three, the gate-keepers said, "Liu Ping has achieved her success through painstaking efforts." The article "Bitter Cold Adds Keen Fragrance to Plum Blossom" introduced me as follows.

Today, Liu Ping is trusted by her leaders, supported by her subordinates and widely acknowledged by her clients. She attributes her achievements to her loyalty to the HO, her enthusiasm in the tourism industry and a good mentality. She doesn't approve of the saying that one should make contributions without asking for repay, which she thinks goes against the principle of distribution according to work. But if what one thinks first before he does everything is what he can get from it, he is not likely to do it well because he cannot maintain his mental equilibrium and would think the world owes much to him.

I Finally Became a Citizen of Beijing

On the first day when I was accepted by the HO and reported for duty at the Personnel Department, head of the department said to me, "Although we accept you, I hope you won't make trouble for me and ask me to solve your *hukou*."

I replied immediately that I would not.

I was very content. I had no *hukou*, but I was an official employee of a large state-owned enterprise. It was very unusual. I still don't understand why I was so favored by fate at one moment. I was sure of one thing: Only leaders as bold as Flying Swallow would discard uniformity of standards in selecting and employing people of talent.

I did what I said and never mentioned my *hukou* problem. My son was only four and didn't reach his school age. So having no *hukou* didn't cause me trouble for the time being. Flying Swallow left HO in 1994 and was given a sentence for corruption before long. If she hadn't left, I would have got my *hukou* earlier.

I didn't think highly of the leader who succeeded Flying Swallow. I cannot even remember if he did something during his term of office which left impression on the employees. He was overly cautious and indecisive. He would never offend anyone. Nor would he defend the interest of someone else. He was transferred away after he worked there for only two years.

When my son went to primary school, I had to pay high extra school fees because of the *hukou* problem. But I still kept my promise and never caused trouble for the HO. When my son finished his primary school, I sent him to a private boarding high school which had no *hukou*-

related restrictions. I just had to pay more money.

I did better and better in my work and occupied a crucial position in the HO. Nobody would believe I was still a "black person" with no Beijing *hukou*.

I thought it was something my superior should consider. If they needed me, it wouldn't be difficult for an enterprise as large as the HO to solve my *hukou* problem.

However, I didn't get a Beijing *hukou* until 1998.

A new vice president came. I knew him through Yang before he came. He was greatly surprised when he heard that my *hukou* problem was not solved after I had worked there for six years. He immediately listed it in his agenda.

The number of people who could get Beijing *hukou* was limited every year. The enterprise was given a limited quota from its higher level authorities. One needed to have a strong backing or background to get a Beijing *hukou* which was usually used as bargaining counters in deals between power and money. According to the policy, exceptions could be made for those who made special contributions for the enterprise. I was perfectly up to the special contribution standard.

In 1998, the leading body of the HO had a quota of two *hukou*. I was given one and finished my life as a "black person". My husband and my son's permanent residence was also registered in Beijing together with mine according to the rules.

I left Guizhou in 1979. After 19 years' hard work, I finally became a citizen of Beijing in 1998.

My Destiny with People to People

People often ask me how I came to know People to People.

Before 1997, I didn't know there was such an organization called People to People International. I was mainly responsible for the Dutch market since I came to work in the HO in 1992. The main business of the European Department One where I worked was doing leisure tours. I always preferred to do something more creative and challenging.

One day in the first half of the year 1997, I encountered People to People by an inevitable chance, which changed my life and my destiny in a way.

An American named Will Berg who used to work with the HO got a job in People to People Ambassador Programs (hereinafter referred to as Ambassador Programs), a cooperative partner of People to People International.

Ambassador Programs was in cooperation with many associations and travel companies in China. After Will Berg joined Ambassador Programs, he immediately contacted someone he knew well in the European Department One and expressed his willingness to cooperate with the HO. Will Berg mailed a large package of materials about Ambassador Programs to the European Department One.

When I saw the package on the desk of the department head, I thought I was the best one for this kind of business which required the person in charge to have wisdom, passion, creativity and political sense. But I did not expect that the head would let me take care of it. Two days later, the head had a talk with me and said he decided to put me in charge of it. He also told me that I was the best candidate for the job because I had experiences working in the government. This was how I got the opportunity to cooperate with Ambassador Programs. There were rumors spreading that I seized the client from other department. I really couldn't accept their "praise" because such a thing was beyond my capability.

As far as I knew, some staff members of Ambassador Programs were not really happy when Will Berg changed business partner in China on his own authority. Ambassador Programs once cooperated with the North American Department of the HO. The HO monopolized the domestic inbound market at that time. They were not interested in the challenging products of Ambassador Programs and gave up the cooperation. I would have lost the opportunity to work for Ambassador Programs if it had not been for Will Berg's perseverance. Will Berg left Ambassador Programs after he worked there for only one year. We lost contact with each other. I was grateful to him. Many staff members of Ambassador Programs became my good friends. They often said jokingly that if it had not been for Will Berg, they wouldn't have met someone as excellent as me.

People to People International was founded in 1956 by Dwight Eisenhower, 34th US President in the hope that world peace could be realized through mutual trust and mutual understanding of people of different countries through dialogue and face-to-face communication. All the previous US presidents have been honorary president of People to People. Mary Eisenhower, granddaughter of General Eisenhower, is the CEO of the organization.

The reason I liked to work for Ambassador Programs is because of its mission. Every year, Ambassador Programs works with government departments, professional institutes, hospitals, universities and other institutions of more than 80 countries holding exchanges in science, culture and technology, etc. The professionals come from fields of medicine, law, science and technology, education, arts, agriculture, finance, architecture, transportation, manufacturing and processing and natural resource development, etc. They come to China to exchange ideas and experiences with Chinese counterparts. They learn from each other and increase their understanding of each other. Many of the delegates have established friendly cooperation with the Chinese counterparts. We call them "People to People Professional Delegations".

There is a big difference between People to People Professional Delegations and other leisure tour groups. Thirty percent of their itinerary is culture programs while 70 percent is professional exchanges and activities, which is a big challenge for Ambassador Programs' business partners abroad.

Ambassador Programs sends about 2,000 professionals to China for cultural and professional exchanges each year. Most of the delegates come from the US and some are from other countries. Before 1997, Ambassador Programs had cooperated with many Chinese travel companies or associations and the quality of their service was at different levels.

Ambassador Programs did not give all of its business to us at the beginning. There was one thing we did that made Ambassador Programs more confident about us. Ambassador Programs contacted one of its partners in Beijing for a story-telling delegation. When the marketing manager of Ambassador Programs was searching on the internet, she found a village named Geng Village in Hebei Province where the villagers had the tradition to tell stories from generation to generation. She talked with her partner in Beijing and asked if they could arrange the delegation to visit Geng Village. The answer she got was negative. She turned to me and I said "yes". Actually I felt embarrassed for I had never heard anything about Geng Village which was over 400 kilometers away from Beijing. I immediately made an inspection trip with my colleagues and realized that Geng Village was the most ideal place for the American story-telling delegation. The visit later made by the delegation was an once-in-a-lifetime experience.

We soon won the trust of Ambassador Programs because our service was far better than that of other travel companies or associations though we also received complaints about too much shopping which was some-thing out of my control because of the system. We became Ambassador Programs' only partner in China for its adult programs one year later.

Since US President Nixon visited China in 1972, Ambassador Pro-grams has organized People to People professional delegations to visit China for 38 years, making great contributions to the friendly unofficial exchanges between the two countries.

Mary Eisenhower was honored as "Friendship Ambassador" by Chinese People's Association for Friendship with Foreign Countries on April 16, 2007 for her contributions to promoting friendship between the Chinese and American people.

Mary Eisenhower and I have become good friends. We are of the same age and have a lot in common. I have made a lot of American friends and friends from other countries since I worked with Ambassador Programs. I am very proud that we have made them understand and love China through our work.

Taking the First Flight to America After September 11

I started working with Ambassador Programs in 1997, but I didn't get the opportunity to visit my client in Spokane, Washington State of America until 2001. I booked the UA flight to Seattle on September 16.

On September 11, my sister called me and asked me to turn on TV to watch the news of September 11. Since then I watched TV all day long even slept on the sofa in front of the TV for fear I might miss any news of it.

I asked the airport if the flights to America would take off as usual and was told all the flights were cancelled. I made inquiries about the flight by telephone every day and still didn't know if I could fly to the US until the day before departure.

The annual motivation show in Chicago was held in September. The State Tourism Administration would participate in the exhibition every year with the local travel bureaus and enterprises. After September 11, the State Tourism Administration cancelled its plan to attend the show and the North American Department that supposed to join the show also cancelled its promotion plan in America.

Ambassador Programs knew that I would go to visit them. If I cancelled my trip because of September 11, it would be too cowardly and inconsiderate. It was not my personality. Even if nobody was willing to go to America for fear of danger, I should stick to my original plan. I believed my American clients needed friendship and support more than ever before. When they asked me if I would visit them as scheduled, I said I would go as long as there was a flight.

On the evening of September 15, I got news there might be a UA flight to America the next day. I reached the airport early the next morning. There was a long queue before the UA counter and the American passengers who had been held up in Beijing for days were eager to take the first flight back home after September 11.

When I was going through the immigration control in Seattle, I was asked to show my invitation letter. It was only then that I found I had forgotten it. The staff member said, "You cannot enter our country without an invitation letter." "Who would like to come to America at this time?" I said. He was stunned for a second and then let me pass.

My clients were grateful and touched that I visited America when everybody else avoided it, which also increased their trust in me and appreciation for me.

Anonymous Letters

The years 1999 and 2000 had witnessed the biggest success in my career life before I started my own business.

Before the Chinese New Year of 2000, president of the HO invited me and another department head for dinner. He said, "Do you know why I just invited you two? Among all the department managers, only the two of you work hard silently without getting me in any trouble and did a great job last year. I can fully trust you."

I was actually deeply hurt in 1999. I offended an operation manager and a tour guide from our Beijing local agent when dealing with a complaint. The operation manager wrote an anonymous letter and sent a copy of it to all the leaders at different levels in the HO. I didn't understand how she could be so stupid. All those who received the letter could tell immediately that it was written by her. What really hurt me was not the letter. It was the fact that she used to be my friend, a girl whom I used to appreciate very much. She was bright, creative and full of feminine charm when she was in good mood. She was 12 years my junior, but she was mature and sophisticated. I often exchanged ideas with her when I had problems in my work. This was why she had a lot of "subjects" to use in her anonymous letter.

She also did another thing which was very immoral. She wrote a letter to my client Ambassador Programs in America. Below was part of the original. I made no change, including her grammatical mistakes.

"Well, the reason that I wrote all this to you is, Liu Ping, made me quit my job, even quit the tourist industry. Two purpose of this message. One is warning you be careful about Liu Ping. i.e. she said that your company paying her pretty high made her big benefit from your groups. She force the branch agencies pay her under the table but add all those money into the groups expenses, then let the Xi'an local agent pay them back. She has been doing this since the first group you work with her."

She was right about one thing. For many years, she couldn't find a job in the tourist circle. The anonymous letter she wrote was destructive with malicious language and was widely spread, but it ruined her reputation instead of mine.

I might have many shortcomings, but my biggest advantage since I entered tourism was that all the clients who had worked with me trusted me very much. After they received the letter, they called me and sent the letter back to me.

I took no action against her.

It happened in the summer of 1999. I was not influenced by it in my work and still scored outstanding achievements by the end of the year.

I did very well in 2000 too. The rumor was widely circulated that I would be promoted vice president of the large enterprise with about 1,000 employees. I didn't care about it. I had no desire for an official post. Again in the summer of 2000, hundreds of copies of two anonymous letters against me were widely spread in the company and every leader at or above department head level received a copy except me. The following was the one with the comparatively less filthy words.

Leaders of the HO,

Do you know what kind of person Liu Ping is? It is really ridiculous that she should have climbed to the post of head of the department. All she depends on to get herself out of the mountains of Guizhou and have today's success is her ability to please men. It is thus clear that the ethical standards of some leaders are not as high as we have expected.

Why Liu Ping works so hard is that she wants to get rid of her lowly origin and rise head and shoulders above others. She ropes in clients for her own interests and cooperates with so-and-so (the real name was mentioned in the letter) *local travel agent for money and for her own company. She has secretly become one of its shareholders and has become the sex partner of Xi, president of the local agent, for a long time.*

Due to disharmony in her marriage life, Liu Ping has sexually harassed many young male employees several times since she joined the HO. She is coquettish before male superiors. When she is refused or fails to get what she wants, she would make a terrible scene or threaten them.

In order to achieve personal purposes, Liu Ping does not scruple to abuse power to win over her subordinates and to retaliate against those who have different opinions. Her behavior during her recent business trip to Europe is really disgusting. Her unbridled nature has been fully displayed in front of some leaders.

As a group of people who loves the HO, we sincerely appeal that shameless people like Liu Ping should be kept from the leadership. Otherwise, the HO would be influenced adversely and suffer losses. We hope you will sharpen your vigilance so as not to be confused by Liu Ping's tricks.

The name of the sender was "a group of people who love the HO".

When the anonymous letters were widely spread in the company, I was the only one kept in the dark. I was preparing for my driver's license test and was not in the company. When someone showed me the letter later, I made no response. I just felt helpless.

The president of the HO called me and asked me what I was doing. I said I was practicing driving. He asked me to come back as soon as possible. When he saw me, the first sentence he said was "How can you possibly be so calm and still in the mood for practicing driving?" "What can I do?" I said.

It happened 10 years ago. Three years ago when attending the motivation show in Chicago, we met the people from the HO and they told my colleague, "Do you know who wrote the anonymous letter? It was so-and-so."

It is not important to me at all.

Asking Underworld for Help

As I have told you previously that I offended an operation manager and a tour guide of a Beijing local agent when dealing with a complaint.

The operation manager was obviously partial to the tour guide. Later I came to know that they were relatives. The tour guide and the operation manager were named Shu and Ying separately.

Shu often worked as the national guide for a group series from America. She was overbearing and didn't get on well with local guides of the other cities. She acted as if she was on good terms with me so that other people dared not offend her.

It was common in the tourist circle that the national guide and the local guide had conflicts in economic benefits. If the national guide was a greedy and arrogant person, the local guide would have to swallow his anger and pride. Certainly some local guides were also not easy to deal with. Only if the national guide and the local guide worked together with one heart could they provide good service to the guests. Therefore, rules and regulations were made by European Department Three to supervise the behaviors of both the national guide and the local guide. The national guides were required to supervise the work of the local guides and the local agents, who were required to do the same to the national guides. The national guide was granted big power. At the same time, rules were laid down to prevent them from abusing power. One of the rules was if a national guide received complaints from three local agents at the same time, an investigation would be carried out. If the complaints were based on facts, the national guide would be disqualified temporarily or permanently.

English tour guides all preferred to work for American tourists for their high gratuity and high enthusiasm in shopping, especially our American group series which was well-known in the tourist circle in China.

On the 2000 annual training session, three local agents complained about Shu. Therefore I made the decision that Shu be temporarily suspended from her post as the national guide. But she could still work as a local guide. Most of the tour guides would accept the punishment and tried to correct their mistakes to regain trust. Shu didn't admit her mistakes but made quite a scene sitting on the desk in the local agent office and cursing me.

Ying was the operation manager of the local agent and was at odds with her boss the general manager Xi. Xi removed her from her post and demoted her to be a tour guide to force her to resign. Ying had no English tour guide certificate, so she couldn't be a tour guide. I tried to persuade Xi not to drive Ying to a tight corner. I knew they used to be on good terms and trusted each other. Actually there was another reason for Xi's decision to remove Ying from her post. She had already accepted an offer from another travel agent before she terminated her contract with Xi. She wished I could cooperate with her new employer. To tell the truth, it was quite possible. I appreciated her work ability and creativity. She was a talent that was hard to come by. But her new employer had no contract with the HO and we were not allowed to cooperate with the local agent that had no contract with us. I told her that I would consider our cooperation as long as her new company managed to get a contract with the HO. When Xi found out Ying was straddling two boats, he removed her from the post.

It was a coincidence that Shu's being punished and Ying's being fired happened at the same time.

I still cannot understand why Ying didn't hate Xi who fired her but gave vent to her anger on me. Someone analyzed it from the point of view of a bystander that Ying thought I would put in a word for her and Xi wouldn't fire her for fear of losing my business. I liked her, but business was business. I wouldn't interfere in the internal affairs of the local agent. We were partners, not superior and subordinate.

I felt sorry for her when I heard she was fired and I wanted to help her get a new job. She didn't know it. It was at this time that she spread several hundred copies of anonymous letter in the HO. Her anonymous letter was menacing and scared all the travel companies in Beijing. No one dared recruit such a "bomb".

The only thing I could do about the anonymous letter was ignore it.

But it was not the end of their revenge.

For a period of time, I would receive harassment calls every early morning and midnight. I thought they would be tired some day and ignored it. But they had amazing stamina and kept harassing me for dozens of days. In the end, they put my house on the ads for house rent and I had to receive numerous calls from house seekers every day.

Ying was a wise woman, but she was stupid this time. She did all the things anonymously, but what she did was full of flaws and made people suspect her without any difficulty. She was the only one among my friends who knew the detail such as the address, the area, the decoration and furniture of my house.

I didn't know when their crazy revenge would stop. My son was young and there were only the *ayi*, my son and me, two weak ladies and one child, at home. I was worried about the safety of my son, so I reported it to the security department of the company. I hoped they could help me solve the problem by legal means. Protecting the employees was part of their job.

I reported it twice to the security department and the reply was I had to be careful myself because they had no other better way to deal with it.

I was driven crazy. I found Xi and said, "You must get it solved. You fired your employee. Your employee hates me instead of you and took revenge against me. I don't know what has happened between you."

Several days later, Xi told me that the problem was solved.

Xi turned to a gangster of the underworld who lived in the district where Shu lived and gave him 10,000 yuan. The gangster intercepted Shu and said, "You had better stop your mean tricks."

"What have I done?" Guiltily, she asked.

"You know what I mean."

Since then, the harassment was gone and both Ying and Shu disappeared from my life. It was just that easy.

Nine years later in 2009, I found Ying was working in a company that was in close cooperation with my company and I happened to know the top leader of the company well. I remained silent.

The Fuse Leading to My Resignation

When it was rumored that I would be promoted vice president of the HO, the anonymous letter was widely spread. Many people in the company had been attacked by anonymous letters. The anonymous letter against me used the most dirty and coarse language and was unbearably offensive to the ear. I didn't want to take any action against it. Since it was anonymous, it was a sinister deal itself.

The president of the HO had a talk with me.

"Do you know who wrote the letter?"

"It is Pi." I said it with great certainty.

"Are you a shareholder of the so-and-so local agent?"

"If you don't believe me, I have nothing more to say."

I actually liked and respected the president very much. He was exceedingly intelligent and knowledgeable. It was out of my expectation that he would ask such a question. How could a non-share-holding state-owned enterprise have shareholders? Besides, he belittled me. None of the travel companies in China were good enough to make me a shareholder for it.

I said, "You can look into it if you don't trust me. I am willing to accept any punishment if you find anything wrong with me."

"You had better write a statement asking for an investigation. Then it will be easier for the leaders to help you on behalf of the company."

I was grateful to him and I knew it was for my good that he said it. I made the following statement.

Respected leaders,

Recently, someone spread anonymous letters in the company, which is a slander and personal attack against me. Therefore, I'd like to make the following statement.

The remark that I am a secret shareholder of so-and-so local agent is nothing but slander against me. What I have done can bear any form of test. I'd like to ask the leaders to carry out an investigation to clarify facts. If there is any problem, I will take all the legal responsibility.

I have never made any remarks in the "Collection of Liu Ping's Remarks" (part of it attached below) *at any time or in any place. I think the sender of the anonymous letter used me as a cat's paw to voice his own opinions. If the person has the guts to stand out, I will confront him face to face at the law court about every sentence in the "Collection of Liu Ping's Remarks". The anonymous letter is a personal attack against me with its dirty and coarse language. I will exercise my rights and defend my dignity through legal means when I find it necessary.*

I have done nothing that I should feel sorry for the country or the company since I came to the HO. I have never done anything harmful to others' interests. I can stand any test. I believe the person who wrote the anonymous letter hurt himself more than he hurt me. He would be by no means in a peaceful state of mind. If he thinks he can tarnish my name with his anonymous letter, he is wrong. I believe there is a steelyard between heaven and earth. The anonymous letter wouldn't change my outlook on the world or my pursuit of success in my career.

The person who wrote the anonymous letter really hated me to the core and called me "the well-known whore of the HO" and described me as having a "pig's head face with the cheeks that looked like two steamed rotten crabs".

Obviously the person wanted to have me destroyed by making everybody hate me. He also spread with the anonymous letters the *"Collection of Liu Ping's Remarks"* in which all the leaders at or above the department level were verbally attacked. Real names were mentioned in the letters. I will use so-and-so instead of the real names when I show you part of the letter here.

The two old vice presidents do nothing all day long and what they do is go abroad to have fun and waste the money we earn.

The stupid pig so-and-so works just to get by and has no ideas at all.

So-and-so has made some achievements and it seems he will be promoted the president of the HO. He is fond of singing and we must invite him to KTV to promote friendship with him.

So-and-so is an idiot and good-for-nothing. His ladyboy-like wife is a damned nuisance. But I cannot afford to offend him.

What capability does so-and-so have except licking boots? He is just lucky. He is bound to fall sooner or later.

So-and-so still refuses to leave although she is already retired as if we cannot do without her.

So-and-so is an idler. All he thinks about is pleasure-seeking and golfing but not his work.

It's said so-and-so is promoted head of the department through her personal link with so-and-so director. She is eccentric and one had better beware of her.

So-and-so (my partner, the deputy Party secretary of European Department Three) *is obediently to me in everything, but in fact he bears many grudges against me. Fortunately, I have evidence against him.*

So-and-so seeks personal gain by opportunism and trickery and should have long been removed.

It's said so-and-so is a shrew. She often glares at me. Maybe she is jealous of me because of my ability.

So-and-so is half disabled (who got cancer) *now and I might as well not mention him.*

The anonymous letter was a failure. Nobody, even those who were cursed in the letter, believed that I had said the above things. I even did not know a couple of the guys mentioned since I always concentrated on my job and neglected those people around. It was not because they all trusted me. I had worked in the company for eight years, and everybody knew it was not my way of doing things. The letter was targeted against me, but it hurt many other people. No one who was attacked in the letter could calm down.

The president called a meeting attended by all the leaders above the department level. He first criticized the despicable act, and then he said, "I have asked Liu Ping if she is a shareholder of the so-and-so local agent. She is not according to what she has told me."

I was so disappointed. The president didn't clarify the facts for me but emphasized "according to what she told me". Since he didn't trust me, I decided to take it seriously. It was the president who asked me to write the statement and wanted to help me. Originally I did not want to take any action, but now I firmly asked for an investigation.

Someone tried to dissuade me, "Liu Ping, don't take it seriously. You are bound to wet your shoes if you often walk near the river."

"I often walk near the river, but I never wet my shoes. Just wait if you don't believe me."

The Party committee of the company and the deputy secretary of our department's Party branch formed a team to look into the matter.

I was anxiously waiting for the result of their investigation. But there was no news.

I asked them, "What's the result of your investigation?"

"You are innocent."

"Why don't you tell me? Why don't you announce it at the meeting?"

"We trust you from beginning to end. So there is no need to tell you or to announce it."

All Chinese people understand the destructive power of an anonymous letter. There used to be a famous saying: eight cents, half year's investigation. Many years ago, the postage of ordinary mail was eight cents. Stick an eight-cent stamp and mail the anonymous letter, you could wait to watch the fun. It would take at least half a year to find out the truth. During the half year, your promotion, pay rise, or travel abroad might be suspended, which was the power of an anonymous letter.

At that moment, I was one of the three newly promoted department deputy general managers. After we were in deputy positions for about half a year, the personnel department decided to promote us and started a public opinion poll on our reputation in the company and talked to us one by one.

The head of the personnel department looked at me smilingly, "Everybody speaks highly of you and there is almost no negative comment. You have got the most favorable opinions among the three of you."

Other personnel cadres present also gave me a lot of recognition and courage.

When the anonymous letter incident happened, the official evaluation made on me by the personnel department of this state-owned company was overthrown. A meeting was specially held outside the company to discuss whether or not I should be made official general manager. The meeting lasted a day and there were strong opinions against me. But they finally reached the agreement to give me the promotion.

A meeting was held to announce the appointment. I was appointed general manager of the department. At the same time, two other women who used to be deputy secretaries were appointed secretaries of the Party branches of their departments. It was widely discussed that it was for the sake of balance to promote three female cadres at the same time. But who knew.

Appointments were announced at the meeting.

The president said, "There is much disagreement over the appointment of someone. But we have decided to approve of her promotion considering the overall situation. We will talk to her and point out her shortcomings after the meeting." Then, the president turned to me with all the other attendees present, "Liu Ping, please stay after the meeting."

The president started his private talk to me with two more staff present from the Party committee of the HO.

"Have you considered why it is always you who are targeted by anonymous letters?"

"Because that I am outstanding and some people are jealous of

329

me." I didn't usually talk like that. But now I didn't want to pretend to be modest.

"Don't you think you are over-confident? Have you never thought that there must be some facts in the anonymous letters? An empty hole invites the wind—weakness lends wings to rumors. "

"If so, I'd like to ask you: The anonymous letter says I am coquettish before male superiors. Have I ever been coquettish before you?"

He made no reply.

"I certainly have weaknesses and this is why I need to constantly improve myself. I like you and respect you. I think you are a very good leader. But why are there still some people who attack you by anonymous letters? Does it mean that you have an empty hole?"

As I have mentioned previously, anonymous letters were not something unusual in the company.

"You are unanimously acknowledged for your excellent work, especially your clients' trust in you."

"Don't you like an employee who does an excellent job and is trusted by the clients?"

I knew I was a bit aggressive during the conversation. I was ready to risk everything. I had nothing to be afraid of. I was not an office-seeker in the first place. A straight foot is not afraid of a crooked shoe.

The two from the Party committee said: "Everybody says Liu Ping is straightforward. But we never expect that you are so straightforward."

The anonymous letter was the fuse leading to my resignation from the state-owned enterprise.

Why Was I So Hated?

Why was I so hated when I worked in the state-owned enterprise? I have examined myself and have tried to learn from my experiences.

In the days of having everyone "eat from the same big pot", one should never make oneself conspicuous. There are many Chinese idioms that teach people to keep a low profile, such as "one who sticks his neck out gets hit first", "a tall tree catches the wind" and "exposed rafters are the first to rot".

But I violated the taboo.

I developed a market that nobody took seriously into one of the HO's top 10 tourist sources.

My department had almost the highest gross profit margin and the lowest arrears by the clients.

Our department achieved high gross profit margin not because that I added a higher mark-up. It was because that I had strict control over the links that might lead to profits flowing into private pockets.

I also made the biggest mistake. I touched others' cheese. I did the American People to People Ambassador Programs and Belgian tourist groups. There were strict market division in the HO and the markets in the US and Belgium were not my responsibility. For some reason, the leader put me in charge of the two clients. No one expected that I would be so successful with the two clients, especially the Belgian market which I started from nothing brought in more than 3,000 tourists annually. The American People to People Ambassador Programs was once refused by the HO because it was too challenging. But I started it up and created a wonder. The heads of the two departments that were responsible for the US and the Belgian markets said to the boss that they wished I would

331

return the two clients to them. But the clients insisted I should be the one that handle their groups. The Belgian client even said if he had to work with someone else instead of me, he would turn to the HO's rival firm.

Unreasonable division of marketing responsibilities resulted in the loss of clients. The cooperation in tourism was based on the trust and friendship between people. I often met with the problem that the clients from the markets which were not under my charge asked me to handle their groups, but I had to introduce them to other departments according to the division of responsibilities, which resulted in the loss of clients. I felt sorry, but there was nothing I could do about it.

The HO attended many international travel exhibitions every year. The buyers and suppliers came from all parts of the world and all of them spoke English at the exhibitions. But according to the market division, the sales managers that could speak German were sent to Germany; those who could speak English were separately sent to the English-speaking countries and those who could speak Spanish were sent to Spain, and so on, so forth. Many opportunities slipped away because our sales managers couldn't speak English at the exhibitions held in non-English-speaking countries.

I once wrote a report to the leaders of the HO and suggested marketing strategy reform. But the traditional practice of several decades was hard to displace.

When I was nobody, I got on well with my colleagues. When I became somebody, I found I lost my popularity. We worked independently and seldom had contact with each other except some greetings in the corridor or in the mail room, especially with those from other divisions. I had my whole heart in my work and was unaware that I had made so many "enemies".

One day, my friend Yang who introduced me to Flying Swallow told me, "Ping, I am calling to remind you that some leader in the HO has very bad impressions of you."

I was surprised! How would I offend some leader since I worked so hard? I was more surprised when I knew that the leader who did not like me was C. Yang once had told me that C was a very nice and fair person and I was very positive about her before I met her. So, whenever I met C in the office building, I always greeted her with a smiling face. We never talked to each other. She didn't know me. I wondered where her bad opinion of me came from.

C used to work in the French division of European Department One. When she returned after working abroad for several years, she became vice president of the HO. Two middle-aged women in the French division were on good terms with C. They often got together and gossiped something. I didn't expect I had something to do with what they gossiped. They said I was ambitious, ingratiated myself with the boss, climbed my way up by treading upon others, and stole others' clients.

I didn't expect the two middle-aged women were such hypocrites. I was a junior to them. Although I had no personal or business contact with them, I showed them my respect and politely greeted them whenever I met them.

Since then, I kept a safe distance from them.

As to C, my attitude to her went to extreme. I didn't think she was a qualified superior. She didn't have to like me. But as my superior, she should be responsible for me. Why did she speak ill of me behind my back without knowing much about me? Why couldn't she point out my mistakes or criticize me to my face like a superior?

I had stubbornness in my character. I ignored C when I met her. I even avoided being in the same elevator with her. Once our department had a party. C was invited. Managers at division chief level and above were seated at the same table with C. I was arranged to sit next to her. I went to another table to sit with employees. The department head asked me to sit back with them, but I didn't listen to him. I thought C could clearly feel my resentment against her.

What C did was certainly unprofessional. She not only spoke ill of me in front of my friends, she also spread unpleasant words against me among the subcontracted local agents of the HO. Many colleagues came to ask me how I had offended C.

I couldn't put up with it any more. I went to the president's office and said, "Please tell C if she is not satisfied with me, she can point it out to me. As a superior and a Communist Party member, she shouldn't violate the rules of Party discipline and make mistakes of excessive liberties, say nothing to people to their faces but gossip behind their backs."

Interestingly, all those who disliked me, no matter how they depreciated me or slandered me, had to admit in the end that Liu Ping was undoubtedly the best in terms of work.

I did better and better in my job and often got praised by the head of the department. Someone suggested I should not be praised so frequently. Apparently, the department head took the advice. Someone said I was ambitious to expand market. Indeed I was. But I tried to restrain my ambitions and played by the rules. In fact, I never touched other departments' market except People to People Ambassador Programs and the Belgian client assigned to me. Many sales managers would rather lose their clients to rival companies than let colleagues from other departments take them over. If they were beaten by their rivals, they could find many excuses, such as that the rivals had offered much cheaper price. If other colleagues took it over and did it better, wouldn't it be losing one's own face? When egalitarianism was practiced, many people were uncomfortable if others outshone them.

Ambassador Programs was a great success. But I kept it low to avoid other people's attention and grudge.

When Li Peng, the former premier of China, was chairman of the Standing Committee of the NPC (the National People's Congress), he received a People to People delegation of senators in the Great Hall of the People. *China Daily* published the news and the photo. If it was done by the North American Department, it would be lauded as a great honor. But it was my achievement, so it was kept low. When I took the newspaper to M who was then the vice president of the company, he took a look at it and handed it back to me without saying anything. I couldn't understand it. It was a collective honor, not an honor of my own.

Although I was unhappy during the 10 years' work in the HO, I could face honor or disgrace with a peaceful mind. I never let other things affect my enthusiasm for work. No matter how some people disliked me, they could only defame me behind my back. They couldn't place the reasons why they disliked me on the table, so they couldn't stop me from advancing in my career. My continuous promotions made me the target of some people's grudge. But they could do nothing about me. My work performance was there for everyone to see.

Later it was rumored that I might be promoted vice president of the HO, which meant I would be superior of those who didn't like me. This was probably why the anonymous letter incident happened.

The French Division chief Pi and the North American Department head Hou were extremely excited about the anonymous letter. It's said Hou was attending a meeting outside and Pi specially found him and showed him the letter. Pi even faxed the letter to the general manager of the HO's Hong Kong office, which was a very abnormal behavior. Pi and Hou had little dealings with each other since they worked for different markets. But they had one thing in common. Both of them didn't like me because they thought I touched their cheese. Many years later after I left the HO, someone from the North American Department told my colleague that the anonymous letter was written by Hou. I believed it was not him. Although he didn't write the letter, it was an echo of his heart.

At that time, I thought to myself, when I had a company of my own, I would develop whatever market as I wanted, the US market, the European market and the market of the whole world. No one could stand in the way then.

Don't you fear that I would be promoted vice president? Ok, I am going to give way to you. I will leave!

I believe no matter you work for a state-owned enterprise or a private enterprise, if the system is good, the employees will be good; if the system is bad, the inherent weaknesses of human nature will be fully exposed. I made up my mind that when I had my own business, I would establish a scientific management mechanism and be a good boss.

Giving Up the Iron Rice Bowl

It's my dream that one day I could set up my own travel company with international standards. I prepared myself mentally when the negotiations of China's entry to the World Trade Organization were under way. But I had no idea when the opportunity would ripen. In 2000, I enrolled in an in-service postgraduate program on the major of Tourism Business Administration at my own expense. The in-service study expenses could be reimbursed for employees of my position. But I was not willing to use the company's money since I had made up my mind to resign.

Although I was treated unfairly, I was still loyal to the company. Loyalty was the basic work ethics for any employee. I don't know if I had the courage to resign if those things hadn't happened. I am the kind who will die for one who appreciates my worth. It was not a bad thing they treated me like that. Otherwise it would have been difficult for me to make the decision to leave.

I handed my resignation at the beginning of November of 2001 and decided to leave by the end of the year. I had my first job at the age of 15 and gave up my "iron rice bowl" of 30 years at the age of 46. It caused a big stir in the company.

At that time, the only female president retired and it was rumored again that I would be appointed her successor. Nobody believed I would resign when reaching the summit of my career. People came in an endless stream to advise me not to quit. Many of them were common employees. They said, "Don't leave. The company will be hopeless if people like you have to go."

All the leaders tried to persuade me to stay, including M who never liked me. He described the bright prospects to me and told me the joint-stock system would soon be adopted and people like me who had made special contributions would become shareholders. By the way, the joint-stock system was finally realized last year in 2009, eight years after I left, but no shares for any individual employees in the HO. Many department leaders left the HO after me, including Hou and Pi who hated me.

I worked out my last annual report conscientiously. I made a detailed analysis of each market and client and tried to lay a solid foundation, so that my successor would enter into her role soon. The annual report was perfect.

The president had a talk with me and tried to persuade me to stay. He asked me to forgive him if he did anything wrong. He asked me to stay another two years if I insisted on quitting. I knew he would be retired in two years. He advised me not to make the decision so hastily. He said he was leading some department leaders on an inspection trip in Vietnam and Cambodia and asked me to go with him and to make the final decision after I came back. I said I wouldn't go and I didn't want to feel indebted to him. And it would hurt his feelings if he still couldn't persuade me and I still insisted on resigning.

He also said it was really a good thing that I joined a non-Communist Party. He was sincere when he said it. I just joined the Jiu San Society, one of the eight non-Communist parties in China, and the society informed the HO by letter. I knew what he meant. If I were a non-Communist party member, it would be much easier to promote me. According to the policy, there should be a certain proportion of democratic personage, women and people from minority groups in the leadership. I met all of the three conditions. I was a Manchu — an ethnic minority, a female and a non-Communist party member. There were only two non-Communist party members among nearly 1,000 employees of the HO. But I was the only one of both a minority and a non-Communist party member. If I hadn't left, I might have led another kind of life. But it is not what I want.

It was not a secret that I didn't like the management system of the HO. A leader promised he would find a post for me in the joint-venture run by the HO and American Express if I stayed.

What surprised me most was the deputy director of the marketing department. She came to me and said her prejudices against me were stirred up by someone else. She was weeping when she told me this. The person she mentioned was the director of the marketing department who was extremely warm whenever he met me. He was promoted deputy general manager and then general manager of the department the same time with me. He graduated from a very famous university with a Ph.D. degree. During a long period of time, I found everyone in the marketing department keeping a distance from me except the director himself. I was not surprised at their attitude towards me. I once reported in a sales promotion report that the gifts made by the marketing department were of poor quality and it would be harmful to the corporate image. A staff member of the marketing department told me after we had traveled together for a ten-day promotion in East Europe, "You are not the kind of person as our general manager has described. He speaks ill of you and asks us to be aware of you." I was shocked. It was completely out of my expectation that he would be such a hypocrite. I thought that he was driven by his desire for power and wealth and desperately wanted to get rid of the obstacles on his way forward.

My resignation was finally approved. The president said, "You will regret." "Please let me regret," I said.

Stories Happening in 2001

Beijing won the bid for the 2008 Olympic Games; China joined the WTO; I resigned from a state-owned enterprise; I divorced; all these happened in 2001.

If the year of 2001 is a turning point in the history of China, it is also a milestone in the journey of my life.

22:08 23" July 13, 2001, this is the moment. When Mr. Juan Antonio Samaranch cast a meaningful glance at the Chinese delegation, time is frozen at this moment. "The host city of the 2008 Olympic Games is — Beijing!"

Chinese people all over the world, men and women, young and old, high and low, are shouting out in delight and excitement. Yes, this is the moment. The long-cherished dream of the Chinese people has come true! We won! We finally won!

It is the commentary of the documentary *We Won! On-the-Spot Report of Beijing's Success Bidding for the Olympic Games.*

In fact, words could hardly express what we felt at that moment.

I was working for my in-service postgraduate program in Beijing International Studies University. We were having dinner with the teacher at the Beer Garden of Ritan Hotel not far from the Tian'anmen Square, eating, drinking and waiting for the result of the IOC vote.

When Mr. Samaranch announced the result of the vote, the whole city of Beijing was seething with excitement.

Everlasting cheers rent the air like thunder. I was too excited to say a word, tears rolling down my cheeks uncontrollably. One of my class-mates was so excited that he broke a glass and blood came out of his hand. I held his hand and my tears dropped into his palm. Blood and tear mixed together, which was how I felt at that moment.

I seldom had any contact with the male classmate. But at that moment, the reserved and shy Chinese people forgot to stand on ceremony, embraced each other, shouted and jumped for joy. Beijing had a sleepless night. It seemed that all the people run to the street to celebrate the victory. Every corner of Beijing was crowded with people, waving the national flag and singing the national anthem.

We have been waiting too long for the moment.

I had never heard that any other cities in the world had such a strong reaction to the success of the biding for hosting the Olympic Games.

I asked myself a thousand times: What would it mean to me?

In 1991, Beijing became a candidate city for the 2000 Olympic Games. In September 1993, the IOC held its 101st plenary vote and Beijing lost to Sydney 43:45.

I was very sad though I didn't think Beijing would be fully prepared in 2000.

Since I worked in foreign affairs, especially in tourism, I have learnt from my experiences that Chinese people are restricted by the social system to fully display our good qualities of kindness, hospitability, diligence, wisdom and humor to the world. The world, especially the West couldn't get a clear picture of China or Chinese people due to many years of the country's isolation to the outside world. Not knowing China's past, Westerners cannot understand what dramatic changes are taking place in China. At the same time, our defects and weaknesses are exposed in every situation to the Western countries, which has aroused their prejudices against China.

I cannot tolerate the Western world's prejudices against my country. As a Chinese, I am aware that China has its own problems. But I hope our country will be treated fairly by the world. No one can be impartial in his judge unless he fully understands a country.

To let the world understand our country as early as possible, there must be a big event to display it. Nothing is better than the Olympic Games.

I was eager to let the world see the best and the most beautiful side of China. I couldn't do it, but the Olympic Games could.

On December 11, 2001, China opened the door of WTO and became its 143rd member.

I didn't know in detail what benefits China would gain after entering the WTO. But I was sure it would give me more opportunities and more space of development.

Long Yongtu, the chief negotiator for China's entry into the WTO was my alumnus in Guizhou University. He was my icon though I didn't know him personally. I was proud that my Alma Mater could produce such an outstanding talent.

I met him at the "Training Session on WTO". When I told him I graduated from Guizhou University, he immediately showed kind attention to me and asked me what job I was doing and how I came to Beijing. It was a pity that I had no chance to have further conversation with him.

China's entry into the WTO is a watershed in my life. When the negotiations were in full swing, I told myself: The day when China joins the WTO will be the day for me to resign.

In December, 2001, I handed my resignation to China's largest travel enterprise and gave up my "iron rice bowl" of 30 years.

The same year, I ended my 16-year unhappy marriage. I got married in 1984 and was never happy in my marriage life. My husband was a soldier on active service when we got married. My love for soldiers lasted from childhood to youth. I didn't marry him for love, but for the military uniform.

My husband and I virtually lived separately since our son was born in 1987. I brought up him alone.

The reason why I didn't divorce earlier was that my son was too young. I once tried to tell him that I wanted to divorce his father. Soon tears welled up from his eyes. Although he had little time together with his father, blood is thicker than water. I decided to endure the unhappy marriage until my son reached 18.

In 2001, my son was 14. One day, he suddenly said to me, "Mom, you can divorce if it makes you happy."

I felt relieved.

I have been much happier since I divorced.

Revenge by M

Although M had a successful official career, he didn't enjoy a good reputation among the employees. One of his biggest problems was being jealous of the worthy and able. If you worked under him, no matter what a good job you did, he would not appreciate you or encourage you. All he did was to upset you and oppress you and make you uncomfortable. I have been running my own business for many years. From the perspective of an employer, I think he is unwise.

My resignation in 2001 aroused a big stir in the company even in the tourist circle. I never realized I would have such an influence.

When I left, I did not take any business, except part of the business of Ambassador Programs, with me.

I always believe if a person doesn't have the ability to develop the market, he had better stay in the state-owned company where he can ensure a safe income.

One of the important reasons why I resigned was that my market development ability was restricted by the management system of the HO. Most of the people depend on large leisure groups from one or two clients, which they took with them, for a living after they left the HO. Few of them have set up a goal or established a professional and canonical private travel enterprise which has a clear market orientation and a corporate brand. They do not like to invest money, spend time or take energy for the market development. Those who are successful all treat their job as a cause, not only a means of making money or livelihood.

I met with a series of sanctions after I left the HO, many of which were schemed personally by M, who was then the vice president of the company.

I accepted the offer of the executive general manager of DB International Travel Service as a transition after I resigned by the end of 2001. My dream was to build up my own company, but the conditions for a private travel company were not ready.

In February and March of 2002, Ambassador Programs sent staff to China for inspection. One of their most important purposes was to find out if I was still qualified to cooperate with them. Although they trusted me, they were a little worried about my financial situation. They were not sure if I could survive the sanctions from my former employer. They must come to see themselves if a small private company was able to challenge a Top-500 enterprise.

I still maintained cooperative relationships with some of the local agents of the HO at their strong request. I had personally trained all those local agents who understood my way of doing business at a certain level and the service standard I required. More importantly, they were all independent enterprises, not subordinate to my former employer and not the exclusive subcontractors of it either. It was not against the law for me to work with them. I was very meticulous and consulted a friend of mine who was a lawyer for everything.

When I worked in the HO, M was mean to me. He wanted to make me suffer, but what I did was faultless and there was nothing he could do. I actually tried to respect him as a subordinate to a superior and supported his work as much as I could. But deep inside, I despised him. He knew it and was harboring a grudge against me.

My resignation was considered to be a threat to the HO. Obviously, M was no less than swallow this tone. He warned all the local agents and hotels not to cooperate with me. Otherwise he would take actions against them. In the beginning, they all promised in all sincerity and seriousness that they would pay no attention to what M said. They thought the HO was beginning to lose its predominance in the tourism industry. More and more people were leaving and it couldn't punish everyone. What they didn't expect was that M was so determined to punish me.

M's call followed me to every city I went with the clients of Ambassador Programs. Ming "ordered" all the local agents, even hotels and restaurants not to work with me. I was really flattered that M, the president of a Top-500 enterprise, would condescend to deal with me personally.

To my surprise, M obtained a detailed schedule for the inspection trip of Ambassador Programs in China. I got to know later that it was submitted by one of our guides who did not want to offend the HO so as to keep a way open for retreat in case I was crashed by M's sanction.

When we arrived in Shanghai, there was only a tour guide to receive us, not the manager of the local agent as scheduled. At midnight, the manager met me in the hotel and told me he wouldn't be able to continue with our cooperation in the future. He looked frustrated. If M was serious about his sanction, the local agents that continued to cooperate with me would lose the HO's business compared with which the volume of my business was not worth mentioning.

When I was already on the trip with my clients to different cities for inspection, I received calls from the local agents one after another and told me that they couldn't receive us. The managers of the local agents would sincerely apologize to me and at the same time express their grievances against the HO. The HO required absolute unilateral loyalty from its local agents, but the loyalty was not paid off. The HO distributed its business to a couple of local agents who were competitors to each other.

M was determined to cut off my livelihood. He warned the local agent in the next city the last moment before we arrived so that I was caught unprepared. He wanted Ambassador Programs to see that I had no way out and no local agent would cooperate with me. Actually I had to thank him for what he did to me. Half of the Ambassador Programs' business was still left in the HO. When they saw such a large state-owned enterprise was so afraid of a small individual, they were more certain of my ability and strength. The sanction was getting more and more severe and it made the inspection trip very difficult. It also got the clients frustrated. When Beijing KL Hotel called me that they were asked not to accept my reservation for the Ambassador Programs' groups, the clients looked at me sympathetically and asked me if there was any bad news. I told them the truth. They said angrily, "What they have done is not only directed against you. They are against us now." M failed to regain the clients. The HO concentrated its energy on its sanction against me instead of winning back the clients through improved quality of service. As a result, they totally lost the client.

Later the legal adviser of the HO threatened to sue me. Actually it had been the only right thing that the HO should do since I left. It was what I wished. I would readily accept the punishment if I violated the law. However, M was only good at playing petty tricks and had no courage to confront me open and aboveboard.

It has been 10 years since I left the HO. The market orientation of my company is entirely different from that of the HO. So the two enterprises are totally unrelated and lack comparability. The team of the local agents we have developed by ourselves has become the most competitive team in China's tourism industry.

The biggest beneficiary of the HO's sanction against me is China's tourism industry. We have developed a professional reception force in the main cities by ourselves. We started everything from the beginning. The force has received our training since 2002 and has developed fast under the influence of our company's management model, marketing concept, innovation and team spirit. We have produced a batch of professionals for China's tourism industry and made contributions to the improvement of the overall quality of the people engaged in tourism.

The economic reform has smashed the monopoly of the HO in China's tourism industry. Lots of employees either in the HO or in the local branches have left to build up their own business.

M has now given up fighting.

Xi's Tragic End of Life

Xi was the general manager of SH International Travel Service (referred to as SH branch hereinafter) based in SH County of B Province. The HO has branch agents in almost all capital cities or tourist cities with famous scenic spots. All the local branches were financially and administratively independent though they shared the same brand with the HO.

A branch agent was set up in SH County because a famous tomb of the Qing Dynasty was located there. There were several branches in B Province just like many other provinces, municipalities and autonomous regions in China. Before and at the beginning of the reform and opening-up, almost all the adult foreign tourists were received exclusively by the HO that had subcontract with its branches. All the travel agents were state-owned enterprises founded and financed by the government. After the reform and opening-up, travel agents were restructured and had to be responsible for their own profits and losses. Business was hard for the branches in cities that were not frequented by foreigners. At that time, all foreign tourist groups needed guide service during the entire journey and many tour guides of the branches had worked as national guides for the HO. Xi also had often worked as national guide. Later, he became general manager of SH branch that could not survive after the reform, so he moved the company to Beijing and engaged in local land service, becoming a business rival of the Beijing branch and the reception department of the HO.

I joined the HO in 1992 and had no idea of the relationship between the HO and its local branches. The HO was still competitive in the international market. The sales managers had no sense of crisis and they were assured as long as they could retain the clients on hand. Competition for market share started, but far from the white-hot situation.

Although many travel companies had been authorized by the government to deal with inbound market directly along with the progress of the reform and opening-up to the outside world, they were not known in the world market. The sales managers in the HO still had advantages and it was easy for them to get business as long as they worked a little bit harder and had a sense of responsibility. I myself was a good example. I started as a layman in tourism, but I won from a competitor without too much difficulty a Dutch client who sent 4,000 to 5,000 tourists over to China each year. After reaching the cooperative agreement with the client, I worked out a report in which I listed three candidates of SH Branch, Beijing branch and reception department of the HO that I delivered to my boss to decide which one would be the best to take care of the land service for this Dutch client.

I was still new in the HO and I did not know the tricks between the HO and its local branches. People from local branches usually neglected me because I did not have business for them. When they realized I might be a potential client for them in the near future, the general manager Xi and vice general manager Yu of SH branch suddenly became unusually warm and showered attentions upon me. Later I knew what happened. Someone tipped them off that I had new business. They wished I would give the business to them. The two managers invited me to an extravagant dinner at Beijing Hotel and I had panopea abrupta for the first time in my life.

It's understandable that SH branch was eager to get the business. But how could the HO disclose secret information to a local branch? In fact, the reason was simple. *Guanxi* (personal connections to one's benefit) was important in China and everyone had his own *guanxi*.

As general manager of SH branch, Xi had final say in the company. He was smart and knew how to please his clients and to cater to their likes. His company was small and had the advantage of flexibility. The HO gave his company a lot of business. One year in the early 1990s, his company made a profit of one million yuan and he personally was rewarded 100,000 yuan. It was a huge sum of money at that time. He was at the same time deputy director of SH Tourism Administration and was chosen a national model worker in the tourism industry. I admired him for his outstanding achievements. I had no idea of the rules of the game in the tourism industry.

When I first came to the HO, I had cooperation with SH branch, Beijing branch and the reception department of the HO. Later I found the service quality of SH branch was much better. The other two were choosy and did not like to receive individual tourists, while SH branch would receive whatever business they got, which was also why it could gain a footing in Beijing. Unable to throw off the airs as large-scale state-owned enterprises, Beijing branch and the reception department of the HO offered worse service and were difficult to cooperate with. Xi's company had to strive for a living in the narrow space between strong competitors and had a much better attitude towards work. As I had more and more contact with Xi, I knew him better as well as the hidden rules in the industry.

I found that Xi spent almost all the time after work on social engagements. Whenever I called him for business, if it was evening time, I could hear background music or noises over the phone. When I was getting familiar with him, I always asked "Are you indulging in dissipation again?" if I heard his voice mixed with the noises. On the one hand, he had to socialize for the sake of his business, on the other hand, he enjoyed this kind of life himself. He was used to spending the company's money after so many years' work in a state-owned enterprise. It was an important part of his job to entertain people from the HO by inviting them to dinner, drinking, singing and playing mah-jong. He had easy and elegant bearing and a great sense of humor. A lot of people enjoyed his company. But when it came to business matters, such as company management and quality control, he became absent-minded. He was not the kind of person who could settle down to work or study. A state-owned enterprise was the right place for him.

Xi's home was in SH County and all his family lived there. He was the only boy and also the most successful one of the family. His parents were very proud of him. He was so busy with and wild about his social activities that he had little time to go home to visit his family. I once asked him, "Does your wife have no complaint that you are always not at home?" He said his wife complained a man who cared little for his family like him should never have married.

After we knew each other for a long time, he would sometimes tell me about his innermost thoughts and feelings. One day, he told me he was upset. A married sales manager of the HO had a mistress and asked him to help them rent a house and pay the rent. I said there should be a bottom line of moral standards in one's mind and there was something one should never do.

If someone from the HO came to SH County for a holiday, Xi's company would cover all the expenses even if they got little business from that person.

Being small with simple personnel structure and low cost, the company offered competitive prices. It was actually reasonable to cooperate with them. Xi spent a lot of time and energy on public relations which were built up by money through beer and skittles. Xi was on close terms with some department heads and operation managers of the HO. He was a tight-mouthed person, so they didn't have to worry about their secrets being let out. Therefore, Xi benefited a lot from this virtue of his.

Beijing branch and the reception department of the HO only liked to receive groups but not individual tourists. My principle was those who cared about my individual tourists would get my groups, which I thought was a fair deal. To make sure my individual tourists would be taken seriously by the Beijing branch, I had specially invited chief of the Individual Tourist Division for dinner to curry his favor, which is unbelievable now.

The problem of individual tourists was solved since I started to work with Xi's company.

Many tourist groups of mine needed to go to cities like Xi'an or Luoyang by train. The number of soft sleepers was limited. Neither the HO reception department nor Beijing branch could guarantee the train tickets. But this was not a problem for Xi's company because they had a special *guanxi* in the railway.

Xi and his team maintained their relationship with the HO with the greatest care so as not to offend anyone and lose business. Some sales managers took advantage of his mentality and used his company as the base to gain personal benefits.

People schemed against each other for power and wealth in the HO and it was impossible for Xi to please all. If he was on good terms with one side, he might offend its opposite side. Sometimes he was like a mouse in the bellows that had to be bullied by both sides and didn't know whom to turn to.

However, I always believed that the state-owned company was the best choice for him who had been spoiled by the big-iron-bowl system. His father was secretary of the Party Committee of SH County and was a veteran revolutionary. Xi lived in comfort since childhood. During the Cultural Revolution, when we children of ordinary families went to the countryside to be peasants or to factories and mines to be workers, he became a PLA soldier who was admired by everyone and was recommended to the People's Liberation Army Foreign Languages Institute to study English. In the small city, he was the child of a high-ranking official, envied by all and was the Prince Charming in every girl's mind. His father paved a broad and smooth road for his career. Joining the army, going to college, being a guide, becoming the general manager of the local branch and at the same time the deputy director of the local tourism administration, step by step, he never suffered any hardship or experienced any setback due to his favorable background. When he came to Beijing, he had to depend on himself and lost the advantage he used to have in the small county. He suffered from discrimination and unfair treatment everywhere. It was easy for him to lose his mental balance. One day, he told me he had left SH branch. A state-owned international travel company in Beijing advertised for a general manager. He applied for it and got the offer.

It was JT International Travel Service subordinate to a ministry. It suffered losses due to poor management and was in need of a talented manager.

I was worried for Xi. I thought he was not mentally prepared for such a challenge. The reason why the travel company hired him was they wished he could help them put an end to deficits. But, was he able to help them turn the tide? When he was in SH branch, he entirely depended on the business from the HO and only did the land service. He had not developed any inbound market by himself. It was a time-consuming and tiring job to develop market. Leading a life of ease and comfort, he wouldn't bear the trouble to do it. JT International Travel Service had no cooperation with the HO, so Xi wouldn't be able to get business from the HO as before. Although he was full of confidence, I didn't think he would succeed. For a long time, the HO had cornered the inbound market. Although competition emerged, the HO still gained the upper hand. We Chinese say that "A starved camel is bigger than a horse". SH branch could survive depending on the business from the

HO. If Xi left SH branch, his future would be unpredictable.

As I expected, Xi didn't mention JT International Travel Service for a long time. After a period of time, he told me that he accepted the offer of another travel service called Q subordinate to some bureau under the government. His purpose was to change the company into a share-holding company and to be one of the shareholders.

I was then the executive general manager of DB International Travel Service which was also subordinate to a ministry. I subcontracted some business to Xi and my company was the only client that provided them with inbound business.

I didn't understand how Xi managed his company. There was always some problem with his cash flow. We prepaid him. But he tore down the east wall to repair the west wall — always in straitened circumstances. The restaurants and coach companies who were suppliers of Xi could never get paid timely. Xi's reputation was going from bad to worse.

I was worried about Xi. I knew our cooperation would come to an end sooner or later. Actually, we didn't need a local agent in Beijing and we could handle our business by ourselves. I wanted to prepare him for it, so I told him that we were going to do the land service in Beijing by ourselves when time was mature. He was obviously worried about it. If his company lost our business, it would be hard for them to sustain. Besides our business, Xi did some domestic tours with very limited profit.

I felt somewhat guilty. When I worked in the HO, I gave a lot of business to Xi. We had a lot of contact on business and we were friends. He was the one that the anonymous letter referred to as my "bed partner". At a meeting when all the department managers were present, the president of the HO asked me to end my cooperation with SH branch. Although I was in a sad plight myself, I still stuck to my principle. I said, "It is unfair to Xi's company. Why should his company suffer due to the anonymous letter against me? Does it mean you believe what is said in the letter? I would accept it if it is your decision. But

I have two questions. Who is going to handle the individual tourists? How can we guarantee train tickets for my groups?" Divorced from the masses and reality, the president knew nothing about the detail of group operation. After listening to my reasons, he decided the groups that needed train tickets and the individual tourists would still be given to Xi's company. Other groups would be handled by the reception department of the HO. Xi suffered losses because of me, so I wanted to help him when he was in the early stage of starting his own business.

In 2003, when I had been doing my own business for one year and two months, China was hit by SARS. Beijing was the most severely hit area. Inbound travel groups were cancelled. All the travel companies sank into a desperate predicament. I decided to find another office with less expensive rent. Xi together with one of his friends bought an office on mortgage loan. In order to save cost, I asked Xi if he could let us use his office for free and he could still have our business after SARS as return. He readily agreed. When we went to his office for an inspection, we found he already had his office divided into several cubes and rent it out.

We found a new office. We ended the cooperation with Xi's company after SARS. When I made the decision, I immediately felt relieved as if a burden weighing heavily on my mind was lifted.

As a business partner of many years and a friend, I still cared about Xi and often asked him how he was doing. Once, he told me he was doing business. A steelworks in SH County produced steel doors and windows and asked him to help find buyers. He said he would soon earn 200,000 yuan as commission. I felt happy for him.

His plan to change Q Travel Service into a share-holding company had no progress. He said he was going to give it up and he had already contacted another travel company.

Many travel companies existed only in name. Being state-owned enterprises, few of them went bankrupt. The doorsill of the travel industry was too high for common individuals to cross over and it was very difficult to set up a private travel company. Many travel companies leased their licenses to individuals and profited from the rent.

After I left the HO, I ran my own business under DB Travel Service. My purpose was also to reform it into a shareholding company. But I failed to reach agreement with its higher level authority and had to give it up one year later.

I was looking for a new company when Xi was going to give up Q Travel Service. I shared with Xi the same financial adviser who suggested that I discuss with Xi and take over Q. I had business and was in a more advantageous position.

Unexpectedly, Xi firmly disagreed with it. He said he wanted to cooperate with me to restructure Q and both of us should be its shareholders. I said, "I cannot possibly work under your leadership. We have totally different ideas on management and our ways of doing business are also different. The shares you want to hold are not proportionate with the possible contributions you are going to make. As time goes on, we will clash with one another and won't be able to run the company well together. Since you are going to give it up, why don't you let me take it over?"

Xi finally agreed to introduce me to Q and gave up the idea of running it together with me.

I did not realize how difficult it would be to cooperate with a company belonging to the government for the share-holding reform if I did not have any *guanxi*. Xi left Q and my cooperation with Q was miscarried for the reasons that are difficult for any Westerners to understand.

Xi and I had less contact with each other since we ceased cooperation. I still gave him a call from time to time, but it was hard to find him. Inbound travel and domestic travel hadn't recovered yet when SARS was just gone. I wondered what he was up to all day long. Once he told me that it was too troublesome to work with a state-owned company for share-holding reform, so he decided to set up a private domestic travel company with the help of his *guanxi* and turn the domestic travel company to an international one later. In China, a domestic travel company is only allowed to handle domestic tourists traveling in China. But it would be easier to set up a private domestic travel company that could be upgraded to an international one later.

One day in March 2004, the sad news came. Xi Died.

Having failed in tourism, Xi turned to some other business. He was doing business with a married couple from Beijing. One day, they went to Tianjin, a neighbor city of Beijing, for business and had a lot of drinking. On their way back to Beijing, Xi drove while intoxicated and dashed into a truck parking by the roadside. Xi and the wife of the couple died on the spot.

His dead body was placed in the undertaker's for a long time. His family had doubts about the accident. According to Xi's wife, some witness said it was the wife of the couple who drove the car. They had paused to ask the direction before the car accident. The husband, the only survivor, made a phone call and soon his friend came from Tianjin to the scene before the police. Xi's wife suspected that they exchanged the seats of the two victims after the accident happened. The police carried out an investigation, but didn't find any evidence.

After Xi's death, his wife found he was in heavy debts which was a huge burden for a family. She received phone calls to press for payment of debt every day from both individuals and companies. Nobody knew if there was anyone who owed him money.

It was not until after his death that I knew he had just left another travel service and was about to set up a domestic travel company of his own. He had worked for the government for his whole life but happened to die during the few days when he didn't belong to any work unit. In China, if you work for a state-owned enterprise, your enterprise will take care of your funeral after you die. Xi didn't belong to any enterprise and his family had to take care of the funeral and cover the expense.

When Xi worked in SH branch, many people of the HO gained

personal benefits from him. Now he was dead, his old friends should at least do something for his family to help them overcome the difficulty. I called everyone who I knew was supposed to be on good terms with Xi and said we should donate some money to help his family.

About 80,000 yuan was collected. Some people made the donation out of their own will, and others did it out of their respect for me. Those who took most from Xi not only did nothing, but intentionally avoided it. Xi's death made me realize the snobbish way of the world. One of his acquaintances said, "Xi had made only one true friend in his life and it is Liu Ping."

I took some of my employees to attend his funeral. The funeral was prepared by his family. His cousin delivered the memorial speech which said Xi died at the age of 50. Actually he was only 47 that year. If he had still been the general manager of SH branch, his funeral would have been ceremonious.

Tears were running down my cheeks when I looked at unrecognizable Xi lying in the coffin. His face became deformed due to being frozen for too long and there was a big crescent-shaped wound on his left face. The heavy makeup failed to cover the shocking wound. He was dressed in a plain jacket which seemed to be forcedly put on his stiff body. He had a great love for brand name clothes and always followed the fashion and trend. If he knew he departed the world in such an image, his soul wouldn't be in peace.

I was worried about his family after Xi passed away. I didn't know his wife well. When I called her to extend my greetings, she mentioned the heavy debt incurred to the family after her husband's death. There was more grudge than sorrow in her tone. I was in sympathy with her. How could she face the future? I said if she needed it, my legal counsel could provide her with legal advice for free. Less than a year later, I heard she was remarried and led a happy life.

The page of Xi has been turned over.

A Private Company — Xin Xin Yi Xiang Was Born

Guakao is a Chinese phrase which is difficult to find a corresponding English translation. It sometimes translates to "affiliating operation" which, I am afraid, is not complete and accurate. *Guakao,* which consists of two Chinese characters *gua* and *kao,* is quite Chinese characteristic. *Gua* means "hang" and *kao* means "lean" or "rely on".

In China, it used to be very difficult to get the license of travel companies and there were no private tourist enterprises. Before the economic reform, there were only three travel companies, China Travel Service, China International Travel Service and China Youth Travel Service, with strict division of responsibility and separately received overseas Chinese including compatriots from Hong Kong, Macao and Taiwan, foreign adults and foreign students. In the early 1990s, suddenly a lot of travel companies, subordinate to different ministries or bureaus at ministry level, emerged. These travel companies were funded and managed by the government when they were founded. The managers of the companies, who knew nothing about tourism, were appointed by the government. It was not a surprise that almost all this kind of companies lost money. The government still tried to help them with some money for the first couple of years, but felt that it was an endless hole that could never be filled up. Without financial help from the government, most of the travel companies subordinate to the ministries could hardly survive. But they have licenses that they can lease to those individuals who have business but not licenses. The practice of the individual who rent the license and operate his tourist groups under the name of the company is called "*guakao*". What the individual has to do is to pay the fee for *guakao*. Whether he would lose or earn money is none of the business of the travel company.

Guakao, though illegal, is a very common practice in China. If one only seeks money instead of long-term development, the most economical way is to find a travel company for *guakao*. Some large-and-middle-scale travel companies in China survive by leasing their licenses. A well-known travel company in Beijing has more than 100 individuals for *guakao*. If it is 100 and each of them pays at least 20,000 yuan a year for *guakao*, there would be a net income of two million a year. Actually the average *guakao* fee is more than 20,000 yuan. It is difficult for the travel company to have control over its *guakao* individuals. In most cases, the travel company just receives *guakao* fees without playing any role in the management of the *guakao* individuals. One can run his own business in the name of the travel company if he pays for *guakao*. If anything goes wrong with the individuals, the travel company would be the one to be sued and it will deal with the individuals afterwards. Some big travel companies have specialized staff responsible for the lawsuit aroused by *guakao*. Even if there is a risk, the practice of *guakao* is still popular. These travel companies have no source of business. Although *guakao* might bring them trouble, it is a source of easy income for them.

I have been against *guakao* though it is probably the best choice for most of my former colleagues who left the HO before or after me. I had worked under two travel companies since I left the HO. The two travel companies will be referred to as company A and company B hereinafter. Both of the two companies were affiliated to ministries. My ultimate goal of joining them was to transform them into share-holding companies or to purchase them. I joined company A in the form of *guakao* on condition that it should not accept any other individual for *guakao*. I didn't want to share the license with other individuals who might not observe law and discipline and ruin my reputation. The *guakao* fee that I paid for company A was 100,000 yuan a year. Both of the travel companies were dying when I joined them.

I met with a lot of obstacles in running my business under company A. I was the executive general manager. The general manager was a government official from the ministry. He was a kind person, but a layman. The vice general manager was a former colleague of mine. He left before me and was offered the post of vice general manager of company A. I signed a one-year contract with the company. One year later, I left with my team.

There were two main reasons why I decided to leave.

First, there was virtually no hope of turning company A into a share-holding company. Company A had no source of business and almost all the business was brought by me. I worked out a proposal for share-holding corporation reform in which I suggested individuals take 51 percent shares.

The deputy director of the department of the ministry who was in charge of the administrative management of company A, after reading my proposal, said, "How can a state-owned enterprise of the government let individuals become the majority shareholders and take a controlling stake? Don't even think about it."

I said calmly, "Many travel companies in Jiangsu, Zhejiang and other provinces have been transformed into share-holding companies. Individual holding is not something new. If travel company A disagrees to carry out the reform, we can part on good terms. Besides, my one-year contract is about to expire."

I felt my words had some effect on him. It might be out of his expectation how fast the travel companies in Jiangsu, Zhejiang and other coastal areas were changing into share-holding companies. The deputy director did not know tourism either. The pace of reform and opening-up in tourism industry was contrarily slower in the capital city of Beijing. It was then hard for the deputy director to give up the state-owned enterprise partly to some individuals, although the individuals could save the company at its last gasp.

The second reason was that the vice general manager and I shared no common principles. He brought with him the incorrect practice and would from time to time do something that filled me with apprehension. Although we used to be colleagues in the HO, we were not in the same department and I knew nothing about him. Many of my former colleagues did not understand that how I could make him a business partner and alleged that we would soon part company since we had totally different ways.

I said to him before the expiration of my contract, "I am afraid I cannot work with you. We might be still friends if we separate or we might be enemies if we continue with our cooperation. Either you or I have to leave."

"I agree with you. I stay and you should leave."

The entire team especially the core operation managers joined the company because of me. If I left, the company would lose the entire team.

We still became enemies after we separated. The vice general manager played many dirty tricks behind my back to slander me and my team.

Then Xi introduced me to the general manger of travel company B who could hardly keep the business going and was looking for a buyer desperately. This was what I wanted—a company of my own with a couple of partners in the same camp. We reached an agreement. Before the purchase of property right, I held the post of the executive general manager of company B in charge of its management. No other *guakao* was accepted.

Later a laughable thing happened. A middle-aged woman came to my office and said in an aggressive manner that she was the vice general manager of company B but she knew nothing about the change. I came to know in our conversation that she had already reached a *guakao* agreement with company B at the cost of 20,000 yuan a year and was entitled vice general manager. The agreement was torn up unilaterally by the general manager of company B since now I was in charge of its management. Obviously she was not a professional in tourism. She said she was hoodwinked by company B. She said she had already developed 10 individuals for sub-*guakao* and each of them had paid her 20,000 yuan. I think now the readers understand what she meant. The minimum *guakao* fee was 20,000 yuan a year. She paid company B 20,000 yuan for *guakao* and she subcontracted with 10 individuals and charged 20,000 yuan each. She could easily earn 180,000 yuan a year without having to do anything else.

The license of a state-owned enterprise could be abused by individuals like that, but the company couldn't be purchased by entrepreneurs like me in accordance with the rules of the market economy.

The general manager of company B knew nothing about tourism. Leaders of state-owned enterprises were all appointed by the higher ups.

I signed a letter of intent with company B and we reached preliminary agreement on the price of acquisition. I paid 50,000 yuan as deposit required by the ministry. I had to pay the general manager as well as to buy insurance for his former employees who were laymen in the tourism industry. The general manager asked me for money from time to time which he said was used to persuade the leaders in the ministry to sell the company to me as soon as possible. I paid him all in cash and did not ask him for receipt because he didn't want others to know about it. Later, agreed by the ministry, he borrowed 150,000 yuan from me in the name of company B which he said would be deducted from the acquisition expense according to the agreement. It was said that the money was spent on the placement of his original employees. According to the letter of intent on acquisition, I was not responsible for the placement of his employees and the placement allowance was included in the acquisition expense. But the general manager deleted it for the sake of his own interest. All the employees of company B were not professionals in the tourism industry. If I accepted them, they would be a permanent pain for the enterprise and it would be no different from the state-owned company.

Due to someone's firm opposition to the state-owned assets falling into the hands of individuals, I did not make the purchase in the end.

Someone named Wu of the ministry questioned why company B should be sold to an individual. Wu said that he could take it over and make it profitable. The ministry dared not sell the state-owned enterprise to an individual if someone of the ministry promised that he could save the company. The ministry let Wu take over the company which still exists today, living on leasing licenses to individuals for *guakao*. The 150,000 yuan Company B borrowed from me has never been returned like a stone dropped into the sea. The general manager had instigated me to sue the competent authority of company B before he resigned. He wanted to sell the company to me and earn some money. His plan was miscarried by Wu's intervention. So he wanted me to make some troubles for the ministry who approved the agreement to borrow money from me. I didn't do it because I didn't want to enter a lawsuit against the government.

As the reform and opening-up pushed forward, individuals could also set up travel companies. Finally I set up a share-holding private company in July 2005 at a much smaller cost than turning a travel company into a share-holding one or purchasing one.

Fortunately, I failed in my cooperation with the two travel companies. If I had succeeded turning travel company A into a share-holding company, I would have had to give away 49 percent of the profits to state-owned shareholders who made no contribution to the company. I would have met with a lot of unexpected difficulties if I had acquired company B. I prefer to run my own business like today lawfully and pay taxes as required.

Companies A and B still depend on others' *guakao* and are struggling to get by.

I have learnt from my experience that it was almost impossible for an individual to try to turn a state-owned enterprise into a share-holding company or to purchase it if he had no strong *guanxi* even if the enterprise was hopeless. But it was easy for those who had no ability but a strong background. Someone from Inner Mongolia with very strong *guanxi* purchased a state-owned travel company in Beijing. He had no ability to run it and invited me to his company to be vice president, which would mean that I did the business and he shared the profit just because he had the license but I didn't.

In fact, natural person was already allowed to build up travel companies then, though difficult. The reason why I couldn't make up my mind to set up a company was that I was worried people like M would abuse his power to make things difficult for me. Many people suggested that I should register my company under someone else's name. I didn't take their advice because I thought it would lead to a lot of trouble in the future.

I made four attempts in total, all ended in failure. I finally decided to set up a travel company in the name of several natural persons.

I handed my application and materials to the department concerned, including a perfect feasibility study report.

My feasibility study report was very convincing because we met all the requirements for setting up a travel company. China was still in its transitional period from a planned economy to a market economy; one was bound to meet with some obstacles to set up a private enterprise.

I had experienced a difficult period of time of three and a half years before I finally set up my own company. I cannot tell you the whole story because of some reasons.

On July 25, 2005, Xin Xin Yi Xiang Travel Service (欣欣翼翔) officially came into being. The name of the company Xin Xin Yi Xiang (hereinafter referred to as Xiang) consists of three names of my niece and two shareholders, which means flying to the prosperous future. The logo of the company is the Chinese character 翔（Xiang） which means so much more than a mere trade mark. 翔 means flying and it is a juxtaposition of the characters 羊（sheep）and 羽（feather）. To me, this is a perfect metaphor: China's policy of reform and opening-up gave a pair of wings and freedom of entrepreneurship to me, who was born in the Year of the Sheep. 翔 also means by pronunciation "good luck" that, I wish, will accompany my team and its families forever.

The English name of the company is China Star Ltd. I will not use the English name in this book to avoid commercialization.

My resignation at the end of 2001 was considered a loss to the state-owned enterprise. Several years later, our company has become a pioneer in the meeting and incentive travel industry in China and has established itself in the world as an industry representative of China. We have made contributions to the development of our country's high-end tourism.

Although *guakao* is still common in our country, there are some people who have successfully built up professional travel companies doing meetings, incentives, luxury and special tour programs and have laid the base for further tourist market segmentation. We have seen hope in the sound development of China's travel companies.

Now it has become much easier to set up travel companies. Let the fittest survive. China's travel companies will catch up with the advanced world level in the near future.

Collisions Between East and West

On July 13, 2001, Juan Antonio Samaranch announced that Beijing would host the 2008 Olympic Games. Seven years later, the 29th Olympic Games was held in Beijing on August 8, 2008. During the seven years, China witnessed its rapid economic development and changes in people's lives and mentality.

When I was on a business trip in London and Frankfurt in April

2008, one of the important things I did every day was to watch the CNN and BBC news coverage on the Olympic torch relay. I saw many scenes my fellow countrymen couldn't see. I was shocked and disturbed at the Western media's one-sided coverage and the fact that Westerners knew so little about the history and present conditions of China. When I saw blond Westerners and their children in the anti-China forces, I felt as if a heavy burden were weighing on my mind. I wished I could carry a five-star red flag and run after the Olympic torch, shouting encouragement and cheering for China and the Beijing Olympic Games. At the same time, I thought our government should reflect on why the Western countries had such prejudices and misunderstanding against our country.

I went to London to attend the European Annual Conference of MPI (Meeting Professionals International). There was an open space session at the meeting which was new to me. I could learn something new every time and this was why I developed an intense interest in attending international conferences of the industry. The open space session was a plenary session and there were about 500 participants. I was the only Chinese.

There was a platform in the middle of the venue. Anyone who wished to discuss some topic could go up onto the platform to raise the topic. There were 10 topics and each topic would be written on a piece of paper and put up on the wall. Participants could join the discussion groups they were interested in.

I walked to the platform and put forward my topic of discussion "How to make the Western world understand China better". I had hardly finished my sentence when I heard a burst of laughter. It was when the Tibet issue aroused a big stir and the Olympic torch relay met with resistance.

My topic attracted the most attention.

To tell the truth, I never expected the Western image of China would be so bad. As the argument got more and more heated, I felt many Western colleagues rose against me. All of a sudden, I even felt lonely and helpless. Several times I had to refrain myself so that tears wouldn't come to my eyes. They probably forgot I was a Chinese and argued with me in a frank and straightforward way that most Chinese were not used to.

The remarks of two Europeans were even filled with "hostility".

The focus of the discussion was the disturbance created by the Tibet secessionist forces during the Olympic torch relay.

"Tibet is an inseparable part of the People's Republic of China. This is my point of view, no matter you accept it or not. Today we have no time to discuss about the history of China. Have you ever considered no matter what we do, we should never hurt the feelings of the people? It's true that not all the decisions made by the Chinese government might be supported by the people. But the majority of the Chinese people support the Olympic Games. And Chinese people and the Chinese government share highly unified stand in the issue of Tibetan separatists' sabotage of the Olympic torch relay. The Tibetan separatists hurt the feelings of the Chinese people even if their purpose was to air their grievances against the government. Why should we hurt the feelings of the majority of the people?"

A Nordic said, "The Chinese government should not beat and crack down the minority groups."

I knew he was referring to the March 14th Incident in Lhasa.

I avoided talking about it directly. There was no time to explain it to a foreigner in a one-hour discussion session.

"Do you know how many ethnic groups are there in China? There are 56. I come from a minority group myself, the Manchu ethnic group. There are Manchu people, Miao people, Dong people and Han people in my family. Do you know that Han people are envious of those who come from minority groups or even wish they were minority members? Because people of minority groups enjoy a lot of favorable policies and can have more than one child and college entrance examination candidates can get extra marks. My son got 10 extra marks. I am proud to be a member of a minority group."

I knew my answer was superficial. I just wanted to convey some information which was general knowledge to the Chinese people while new to Westerners.

Speaking of the Olympic Games, I said China would overcome all obstacles and host a very successful Olympic Games. Then I added immediately, "The most successful Olympic Games."

"The most successful Olympic Games? How can you be so sure?" It was a question from a Dutch. I sensed doubt and sarcasm in his tone.

"Because I know my country well."

When our discussion was drawing to a close, I found the discussion of many other groups already came to an end and many participants of other groups joined us.

I received the most thunderous applause in my life. Some people said they respected me for my patriotic passion. Someone even said I was her idol.

The session chair praised me for my performance. I said I couldn't fully express myself within a short period of time due to the language limit. She said that I had made my point of views clear enough and the language was not a problem.

We didn't go deep in our discussion.

The experience made me realize that I had much to learn to speak at the international stage. I think one should have the following qualities to make oneself heard at the international stage.

Have the ability to speak English and be good at it;

Have profound knowledge in politics and history;

Understand the thinking and attitude of Westerners and speak in a way that can be accepted by them; and

Listen to different voices in a peaceful state of mind.

I was interviewed by CIM magazine of Germany.

Question:

In the Open Space Session at MPI's major European conference in London you discussed passionately with colleagues about the Western image of China. Why did you do this and what did you learn?

Answer:

I have heard too many negative comments about China this time when I have been traveling in Europe. I felt so bad when I saw what happened with the global Olympic Torch Relay worldwide and the spirit of Olympics was mixed up with political issues. I was surprised to realize how much the Western world misunderstand China. China is not perfect and neither is the Chinese government. However, who can say that their systems and their governments are perfect? The media coverage in Europe and North America is too much one-sided. I want the Western world to understand China better. I would like to invite as many people as possible to come and see China on their own. At the MPI conference, someone said that the Dalai Lama was her role model. I do not think that she is wrong to have her own belief. But I really ask myself how much Westerners know the history of China and what we can do to make the Western world understand China better.

I have been struggling very hard to run my own travel company which can serve as carrier for me to change the image of China. As a Chinese, I feel that it is my mission and responsibility to tell Western people the real situation in China though I am not powerful enough as an individual.

Things in China are complicated for Westerners. We have different political systems and histories. I don't expect all Westerners to like China. I just hope they don't have prejudices against our country.

Take the Olympic Games as an example. In 2001, the whole nation was united to celebrate the success in bidding for the Olympic Games, holding high the national flag and singing aloud the national anthem. It is true.

During the 2008 Olympic Games, some people expressed their discontent and complaint with the government for the inconvenience caused by some policies such as the traffic control, restrictions on movement of population and public security measures. They once were in the parade holding high the national flag and singing aloud the national anthem. It is true.

We were proud of being Chinese when the whole world was watching the extraordinary opening ceremony of the 2008 Olympic Games. Our eyes were brimming with tears when we gazed at the national flag rising slowly in the Olympic venues. It is true.

Some of us raised doubts if it was worthwhile to spend the money of taxpayers on such a grand and magnificent Olympic Games while there were still many impoverished and backward areas in our country. It is true.

One may on the one hand fully support the Beijing Olympic Games; while on the other hand has different opinions of it. It is true.

Personally speaking, I am proud of the Beijing Olympic Games. I went to Europe on a business trip not long after the Olympic Games. For the first time I felt I was so confident and unafraid. No matter what people in the world think of China, the Beijing Olympic Games would surely arouse Westerners' curiosity about her and make them eager to walk close to her and to understand her. It is absolutely true.

From Asian Games to Olympic Games

I wrote the following short article during the Beijing Olympic Games in 2008.

"The biggest honor in my life was that I personally got an opportunity to work for the Beijing Olympic Games.

Prior to the Olympic Games, the biggest sports event held in Beijing was the 11th Asian Games.

The 11th Asian Games was held in Beijing between September 22 and October 7, 1990. It was the first international sports competition held in China and the first Asian Games hosted by China since it came into being 40 years ago.

There were 18 years between the two sports events. During the 18 years, there was a tremendous change in my life.

All I can remember about the Asian Games are miserable experiences except the mascot panda and the theme song *The Spirit of Asia*.

Eighteen years ago, I had no Beijing *hukou*, no house and no money, and was struggling with hard life.

Eighteen years has passed.

Eighteen years later, I have Beijing *hukou*. I have a company of my own. I have an apartment house of my own. I have a car of my own and a credit card of my own.

Eighteen years later, my son became a university student.

Eighteen years later, I travel around the world in first-class or business class cabin.

Eighteen years later, the Olympic Games is held in Beijing and my company has the honor to provide service to the important international clients of the Olympic Games.

Eighteen years later, I am running for the board of directors of an international industry association.

For 18 years, I have witnessed the changes China has experienced thanks to the reform and opening-up.

When Beijing won the bid for the Olympic Games in 2001, I didn't expect a private enterprise could serve for the Olympic Games. But the truth is we have gained the opportunity to provide service for about 4,500 international guests coming for the games.

China's reform and opening-up has provided to a certain extend equal opportunities for private enterprises and state-owned enterprises. I always say, "I have benefited a great deal from the reform and opening-up."

Facing the Test of Crisis During Beijing Olympic Games

On August 9, 2008, two American tourists were attacked in Beijing. One was killed and the other was injured. The tour guide was also injured. The assailant committed suicide by jumping from the Drum Tower and died instantly.

The two American tourists came to Beijing to watch the Olympic Games through a Canadian company who was our business partner.

At noontime of August 9, our tour guide Duan Rong accompanied three tourists Todd Bachman (victim), Barbara Bachman (victim's wife) and Elisabeth Bachman Mccutcheon (victim's daughter) to the Drum Tower, a famous tourist scene in Beijing .

When they climbed to the top of the tower and stood on the terrace, suddenly a man took out a dagger and stabbed at the daughter Elizabeth but missed it. Duan Rong called out for help. The assailant turned to her and stabbed her in the right chest. Then he continued with his attack against the couple. Duan Rong immediately called 110 and 120 and reported it to the company. The company soon called the police and reported it to the higher competent authority of travel companies.

I also called Liu Yanxiang, president of the company and asked him to hurry to the scene. He was on business in Hilton Hotel which was relatively nearer to the scene.

Chen Qu, the operation manager who was responsible for the tour programs of the American guests burst into loud sobs. We did our best to comfort her. All the employees were exhausted in the preparation before and the reception during the Olympic Games. Our company received about 4,500 guests from the United States, Canada, South American and European countries during the Olympic Games including many celebrities, athletes and internationally well-known companies. The young employees born in the 1980s were the backbone of the company. They each were responsible for different clients and worked overtime every day. There was hardly time for sleep sometimes. Everyone was stressed by the responsibility. It was all out of our expectation that such an accident would happen when the Olympic Games just began.

I said, "What is the use of crying now? Since it happened, we have to deal with it. I would hold it up if the sky collapsed."

I was not talking big. Certainly I knew how serious the matter was and how grave the consequences would be if our company was at fault. All our employees were young. They were frightened and they needed comfort and backing.

Chinese President Hu Jingtao and US President George Walker Bush all showed their concern over the accident.

The deceased Mr. Todd Bachman was the father-in-law of the coach of the American men's volleyball team.

The police came to our company that afternoon for an investigation. As the legal person and CEO of the company, it was my obligation to cooperate with the police and relevant authorities in the investigation.

Most of the policemen treated us with respect and asked questions politely not in an interrogating tone of voice. But there were still few of them whose attitude and way of work were quite unacceptable.

Chen Qu and I were questioned in separate rooms. I was calm during the whole investigation. We provided whatever material they asked for. I believed that the rigorous management of the company could bear the test at this critical moment.

I was particularly fond of a policeman who was the team leader. We were all touched and relieved by what he said before he left. He said, "It seems that your company has nothing to do with the accident."

August 13 Beijing News:

According to Wang Zhihua (deputy director general of National Tourism Administration), it has been verified the American tourists' being attacked in Beijing is an isolated and accidental criminal case which has no immediate connection with tourism organizations or the Beijing Olympic Games.

Although it was extremely busy in the company, the whole team of the company management was involved in dealing with the problems arising from the accident.

Duan Rong displayed bravery and calmness when faced with danger. As Chen Qu who answered her phone call at that time told us, she was steady and calm and gave a very clear account of the accident. We had a great admiration for her.

We arranged Duan Rong in the best ward of the hospital. The company took care of all the extra expenses which were not covered by the insurance. Her parents were sincere and honest people. They demanded nothing from the company. We felt sorry for the young girl and cared for her as much as her parents did.

I called a meeting after the accident. I said, "You may have resentment and think the company leaders are fastidious when we are strict with you. But now you should understand the company actually has benefited a lot from the strict management which has enabled us to stand the test of the accident."

Everyone nodded his agreement.

After the accident, the incumbent authorities of travel companies repeatedly asked us if Duan Rong had received training from the company.

In fact, since April of 2008, our company held many training sessions on anti-terrorism and matters needing attention during the Olympic Games. We attended all the trainings and meetings hosted and organized by Beijing Tourism Administration and we reiterated and emphasized the main ideas of the trainings and meetings at our own training sessions or company meetings.

The last training of the company was held on August 6. No one expected three days later a case would happen which startled the whole world.

Although what Duan Rong did was what a professional tour guide was required to do, no one dared say he could do as well as Duan Rong when in the same situation.

When Duan Rong was hospitalized, the leaders of the National Tourism Administration and Beijing Tourism Administration went to visit her and praised her for her outstanding performance.

The victim's wife and daughter called Duan Rong when they left Beijing and expressed their gratitude to her for what she had done for them in the dangerous situation. The conversation went on in sobbing and those who were present were all moved to tears.

The American Ambassador to China also visited Duan Rong in the hospital.

We often discussed what lessons we could draw from the August 9 accident. Although we had no fault, we had fear after it. If the tour guide lacked a sense of responsibility or was lazy and asked the guests to climb the Drum Tower by themselves and she was waiting downstairs like some of the irresponsible guides did, there would have been no one to call the police and ambulance and the rescue of Mrs. Barbara Bachman would have been delayed. If the tour guide was not there calling for help, the murderer wouldn't have been deterred and would have hurt more people. Then our company would have had a grave responsibility. I was by no means deliberately exaggerating so as to create a sensation.

We set a good example for our partners all over the country in the following aspects.

Firstly, we have signed work contract with both official and freelance tour guides.

Secondly, we have bought accident insurance for tour guides.

Thirdly, we have carried out trainings for tour guides.

Although the above are basic requirements for travel companies, not all do them.

There is another thing I'd like to mention that we must remind the tour guide not to desert his post or leave his group alone during sight-seeing.

When Todd Bachman's family went to law against the Canadian company, there was a question about whether the tour guide was on the scene when Mr. Todd Bachman was attacked. the true story was that our tour guide was also injured, but she called 110 and 120 without any delay. Otherwise, the life of Mrs. Barbara Bachman would have been in danger because of a delay in her rescue.

Peter V. Ueberroth, president of the US Olympic Committee and I are good friends. We talked about the accident many times and he gave me much comfort during those tough days. He asked me to send his regards and his heartfelt thanks to Duan Rong.

Someone said our company had too bad luck. I didn't think so. If it happened to some travel company that didn't strictly observe law and discipline like us, the consequences would have been much worse. Fortunately, what we did in dealing with the emergency didn't bring disgrace to our country. We are Angels, so God entrusts us with the most difficult task.

When my younger brother who was far away in Guizhou heard about the accident, he called all his friends and said, "My sister is in big trouble this time and her company may have to compensate a lot of money. I may have to borrow money from you." None of his friends hesitated and all got the money ready to support me. One friend even decided to put off his plan to buy a house to help me.

God will not make things difficult for good people. Our company and tour guide Duan Rong got commended by governments of all levels for our outstanding performance in dealing with the emergency.

Duan Rong was a freelance tour guide before the accident happened. After the accident, she was accepted as a regular employee of our company. By the way, she became a mother of a baby girl in July 2010.

Wish her health, peace and happiness!

Chapter Six

Stories of Common Chinese

I ended the previous chapter in the year of 2008 when we celebrated the 30th anniversary of Economic Reform and Opening-up.

In this chapter, I will lead the readers travel back and forth from the old days to today to see the difference in the life and ideology of me and the people around me.

The stories are about common Chinese people. Many of them will find the reflection of their own life in the stories.

Years Short of Supplies

One day in my childhood, two bachelors used our stove and wok to cook shredded pork with spicy green peppers. My younger brother and I were standing beside the stove drooling. They left a tiny portion of the dish in the wok for us. The delicious flavor still lingers in my memory today.

In those years, almost all the goods and materials related to people's livelihood were supplied based on ration coupons—grain, clothes, cigarettes, cooking oil, salt, soaps, matches, and thread, etc. We never had enough to eat and always felt a lack of grease in the stomach.

Everyone was rationed only half a *jin* (1 *jin* equals 0.5 kilograms) cooking oil every month. People had to economize with the oil when cooking. If one used a little more for a meal, he might end up having no cooking oil for half a month.

Most of the cooking oil supplied was roughly processed colza oil which sent out a strong vegetable smell and a lot of fumes when cooked. We were used to colza oil since we had every meal cooked with it and we liked it.

The following story happened when I was a child. I can still remember it with vividness and anguish.

There was a grain shop near our house that purchased farm produce such as grain and colza oil from peasants. One day, an old man was passing in front of our door carrying two jars of colza oil on a shoulder pole. It was raining. The old man tumbled on the slippery ground and broke the two jars. The oil spilt all over the ground and flew into the bumps and hollows. The old man picked up a piece of the broken jar and scooped the oil mixed with mud into the bottom of the jar. I was looking on nervously. What a big disaster to have spilt two full jars of colza oil! Although I was a small child, I felt terribly sorry for the waste. I was sympathetic with the old man too. The two jars of colza oil belonged to the commune and the old man had to compensate for it with many work points.

Our neighbor had three boys who were all big eaters. Every month when the family ran out of colza oil, the mother would shout, "Xiao Er (the second son), we are out of oil." Xiao Er would take up a clean cotton ball which was used in the factory to wipe machine and run out. The mother would place the wok on the stove. In a few minutes, Xiao Er would run back, dash into the kitchen and wring the cotton ball. Then a stream of colza oil would flow into the wok. It turned out that the place he ran to was the grain shop near his home. He quickly dipped the cotton ball into the oil barrel when the salesperson took no notice of him and ran back home.

There was a small state-run restaurant in the Yang Water Valley where we lived. Sometimes when we were too greedy, my father would ask me or my brother to buy a portion or two portions of pork meat from the small restaurant. My mother would cook a large pot of vegetable with the meat and the whole family would sit around the oven and enjoy the delicious meal. How could the meat be so delicious at that time! I remember a portion of meat cost 60 cents. The waitress was the mother of one of my classmates. Whenever she saw me, she would put the ladle deep into the basin and scoop a full ladle of meat into my bowl and then add a ladle of gravy. If the classmate's mother was not on duty, I wouldn't be so lucky.

The meat vendors at that time were regarded as the most powerful people who were flattered by everyone. The female meat vendor in the phosphate mine was an illiterate woman named Cai. Everyone curried favor with her and she enjoyed high prestige in the small valley for more than 20 years. Whenever we met her, we would greet her warmly with smile on our face. Everyone called her Mother Cai. She was always wearing a cold expression as if treating all alike without discrimination.

With the power of meat selling, Cai became a celebrity of the mine. We often saw her walking arm-in-arm with the wife of head of the mine in the street, talking and laughing happily and ignoring others' greeting.

When food supply was in great shortage, people could only buy foodstuff during limited period of time. The place where Cai worked was called Vegetable Company (today's grocery). Whenever meat was available, people would run back home to get the meat coupon and money and rush to the Vegetable Company to queue for the meat. My middle school teacher named Chen Zhong fainted when queuing to buy meat due to standing for too long.

Cai cut and weighed the meat slowly without even lifting her eyelids. Everyone wanted good parts of the meat. If it happened to be the pig's neck, one had to accept the bad luck without complaint. Everyone curried favor with Cai in the hope of getting a good piece of meat.

When my mother was making lard, we small children would stand around the stove and stare at the fat meat in the wok. When oil was extracted, we would share the delicious cracklings. Sometimes we couldn't wait and picked up a crisp bit that still contained oil in it and put it into mouth. How delicious it was! The lard was stored in a jar for cooking.

When I was a teenage girl, I had the hardest times. For teenage girls, there were some necessary articles for daily use, such as soap, toothpaste, shampoo and straw paper. The country was poor and everything was supplied in limited quantities. Toilet paper was a luxury. People used old newspapers or leaflets. Only women used a kind of yellow straw paper which was made of wheat stalk during the period. It had a rough surface and wheat straw could be clearly seen. There was a supply and marketing cooperative near my home. It was the only place one could buy straw paper. When the straw paper came, a long queue would form up in front of the counter, all women.

The shop often ran out of toothpaste, soap and shampoo powder, sometimes for several months. Many children simply didn't brush their teeth. I used tooth powder or salt to brush my teeth and my gum often bled. There was no shampoo and we used soap or washing powder to wash our hair. When soap and washing powder were not available, we would decoct the fruit of honey locust we bought from the peasants and used the water to wash hair.

Sometimes the Vegetable Company had salted pork or salted fish on sale. Once in a summer, the salted fish was not sold out and went bad. They piled the salted fish in the open space to dry. Many flies were attracted and the smell was terrible. They decided to throw them away. A friend and I went to pick some salted fish every day. At first I was reluctant because I thought the fish was too dirty. My friend said, "*yi shui wei jing*" which meant that any dirty stuff could be cleaned with water. Later I motivated other friends to pick the fish and also said to them "*yi shui wei jing*" if they disliked the smell and dirty fish.

Another thing I can remember clearly is buying tofu. I had to get up very early before dawn to go to the tofu shop in a valley called Big Water Ditch. There was always a long queue. If I got there late, there would be no tofu left. If I got there too early, the tofu was not ready yet and I would watch the master making tofu. I always bought jellied tofu. A large bowl for one coupon and was enough for one meal of the whole family. I had to walk several miles' rugged mountain road holding a basin of jellied tofu in my hands. We also had tofu dregs which could be bought by money without coupon. Tofu dregs were usually used to feed pigs in the countryside.

Food supply shortage lasted long, from the 1950s to the 1980s.

In the 1970s, I studied in Guizhou University and my father attended classes in Guizhou Party School which was near our campus. The meals offered in the Party School were relatively better. On the weekend, father would buy some meat dishes, put them in an aluminum lunch-box and brought it to me. We would collect some dry branches, make an outdoor fire near the dormitory building, heat the dishes and take them to the dormitory to share with my classmates.

In the early 1980s, I accompanied an American and a British man on an inspection trip to Kaiyang Phosphate Mine. When we arrived there, we were surrounded by people who had never seen a foreigner before. I was envied by everyone because I was the first to bring foreign guests from Western countries to the mine.

Another translator accompanied the foreign guests for lunch with the leaders of the mine. I returned home to have lunch with my parents. My mother went to the Vegetable Company to buy meat. When Cai saw my mother, she lavished her praise for me such as I would have a bright future, and cut the best part of meat especially for me and handed it to my mother.

During the early days of the reform and opening-up, commodities such as desk clock, watch and white and black TV set began to appear in shops. The coupons for such commodities were limited. Every work unit was allotted only one or two coupons for each quarter and one didn't know in advance what commodity the coupon was for. Those who were capable of finding coupons by *guanxi* were admired by everyone. It was then considered important for a family to prepare three major items for the children's marriage. They were watch, bicycle and sewing machine. Those who were getting married would try every means to get the coupons for the three items. The family who prepared the three-major-items for their son or daughter's wedding would be considered well-off and fashionable.

Things are different now. People can buy whatever they want to buy or whatever they want to eat as long as they can afford it. I have become virtually a vegetarian and seldom eat meat. The cooking oil I use now is expensive imported olive oil. Even if I live in comfort now, I still rack my brains to lose weight.

Cai enjoyed prestige for many years. Later when people could buy meat as much as they wanted from the free market, nobody paid attention to her or greeted her when meeting her in the street. I heard she was rather frustrated for a period of time.

Housing in China

On July 15 of 1955, I was born in a small house in the pyrite mine in Benxi County of Liaoning Province in northeast China, and one year later my first brother was born. My parents were employees of the mine and the mine allotted a house to each family. Our family of four members had lived in the small house which had no kitchen and toilet for two years till August 1957. I returned to the place where I was born for the first time during the Chinese New Year of 1994. I was quite surprised to find the house, which was as shabby as the houses in slum, was still there and was occupied.

The house was about 30 square meters. It was divided by a wall into two parts. The outer space of 10 square meters was used as kitchen and the inner space of 20 square meters was the living room. A *kang* was built in the living room which was the bed for the whole family. The public toilet was far away and it was a miserable thing to go to the toilet in winter.

My parents were recruited from the countryside and they were content with the shabby house.

In 1957, my parents were transferred to Jinping Phosphate Mine in Lianyungang City of Jiangsu Province. The mine allotted a house to my parents which was about 30 square meters and had the same layout as our house in Benxi.

Recently, my cousin who lives in Lianyungang sent me a photo of our old house there. Half a century has passed and our old neighbors still live there. I cannot imagine how they manage to live in such an ill-conditioned house for 50 years.

In 1958, my parents were transferred to Kaiyang Phosphate Mine of Guizhou Province in southwest China. The construction of the mine was not finished yet and there was no residence for the employees. We lived in the thatched shed of a local villager's home. Thatched houses can still be found in the remote mountains in Guizhou Province.

With the development of the mine, we moved from the thatched house to a tile-roofed house and from the tile-roofed house to an apartment building. When we lived in the thatched house, the toilet was a pit dug in the ground fenced with corn stalks. The manure was collected and spread in the field. Many households lived in rows of tile-roofed houses and used the public toilet and the outdoor tap water.

Between 1963 and 1973 before I went to college, my family lived in an apartment of 50 square meters on the second floor of No. 13 Apartment Building. The inner room was smaller and was the bedroom of my parents. Two bunk beds were placed in the outer room for me and my two brothers and a sister. I always slept on the upper bed.

The apartment at that time was all simply-constructed with a small kitchen and a toilet. We burnt coal for cooking and the kitchen was always dusty with coal ash. Domestic water was always in shortage and was still supplied in limited quantities and for a limited time when I left home in 1979. Due to the inadequate pressure, there was even less water for the households living above the second floor. When I came back home during holidays, I always carried a large tub of dirty clothes to find a place with water to do the laundry. The Yang Water River was not far from my home and I always went there to clean the mop. I had to go between home and the river several times before I could clean the floor. I mopped the floor several times a day and often cleaned the mop in the Yang Water River at middle night. The river water used to be crystal-clear. With the development of the mine and the increase in population, industrial and domestic sewage was poured into the Yang Water River. I also fetched the contaminated water in bucket to clean the toilet. There was always a terrible smell in the small and dirty toilet for lack of water. I never dreamed that one day I could use a spacious, bright and clean bathroom with a bathtub and a shower with fragrance.

My sister and I left Guizhou separately. My parents had lived in the apartment for 30 years before they moved to Beijing to stay with me. When we went home to visit our parents, we still slept on the bunk bed.

From the founding of the People's Republic of China to the beginning of the 1980s, welfare-oriented public housing distribution system was adopted in cities and towns. That is to say the house was provided for free by the work unit you worked with; no matter you were a worker, an intellectual or an army man. This planned housing distribution system caused a heavy fiscal burden on the government.

For people from Western countries where education, medical

care and housing are social welfare or money-making practices, it is difficult to understand. Government organizations, enterprises or public institutions were a complex comprising production, residence, hospitals, schools, kindergartens and shops, etc.

Single employees lived in dormitories. Only married couple who worked in the same work unit were qualified for the housing distribution. Normally there were not enough houses, so houses were distributed among employees by seniority of position, length of service, age and family members based on *hukou*. Many young people got married hurriedly for a house instead of love.

If a couple didn't work in the same place, under most circumstances it would be the husband who was allotted the house. One of my father's subordinates and her husband lived separately in different places. She still lived in the dormitory after she had a child. It was cold and humid in the winter and there was no heating. There was no paper nappy at that time. All the diaper was made of old clothes or towel and it took several days to dry them. When there was no dry diaper, she would put the wet diaper around her waist to dry it.

The dormitory had no kitchen and the unmarried employees ate in the public canteen or cooked themselves in the dormitory with small kerosene stoves.

Housing distribution and corruption were always related. People with *guanxi* would have priority in getting houses.

I lived in the dormitory since I was transferred to Hebei from Guizhou in 1979. I had no house of my own when I got married in 1984. My roommates moved out one after another and I made my home in the dormitory.

Since there was no housing shortage in the place where I worked, I should have been allotted an apartment. According to the state policy, those who had worked for long years or had late marriage and late childbirth or whose spouse was a soldier in active service should precede others in housing distribution. I met all the requirements. I started my first job when I was 15, earlier than most people. I got married at the age of 28 and gave birth to my son at the age of 32, all very late at that time. My husband was a soldier in active service.

There was a Property Division in most work units and the division chief usually had power and influence because everybody had to fawn on him or her.

It has been a difficult thing for me to flatter. Since there were state rules and regulations concerning housing distribution, we should act according to them. If I bribed the leader, I would not only be ashamed of myself, I would feel embarrassed for the leader too. I would feel ill at ease whenever I had to ask the leader a favor. I had to hesitate for a long time before I plucked up my courage to knock at the door.

The chief of the Property Division was a retired military officer who pulled a long face all day long. Everyone greeted him with a broad smile.

New single employees were coming and the division chief asked me to move out of the dormitory. I asked him where I should live. He said I could share a dormitory with other single employees. My husband was in service and returned home every weekend. If I shared a room with others, my husband would have no place to live when he returned.

The quarters for the single were on the fourth floor of the office building and the first three floors were offices. I found that a public toilet on the third floor was made a storehouse and a lot of broken furniture was piled there. I asked the division chief if he could allot the toilet to me to live with my husband. He said no. Although I felt embarrassed, I refused to move out of the dormitory. I lived in the dormitory during my pregnancy.

When I was 34, I was temporarily transferred to work in the H Ministry. At first, I lived in a dormitory with my son. Then we moved into a 20-square-meter room in a shabby tube-shaped apartment. The toilet and the kitchen were shared by many households. The living environment was dirty and messy and nobody was willing to clean the public toilet or the kitchen. Since I moved there, I did all the sanitation work and kept the environment as clean as I could. I did it so that I could endure living there. Cockroaches ran rampant in the apartment building. There was a crevice in the wall in my room. One day, the wall paint came off and a swarm of cockroaches fled out of the crevice in all directions, the sight of which raised goose bumps on my skin. Once I invited two friends to my home for dinner. I stewed pork ribs in the pressure cooker. When I put the cooker on the table and was about to open it, I was scared by some cockroaches as small as ants that crept out from the gap in the handle. I blushed and felt much embarrassed.

When I was transferred to the HO, I didn't dare to raise the house request for fear it would affect my being accepted by my new work place.

The tube-shaped apartment building where I lived belonged to the H Ministry. Half of the householders no longer worked in the ministry, but they still lived there. This was also a kind of Chinese characteristics. It was difficult to get a house, it was also difficult to move out the residents who had changed jobs and worked for different work units. Several of my neighbors had changed their jobs and no longer worked for the Ministry for several years or even a dozen of years, but they still occupied the houses belonging to the Ministry. No one pressed them to move out because they had special *guanxi*.

The chief of the Property Division in the H Ministry was a middle-aged woman. I didn't know her. Since I was transferred out to the HO, she always sent someone to force me to move out and even threaten to break the lock and throw my things out. I didn't understand why she was so mean to me. Later someone pointed it out that I should send gifts to her.

I thought it was embarrassing to send gifts. If someone gave me gifts in order to ask me to do something for him, I would feel insulted. But still I sent gifts to the Property Division chief. It was the first time I saw her personally. Maybe my gift was too small and it didn't work.

I didn't intend to occupy the house for long. I just needed a transition before I could put forward the housing problem to my new employer after

I made some achievements. I was driven from pillar to post by the female chief and I had no alternative but to force myself to talk with my leader at the HO to allow me to live in the dormitory.

The HO had plenty of houses, but the houses were never enough to be distributed among the employees. A lot of officials had more than one suite and their offspring didn't have to worry about houses. Those who were on good terms with the leaders had an advantage in getting houses or big and good houses regardless of their seniority.

For some reason, the leader didn't consent to my living in the dormitory but allotted me a nine-square-meter house in a compound like slum. No kitchen, no toilet, no heating. There was only one water tap in the courtyard shared by many households. It was unbearably dirty and disorderly. When I looked around the courtyard, I got a nasty shock. I didn't know how I could manage to live in such an environment with my four-year-old son. Although my former living conditions were not good, they were not that bad.

Since many Beijingers live in the compound, I should have nothing to complain. But I was not a Beijinger and had no relative there. I had to work at least 12 hours every day. I had no time or energy to bring up my son in such bad living conditions without help. I had no choice but to send my son again to his grandma in Hebei.

I didn't accept the house. The previous occupant was a boiler worker of the company. He told me he had a terribly hard time when he was living there and advised me not to accept it.

It was strange. The company had spare houses at that time, but just didn't want to give me one. The leaders were at odds because of different opinions on housing distribution and we became the victims of their conflict.

I was a new comer and made no contribution to the company which could prove my value. I found it difficult to bring up the matter of my house problem. Besides, the leaders in charge of housing distribution would take full advantage of their power and wouldn't let you get the house easily. I was only an office worker, and it was beyond my ability to establish private relationship with leaders after work.

The Property Division chief of the H Ministry forced me to move out every day and threatened to throw my things out. I had no choice but to constantly plead with the deputy president of the HO who was in charge of logistics. Several times I failed to suppress my sadness and shed tears in front of him. Finally I got a new apartment which was about 40 square meters in floor space.

Later I became a backbone of the company and the money I earned for the company was enough to buy many houses. Although I hadn't worked there long, I created more economic benefits than those who had worked in the company all their lives. I didn't move out of the small apartment until my son went to high school. I hired an *ayi* to help me look after my son and do the housework. There was only one bedroom, so I had to find a place for the *ayi* in the corridor. My son still shared a bed with me when he was a teenage boy.

Due to my hard work and outstanding ability, I soon distinguished myself in the company. I won the leader's recognition and got promoted continuously, so I was qualified for an apartment of over 100 square meters. However, seniority was more important. I made great contributions to the company, but I hadn't worked there for long. There were many people in front of me queuing up for bigger houses. Moreover, the squeaky wheel gets the grease. Working in a state-owned enterprise, if you didn't ask for it yourself, you would be forgotten. The company allotted another 40-square-meter apartment to me at my request. I had two apartments, each of 40 square meters. Although I didn't get what I should have at my position, I was content.

During the time of the housing reform, I purchased the two apartments at 60,000 yuan. I had my first job at the age of 15 and had worked for 30 years by that time. Seniority was money. I didn't understand the housing reform in detail. I only had to pay that much money for my two apartments after my and my husband's seniority was converted into money.

I was then head of a department. The housing standard for department general managers was 130 to 160 square meters. When others were busy about getting bigger houses, I buried myself in my work and knew nothing about it.

Some colleague told me the news and added that there were 10 apartments left while only the houses of three department managers were below the housing standard.

I was then a professional backbone and general manager of the department. I went to the leader, "Is there any possibility I could get a new apartment?" "No." Many retired cadres were in the waiting list and the 10 apartments were all occupied. The leader also asked me, "What were you busy with earlier?"

What was I busy with earlier? I was busy with my work! Otherwise I wouldn't have caught up from behind and made all the contributions to the company.

Since the leader said there was no possibility, I simply gave up the idea entirely. I felt somewhat relieved instead. If there was hope, I had to talk with this or that leader. I was not good at that.

When I made up my mind to leave the state-owned enterprise and to set up my own company in 2001, I bought an apartment of 138 square meters on loan. I thought I should depend on myself instead of the government to improve my living conditions. I purchased the apartment at the age of 46 with the repayment period of 15 years. When I moved in the new apartment, I thought I would live in it the rest of my life.

I resigned from a large state-owned enterprise, gave up my iron rice bowl and promotion opportunity and purchased an apartment on loan. I wondered where I got the courage.

I lived with my son and my parents in the comfortable apartment. I was very happy. I would never have had the courage to purchase a house on loan if there hadn't been the reform and opening-up. I had confidence in my future, so I made the bold decision. I feel my life has been prolonged for 20 years because of the reform and opening-up. Many of my old classmates in high school retired at early age and most of my university classmates are retired too. I am still working energetically to develop my own business. I believe I have a bright future. I am still young in the industry in which I am engaged.

My parents were worried about me. People of their generation would never borrow money to buy a house. Every morning when they woke up, the first thing that came into their mind was their daughter was in heavy debts. They found it hard to accept. Since then, I report only the good news while concealing the bad from them.

Half of the employees in my company bought houses on loan and the other half of unmarried employees rent houses. The company provided them with rent allowance or paid the rent for them. I had my two small apartments renovated and provided them as free accommodation to the employees, their families or college student interns. I hoped they didn't have to experience the mental burden of having no place to live that I had experienced.

Up to 2007, I earned enough to buy another apartment of the same size in the same building. I gave my previous apartment on the second floor to my parents and moved to the new apartment on the seventh floor with my son. My parents were happy to have an apartment to their own. They could invite their friends and relatives to home as they pleased without having to worry that it would bother me. I was happy that I could provide my parents with spacious and comfortable living conditions in their later years.

I am proud that I have improved the quality of life for myself and my family through my own efforts.

I always say that I have benefited a lot from the reform and opening-up which enables me to earn more through hard work. But it would never happen when egalitarianism, with everyone "eating from the same big pot", was practiced.

Stories of Zheng Han and Xin Xin

Zheng Han is my son and Xin Xin, whose name is part of the company name, is my niece. Their stories are a reflection of the status quo of students in China.

When my son was in primary school, one day, he said to me, "Mom, why don't you send me to America? Children there are very happy because they don't have to study." I wondered where he heard of that.

Chinese children have to work very hard. They have a short childhood which ends as soon as they finish primary school.

During those years, I overworked myself to change my destiny and to improve the life for my son and for the whole family. I had no choice and could rely on my husband for nothing. I had no time to take care of my son. Zheng Han was too fond of playing games since he was a child and had no interest in study. My heart was torn with anxiety. I often wept through anger for his poor performance in study. I even spanked him when he didn't do his homework and lied to me. Sometimes I hit him too hard that my fingers got swollen. My heart ached. I tried to look on the bright side of things, but the pressure kept coming from the school and the society. I was always scolded by the teachers because of my son's poor school record.

Spanking didn't work either. Once I was so angry and didn't know what I was going to do with my son; I ran away from home and left my son with the *ayi*. I stayed over at my sister's home.

Zheng Han called up my sister, weeping, "Small Aunt, is mom at your home?" My heart was bleeding. I wanted my son to have a happy childhood and have enough time to play. But it was impossible in China because of the examination-oriented education.

Once, my son told me, "I want to be adopted by Bill Gates." "Me, too." I said.

In fact, what I really cared was not his grades but his attitude towards study. If he had worked hard but still couldn't do well in his study, I would feel sad but I wouldn't have blamed him. What I dreaded most was to attend the parents' meeting. From primary school to his first year in senior high school, I never heard any word of praise from his teachers. I felt I was a guilty mother in front of the teachers.

Our neighbor's son was of the same age as Zheng Han. I often saw the mother helping her son with his study, playing with him and going with him to learn the musical instrument or to the tutoring center. I had no time to spend with my son. I was in an agony of guilt.

When I went abroad on a business trip, I asked a colleague to come to help Zheng Han with his English lessons. During the dictation, Zheng Han copied the words on the newspaper beforehand and put the newspaper under his exercise book. He glanced stealthily at the newspaper from time to time. My colleague found it out and took away the newspaper. Zheng Han then copied the words on his arm and was detected again. The colleague just graduated from college and was familiar with the little tricks. "I have played the tricks before. Don't you try to fool me! Since you have time for the tricks, why don't you take the time to memorize words?"

Zheng Han promised to my face that he would study hard, but hid a comic book between his English textbook. I took time to record his English lessons before I went to see a client and asked him to read after the tape recorder. But he forgot about his promise and began to play as soon as I turned away. My younger brother stayed at my home when he came to Beijing on business and saw what happened between my son and me. He said to Zheng Han, "Your mother is too pathetic." My son hated my brother because he reported to me when I was home.

I worked hard at school, but Zheng Han didn't take after me. I was grieved whenever I thought about it.

Zheng Han had a bright and cheerful personality. He was a happy boy always with a sunny smile on his face. But as soon as you mentioned study, his eyes would be brimming with tears. To study seemed like to suffer torments in the purgatory to him. I was so worried that I took him to see a psychiatrist. After having a conversation with Zheng Han, the psychiatrist made the following conclusion: Zheng Han is perfectly mentally healthy, even healthier than most of the children and have a brighter future than those bookworms who study mechanically and do well in study.

How can a person have a promising future if he has received little education?

"Since he is mentally healthy, why does he hate study so much?" I asked the psychiatrist.

"When he grows up and becomes more mature, he will realize the importance of study and take it as his responsibility and something he must do even if he doesn't like it."

I asked how long I had to wait. The psychiatrist said it depended and she was not sure. I thought I must have done too many evil things in my previous existence and have owed Zheng Han too much that I have to pay him back this life.

The most horrible thing was that Zheng Han failed in his senior high school entrance examination. The high school of Zheng Han was a private boarding school, which decided to give Zheng Han a chance and allow him to finish the first year on probation.

Zheng Han didn't work hard and always came last in his academic performance. The more he hated study, the more he lagged behind; the more he lagged behind, the more he hated study.

Zheng Han had no confidence in himself either. He felt he would fail the college entrance examination. One day he told me he wanted to go to an art vocational school after graduating from high school.

I flew into a rage as soon as I heard it, "What special talent do you have to be admitted by an art school?"

I felt terribly sorry when I said something like that. It was my fault that he had no exceptional talent. All the parents in cities paid attention to the development of their children's special talent. But I failed to do it.

After Zheng Han went to senior high school, I got him a home tutor. He was tutored at home every weekend in mathematics, physics, chemistry, English, almost every subject.

I spent a lot of money on his private boarding school fees and home tutoring. I took care of all the costs myself. I was proud that I had the ability to bring up my son on my own. What made me sad was that I couldn't get him to work harder.

Why is life so unfair to me? I don't have great ambitions for my child. But I hope Zheng Han will receive higher education and have the ability to change his fate through knowledge.

What happened later proved that life was not unfair to me, I just needed more patience.

Things took a favorable turn when Zheng Han was in second year.

Miracle happened. Zheng Han suddenly changed to another person in the second half of the year in senior high school. He studied hard, respected teachers and cared for classmates. He was generous and warmhearted and was elected class monitor. Physically, he grew into a big boy 1.84 meters high. What happened on Zheng Han made me believe there were miracles in the world. His teachers kept exclaiming, "Zheng Han is a miracle! Zheng Han is a miracle."

The college entrance examination was only one and a half years away. Although he had made remarkable progress, it was still difficult for him to pass the college entrance examination. I was mentally prepared for it. Since his attitude towards study changed for the better, the result was not that important.

The admission rate of private high schools was low. Being a newly-established school, the school hoped more students could be admitted by colleges and universities to create a more favorable condition for future enrollment. His teachers all had high expectations on him.

For the first time since primary school, Zheng Han wished I could go to attend the parents' meeting because I could finally hear words of praise from his teachers.

The home tutors also looked forward to his success.

I was mentally prepared for Zheng Han's failure in college entrance examination and planned to let him repeat the last year of high school. Although he came to realize the importance of study, he fell too far behind and there was not enough time for him to make up the missed lessons.

I was under no pressure before and during the national college entrance examination. Zheng Han was also in a peaceful state of mind. I went to work as usual during the two days of the examination. I didn't call him up to ask about the result. I didn't want to make him nervous. National college entrance examination is a matter of prime importance in China. Everything has to give way to it during the days of the examination. The parents are even more nervous than the examinees. Many parents escort their children to the place of examination and wait outside. I think it virtually adds to the pressure of the examinees.

I failed to fulfill my responsibility to my son; at least I could give him a good mood when he was taking the examination.

Zheng Han checked his score on the internet before 8:00 on the morning of June 23, 2006. He got 502! His total score was 512 including the extra 10 marks for minority groups. He was admitted to the Department of Communication of Capital University of Economics and Business, one of Beijing's key universities.

502 was a score not worth mentioning for excellent students. But to Zheng Han, it was a miracle. He was made an example and was often invited back to his school to pass on his successful experience to the students in lower grades. His home tutors also had a rise in their reputation because they sent a backward student to college.

College life in China is very easy and different from that in other countries. In China it is difficult to get into college, but easy to graduate from it. Zheng Han had four years easy time in the university and obtained his bachelor's degree without much difficulty. He just graduated in the summer of 2010 and got a job in the newspaper of *Beijing News*. He loves his job and his colleagues and works very hard.

Now my heart aches for my niece Xin Xin.

Xin Xin is completely different from Zheng Han.

Xin Xin is a highly self-disciplined student. She doesn't need to be pushed to study. On the contrary, her parents always urge her to take a rest. She is now a sophomore in Beijing No. 5 High School.

Xin Xin suffered an ordeal in the summer of 2010. As one of the best students in the school, she failed in the senior high school entrance examination and didn't reach the scores for the schools she was supposed to enter easily. What made her feel more miserable was that a couple of her classmates who had been much far behind her in study did a better job in the exam and were recruited by her target school. In China, the entrance exams for middle schools and high schools are as important as that for universities. Three years of extremely hard work in the junior high school is a preparation for the entrance into a good senior high school which means that a good university is guaranteed. Xin Xin cried her heart out. Her teachers were as sad as she was and were so worried about her. We, the whole family, our friends, and even my employees, all tried to comfort her, but we all knew this kind of pain was too much for a girl of 15 in China where examinations decide everything.

I always encourage Xin Xin to join some social activities and do something for the community, but it is so difficult for her who has to do homework everyday till very late at night, otherwise she cannot finish it.

Beijing No. 5 High School is also one of the key high schools in Beijing. Xin Xin does a good job in the new school and studies even harder. Seeing that Xin Xin is under such a heavy burden at such a young age, I always hope time would pass more quickly so that Xin Xin could go to college for an easier life and have fun as a young girl.

Xin Xin gets up at six every day and leaves home at seven. The class begins at eight and there are nine classes a day. There is no time to relax except the physical exercise class of 45 minutes. She returns home at six in the afternoon, hurriedly finishes her supper and starts to do homework at seven, then goes to bed at 11. She can only sleep six or seven hours every day.

Xin Xin's school bag is as heavy as 10 kilos.

Weekends are not easy for Xin Xin either. She has to take two hours' physics class and three hours' mathematics class in a tutoring center outside school every Saturday. Despite repeated injunctions from the Ministry of Education, tutoring classes after school never cease to exist. The teachers also encourage their students to take extra classes on the weekend. On Sunday morning, Xin Xin has to learn English with a foreign tutor for two hours.

Xin Xin has to take tests almost every day and the students are ranked according to their grades. There is also a test at the end of each month and classes will be ranked too. The teacher will have extra bonus if his class ranks the first three places in the monthly examination. If the class always lags behind, the teacher would be fired or demoted to lower grades. The teacher who teaches Xin Xin Chinese is their fourth teacher.

Teachers are under greater pressure than students. Even the students are sympathetic with their teachers.

Places in the examination have become the only criterion for the students' academic performance and the teachers' work ability. It is the result of China's examination-oriented education system. The examination-oriented system is widely criticized in the country, but it is a problem that cannot be solved in a short period of time. For parents in China, the only hope of their children's future is a good university.

Xin Xin respects and likes her teachers very much. She thinks the teachers care so much about the students' places in the examination not for the bonus but for a sense of accomplishment. They hope their students will have a promising future. Xin Xin's Chinese teacher is already

70 years old. The old teacher would weep if Xin Xin's class doesn't do well in the Chinese examination. Xin Xin's mother often receives short messages from Teacher Huang who is in charge of Xin Xin's class. Teacher Huang often encourages the students and their parents in short messages which fully express his care and love for the students.

Xin Xin does very well in the new school and often comes first or second in the examination. I once asked Xin Xin if her classmate who got the last place felt painful. She said the first place was as painful as the last place because one is likely to feel desolate if he is outstanding. Seeing that children in China have to bear such enormous mental pressure at such a young age, I really feel sorry for them.

Xin Xin has two and half years' more difficult senior high school life ahead of her. For a 15-year-old girl, study is her whole life. Xin Xin has displayed special talent in dancing and drawing since she was little. But she gave up the hobbies since she started high school.

According to the educational guideline, students should develop in an all-round way — morally, intellectually and physically. But now most schools concentrate on the intellectual development of their students.

I never stopped learning. I always feel the education I have received is far from enough. It has been my dream to pursue my study to doctor's degree; however it will not possibly come true. I first placed my hope on my son Zheng Han, but he had no interest in pursuing his studies after obtaining his first degree. Then I placed my hope on my niece Xin Xin. But Xin Xin has decided she would not continue her studies after she has obtained her Master's degree. Chinese children are too tired from studying.

Some of her classmates have gone to study in America. When they chatted online, the classmate said, "America is the paradise for students."

It is paradise because the students have time to play and have no heavy burden.

I told Xin Xin that Chinese students could easily become top students when they studied abroad because they had laid a solid foundation. I also told her she would experience it herself if she had opportunity to study abroad in the future. The educational system in China has its strengths and weaknesses.

I hope Xin Xin can study abroad for her postgraduate programs and see the outside world.

It has been Xin Xin's dream to be a movie star and she wants to be admitted by a film academy. Art schools are popular in China. Every year, there are hundreds of thousands of examinees, but only a small number of them will be admitted. I said to Xin Xin, "What you should do now is study hard and get admitted to a university. Even if you failed to go to a film academy, you could still realize your dream. Earn money to invest in your movie and be the director or play the leading role yourself."

I hope Xin Xin will grow up healthily and happily. It is not important what university she attends. My university lies in the underdeveloped Yunnan-Guizhou Plateau and lags behind those good universities, but it did not prevent me from becoming a successful person.

From Country Boy to Industry Leader

This chapter is about changes of times. It has been 44 years since the Cultural Revolution began. Real changes happened in China after 1978 when the reform and opening-up was carried out.

My colleague Yanxiang was born in 1977 and grew up with China's reform and opening-up. His story is a typical example of the stories of people of his generation.

Yanxiang is impressively handsome with easy and elegant bearing and is nicknamed "China's Tom Cruise" by our Western clients. However, no one would imagine he was brought up in destitute circumstances.

Yanxiang's hometown was Beidianzi Village in Jilin City of Jilin

Province in northeast China. The village had a population of about 1,000 and most of the villagers made a living by growing vegetables. Yanxiang was the only child in the family, which was rare in rural areas at that time.

Yanxiang's mother suffered from congenital heart disease. The family was poor and couldn't afford the operation, so his mother missed the best time for treatment. His mother should not have had childbirth under her physical conditions. He took his mother to all the big hospitals in Beijing after he earned money. All the doctors said it was a miracle that his mother gave birth to him safe and sound. They admonished Yanxiang to treat his mother with filial piety.

Yanxiang's mother was in poor health, so his father had to do almost all the work, growing crops, feeding pigs, grazing cattle and doing some odd jobs to provide just enough for the family to eat and wear.

When Yanxiang was six years old, the old house was too dilapidated to live in, so the family decided to build a new house. It then took 3,000 yuan to build a new house in rural areas in the northeast. But all the family had was 400 yuan. The family had many relatives in the village. They borrowed from different relatives to make up the sum. The house was built but the family was in heavy debts.

When Yanxiang was five in preschool class, he had to walk two kilometers to get to the school. Simple dormitories were provided to students for the noon break. Students had to pay five yuan for the bed. Yanxiang was always in arrears with the noon break fee. The teacher often scolded him or ridiculed him. One day the teacher asked him to go back home if he still couldn't pay the money. Without saying a word, Yanxiang went back to his dormitory, collected his bedroll, put it under his arm and went home.

When our fathers talk about the hard times, they often start with "before liberation (before New China was founded in 1949), while people of my generation would say "in the 1950s" or "in the 1960s". The story of Yanxiang happened in the 1980s, not far from today.

Since Yanxiang told me the story, the picture of a small child walking on the country road carrying a bedroll under his arm would always come to my mind.

Yanxiang was a bright child. He got admitted by the best high school in Jilin City.

Yanxiang felt he was not treated equally as his classmates who came from well-off families in the city. Once he had a fight with a classmate. It was obviously the classmate's fault, but the teacher was partial to the wrongdoer because his family was wealthy and influential. Yanxiang got a punch on the nose. Seeing the bruise on his nose, his father asked him what happened. Yanxiang said he hit the basketball stand. His father gave him a good dressing-down, which made him feel more grieved. The physical pain was nothing compared with the insult he suffered. He felt his self-esteem was hurt.

Yangxiang was a naughty boy who cared for nothing but playing. After it happened, he made up his mind that he must go to college and stand above others.

From then on, Yanxiang studied very hard and got better marks in school day by day. His relatives were happy to see his progress and offered financial assistance to help him finish his high school.

In 1995, Yanxiang was admitted to one of China's best universities — University of International Business and Economics and became the first university student in the history of the village. According to the old Chinese saying, there must be a wisp of blue smoke emitting from the ancestral grave of the family, which means that the ancestors blessed Yanxiang who brought prestige and honor to his family and clan.

Yanxiang's family entertained the fellow villagers to a big banquet to celebrate their son's success in the courtyard of their house. About 700 people came and the banquet lasted from noon to evening.

Yanxiang is the pride of Beidianzi Village. Adults take him as a fine example to teach their children. Every time he returns home to visit his family, there will be fellow villagers waiting in line to invite him to their homes to pass on his experience to their children.

In the spring of 1999, Yanxiang was about to graduate from university and started to find jobs. The HO went to his university to recruit new employees. A team was formed to be responsible for the recruitment. I was one of the interviewers and met him for the first time.

I read his curriculum vitae: Communist Party member, president of the student union, basketball team leader and ballroom dancing team leader. The first idea that came to my mind was "Does he have time for his study?"

The European Department Three under my leadership only needed one university graduate. I selected one of Yanxiang's classmates Zhaolong.

Several days later, a colleague from the personnel department came to me, "I suggest you give Yanxiang a chance. He is a good student with all-round development. If you don't want him, we have to send him to be a tour guide. It will be a waste."

I accepted Yanxiang reluctantly.

Before Yanxiang and Zhaolong came to my department, they failed to be chosen by North American Department. Although it was not the department with the best achievements, it was given the priority in everything only because it was in charge of the North American market. The whole department, from the director to common employees, all had a sense of superiority.

Yanxiang and Zhaolong vowed to work hard and make the North American Department regret their decision.

One day Yanxiang came to my office and said he wanted to be a tour guide. I asked him why. He said with tearful eyes he might need 100,000 yuan for his mother's heart operation. He thought tour guides earned more money. Although I made no promise, I decided if his mother needed the operation, European Department Three wouldn't stand by unconcerned. It turned out the operation was not suitable for his mother considering her condition.

When I resigned in 2001, nobody knew my plan for the future.

Yanxiang came to my office and said he was going to quit too.

"Why?" I asked him.

"Since you are leaving, I think the job is not worth doing."

I didn't intend to take anyone with me. Hearing what he said, I decided to take him. I told him I wanted to build up an incentive travel company of international standards. Yanxiang decided to follow me. It was not easy for him to make the decision. He didn't know what would wait for him. He just followed his instinct. Besides, he had to consider his parents' opinions. The whole family was proud of him who found a job in a large state-owned enterprise though he grew up in the countryside. They all worried about him when they heard he was going to resign.

Over the years, Yanxiang got married and had a son. His parents have also come to settle down in Beijing.

Yanxiang's wedding was designed and prepared by the company. I hope every employee will receive good care and feel warm being a member of the team.

Yanxiang's mother receives conservative treatment and is often hospitalized. Neither of his parents has medical insurance, so Yanxiang has to bear all the medical care expenses. His parents are worried about such a heavy financial burden on their son. Every time when I go to see his mother in the hospital, I would comfort her, "Don't worry. Money is not a problem."

Yanxiang is confident in his future.

Our company holds a nationwide training every year. During the training session in 2003, the company made slides with the photos of the employees taken in their childhood and asked the participants to guess who was who. Yanxiang took out the only photo of his childhood for the game. The photo was taken when he was 100 days old. He was a chubby and cute baby in the photo. Children in the countryside had little chance to take pictures. The photo was very precious.

One day, Yanxiang told me his photo was lost by the IT engineer of the company. I felt terribly sorry for him. I had many sleepless nights thinking about the photo.

When the company held the annual training in 2007, it happened to be Yanxiang's 30th birthday. We prepared a surprise for him at the evening party. Because of the training, his family did not plan to celebrate his birthday. His wife was then nearly six months pregnant. I invited her to the party and asked her to keep it secret.

Yanxiang's only photo of his childhood was lost. The slide couldn't be found as the IT engineer who did it had left the company. My computer broke a couple of times during the years and some data were also lost. I was overcome with sorrow whenever I thought Yanxiang's child wouldn't know what his or her father looked like when he was a child.

I was very busy those days, preparing for the speech I was going to make at the training. At the same time, I was still trying to find the slide with his photo in it in my computer. One day it came to me that there might be some image of the photo in the video of the training session. I took an image of the photo from the video, but it was very vague.

One day before the training, I was still looking for the slide in my computer. When I was almost despaired, I suddenly found it.

On January 27, 2007, over 100 colleagues and partners from all over the country attended our evening party held in 798 Art Zone in Beijing. Halfway through the party, the birthday song was played, Yanxiang's 100-day-old photo appeared on the big screen, his beautiful wife wearing a maternity dress and holding a bunch of pink roses gracefully walked into the banquet hall, followed by a young girl employee holding a birthday cake with three candles in it.

I told the story of the photo. I was moved to tears when I was telling the story. Yanxiang was very excited to have regained his lost photo. Seeing the photo of her beloved husband's childhood for the first time, his wife was so touched that her eyes brimmed with tears.

I finally took a load off my mind. Yanxiang's unborn child would be able to see what his father looked like when he was a child.

Strictly, Yanxiang and I belong to two different generations although I am his son's godmother. We are different in many ways, but we have one thing in common: We want to improve the living conditions of our parents, our children, and ourselves through our own efforts.

China's reform and opening-up has provided us with the opportunity.

Shortly after Yanxiang and I left the HO, Zhaolong went to America to further his studies. He found a good job in the Chartered Bank after graduation.

On March 5, 2010, Chinese Premier Wen Jiabao made his government work report at the third session of the 11th NPC in the Great Hall of the People. He said, "Everything we do is enabling our people to live a happier life, to have more dignity and to make our society juster and more harmonious."

As an individual, I cannot accomplish something big. But I can set a goal for myself, which is to enable my family and my colleagues to lead a happier and more honorable life with dignity, and to lead my team to do our bit to build a harmonious society.

Yanxiang shares the same thoughts with me. After many years' hard work, he has become president of the company, standing out among his contemporaries as a young leader in the incentive travel and meeting industry.

The Boy Bearing the Heavy Responsibility for Keeping the Family Line

I was born in July 1955. At that time, the Chinese government encouraged childbirth, the more the better. My big younger brother was born in July of 1956. The girl who was born after him died. My second brother was born in July of 1959 and my youngest sister was born in

June of 1963. Four children were not too many for a family. Our neighbor had seven children. The more children a mother had, the more glorious she was. The mother who had many children was honored as "a hero mother".

In 1953, China conducted its first national census. The result was the population of our country was 0.6 billion by the midnight of June 1st, 1953. At the Supreme State Conference, a famous demographer Ma Yinchu pointed it out in Mao Zedong's presence, "Over-population is our biggest problem. It has reached 0.6 billion according to the census in 1953. If the net increase rate is 20‰, the population will reach 0.8 billion in 15 years and 1.5 billion in 50 years. This is not just alarmist talk."

Mao Zedong didn't pay attention to Ma Yinchu's opinion. Uncontrolled childbirth resulted in population explosion and the country could hardly bear the population burden. The Chinese government decided to adopt Ma Yinchu's suggestion to control population growth at the end of the 1970s and a nationwide family planning campaign was launched.

When Hu Yaobang, then head of the Organization Department of the CPC Central Committee, reviewed relevant materials about Ma Yinchu, he exclaimed, "If Chairman Mao had listened to Ma Yinchu, how could China's population have exceeded one billion today!"

In September, 1980, the Central Committee of the Communist Party issued *An Open Letter on the Control of Population Growth of Our Country to All the Communist Party and the Communist Youth League Members*, which called on all the Communist Party and the Communist Youth League members to take the lead in response to the call for "one couple one child".

According to the third census in 1982, the country's total population reached 1 billion. In September, 1982, the Party's 12th National Congress was convened which set family planning as a basic state policy of our country. *Population and Family Planning Law of the People's Republic of China* was put into effect on September 1, 2002.

Since the implementation of the family planning policy, a population increase of 0.4 billion has been prevented which equals the total population of half of Europe.

The children of my generation were all born after the family planning policy. My two brothers, a sister and I have in total two boys and two girls. Two boys have graduated from university, one girl is in college and the other girl is in high school.

I like children, but I am in favor of the family planning policy. As far as we can tell now, China's family planning policy not only has made contribution to China, it has also made contribution to all mankind. Natural resources of our planet are limited. The larger the population is, the more resources are consumed and the worse our living environment will become. If China hadn't done anything about its population growth, it would have been accused of excessive consumption of natural resources.

During public holidays especially the Chinese New Year, long-distance bus stations, railway stations and airports are extremely crowded with people, migrant workers, college students and white collars who are going back home for a family reunion. It is common for people to queue up for several hours or even days amid the piercing chill or under the scorching sun for a train ticket. Although the government has taken many measures such as building more railways, highways and airports, traffic is still a tough problem. Most ordinary people still travel by train which is the most economical means of transportation. The carriage of the train is overcrowded. People have to stand in the aisle for several or even dozens of hours if they fail to get tickets for seats. They dare not drink or eat because they could not get rid of the crowd to the toilet.

I always think if those Westerners who don't understand China's family planning policy came to China to live for some time among the ordinary people, went to railway stations to take a look or to buy a train ticket and get on trains to experience the disastrous effects of overpopulation themselves, they must approve of and support the family planning policy. It is difficult to imagine the tribulation without experiencing it personally.

The state policy of family planning is even more correct if it is raised to the height of human rights. Chinese people have the right to improve their quality of life. Otherwise, we cannot live with dignity.

Someone would say: We are not against the family planning policy; we are against the strong measures adopted in the execution of the policy.

I am against it too. But in such a big country, errors are inevitable when the policy is being carried out from top to bottom. In a country where the rural population accounts for 80 percent of the total population and the feudal idea of valuing the male child only is deeply rooted for thousands of years, it is not easy for China to get today's result.

The story of Chen Family is a good example.

My maternal grandparents had five children, four daughters and one son. The responsibility to carry Chen Family on was placed upon my uncle, the only son of the family.

My uncle went in for farming as soon as he finished primary school. He had been a peasant all his life and was the only one among the five children who lived in most straitened circumstances.

The story of my uncle is repeated in his next generation. Uncle also had five children, four daughters and one son. The only son my cousin Xiaodianzi naturally became the only hope to carry on the Chen Family line. Just like his father, Xiaodianzi is the only child that stays in the countryside. According to the tradition in rural China, it is the son's responsibility to carry on the family line and to support his old parents. When the daughter gets married, she will move out and belong to the husband's family like water splashed away.

According to the family planning policy of Liaoning Province, if the wife is a rural resident, the couple can have a second child if their first child is a girl. Xiaodianzi and his wife are both rural residents and their first child who was born in 1984 was a girl. Five years later, their second child was born, another girl. It meant the family line would break. It would be against the state policy if Xiaodianzi had another child. Uncle decided to break the law and pushed his son to have one more child. His decision was supported by my mother and my three aunts.

My mother joined the Communist Party in the early 1950s and has received education from the Party all her life. But she still views sons as better than daughters. It thus indicates how difficult it has been to carry out the family planning policy in China.

Xiaodianzi's wife got pregnant again. Although she hid herself from place to place, she was still found out when she was seven months pregnant and was forced to have an abortion. It was a boy this time.

To be forced to have an abortion when one is seven months pregnant is something that cannot be accepted by anyone. I had contradictory feelings on this matter. I am against the conventional idea that boys are superior to girls, which can be found in my cousin, his wife, and other family members including my mother. At the same time, I was indignant at the barbaric act in implementing the family planning policy. It happened over a dozen years ago. Nowadays, people seldom hear of such a thing.

The whole family cried their heart out. My mother also wept.

I have always been against the feudal thought and held the idea of "carry on the family line" in contempt. I asked my mother, "Why must Xiaodianzi have a son? I am a daughter. Am I any inferior to a son? Why cannot Xiaodianzi just have two daughters and give them better education? The poorer the family is, the more children they want to have; the more children they have, the poorer they become."

But nobody listened to me. Xiaodianzi's wife was pregnant again. She was hidden safely this time and escaped people's notice. She gave birth to a son. Finally the Chen Family's wish was fulfilled.

The family shouted and jumped for joy for getting a son. Nobody considered the price they had to pay for the son. The price was high. The two girls were deprived of their rights to receive more education, which seriously influenced their future. They dropped out even before they finished junior high school. According to my mother who tried to find excuse to prove the decision to have a boy was correct, the two girls didn't want to go to school on their own will. Their eldest daughter told me the reason why she dropped out was her self-esteem was hurt. The family was poor and had to pay the fine for having a child outside the state plan. She suffered the teacher's sarcasm when the family couldn't afford her tuition. She was too upset to concentrate on study, so she decided to drop out. The family was fined 20,000 yuan for the boy. It was a huge sum for the poor family. Although I resented their behavior, I helped my cousin financially and paid part of the fine for the family.

In fact, the traditional concept that "boys are better than girls" is not only common in rural areas, but also in cities. Before I gave birth to my son, my parents-in-law said it didn't matter if it was a boy or a girl. As soon as they knew it was a boy, they said happily that I made a great contribution to the Zheng family. My husband's brother was very happy because he was relieved of the pressure to carry on the family line. Later he had a daughter who was named Yuanyuan. When my father-in-law passed away, my husband's cousin came from his old home to attend the funeral. The cousin said to me "Zheng Han is the true descendant", implying that Yuanyuan was not. After learning of my divorce, the cousin said he could help me pay for my son's college tuition if I had difficulty.

It has been a tradition for several thousand years in China to "raise sons to provide for old age". However, my parents live with me, their daughter. Even so, I cannot change their idea of "boys are better than girls" that is deeply rooted in their soul.

China now has a total population of 1.3 billion. The state policy of family planning will be carried on and the tradition of carrying the family line on will come to an end sooner or later. Even the family of Mao Zedong, a great figure in history, is faced with the same problem. Mao's grandson Mao Xinyu is the only child and his great-grandson is also the only boy. If the only boy gives birth to a daughter, the line of Mao Zedong's family will stop.

Most of the people who have received higher education can face it properly. Now, there are a lot of successful women in our country. What does it matter if you have a son or a daughter?

Both of Xiaodianzi's daughters are now working in Beijing to earn money to support their parents and to pay for their younger brother's schooling. I hope the hard-won boy will live up to the Chen Family's expectation, study hard and have a bright future. I hope Xiaodianzi can get rid of the old ideas and will not transfer the pressure of carrying on the family line to his son.

My uncle died in his sixties, while all his sisters still live healthily and happily.

One day at the end of the 1980s, my uncle unexpectedly paid a visit to my home. I hardly recognized him when I saw an old man standing outside the door in rags. My mother bought new clothes for him from head to foot and from outside to inside. My uncle suffered from headache and took handful of painkillers. We didn't know it was a premonition of cerebral hemorrhage. In fact, he had long had high blood pressure. It would have been cured if he went to hospital and took medicine. He was a peasant who had not received any education and had no money. Besides, he had to bear the fine for his extra grandson. Otherwise, he would have lived a longer life.

It has been more than 30 years since the family planning policy was carried out in China. The broad masses especially women of childbearing age have made sacrifices for and great contributions to the implementation of the state policy. The cold and stiff slogan of birth control "first the loop, second the ligation or vasoligation and third the fine" is a reflection of the neglect of birth ethic and respect and care for life, which directly influences the image of the family planning policy and the image of our country.

However, it is a comfort to see that China is learning from experience and making progress. More civilized and warm slogans such as "Our mother earth is too tired to hold more children" and "If the baby is of high quality, there will be fewer worries in life" have appeared. The focus of the birth control policy has shifted from punishment to reward for those in the countryside who prefer to have only one child. All these have shown that China has made progress in respecting life and human rights.

Time has changed. Daughters are as good as sons. From the perspective of my ex-husband's family, my son Zheng Han bears the responsibility of carrying on the family line. But for me, it doesn't matter at all if he has a son or a daughter or opt for a DINK lifestyle as long as he is happy and becomes a person useful to the society.

Our generation's efforts have brought evangel for the next generation. The only-child generation has grown up, married and had children. According to the new policy, if both of the couple are the only child, they can have a second child at least five years after the birth of their first child.

Who Will Watch the Ancestral Grave in the Future?

My family had been farmers for generations before my parents.

The earliest to leave the village was my Big Uncle Liu Shijun in 1948. Then my father left in 1950. Old Uncle Liu Shiliang was drowned in 1964. My three aunts left old home after they got married. Only Third Uncle Liu Shizhen has stayed in the village as a farmer all his life. He has two sons and three daughters. All his children have left the countryside except the oldest son Liu Shuan.

In the Chinese New Year of 2006, my father had herpes zoster. At first, he paid no attention to it. As it got worse and worse, he went to see a doctor. He suffered great pain. Sometimes when the pain became unbearable, he thought he was going to die. One day at midnight he began to rave, "Is Heping back yet? Ask Heping to come back."

My father began to have mental problems due to suffering the pain for a long time. He had depression. Not even a psychiatrist could help him.

My grandma died at the age of 98 in 2004. In the summer of 2005, Liu Family set up tombstones for all the ancestral graves. My brother Liu Gang's son Liu Chang was admitted to Beijing Jiaotong University. So my parents decided to wait for Liu Chang to come to Beijing from Guizhou and cancelled their original plan to go back home for the tomb sweeping. When the tombstones were set up, the whole family was there except my father.

My father believed his illness was a punishment from his ancestors because he was absent from the tombstone set-up ceremony. I made a decision when I saw my father's mental sickness was deteriorating.

I hadn't been to my hometown in the northeast for many years. I decided to go to our hometown for the tomb sweeping to fulfill my father's wish.

I said, "I have decided to go to our hometown to pay respects to our ancestors on behalf of father. Father gave life to me and brought me up. Now I am successful, I can return home with fame and fortune and bring honor to my ancestors. It is because our ancestral grave is located in a place with good *fengshui* that I can have today's success. So I should go back home to pay respects to our ancestors on behalf of father."

My father's spirits immediately rose up when hearing my decision.

My American friend Tom Crossan happened to be in Beijing. I asked him if he would like to go with me to my hometown in the northeast to see the real rural China. It was a rare opportunity for him. He would be the first foreigner to visit there.

I decided to go back home driving my Audi A6. On a Friday morning, the four of us left for my hometown, my sister, Tom, the driver and I.

It took us one day to travel to Dandong, a city bordering with the Democratic People's Republic of Korea, which is about 1,000 kilometers away from Beijing. We stayed in Dandong for the night and the next morning we drove to Tongyuanpu, a town with a population of a few scores of thousand. My Big Uncle's daughter Liu Fu lived here with her family. Liu Family River Village was over 25 kilometers away from Tongyuanpu, all mountain roads. Liu Fu's husband He Wu said the mountain road was very bumpy and the chassis of my car would be smashed. I said I wanted to drive the car to the village so that ancestors of Liu Family could know they had an offspring who had brought honor to the family. I didn't do it out of vanity. I knew my father would be happy and the fellow villagers would be happy.

We drove along the mountain road and enjoyed the beautiful scenery. Decades had passed, yet little change took place here. It was still a poor village. The ecological environment was well preserved because no economic development was carried out here.

Our car drove into the courtyard of Liu Family. All the relatives who lived nearby also came. Scores of them were waiting for us in the courtyard.

My cousin Liu Shuan, who was several years younger, looked at least more than 10 years older than me. Tough life in the countryside and hard toil had ploughed deep furrows on his brow.

According to the local customs, tomb sweeping should be finished before high noon. Otherwise it would be inauspicious. After we greeted the uncles, aunts, uncles-in-law, aunts-in-law, cousins, nephews and nieces, we went to the graveyard of Liu Family in the Cornfield Ditch. Tom would take photos and the driver would do the video recording.

Ancestors of Liu Family were buried in Cornfield Ditch which was chosen by my great-grandfather Liu Fengge. My great-great-grandfather Liu Qingtai was buried separately in the field of the family, far away from the ancestral grave. Someone once suggested the grave of great-great-grandfather should be moved to the ancestral grave of Liu Family. My grandma disagreed. A *fengshui* master, after studying the grave, told my grandma that the *fengshui* of great-great-grandfather's grave blessed the second son of Liu Family. The second son was my father Liu Shijie. My father was indeed the happiest child of the family. He has two sons and two daughters all of whom have received higher education and live a comfortable life. He has two grandsons and two granddaughters. Two have graduated from university, one in college and one in a key high school in Beijing. According to fellow villagers in our hometown, my parents are "*quan huo ren*", meaning they have sons, daughters, grandsons, granddaughters, daughters' sons and daughters' daughters. There will be no "*quan huo ren*" in the future because of the family planning policy. My father lives a happier life in his later years. He and my mother support each other and live in a comfortable house of their own in Beijing with their two daughters near them. They don't have to worry about medical expenses when they get ill because their sons and daughters can pay the extra part that will not be covered by the medical insurance. Every year, they travel to Guizhou and the northeast to visit their family members, old colleagues and old neighbors. They are envied by their contemporaries for their comfortable life. My father believes he is blessed by his great-grandfather who was buried in a place with good *fengshui*. I believe it too.

As my sister and I tried to tell which grave belonged to whom, Big Uncle, Third Uncle and cousins all made explanations at once.

Under the coaching of Big Uncle and Third Uncle, my sister and I presented the bouquet and kowtowed to the graves one by one. Cousin Liu Shuan was busy adroitly cleaning the graveyard, burning paper and lighting firecrackers. I felt grateful to him. Liu Shuan was the only one of our generation who has stayed in the countryside. He is also the one living in poverty. He has taken on the responsibility of looking after the ancestral grave with his father, my Third Uncle. They always do it for us, the family members who are far away from hometown.

I was worried that water loss and soil erosion which might happen in the future would damage the grave. Since there was no vegetation in front of the graveyard, I wanted to have some trees grown around it and

I would take care of the expense. Cousin Liu Fu said it was inauspicious to plant trees in front of the grave.

My sister and I dressed ourselves in brand "White Collar" woolen coats and high-heeled boots instead of casual wear and sports shoes as city people's sense of fashion doesn't appeal to the taste of clansmen, and we wanted to make them happy.

Everyone was excited to see blond blue-eyed Tom, the first foreign guest Liu Family River Village had. Tom was even more excited. I introduced Tom to Big Uncle. Hearing that Tom had been a soldier, Big Uncle kept telling him that he had fought against the Americans brilliantly in the Korean War. Tom just giggled.

My aunts and my cousins' wives got lunch prepared after working in the kitchen for a whole morning. There were 20 or 30 people in the big family. According to the local customs, men sit at one table and women and children another table. My sister and I were seated at the men's table, a VIP treatment. Everyone was in high spirits. Third Uncle said, "Today, I am happier than in the Chinese New Year."

My sister and I drank a lot and talked a lot. At the end of the meal, brothers and sisters toasted each other joking and laughing happily. Uncles, aunts and small children watched the fun smilingly. Everyone's face shone with happiness. I loved to see the joyous atmosphere.

Tom's visit brought a lot of pleasure to the family. Tom and my cousins called each other brothers and played drinking games. They asked Tom a lot of questions about his country. America was too far away for people in Liu Family River Village. But today they could sit on the *kang* with an American guest drinking and chatting with him. How wonderful!

Tom said he would like to use the toilet. We all got nervous. You can imagine what a toilet is like in a small village in northeast China. I said to Tom, "You'd better be prepared for it." Tom smiled. One of my cousins led him to the toilet.

I said jokingly, "Liu Family River Village will surely have a bumper

416

harvest next year because ingredient imported from America is added to the farmyard fertilizer."

Tom came back smilingly. When everybody asked him how it felt, he said, "It is OK." He was a likeable man for his good personality.

Time passed quickly. Before leaving, I slipped 1,000 yuan to Third Uncle. He accepted it gladly. I would have been sad if he had refused it. I could see pride and satisfaction on Third Uncle's face.

When we drove out of the village, it was quiet in the car except sobs. Tom's eyes were brimming with tears. My sister and I also sobbed and wept. We couldn't tell exactly what our feelings were. We just kept silent. I thought Tom was touched by the simple and sincere Liu Family who treated him like family and their life of hardship and poverty.

My sister and I had more complex feelings. The question that frequently came to my mind was: Who will watch the ancestral grave of Liu Family in the future?

Third Uncle's family is the only family that still lives in Liu Family River Village. The younger generation has all left their hometown going to college or making a living in cities. Liu Shuan should be the last one to live in the old home.

My parents began to consider their final resting place as they were growing older. Mother was strongly against the idea of returning home while father insisted on going back to Liu Family River Village. Their places are reserved in the ancestral grave in the village. Mother even threatened that she would divorce father if he was stubborn and did not change his idea. She is worried that there would be no people to take care of their tomb in the future since all the family members of the younger generation have left there; it would be so lonely in that remote village.

I had decided to have my bone ashes scattered in nature, but I changed my mind for my parents when I heard the endless argument between them. Someone in the family had to solve their problem. I knew they were waiting for the reaction of their children. According to the

Chinese tradition, it should be the sons to take care of this kind of matters. My parents wouldn't complain if I kept silent. But my two brothers live too far away in the southwest China to be able to help.

The family members of my older generation are getting older day by day. Recently the senior people in the family got sick one by one. Both Third Uncle and big aunt, sister of father, got cancer and had surgeries recently. My mother was also sick with cancer and took a surgery not long ago. Though their treatment was paid about 70 percent by the medical insurance, I still gave each of them a generous financial support. I want to repay my relatives at our old home for taking care of the family graveyard, and my mother for giving me my life and bringing me up.

When mother recovered from the surgery, she started to argue with father again about their final destination and this time they became more serious. I knew that I was the only one who could solve the problem and it was the time. I did not think that my parents would like to be buried in Guizhou where they had worked for almost their whole lives and where my two brothers live now because that it is too far from their old home.

I made a hard decision against my will and told them that I was going to be buried with them and would buy a small piece of land in a cemetery with good *fengshui* in Beijing for all three of us. They immediately stopped arguing and both agreed with me. Father told everyone that it was also the idea of grandmother who had told father when she was alive that my parents should stay with me. Father secretly told his and mother's bothers and sisters, if they went back to the old home, I would have no place to go because I was divorced with no husband. Another reason that makes them happy with my decision is that they love to be buried not far from the Manchu Qing emperors.

Country and City

Local peasants lived a primitive life when the construction of Kaiyang Phosphate Mine started in 1958. When the first truck drove into the mine, all the fellow villagers came to see the strange thing and someone even fed it with grass.

Although life was hard at that time, we still had obvious superiority because the peasants who lived in the same mountains led a much more difficult life than us.

We lived in the same environment geographically. But there was a world of difference in our status. We were workers while they were peasants.

Workers were superior in the planned economy era. Politically, the working class was the leading class. Economically, factories and mines were financially supported by the government. There was no bankruptcy. Workers had housing, salary, benefits, and coupons for grain, subsidiary food and daily necessities. The factories or mines had hospitals, kindergartens, schools, clubs and shops, etc. Everything was taken care of by the state.

Peasants led a completely different life. Over the years, they toiled in the field, living at the mercy of the elements.

It was easy to distinguish the children of employees of the phosphate mine from those of local peasants. Many of the employees came from big cities such as Beijing, Shanghai and Nanjing. Their children were dressed in cotton print clothes and gym shoes. Girls bound their hair with bows and ribbons. Later they had nylon socks and plastic sandals. Peasants' children were in ragged homespun clothes and cloth shoes or straw sandals or barefooted. When it rained, children of the mine held umbrellas and wore raincoats and rubber boots. Peasants' children wore straw hats, straw rain capes and straw shoes or simply barefooted.

We had a strong sense of superiority in front of peasants' children. We called them "peasants' children" while we were called "workers' children". Peasants' children might be peasants too all their lives while we would never become peasants. The peasants called us the government's people.

Most of the peasants' children didn't receive much education. During the years when I lived in the phosphate mine, few girls from peasant families went to school or they dropped out after they finished three years of primary school. Some boys could finish their primary school. Very few of them could go to high school. There was no high school in the villages near the mine. Peasants' children had to study in the high school of the mine. When I returned to the mine to be an English teacher in the high school after I graduated from university in 1976, there was only one boy from a rural family in the third year of senior high school. Rural families needed labor force and their boys started to work in the field at a young age. Girls were married off when they were young.

Children of the phosphate mine's staff could continue their studies as long as they wanted. When colleges and universities were closed in the Cultural Revolution, most of them followed their parents' occupation after they finished junior high school and became workers.

Most of the peasants who are our contemporaries still remain peasants today.

Kaiyang Phosphate Mine was surrounded by villages. On the hillside opposite No. 13 Apartment Building where I lived for 10 years was the farmland of peasants. Fifty meters away was a supply and marketing cooperative for the peasants. I grew up in a place that combined industry and agriculture. When the harvest season came, we helped the peasants getting in the crops. So today I still say I grew up in the countryside.

When I was in primary school, there was a girl named Biyu in my class who was the only classmate that came from a rural family. I was class monitor and she was deputy monitor. We were good friends. I often followed her to walk several kilometers to her home which was half way down the hill and played with her and help her feed pigs. Sometimes I stayed there for the night if it was late. Her family was very poor. The wooden house they lived in was dingy and smoke-discolored. There was no electricity. There were her parents, her elder brother and her brother's wife in the family. They all treated me well. I had dinner with them. Most of the time, we had steamed corn rice and green vegetables from their field. There was also a dip sauce made of dry fried chili pepper and salt. I enjoyed the meal very much. I hit my chopsticks at the bowl to get rid of the sticky corn rice before picking up the dish and dipping it in the sauce following the example of Biyu. Local peasants had corn rice all year round, so they all had the habit of knocking chopsticks at the bowl before picking up food. Biyu stayed at my home from time to time. We cooked rice for her. Rice was a luxury for the peasants who could only have roughly processed corn rice every day.

Biyu dropped out when she was in the third or fourth year. Occasionally I met her in the Sunday market where she was selling vegetables. I would invite her to my home for lunch and she would come with a cabbage or some radish. Later I seldom saw her. I heard she got married at a young age. I knew she wanted to go to school very much. The biggest wish of a rural family was that their daughter could marry a worker and enjoy a happy life. Population flow was restricted by the household registration system. If one married a peasant girl, it would be a burden to him because his wife would have no grain allowance, no job and their children would be registered as permanent rural residents. Few workers wanted to marry rural girls.

There were, however, exceptions.

In the mid 1970s, a truck of the mine ran over a boy from a rural family. The attitude of the boy's family would be critical in determining the driver's sentence. The boy's parents said they wouldn't bring the case to court if the driver married their daughter. The driver's family and his leaders all advised him to do so. In the end, the driver married the peasant girl and avoided being thrown into jail.

When I was a child, whenever I saw a beautiful peasant girl, I would feel sorry for her. Why should such a beautiful girl be born in the countryside?

When I was 16 years old, I worked in the explosive magazine of Kaiyang Phosphate Mine. I always came across two sisters on my way to work. The elder sister was about my age and the younger sister was much younger. Both of them were very good-looking. I got to know the younger sister first and always took her to the bathhouse at my work place for a bath. I helped her comb her hair and often gave her some small gifts. One day, the two sisters were waiting for me on the mountain road. The elder sister thanked me for looking after her younger sister and gave me a basket of fresh vegetable in return. The elder sister also said she envied me because I was a worker. She said she had a sad fate and wished she would be born in a worker's family in her next life.

During the Cultural Revolution, I was invited by the Mao Zedong Thought Propaganda Team of a nearby village to help them rehearse programs and to teach them the dance "The Red Army fears not the trials of the Long March". A boy had a gift for dancing and was handsome. I often praised him. He was very happy.

He admired me very much because I was good at dancing. Wherever he met me, he would run over to greet me warmly, with a big smile on his face. I would smile to him in return and was very nice to him. I didn't want him to have a feeling of inferiority being the child of peasants.

The army came to our mine to recruit soldiers. The new recruits gathered in front of the office building to get on the truck that would take them to the railway station in the capital city. Their parents, brothers, sisters and classmates all came to see them off. A dozen young people stood in a row in brand-new military uniforms. Nobody could tell who was a child of peasants and who was a child of workers. Suddenly I saw a face in the team smiling at me. It was the dancing boy. He was also recruited.

If the child of a rural family joined the army, he would be called a "rural soldier". If the child of an urban family joined the army, he would be called an "urban soldier". If the rural soldier didn't get promoted to an officer after three years in the service, he would be demobilized and go back to the countryside to be a peasant. If he got promoted to be an officer, he would be assigned a job and be transferred to civilian work after his service in the army. For urban soldiers, no matter they got promoted or not, they would return to the cities, factories or mines and be assigned jobs there after they were demobilized.

I didn't know what became of the dancing boy.

Peasants' children would no longer be peasants if they went to college. Their rural household registration would be changed into urban household registration in the city of the university and his farmland would be cancelled. After graduation, he would have his household registration changed to the place where he would work and would be no longer a peasant.

Joining the army and getting promoted, going to college or becoming a worker were the main ways for peasants and their children to change their residential status. If my parents hadn't become workers when New China was founded, they would still have been peasants today.

Of the total population of 1.3 billion of China, 900 million are peasants.

Since the early 1980s, the surplus labor force in China's rural areas has moved into cities. It was after 1992 that large quantities of migrant workers began to seek jobs in cities. The system that food and daily necessities should be supplied by coupons was cancelled in 1992. Migrant workers could buy food and daily necessities with cash only.

There are three reasons for peasants to go to cities to seek jobs. First, there is substantial surplus labor force in rural areas. Second, a lot of cheap labor is needed in the urban construction. Third, urban-rural differences make peasants long for city life.

One example that I am familiar with is the "basket carriers" in Guizhou.

In the streets of Guiyang, capital city of Guizhou, you can find special groups of people of two or three, old or young, dressed in dirty ragged clothes, with dust all over the face and carrying a basket on their back. Guiyang citizens call them "basket carriers". "Basket carriers" come from remote mountain areas or the countryside and make a living by helping people carry heavy things.

"Basket carriers" are the most helpless group. They have no education or skill. All they have is their strength. They are cheap labors. Most of them don't solicit business. Instead, they just wait for their chance.

Walking in the street, you can often hear someone shouting, "basket carrier", like calling a taxi. Instantly, he or she would be surrounded by a group of basket carriers.

If business is good, some basket carriers can share a room. Otherwise, they have to spend the nights in the streets.

Many apartment buildings with seven or eight stories have no lift. Basket carriers climb to the top floor with a heavy load on their back and can only earn two yuan.

My two brothers live in Guiyang. They often call a basket carrier after they have done some shopping even if they can perfectly handle it themselves. They want to give the basket carriers a chance to earn money. My brothers are kind people. They usually pay them more than they ask for. It has been over a dozen years since the special group first appeared in Guiyang. Over the years, great changes have taken place in this city. Part of the city has become very modern and the living standards of urban residents have dramatically improved. But there has been little change in the lives of basket carriers.

When I first came to Beijing, the city always reminded me that I was a stranger. Growing up under the feet of the Emperor, the local Beijingers felt themselves superior and normally would not marry those from other places because of the restriction of *hukou* system.

In the early 1980s, when I worked in Z County of Hebei Province which was about 70 kilometers away from Beijing, a boy from Beijing took a fancy to me. But I had no feelings for him. Many people tried to persuade me, "It is your good fortune to be liked by a boy from Beijing. If you married him, you could have your *hukou* in Beijing."

With the deepening of the reform and opening-up, more and more people who have come to Beijing from other places have succeeded in business. In Silver Maple Garden where I live, most of the households are from other places. Many successful people well-known in the city also come from other places. Beijing has truly become the capital of all the Chinese people.

Migrant workers, who are called "peasant workers" in China, and people from other places are two different concepts. Migrant workers used to be peasants, while people from other places refer to non-agricultural population whose permanent residence is not in Beijing. They call themselves "drifters in Beijing". "Drifters in Beijing" can be Zhang Yimou, the world-famous movie director, or someone who makes a living by singing in the underground passage. With no restriction on *hukou*, they can drift to Beijing as long as they like. Many employees of my company are "drifters in Beijing".

Many people think the form of address "peasant workers" is derogatory and discriminative. But I don't think so. I think it just defines a group of people.

It is said that there are six million peasant workers in Beijing. China is comparatively backward in statistics and one can find several different answers when searching information online. Anyway, it is not important.

How many peasant workers are there in cities? How do they influence the life in cities? We can find the answer when the Chinese New Year comes.

During the Chinese New Year, urban residents suddenly feel life become inconvenient. They cannot find someone to repair shoes, fix bikes, help them with the housework, grind keys, send drinking water or do facial massage or foot therapy because the peasant workers have gone home for family reunion.

Peasant workers have become an indispensable part of city life.

The peasant workers in China are really great. They live at the foot of the social ladder and do the dirtiest and most tiring jobs.

During the past 20 years, nine girls from the countryside have worked for my family or my sister's family as *ayi*. Five of them are our relatives that come from our hometown in northeast China.

The nine girls have one thing in common, low educational level. Some of them just finished primary school; some dropped out from junior high school. Their contemporaries in cities generally have received good education. My contemporaries who have walked out of the countryside all provide their children with good education opportunities. But the children, especially girls of my cousins who still stay in the countryside, haven't received much education. My cousin Liu Shuan's son was admitted to a university. Strictly speaking, he is the first college student of Liu Family that has walked out of the village.

These peasant girls never want to go back to the countryside after they have lived a better life in the city and seen the world. After they work at my home or my sister's home for several years, we will find them jobs. Although their educational level is low, there are still many opportunities in the city for them. Some of them run their own small business and some work in restaurants. If they married a diligent man, they could live a happy though simple life.

Due to their low educational level, they still have limited opportunity for personal development, which means they might have to work hard all their lives.

When I chatted with these girls, I found they were very optimistic. Time has changed. They can live in the city legally without having to worry about being driven back. But they will face many challenges to survive in the city. They must adapt themselves to the development of the city and master more skills. Otherwise, life would be hard for them.

When I lived in Z County of Hebei Province, the first two *ayi* were relatives from my mother-in-law's hometown in Sichuan. They are in the early forties now. They got married and settled down in Z County. Their husbands are also peasant workers. They depend on some small business for a hard living. However, life is much better than when they were in the countryside. They put all their hopes on their children.

The first *ayi* my sister's family had was only 14 years old when she came to Beijing in 1995. The girl was called "Zhu Lao San" (the third child of the Zhu family) and came from the village near Kaiyang Phosphate Mine. She had two elder brothers and a deaf father. The family was very poor. When she was a small child, her mother ran away with another man. She dropped out when she finished the third year in primary school. She had to work in the field, feed pigs and chicken and help take care of the kid of her biggest brother. Her sister-in-law was mean to her and sometimes abused her.

My sister was about to give birth and needed an *ayi*. My father was on good terms with the local peasants. When the village head heard that my father was looking for *ayi*, he took Zhu Lao San to my father and asked him to find a place where she could have enough to eat.

When she came to Beijing, my sister's family treated her as a child since she was too young. My mother helped my sister take care of her baby. Zhu Lao San just needed to do some simple housework. They also taught her to read and write so that she could grow up in a relatively good environment.

When Zhu Lao San was 18 years old, she returned home to visit her family. Someone found her a date, a rural young man. She didn't come back to Beijing. Two years later, she got married and gave birth to a son. The family lived in poverty. My sister would send her money and some toys and clothes for her child during festivals. To get rid of poverty, the couple left their son with his grandparents and went to seek jobs in Shaoxing of Zhejiang Province. Her husband does manual labor in a factory. She makes buttonholes in a tailor's shop.

It is a common phenomenon in rural China. Young couples seek jobs in cities and leave their young children in their parents' care at home. With money earned by hard work, peasant workers have new houses built in the village. But only their lonely old parents and children live there. Left-at-home children and empty-nest old people have become a serious social problem these years.

Recently, Zhu Lao San and her husband went back home. They are going to build a new house with the money they earned over the years. I hope they can find jobs in their hometown and live happily together with their parents and child.

Some couples take their children with them to the city, but life in the city is hard for both adults and children. With no urban residential status, it is a problem for them to find a kindergarten or a school for their children. So, most of the peasant workers still prefer to leave their children at home in the countryside. Xiao Zhang, the cleaner of my company is an example. Xiao Zhang, her husband and her son work in Beijing as peasant workers. Her daughter who is still in primary school is left at home in Sichuan with her grandparents. Xiao Zhang can only see her daughter once a year at most.

Most of the peasant workers live in temporary shed or rent a small bungalow where there is no heating or air conditioner. Several households have to share a public toilet and a tap.

Peasant workers are a huge group who live in the city but out of city life.

The Chinese government has realized the peasant worker problem and has worked out many policies to improve their living conditions. It is said China has more than 200 million peasant workers. It will be a long process to solve their problems.

On February 28, 2010, when Premier Wen Jiabao exchanged ideas with netizens through www.gov.cn, he said, "The problem of peasant workers' children going to school in the city has been of great concern to the government. Our principle on this matter is equal standard and equal opportunity. But now it is difficult to achieve this goal because there are not enough schools in cities to hold all those students. It is a long way to go. However, we have set a clear direction which is to gradually expand the construction of schools so that more children of peasant workers can go to school and enjoy the same and equal educational service as children in cities do."

Another problem is the guarantee of subsistence for peasant workers. Although the government has repeatedly required that employers should buy old-age insurance, health care insurance, unemployment insurance and work safety insurance for peasant workers, very few of them really follow the requirement and buy insurances for peasant workers. Xiao Zhang is treated as a regular employee of my company and she is covered by all necessary insurances. None of the cleaners who work for other companies in the same office building has any insurance. Xiao Zhang asked if we could directly give her the money instead of buying her the insurances. Certainly we couldn't. Most peasant workers are not aware of the importance to take preventive measures. What they need more is cash. In reality, we often hear that peasant workers cannot afford medical treatment when they get work-related injuries or fall ill.

With a population of 1.3 billion, China still has a long way to go to narrow down the difference between the city and the countryside.

I like to make comparison between the new and the old. Before the reform and opening-up, people in China were not free to move about. The great majority of peasants ended up living in the same place from generation to generation and never experiencing city life. By comparison, today's peasants are luckier. At least, they are free to choose their way of living. At least they see hope.

Urbanization is inevitable in China.

Taiwan Compatriots — My Blood Brothers and Sisters

On September 3, 1945, the Chinese people won the final victory in its war against Japanese aggression. In less than a year, a civil war broke out between the Communist Party led by Mao Zedong and the Kuomintang led by Chiang Kai-shek in June of 1946. The war ended with the all-round victory of the Communist Party and the founding of the People's Republic of China in Beijing on October 1, 1949. The government of the Republic of China led by Chiang Kai-shek fled to Taiwan after their defeat that year. The reason why Chiang Kai-shek decided to retreat to Taiwan was because of its geographic position. Taiwan was separated from the mainland by a strait. Defended by natural barrier and depending on its navy and air force, the Chiang Kai-shek clique thought they could contend against the Communist Party which had no navy or air force then and wait for a chance to launch a counter-offensive.

About 1.2 million Kuomintang military personnel, their families, students, entrepreneurs and civil servants moved to Taiwan with the Kuomintang regime. Among them, 600,000 were soldiers.

Some of the Kuomintang officers, entrepreneurs and civil servants took their families with them. The 600,000 soldiers were not that lucky. They fled to Taiwan, leaving their parents, brothers and sisters, wives and children behind. Many of them were captured by the Kuomintang in the field, at their home or on the way to school when the army was withdrawing. They were aged between 13 to over 50. No one knew that they would be separated from their families for decades without getting any news. Since then, the two sides of the Taiwan Straits were in confrontation and all traffic and communication were cut off. People

430

were separated by the Straits, so near to each other, but could not meet.

When we were young, we knew there was a beautiful island called Taiwan which was still occupied by the Kuomintang and was not liberated. People there lived in extreme misery and the suffering children were waiting for us to rescue them. Posters and slogans saying "Liberate Taiwan" could be seen everywhere. We saw many anti-spy movies telling the story that spies were sent to the mainland from Taiwan to gather information and their plot was uncovered and they were caught by the People's Liberation Army.

Across the Straits, Chiang Kai-shek said he would counterattack Chinese mainland within three years and the slogans could also be seen everywhere. Those who fled to Taiwan with the Kuomintang believed they would fight back to the mainland soon and wouldn't have to stay in Taiwan for a long time.

We felt sad whenever we thought of the children in Taiwan. We grew up with the ideal that we must liberate Taiwan. We didn't think it was a difficult thing to liberate Taiwan. We never expected that the two sides of the Straits would be separated for such a long time and the Taiwan issue would become more and more complicated as time went on.

Due to the education we received, we felt sympathetic with the people in Taiwan and felt lucky and proud that we could live in the socialist mainland.

During the Cultural Revolution, most of the people who had relatives in Taiwan suffered persecution. Nobody dared mention their family members in Taiwan because it would mean they were related to the Kuomintang and would be suspected of being spies. People were forced to write a statement to break with their relatives in Taiwan. In fact, since the Kuomintang retreated to Taiwan, family members were separated from each other by the Straits and lost contact ever since.

In 1973, a song *Taiwan Compatriots — Our Blood Brothers and Sisters* got very popular. The first part of the song expressed how people in China's mainland missed Taiwan compatriots. The latter part expressed the Chinese government's resolution to liberate Taiwan.

> *Standing on the coast, I look into the distance for Taiwan Province of my motherland.*
>
> *The waves of the Sun Moon Lake are rippling in my heart, the wind blowing through the Ali Mountain forests is echoing in my ears.*
>
> *Taiwan compatriots, our blood brothers and sisters, we miss you day and night.*
>
> *Ah, people of the whole nation, unite, in one mind, struggle together and work toward the same goal.*
>
> *Liberate Taiwan and reunify our motherland.*
>
> *Let the sun shine upon Taiwan.*
>
> *The tide of revolution is unstoppable. Taiwan compatriots are sure to get together with us.*
>
> *We must liberate Taiwan!*
>
> *Let the sun shine upon Taiwan!*

For a long time, the US government's sanctions on China and its support for Taiwan have made the cross-Straits issue more complicated.

China and the United States established diplomatic relations on January 1, 1979. The US government recognized the government of the People's Republic of China as the sole legal government of China; there was only one China in the world and Taiwan was a part of China. The US government ended its diplomatic relations with Taiwan. The same day, the Chinese government issued *A Message to Taiwan Compatriots*, hoping that direct trade, postal, air and shipping services between the two sides of the Taiwan Straits would be realized as early as possible and welcoming Taiwan compatriots to the mainland to visit friends and family and to engage in cultural, sports and academic exchanges. When Deng Xiaoping visited the United States in January 1979, he said, "We will stop using the term 'liberate Taiwan'. As long as Taiwan returns to the motherland, we will respect the reality and existing policies there. On the one hand, we respect the reality in Taiwan; on the other hand, we will

432

make sure that Taiwan will return to the motherland."

In about 1983, I found there were some changes in the lyrics to the song *Taiwan Compatriots — Our Blood Brothers and Sisters*, for example, "liberate Taiwan, reunify the motherland" was changed into "the early return of Taiwan to the motherland"; "the tide of revolution is unstoppable" was changed into "realize reunification of the country", and "we must liberate Taiwan" into "work hand in hand to build up our splendid motherland".

Since the reform and opening-up launched in 1978, there were overseas Chinese who came back to the mainland to visit relatives or for sightseeing. Some veterans in Taiwan secretly asked their friends in Hong Kong or foreign countries to get news about or to find their relatives left in the mainland or to send messages to them. Some even secretly came back via Hong Kong.

The following story happened at the Beijing Capital Airport in 1986. There was an old man in his seventies on the same plane with me, who was coming back from the United States to visit his family in the mainland. The old man used to be a Kuomintang officer. He went to Taiwan in 1949 and later went to America. It was the first time he came back to see his family since he left 36 years ago. He was full of tears while embracing his children who came to meet him at the airport. His children were in middle ages and looked very much like their father. As a spectator, I was also moved to tears. The moving scene lingers in my mind and heart. I often imagine myself to be the daughter of the old man. I believe it is an unbearable pain to part with one's father for 36 years while not being able to get any news of him.

In 1986, I went with a project delegation of the mining bureau of the H Ministry to Florida of the United States. One of the colleagues was an engineer surnamed Fang. His father was captured by the Kuomintang and taken to Taiwan in 1949. He was only several years old then. His mother suffered a lot of hardships and brought him up alone. After he graduated from college, he became a mining engineer. In the mid 1980s, his father managed to find him and his mother via a friend in Hong Kong. At that time, there was no direct telephone communication between the mainland and Taiwan. So he took the chance to speak with his father over the telephone when he visited the United States. He hadn't seen his father for 37 years. Fang couldn't speak English, so I helped him get through to his father via the American operator. I was listening while they were talking over the telephone. My heart was thumping with emotion. I was more excited than Fang. His father asked him a lot of questions about his hometown to see if he was really his son. They talked in their native dialect which I couldn't understand. I was so touched when Fang called "father! father!" repeatedly that tears came into my eyes. Seeing no hope of returning to the mainland, his father married a local woman and had children after staying in Taiwan for more than 10 years.

People in Taiwan were not allowed by the Taiwan authorities to go to the mainland to visit their family until the end of 1987.

Since 1988, the veterans who had been separated from their relatives for nearly 40 years began to return to the mainland. We often saw on TV or heard on the radio heartwarming stories of Taiwan veterans coming back to the mainland to visit their relatives.

Fang's father finally returned home and saw his wife and son after 40 years' separation. Being a grass widow all her life and waiting for her husband for several decades, Fang's mother was told her husband had married another woman. Many Taiwan veterans had the same story. Few of their wives complained. The wife of a veteran said in a TV program that she was actually happier to hear that her husband had married another woman in Taiwan. Otherwise her husband would live lonely in harder times. She was a typical traditional Chinese woman. She took care of her in-laws for her husband and brought up her children alone without any complaint. The veteran's wife in Taiwan was a reasonable woman. She went with her husband and their children to the mainland to see his husband's first wife and children. More veterans spent all their life alone. They were not allowed to get married when serving in the army. After they were retired, they had no job skills to support themselves, let alone get a wife and support a family. Whom they missed most were their parents. The luckier veterans finally saw their old parents or one of them. More often, their parents died before the day of reunion.

A Taiwanese poet Yu Guangzhong wrote a poem *Homesick* in 1971.

When I was a child, my homesickness was a small stamp
Linking Mum at the other end and me this.
When grown up I remained homesick but it became a ticket
By which I sailed to and from my bride at the other end.
Then homesickness took the shape of a grave,
Mum inside of it and me outside.
Now I'm still homesick but it is a narrow strait,
Separating me on this side and the mainland on the other.

His eyes were brimming with tears when he finished the poem. Yu Guangzhong went to Taiwan with his parents in 1949. According to him, he had been in Taiwan for over 20 years when he wrote the poem. It was during the Cultural Revolution and there was no sign that he could possibly return to the mainland. He was so sad and wrote this poem.

Although I have no relatives in Taiwan, I have paid special attention to the historic tragedy. Big Uncle had served in the Kuomintang army and later came over to the Communist Party. I was grateful that Big Uncle broke away from the Kuomintang. Otherwise he would have gone to Taiwan too. I cannot imagine if Liu Family could have borne the pain. This Chinese New Year, 85-year-old Big Uncle came to see us in Beijing. I asked him if he could choose again, which would be his choice: to go to Taiwan with the Kuomintang and be separated with his family for 40 to 50 years, or to reunite with his family after being unfairly imprisoned in China's mainland for 13 years. He said without any hesitation that he

435

would choose the latter.

Maybe because Big Uncle had the similar experience, I couldn't help sympathizing with the Taiwan veterans and their families. Their sufferings often make my heart sore.

During the Cultural Revolution, people avoided talking about their relatives in Taiwan. But after it, more and more people talked about their relatives in Taiwan and showed off the color photos sent by their relatives from Taiwan to other people. At that time, mainlanders were poor and they thought Taiwan was more prosperous than the mainland. Actually most of the veterans were poor people in Taiwan. When they were allowed to come back to visit their relatives, most of them were in their sixties or seventies. I heard the stories of veterans who came back to their hometown in Guizhou to visit their families. They pinched and scraped and came home with big and small bags of gifts for their family members. Someone said he would not come back again because he didn't have enough money to buy gifts for all the family members and didn't want to see them at odds with each other over the distribution of gifts.

The first group of people that returned to the mainland was those from the show business in Taiwan.

In the CCTV New Year's Gala in 1984, a Taiwanese called Huang Ayuan appeared on the stage as an emcee. In September of 1983, he came to the mainland via Japan with his wife and three children, becoming the first Taiwan compatriot to return to the mainland. It was not easy for CCTV to decide to invite him as an emcee because they were fearful he would be assassinated by Taiwan spy. Appearing with him on the stage of the New Year's Gala were two men Huang Zhicheng and Li Dawei who broke away from the Kuomintang air force and flew the planes to China's mainland in 1981 and 1983, respectively. They said the reason for their uprising was that they supported the reunification of the motherland. They were warmly welcomed by both the Chinese government and the people. Certainly, for the mainland,

436

what they did was uprising; for Taiwan, what they did was defection.

A singer named Fei Xiang (Kris Phillips) appeared on the stage of the CCTV New Year's Gala in 1987. Fei Xiang was born in Taiwan. His mother was Chinese and his father was American. His mother went to Taiwan in 1949 and was not able to come back to see her mother in the mainland until 38 years later. Fei Xiang was the first Taiwanese singer that crossed the Straits to develop his career in the mainland. Before singing the song *Hometown Cloud,* he said, "I have seen my grandmother for the first time during this visit to my motherland." The audience gave him enthusiastic applause. Fei Xiang's grandmother stood up in the audience. Fei Xiang went forward to kiss her on the cheek and said, "Please allow me to sing a song *Hometown Cloud* to dedicate it to my grandmother, my mother and my hometown." When the tall, handsome and blue-eyed man was singing "come back, come back, the wandering son, stop wandering", he won the hearts of hundreds of millions of mainland audience. His eyes glistened with tears when he was singing. I was also moved to tears watching it on TV. His words "visit my motherland" warmed my heart. Overnight, Fei Xiang became very popular all over the country and won innumerable fans.

There was another singer in Taiwan. She had never been to the mainland, but the influence she had on the mainland people was incomparable to any other overseas Chinese. She was Deng Lijun (Teresa Teng). The Cultural Revolution ended not long before Deng Lijun's songs were spread to the mainland at the time when only the impassioned revolutionary songs were popular. During the early stage of reform and opening-up, her songs flew into the mainland through abnormal channels. When I first listened to her songs, I was shocked: Songs can be sung in this way! Deng Lijun's songs were all about love and bourgeois sentiments, which were denounced in the Cultural Revolution. When the songs spread in the mainland with an irresistible force, relevant government departments ordered a ban on dissemination of Deng Lijun's songs which were labeled obscene songs and soft melodies that would contaminate the minds of the mainland people. Even so, Deng Lijun's songs still became a national craze, which was best described in the fashionable remarks "listen to old Deng (Deng Xiaoping) in the day and listen to young Deng (Deng Lijun) in the evening". At that time, not much cultural pastime was available. People, especially young people could hardly find any literature or art to express their feelings or personality. They found it in Deng Lijun's songs, so they pursued her fanatically.

In the early 1980s, I had my first tape recorder. It was a single cassette recorder in the shape of a brick. I used it to listen to Deng Lijun's songs besides English.

Today, if I go to a Karaoke bar, I would sing either revolutionary songs or Deng Lijun's songs.

With the deepening of the reform and opening-up, the songs of Deng Lijun and other pop singers from Hong Kong and Taiwan were gradually accepted by the relevant government departments. Since the market for cultural products was opened to Taiwan, more and more Taiwanese singers and stars have come to do performances, movies or TV series, traveling back and forth between Taiwan and the mainland. Some of them had numerous fans in the mainland.

The biggest regret of Deng Lijun's mainland fans is that their pop idol hadn't been to the mainland before she died. On May 8, 1995, when the news of Deng Lijun's death came, people in the mainland were shocked. Many people shed tears of sorrow. This year is the 15th anniversary of Deng Lijun's death. All kinds of commemorative activities have been held in Taiwan, Hong Kong and the mainland in honor of her.

Since the mid 1980s, more and more Taiwanese have come to do business, work and study in the mainland. The cultural and business exchanges and cooperation between the two sides of the Taiwan Straits have greatly increased. But direct links of mail, air and shipping services between the two sides were not established until 2009.

Our compatriots in Taiwan have long been able to come to the mainland for visits or tours. But Taiwan was not open to mainland tourists until July 2008. Ironically, Jinmen which faces Xiamen City of the mainland across the sea used to be Taiwan's important defensive position, but now it has become a popular destination for the mainland tourists.

From military confrontation to economic dependence on each other, we have experienced a long period of 60 years.

In the 1980s, when Taiwanese especially businessmen and people from the show business came to the mainland, they had a sense of superiority. On the one hand, they were received by mainland people with great warmth, who treated them as family; on the other hand, Chinese mainland was relatively backward and life here was relatively hard while people in Taiwan led a much more affluent life.

But now China's mainland isn't what it once was. Dramatic changes have taken place in cities like Beijing, Shanghai and other coastal cities which are the centers for Taiwanese. Mainlanders and Taiwanese do business with each other on an equal basis. Although there are frictions between the two sides sometimes, they can seek common ground while reserving differences and live in harmony. I think it is normal, just as Beijingers and Shanghainese sometimes mock at each other.

Mainlanders and Taiwanese can be very good friends, do business together or be related by marriage. However, no matter how good their relationship becomes, there is a bottom line between them which is the sovereignty issue. Taiwan is forever an inalienable part of China.

Some Taiwanese pop singers and movie stars have many fans in the mainland who love them more than themselves. They will forgive their idols no matter what mistakes they make except "Taiwan independence"-related mistakes. If some pop star said something improper in public such as calling Taiwan a country or saying that going to the mainland or Hong Kong is going abroad, even if it was a slip of the tongue, it would incur the fans' disfavor and the netizens' scolding. The fans and netizens even call on the government to force him or her out of the show business in the mainland. It is a conscious activity of the people in the mainland to oppose Taiwan's independence. We will never accept or even imagine that Taiwan becomes an independent country.

Taiwanese entertainers understand they cannot afford to lose their market in the mainland. If they supported Taiwan's independence, they would suffer boycott from the mainland audience and pay high prices. Certainly, they are free to have their own political views. But my suggestion to those who are in favor of Taiwan's secession from China is they had better not come to the mainland for career development because they will not be accepted by the mainland audience.

Government officials are more sensitive to the Taiwan issue than ordinary Chinese people. In the early 1980s, a minister led a government delegation to visit the United States. A dinner was arranged in a Chinese restaurant by the American host. When the minister saw "made in Taiwan" on the bottom of the plate he immediately rose to leave, which made the American host very embarrassed.

Although such extreme things are not likely to happen today, government officials still pay special attention to matters of principle. For example, when I attended the annual conference of some international association with a government official who didn't understand English, the official would immediately become alert when the conference host mentioned Taiwan. He would ask me, "Is Taiwan called a region or a country?" It happens that the conference host forgets to add the word "regions" when listing the countries attending the conference. I often tell the person in charge of the conference to remind the speaker to refer to Taiwan as a region instead of a country. I do this not because that I am a fussy woman. I can understand the conference host or the speaker's slip of the tongue. Not everyone knows the problem concerning the cross-Straits relations. Whenever I reminded them, they would respect my opinion.

If an international association or society admitted that Taiwan is a country, we would never join it. People in the mainland take the absolutely same stand with the Chinese government on the Taiwan issue.

I understand Taiwanese's difficulties and discomfitures. Taiwan has always been active in international professional associations. Organizations and individuals from Taiwan joined the associations many years before the participation of their counterparts in the mainland. Many of them have long been the only representative of China in these associations. So not many people cared how Taiwan was addressed. With the deepening of the reform and opening-up and the rise of China's international status, more and more organizations and individuals from the mainland have joined international organizations. It has become a sensitive issue to call Taiwan a region or a country. No issue concerning sovereignty is small.

In the international organizations which only accept sovereign nations as its members, such as the UN, the People's Republic of China is the sole legal representative. As the cross-Straits relations have improved, the Chinese government has relaxed on Taiwan's joining international organizations. For example, Taiwan attended the annual meeting of the WHO (World Health Organization) as an observer and joined the WTO as China's Taipei Separate Customs Territory. Judging by the trend of the development of the cross-Straits relations, many things are negotiable as long as the principle of "one China", "Taiwan is an inalienable part of Chinese territory" and "the government of the PRC is the sole legal government representing the whole of China" is not violated.

As a mainlander, I am sometimes in the same awkward position. I have to be particularly careful with what I say when in international settings. When there are attendants from Taiwan, I would say I come from Chinese mainland. I would never use "your Taiwan" or "our China" or something like that.

Kitty Wong, president of a Taiwan company — K&A International and I are partners and good friends. We were born in the same year and now are in the same business. She was born in Taiwan while I was born in the mainland. Her father went to Taiwan in 1949. When I told her stories about my life experience, she was thinking what she was doing at that time and making comparisons. We grew up in entirely different social and political backgrounds.

Sometimes, we would have different opinions. Kitty would say to me, "You have been brainwashed." "You too," I would retort.

We both have been "brainwashed" because we live in different social systems under different political influence and have received different education. Chiang Kai-shek once claimed that the Taiwan-based Republic of China was the true representative of the 700 million Chinese people in the mainland. People in Taiwan believed we were living in misery and waiting for them to rescue us. The children who grew up in Taiwan were educated by the Taiwan authorities just as the mainland children were educated by the Communist Party.

As we have entered the 21st century, I think the relationship between Kitty and I can well represent the goal of the development of relations across the Straits, which is to seek common ground while reserving differences.

At the 2009 annual conference of ICCA (International Congress and Convention Association), representatives of Asian countries developed strategic partnership by setting up an "Asia Alliance of Professional Meeting Organizers". The initiators came from seven countries and regions including India, Singapore, Malaysia, South Korea, Japan, Taiwan and China's mainland. Kitty was an active ICCA member and the main advocate of the alliance. When I read the draft of the press release, I found "seven countries" instead of "seven countries and regions" was used.

I said, "I am sorry. No matter how good friends Kitty and I are, the question of how to address Taiwan is a question of principle. Taiwan must be called a region not a country."

It was not Kitty's first time to meet with such a situation. She accepted it calmly. I was very grateful to her. The Taiwan issue is an unavoidable question in our cooperation, which sometimes put us in an awkward position. But now there is no better way to deal with it.

In February, 2010, I invited Kitty to Beijing to be a speaker at the training session of my company. I introduced her as my long lost twin sister who came from Chinese Taipei in front of all the participants and the American guest speakers. She laughed heartily about my introduction.

The Taiwan issue has made our life more complicated.

Although we always hear "the reunification of the country is the common wish of people on both sides of the Taiwan Straits", we also hear different voices from Taiwan from time to time. Under the influence of the "Taiwan independence" forces led by the pro-U.S. and pro-Japanese Lee Teng-hui and Chairman of the Democratic Progressive Party Chen Shui-bian, it is not surprising that some Taiwanese are in favor of "Taiwan independence".

Taiwan's leader Ma Ying-jeou, who is also the chairman of the Kuomintang Party, advocates "no unification, no independence and no military confrontation", only cultural and business exchanges and no political negotiation.

In view of the current situation, I think the principles of "peaceful reunification" and "one country, two systems" are in the best interests of people on both sides of the Taiwan Straits.

Some of my friends from Western countries doubt the Chinese government's determination to reunify the country. They asked me, "What if Taiwan insists on its independence?"

"The Chinese government will never allow it to happen," I answered.

As a Chinese who grew up in the mainland, I know perfectly well the Chinese government and ordinary people's attitude towards the Taiwan issue. The Chinese government will never allow Taiwan to secede from China and become an independent nation. Nobody wants to be accused of splitting the country and become a sinner of the offspring of the Chinese nation. The Taiwan issue is the issue of sovereignty and the issue of sovereignty is not open to compromise. If the separatist forces were determined to get their own way and declared independence, the consequences would be very severe.

I am proud that tourism has played a positive role in relations across the Taiwan Straits. Now tourism has brought ordinary people on two sides of the Straits in contact. We can have better understanding of each other through face-to-face communications. We don't have to listen to inflammatory speeches by politicians. My brother and some friends who have traveled to Taiwan said most of the people in Taiwan are friendly and hospitable, even in Tainan, the headquarters of the separatist forces.

I remember in primary school, our teacher Lu Jinghua used a figure of speech to compare the areas of China's mainland and Taiwan by describing the mainland as a dustpan and Taiwan a mung bean. Since Taiwan opened its tourist market to the mainland, more and more tourists travel from the dustpan to the bean. It's estimated that the number of tourists to Taiwan from the mainland reached one million by 2010. But it was just the beginning. Chinese mainland with its large population of 1.3 billion means an inexhaustible tourist source market to Taiwan. Taiwan will become more and more dependent on the mainland for its economic development.

A netizen in Taiwan shared his experience of watching the 2009 National Day parade with others in his blog. It was an interesting story.

An elder, about 60 years old, veteran Kuomintang member, anti-separatism and anti-communist, loyal to the Kuomintang and Chiang Kai-shek, was watching alive the National Day Parade (for the 60th anniversary of the founding of the People's Republic of China) with me with an evident mixture of feelings. When a giant photograph of Sun Yat-sen appeared on the screen, I said, "Look, the father of our nation is reviewing troops." He glanced at me, lost in his thoughts. After a while, he began to clap his hands and shouted "bravo!" and clenched his fists. Opposition to communism was left behind. He was touched by the military bearing and the strength of the country. He was proud of being a Chinese.

The parade touched the heartstring of every Chinese and aroused their enthusiasm and reverence. A powerful China has become their inner resource. We are all Chinese!

The majority of Chinese people feel proud of the glory of a strong China.

What is the glory and pride of the separatist forces? Is it the strength of America and Japan? Are you sure you are recognized by them? Are you sure you wouldn't be detested when you try to kiss their ass?

It is more important for the Chinese government to concentrate its efforts in developing the economy, improving people's living standards and increasing the country's strength. The political, economic and social systems should be improved to achieve full freedom and democracy and to make the mainland a dream place for people in Taiwan.

Political Organization Complex of My Generation

Many people of our generation have "organization complex". In China, citizens of every age group can find their own political organization. Young Pioneers is the organization for children aged between nine and 14. The Chinese Communist Youth League is the organization for youths aged between 14 and 25. The organization for people over 18 years old is the Communist Party.

Like most of my contemporaries, I joined the Young Pioneers and the Youth League. I applied for Party membership but was not accepted. Whenever I thought that I would belong to no organization if I was still not admitted by the Communist Party before I withdrew from the Youth League after I was 25 years old, I would feel sad.

The Young Pioneers was founded on October 13, 1949, by the Communist Party and was under the leadership of the Chinese Communist Youth League. According to the latest rules, all children aged between six and 14 can join the Young Pioneers. But when we were children, only good students could be Young Pioneers. It was an important matter for us to join the Young Pioneers. When the red scarf was put around our neck for the first time, we felt proud of ourselves from the bottom of our hearts. The teacher told us the red scarf was one corner of the Five-star Red Flag and it was dyed red with the blood of revolutionary martyrs. For a long period of time, I really believed the red scarf was dyed red with blood. Although most students joined the Young Pioneers, there were some trouble-makers who were not admitted even when they reached 14. Those children who constantly failed to get admitted by the Young Pioneers were disdained. The red scarf was a symbol of good children. The Young Pioneers was defined as "the mass organization for Chinese children, the school where the children learn communism and the reserve team to build socialism and communism". When I was a child, I firmly believed I was a successor to communism. I thought communism would be realized when I grew up. During the Cultural Revolution, I asked a PLA Representative when communism would be realized. He said he would not live to see it and I might be able to see it before I died, maybe not. I was sad when I thought I might die before communism was realized.

When the Cultural Revolution just began, the Young Pioneers and Little Red Guards co-existed for some time. I was then in my third year of primary school. I felt quite good about myself with a red scarf around my neck and a Little Red Guard armband around my arm. Not long after that, the Young Pioneers was replaced by the Little Red Guards. In October of 1978, the Communist Party resumed the Young Pioneers.

The Chinese Communist Youth League was established in August, 1922. It is the Communist Party's assistant and reserve force. All Chinese youth aged between 14 and 25 can join it. The Youth League was also replaced by the Red Guard organization during the Cultural Revolution and was not officially resumed until May 1978.

Soon after I had my first job at the age of 15, I applied membership in the Communist Youth League. I worked very hard and people all spoke very highly of me. But I was not among the first batch to join the

Youth League. The first reason was still because of my Big Uncle's historical background. The second reason was that I had always been a proud child, which was very negative in other people's mind. Chairman Mao said, "Modesty helps one to make progress while conceit makes one lag behind." Although my failure to join the Communist Youth League in the first batch was a terrible blow to me, it didn't affect my work enthusiasm. I still did the intense work conscientiously. I found some fellow workers who handed in their application for membership suddenly became more active in work. They all hastened to work and arrived at the workshop early to do the cleaning or fetch boiled water. Their pretended enthusiasm worked and they were among the first to join the Youth League. As soon as the oath-taking ceremony was over, they showed themselves in the true colors. I held them in contempt. That was why we were often educated to join the organization inwardly first.

In today's China, parents are still quite concerned with their children's joining the Young Pioneers or the Communist Youth League. The day when they join the organization is important for the children themselves as well for their parents. According to the constitution of the Young Pioneers, the goal of the organization is to unite and educate children to listen to the Party; love the motherland, the people, labor, and science and take good care of public property; study hard, do exercises, take part in social activities, develop one's ability, aspire to build our country into a modern and powerful socialist country; grow into qualified personnel for the socialist modernization and successors to the cause of communism. The words may sound quite hollow; most of them are in line with the parents' expectations on their children.

My son applied for membership in the Communist Youth League when he attended high school. I cared a lot about it. When we were young, we took joining the Youth League or the Party as our political mission and a goal in life. At that time, if you were a Youth League member or a Party member, it meant you were politically reliable. People had higher expectations on you. If you did something bad, people would say, "What kind of a Party member (or Youth League member) are you?" Youth League members and Party members had privileges. For example, they could go to college, get promotion, join the army, or go to work or study abroad before non-League or non-Party members. Now, things have changed. It wouldn't affect one's future career whether or not he is a League member or a Party member, unless he enters politics. It has been much easier now to join the Youth League or the Party, but people seem not to be as enthusiastic as before. Even so, I still believe there are no parents who encourage their children not to join the Communist Youth League. They think it is good to have an organization to restrict and direct their children's behaviors.

When my son was in college, one day he came home and told me he wanted to join the Communist Party. Since he has grown up, I am stricter with him. I asked him if he believed in communism. He said, "Nowadays, how many people join the Communist Party because they believe in communism?" I told him I believed in communism when I applied for Party membership and I decided to devote my life to the cause of communism. I asked him to think it over before he applied to join the Party. He thought I was taking it too seriously.

The oath of joining the Communist Party:

I volunteer to join the Communist Party of China, uphold the Party's program, observe the Party Constitution, fulfill a Party member's duties, carry out the Party's decisions, strictly observe Party discipline, guard Party secrets, be loyal to the Party, work hard, fight for communism throughout my life, be ready at all times to sacrifice my all for the Party and the people, and never betray the Party.

I told my son I would support him if he was sure he could keep his oath after joining the Party. "To fight for communism throughout one's life and be ready to sacrifice all for the Party and the people" was by no means a light promise. I didn't want my son to be a person who said one thing and meant another. Think about all the corrupt officials in today's society.

They once stood under the Party's flag and took the oath, but what they have done brought disgrace on the Party. I didn't want my son to be one of them.

According to the Party Constitution, Party members should "in time of difficulty or peril stand up for the interests of the country and the people. Fight bravely and fear no sacrifice."

Not everybody can do it. Some people did it and became the heroes of their period. I hoped my son would be prepared ideologically before joining the Party. Later he admitted his motivation of joining the Party was that he thought it would help him get a better job. He decided to learn more about the Party before he took the next step.

There are many young Party members in my company. They joined our private enterprise after graduation from college. State-owned enterprises in China all have their own Party organizations. There is no or incomplete Party organization in private enterprises. No matter what their motivation was when they joined the Party, I didn't want them to be in an unorganized state not long after they joined the Party. At my suggestion and under my supervision (It is one of my missions to supervise the Communist Party as a non-Communist party member myself), a Party branch was set up in the company with Liu Yanxiang, president of the company, as the Party branch secretary. I think it is not a bad thing for the company that the young employees are required to fulfill the duties and observe discipline as Party members besides being subject to the rules and regulations of the company and the laws of the state.

I Am a Non-Communist Party Member

Whenever I told my foreign friends that I was a non-Communist party member, they looked surprised. Many foreign friends don't know

China has eight parties besides the Communist Party.

The Communist Party of China (CPC) is the party in power. The other eight parties work in cooperation with the CPC and participate in government and political affairs. Relations between the Communist Party and other parties follow the guideline of "long-term coexistence and mutual supervision, treating each other with full sincerity and sharing weal or woe". There are no parties out of office or opposition parties in China. The multi-party cooperation and political consultation system under the leadership of the CPC is a basic political system of China.

The participation in state affairs of non-Communist parties mainly takes the following forms: participating in the exercise of state power, consultation on fundamental state policies and the choice of state leaders, the administration of state affairs, and the formulation and implementation of state policies, laws and regulations.

China's democratic parties are organizations of particular groups of people and are all smaller-sized. The non-Communist party Jiu San Society I am in has about 80,000 members, a little more than a thousandth of the Communist Party members.

In 2000, when I was pursuing my graduate degree in Beijing International Studies University, a classmate who was a Jiu San Society member initiated me into the society. She introduced me to some other members and leaders of the society. Some of them who had just met me said, "We should admit Liu Ping into Jiu San Society as soon as possible. Otherwise, outstanding elements like her would be seized by other parties." Although they said it jokingly, I felt warm. I was tested by the Communist Party for 10 years since I was 18, but had never reached the standards for a Communist Party member.

One day in the early 1990s, when I was still working in the Foreign Affairs Department of the H Ministry, a meeting was convened to solicit opinions from people like me who were not affiliated to any parties. I said, "Many outstanding people wish to join the Communist Party and are working hard for it, but have been continuously rejected. These people may have shortcomings, but as long as they are of fine character and believe in communism they should be admitted. I think the Party shouldn't be excessively concerned with petty details when judging someone if he meets the requirements for the Party membership."

"The reason why I don't want to join the Party now is that I am beginning to believe in God," I added.

That day, the department chief W called me to his office and said, "Liu Ping, what did you say at the meeting today? Don't say it anymore."

Twenty years ago, democracy was not as developed as it is today.

The Jiu San Society comprises of senior and middle-level intellectuals engaged in science and technology. I worked in the tourism industry. When the eight non-Communist parties were founded, there was no tourism in China. So there was not a party for people like me in the industry. I was organized into the No. 5 Branch directly under the supervision of Beijing Municipal Committee of Jiu San Society.

It was first founded in Chongqing with the name of Democracy and Science Society by a group of progressive scholars in the spirit of carrying forward the anti-imperialist patriotism of the May 4th Movement in 1919, the first mass movement in modern Chinese history. It was renamed the Jiu San Society on May 4, 1946 in commemoration of the victory of the Anti-Japanese War that fell on September 3, 1945. Jiu San means September 3.

The non-Communist parties suffered a devastating blow during the Cultural Revolution. In the summer of 1966, the Red Guards in Beijing issued their ultimatum to all non-Communist parties, ordering them to disband themselves within 72 hours and announce it in the newspaper. Many democratic personages were cruelly persecuted. The eight non-Communist parties gradually revived after 1978.

My son often told me that his classmates all admired me when they heard I was a Jiu San Society member. It is common in China that people admire or at least respect democratic personages. I think there are two reasons. First, there are fewer non-Communist party personages in China than the Communist Party members and it is relatively more difficult to join the non-Communist parties. Second, non-Communist parties are organizations of senior and middle-level intellectuals who are highly respected and have some influence in our society. When I joined the Jiu San Society, my professional title was associate translation editor which is equal to associate professor. Most of the middle-level intellectuals are in their thirties or forties. Senior-level intellectuals are older. So the average age of non-Communist party personages is quite high. When I first took part in the activity of the organization, I was surprised to find out that I was very young among them. Things have changed now. The reform and opening-up has given the young intellectuals many opportunities. They can make great achievements in their fields and enter the ranks of senior and middle-level intellectuals earlier. In the group of non-Communist parties, there are more and more young people abounding with vigor and vitality.

Why did I join the Jiu San Society? What was my motive?

First, although I am not interested in an official career, I love my country and I am concerned about national affairs. Joining the non-Communist parties provides us with a platform to exchange ideas with people in the same party and to better understand what is happening in our country every day.

Second, from the Young Pioneers to the Communist Youth League, I was used to belonging to some organization. Since I withdrew from the League at the age of 25, I didn't belong to any organization nor have any other beliefs. I needed to join a non-Communist party to regain the sense of belonging.

Third, seeking protection from the organization. As an active member in the reform and opening-up, it is inevitable for me to get involved in conflict with the forces of old traditions. I hope there is some place I can turn to when I meet difficulties or suffer injustice.

Fourth, learning knowledge. The Jiu San Society mainly comprises of senior and middle-level intellectuals engaged in science and technology. I hope I can exchange ideas with more people outside my profession to get more information, to broaden my horizons and to look at problems all-sidedly.

Fifth, participating in the administration and discussion of state affairs. It seems quite an ambitious purpose to me.

Certainly, the above motives are just my wishful thinking.

In fact, during the 10 years since I joined the Jiu San Society, I seldom took part in its activities as I was always busy with my work or traveling on business home or abroad. Even if I took part in the activities of the organization, I found what I could do was very limited.

The system of multi-party cooperation and political consultation under the leadership of the Communist Party of China is the basic political system of our country. To what extent can the system ensure democracy and freedom of a country or a nation is of little concern to me. No matter how many advantages and disadvantages the system has, it doesn't make any difference to me, because it is beyond my ability to make any change. I only care about real-life problems. I would be content if, as an entrepreneur, my daily work can help make our society more open and democratic.

To Be a Good Person

I have no religious belief. Although I have no religious belief, I would burn incense whenever I meet a temple or pray whenever I meet a church. Some friends said I should not pray to whatever god I met. Otherwise, no god would bless me. Sometimes when we visited a temple, someone would say, "You must burn incense and pray to every god. If you leave one god out, you would offend him and would be punished." I didn't think so. Most religions in the world advocate philanthropism and forgiveness and teach you to be a good person. If the gods of different religions were not able to accept each other, why should we have faith in them?

Someone said although I had no religious faith, I was born with enlightenment and I had predestined affinity with Buddha. I am not sure if it is true. But I believe one needs to believe in something to have a goal in one's life. Belief can also help people overcome psychological problems.

I once suffered from acute depression. It was getting much better later but I would have a recurrence of it from time to time. Many years ago, when there was something weighing heavily on my mind and I couldn't get rid of it, I would go to the Yonghe Lamasery to burn incense to get a peace of mind. Someone asked me, "In this case, why don't you become a Buddhist?" It is not that I don't believe in Buddhism. I just know too little about Buddha. For the time being, I don't have the time to read about Buddhism or to understand the true meaning of Buddhism. To believe in religion is not to follow the fashion. I will not have faith in it unless I fully understand it. I have no religious belief now. But I am convinced about one thing: One should first be a good person and do good and accumulate merit no matter he has religious belief or not.

Religion is a very complex issue in China.

On the one hand, the Constitution stipulates, "Citizens of the People's Republic of China enjoy freedom of religious belief. No State organ, public organization or individual may compel citizens to believe in, or not to believe in, any religion; nor may they discriminate against citizens who believe in, or do not believe in, any religion. The state protects normal religious activities."

On the other hand, religious issues are sensitive issues because they are easily confused with political issues and used by people with ulterior motives.

According to official figures, there are 100 million people in China who have religious beliefs. But some scholars believe the number should be 300 million. The main religions of our country are Buddhism, Taoism, Islam, Catholicism and Christianity.

In China, not so many people, especially government officials, Party members and League members talk about religion in public because the communists are atheists. But there are many big and small temples in the country that have become a crowded place of public worship. Many of the worshippers are Party members who are supposed to believe in communism.

Government officials show different levels of competence in the administration of religious affairs and the interpretation and implementation of religious policies. Some officials adopt passive attitude towards religious affairs to avoid trouble.

The story of Changjiao Village in Guizhou Province is a typical example.

The village has less than 1,000 villagers. Most of them are Bouyei people, one of the 56 Chinese ethnic groups. The annual per capita income of the village is less than 1,000 yuan. But there is a Catholic church in the poor village. Most of the villagers are Catholics. On the black wall of the villagers' shabby and ill-lit bedrooms, there is always a portrait of the Virgin Mary. The Bouyei people have no unified religion. They worship ancestors and believe in immortality of the soul.

I grew up in Guizhou and it has always been my wish to do something for my second home. I convinced American People to People Ambassador Programs to send professional delegations to Guizhou for professional exchanges. With the help of the local government, we decided to provide long-term financial aid to primary schools in Zhenning Bouyei and Miao Autonomous County in Anshun City. Changjiao Village Primary School was one of them. My company Xiang and People to People Ambassador Programs jointly donated a three-storey school building to Changjiao Village Primary School as well as books, bookshelves, TV sets and sports items.

Every time I visited Changjiao Village with the American delegations, I was deeply moved. The villagers were grateful and were especially warm and hospitable to the American guests. They would hold each others' hands and keep talking with sincere smile on their faces, though they couldn't understand each other. The American guests were often moved to tears.

Unable to communicate with the foreign guests with words, some of the villagers would make the sign of the cross with their hands. Once a little girl pull out the cross round her neck and showed it to me and the guests.

I hoped the American guests could visit the church in the village so that they could understand the status quo of religious freedom in China. In such a poor Bouyei village in the remote mountainous area, villagers are free to believe in God. Isn't it a strong indication that the constitutional right of religious freedom has been well guaranteed in our country? Isn't it a good opportunity to let Westerners understand the religious freedom of our country?

In fact, I was told the American guests could visit the primary school, but not the church. Whenever we walked to the village, the local officers would come to remind our guide to stop the guests from moving on. They didn't want the American guests to see the church. During our visit, the church was closed most of the time. In order that our guests wouldn't feel they were restricted in their movements, we told them there wasn't enough time and we must leave for the next destination.

Every visit of each American delegation to Changjiao Village needs to be approved by the local government.

On September 2, 2007, Changjiao Village School started a new semester and the school building we donated was almost finished. An American delegation happened to be in Guiyang those days, so we arranged them to attend the school's opening ceremony. The vice president of People to People Ambassador Programs specially came for the opening ceremony. He brought every schoolchild a pencil-box filled with pens and pencils. Our company and some Guiyang citizens also donated stationery, sports items, books and bookshelves. Everything went smoothly as it was arranged by the local government.

On October 14, 2007, the school building was completed. Another delegation happened to be in Guiyang. So we arranged their visit to Changjiao Village Primary School. I flew to Guiyang to join the delegation in their visit to the school.

Our local agent in Guizhou directly arranged the visit without getting the local government's approval. But I didn't know it.

Without the participation of the local government, the atmosphere was more unconstrained. Inside and outside the school, the American guests and the schoolchildren and villagers were holding hands and talking cordially with each other, body language and smile were more effective than words. Our guide was hardly needed to help with the interpretation. Many villagers spoke Bouyei language which even our local guide couldn't understand.

Then, the township head came; the female official of the Bureau of Ethnic and Religious Affairs of the town came; the police also came on their motorbikes.

The official of the Bureau of Ethnic and Religious Affairs asked me if I was the organizer. She looked worried and kept saying, "There is going to be trouble. There is going to be trouble."

I asked her, "What is it?"

"The villagers are in too close contact with the foreigners and something bad is going to happen."

The officials scolded the headmaster who was honest but slow of speech. I explained immediately that it had nothing to do with the headmaster.

The villagers started to talk about it among themselves and told our guide that the officials came to cause trouble because they didn't get any benefit from it.

It was regrettable that our officials gave the villagers such a nega-

457

tive impression.

I didn't expect the government officials of such a remote mountainous area could perfectly interpret and implement the country's religious policies. Besides, our local agent was on the wrong side. I wanted to soothe things over, so I asked the American guests to get on the bus first.

I said to the female township head in a low voice, "Please smile and don't look so serious. Otherwise the American guests would feel puzzled."

Actually, they had already sensed it. They asked me, "What are the police doing here?"

"They are here for our safety. After all, we are in a remote mountainous area."

To be fair, the police were polite and civilized. They just stood there quietly with friendly expression.

All the American guests got on the bus. The local guide and the female township head started to quarrel with each other in front of the bus and kept screaming louder and louder. I went over and stopped the quarrel, "You are making a spectacle of yourselves quarreling in front of the foreign guests. Would you please let the guests leave first and I will stay to deal with the problem."

The guide and the American guests left the village. I stayed.

I explained the whole thing to them for more than an hour and kept apologizing to the township head. I admitted that I was wrong to have arranged the visit without getting the local government's permit and it was a severe violation of the disciplines related to foreign affairs.

"The guide dared to argue with me! I could have asked the police to arrest him."

"That's right. That's right. Thank you for your willingness to forgive the guide. I will report it to his superior and he will be criticized for it."

Later I talked to the guide, "You didn't apologize for breaking the rules and you even dared to argue with the government official."

After I returned to Beijing, I wrote a letter to the township head to further offer my apology.

Later when we arranged the American delegations to visit Changjiao Village Primary School, our requests were rejected for different reasons. Our plan to provide long-term financial aid to the school also couldn't be carried out.

A few American guests, ignorant of Chinese people's customs, gave the disposable toothbrushes and soaps they took from hotels to the students as their gifts. It was one of the local government's excuses to reject the delegations' visit. We apologized to them on behalf of the American guests several times and asked the American guests not to do it again in the future.

The local government's biggest misgiving about foreigners' visit was the Catholic church. Their misgiving was not groundless. It's said some Westerners without approval of any department directly rushed into a village school somewhere in Guizhou for missionary work, which caused great trouble for the local government.

Some Westerners even came to promote religions under the banner of charity. No wonder the local government was so nervous about accepting donation from foreign countries.

We were also told by the primary school that the T-shirts sent to them by the American guests were taken by the township government to check if the logo on the T-shirts had any political implication.

The Chinese government does not welcome any foreign missionary in China according to our Constitution. There are historic reasons behind it. In the modern history of China, Western missionaries were involved in imperialist powers' aggression of our country. For example, they joined in the Eight-Power Allies Forces' burning, killing and looting in Beijing in 1900, especially burning Yuanmingyuan (the Winter Palace), which resulted in a monstrous offence to Chinese people.

According to China's Constitution, religious bodies and religious affairs are not subject to any foreign domination.

No matter you agree or disagree with our Constitution, you have to abide by the Constitution as long as you are in the territories of the People's Republic of China.

Recently, things took a turn to the better. Some open-minded government officials showed their support for normal international exchanges. Our foreign delegations could visit Changjiao Village again.

One of the high-ranking officials of the province said, "It is a good thing for Westerners to come to visit and know that there is a Catholic church in such a remote village. We talk about religious freedom every day. Isn't it a good indication of religious freedom in our country?"

However, the Catholic church of Changjiao Village is still not fully open to foreigners. I have always thought it is very regretful.

So far, we haven't found any foreign guest who has visited Changjiao Village hostile to our country. It is totally unnecessary for our local government officials to stop eating for fear of choking.

Although I have no religious belief, I have my principle. One may not believe in a religion, but mustn't blaspheme against it. I would never say anything disrespectful about religious belief, as long as it is not a cult.

Many of my family members and relatives believe in Christianity. My grandma was a pious Christian when she was alive. All my paternal aunts are Christians. They fully enjoy the freedom of religious belief.

I asked my father how grandma came to believe in Christianity and learnt that Christianity was not my grandma's first belief. Before liberation, grandma led the whole family to believe in I-Kuan Tao. Life was extremely difficult with seven children to bring up. My grandpa was addicted to opium and couldn't give it up after several attempts. How could my grandma live without spiritual sustenance under that circumstance? The family lived in a remote village and no other religion was spread there. Influenced by a neighbor who brought in I-Kuan Tao to the village, grandma began to believe in it and led the whole family to chant sutras secretly at home every day. I-Kuan Tao advocated vegetarianism, which was apparently a relief for the family since they couldn't afford meat.

During the early days of liberation, my father joined the Communist Party. He asked grandma and other family members to give up their belief in I-Kuan Tao after he learnt it was a cult. At first, grandma wouldn't listen to my father. When my father told her that I-Kuan Tao was against the Communist Party, grandma soon agreed to give it up. Grandma had a deep love for the Party because it was the Party that helped grandpa give up opium smoking. Grandma told everyone how good the Communist Party was.

I-Kuan Tao was founded in 1877 by Wang Jueyi who came from Qingzhou City of Shandong Province. It was banned by the Chinese government in 1950.

All religious activities came to a halt during the Cultural Revolution. Sites for religious activities were gradually reopened after the Cultural Revolution.

It was in the mid 1980s that grandma started to believe in Christianity. Grandma lived with her biggest daughter, my big aunt, in Dandong and went to church with her every Sunday.

I left my hometown in northeast China when I was only one year old and after that I seldom met my grandma. Grandma enjoyed high prestige in the big family and was widely praised by the fellow villagers. I have told you in previous chapters the tragic stories of the family and the hardships my grandma experienced all her life. Grandma set a good example for the whole family with her strong will. I thought it was after grandma believed in Christianity that she really relieved herself from mental suffering. She became very optimistic. She repeatedly told people that she was not afraid of death and she would go to heaven after she died. Grandma was a devout Christian, but she never forced others to believe in it. When I visited my hometown in the mid 1990s, grandma asked me amiably and softly why I had no religious belief. She said it was good to have a religious belief and the whole family would benefit if

461

one person of the family was religious. Grandma died after she had her 98th birthday. On her birthday, she was sitting on the *kang* under a red blanket, a gift from me, surrounded by her children and grandchildren. Shortly after her birthday, grandma left us in peace.

From the dinner after the funeral, each of the relatives or villagers took away something, a bowl, a plate, a pair of chopsticks, a glass etc. to the memory of grandma and most importantly to gain some good luck from grandmother who was regarded as a saint. The dinner finished with nothing left.

Since Grandma passed away, I can always feel that there is a pair of eyes looking at me from heaven and a soul blessing and protecting me.

As I have mentioned previously, I respect religious people and would never despise any religion. But *Falun Gong* is an exception because I don't think it is a religion.

In the mid 1990s, I had the hardest period of time in my life. My son was in primary school and I had to look after him alone. What I dreaded most was that my son got ill. Once my son was ill for a long time and didn't get any better. Someone recommended me a hospital of Chinese medicine. It was very crowded in the hospital. I was carrying a backpack and there was 5,000 yuan in it, which was the bonus I just got and a large sum for me at that time. After seeing the doctor, we went back to the neighborhood where we lived. A group of old men and women were doing some propaganda in the courtyard carrying some banners. After enquiry, I learnt they were publicizing *Falun Gong*. It was the first time I heard it. They tried to persuade me to buy a copy of the book *Turning the Wheel of the Law*. I was curious. At the same time, I needed spiritual sustenance. So I decided to buy one. When I looked for money in my backpack, I found my bonus was gone. Then I recalled when I was waiting outside the hospital pharmacy, I felt a tug at my backpack. The money must get stolen at that moment. I took out the only 10 yuan note left in my pocket and bought the book. The book was priced at 12 yuan, but I was only charged eight yuan. They told me the wholesale price was eight yuan and they did not want to cheat, so they sold the book at eight yuan. I often jokingly told my friends that I bought a *Turning the Wheel of the Law* at 5,008 yuan.

I read the book. It is still in the drawer in my office. I just don't understand how such a ridiculous book attracted so many followers. Readers can judge by themselves from the following stories described in the book.

When Li Hongzhi (founder of *Falun Gong*) *was a child, he played hide and seek with other children. He said in his thoughts "Nobody can see me now." Other children really couldn't see him and he became invisible.*

When he was in the fourth grade, one day, he left his schoolbag in the classroom. When he went back to get it, the classroom was already locked and all the windows were closed. At that moment, an idea came to his mind "I wish I could get in". As he thought so, he found he was already in the classroom. The next moment, he was outside the classroom.

Li Hongzhi said that Falun Gong could help people cure every disease, stay fit and healthy and become young again. Some old women even had menstruation again after they believed in Falun Gong.

I had direct contact with an overseas *Falun Gong* believer.

A Chinese American went to the office of my client People to People Ambassador Programs and asked to join a delegation to come to visit China. She made it clear that she was a *Falun Gong* believer. My client understood the Chinese government's attitude towards *Falun Gong*. Certainly they couldn't receive her. The woman refused to leave and placed a sleeping bag in the courtyard in front of the office building. The client called me and wanted me to talk to her. When we talked over the telephone, most of the time she was preaching the value of *Falun Gong* and tried to persuade me to believe in it. So we had the following dialogue.

"Since you advocate religious freedom, why do you force me to accept your ideas?"

"I am an overseas Chinese. I have the freedom to go to China and to promote *Falun Gong* in China."

"You can come to China in other ways. It is not my business. But you won't be able to come to China with my delegation. My delegations come to China to promote the China-US friendship, fundamentally different from your purpose of coming to China. You have the freedom to believe in *Falun Gong* and I have the freedom not to believe in it."

Later I came to know that she really planned beforehand to come to China to promote *Falun Gong*. She had a doctor's degree. She said it was *Falun Gong* that helped her obtain her doctorate. Before she practised *Falun Gong*, she made several attempts but all failed. I didn't know what to say.

A Beijing girl who I know married a Westerner. She worked as tour leader for leisure groups from a Western European country and often came to China with the groups. She became a *Falun Gong* practitioner. She had a child when she was over 40 years old and said it was *Falun Gong* that sent her the child.

In recent years, she took every opportunity of coming to China to promote *Falun Gong*. She instigated Chinese tour guides to withdraw from the Communist Party or the Youth League. She said she would take care of it and just needed to make a statement of withdrawal on the internet on behalf of them. If the tour guide said he was neither a Party member nor a League member, she would ask, "Have you joined the Little Red Guards? That case, you can declare your withdrawal from it on the internet." What nonsense! The Little Red Guards was a product of the Cultural Revolution. Since the Cultural Revolution was over several decades ago, how can the Little Red Guards still exist today? Was it something a normal religious believer would do? It really puzzled me why she did all these. What were her real purposes? Chinese tour guides all disliked her and were unwilling to work with her.

She often brought unlawful propaganda materials about *Falun Gong* into the country. In 2009, she was investigated by the state security department.

I read her article on the internet. It was about her being trial in June, 2009. I was in no position to comment on the propriety of law enforcement or the truthfulness of her story. She said she didn't break the law. But in fact, she did. She brought in unlawful propaganda materials and promoted *Falun Gong* which was a cult and was banned in our country. She didn't mention it in the article. Overseas *Falun Gong* organizations made much of it and asserted she had been kidnapped in China. The truth I knew was that she was expelled from the country. I was sympathetic with her. It is very sad if a person is used by politics.

However, we need to self-examine and rethink, how could such an absurd cult stir up such disturbances and have quite a number of followers?

Personally, I think religious belief will prove valuable to building a harmonious society. In July, 2009, when I went to the Salt Lake City to attend an international meeting with my son, I was impressed by the city's friendliness and harmony and felt it was different from other cities in the United States. My son had the same feelings too. My son practices kick boxing. He got help from many strangers when he was looking for a fitness club in the strange city. A taxi driver even drove him to the club for free. According to online information, more than half of the population of Salt Lake City believes in Mormonism. Salt Lake City has the lowest crime rate and divorce rate among the big cities in the country.

The Chinese government has paid more attention to "religion promotes harmony". As an ordinary Chinese who has no religious belief for the time being, I sincerely hope that the religious atmosphere will become more harmonious in our country and that religion will make contributions to building a harmonious society.

As I grow older, I am becoming more and more fatalistic and I need some support in my spiritual world. I will probably have some belief in the near future.

I am sure for one thing: You have to be a good person if you want to be blessed by your god.

I Am a Manchu Princess

In China, minority ethnic groups are admired by the Han people. Many Westerners don't understand it. I met some Westerners who were extremely biased against China and they thought minority groups were discriminated and persecuted in China. When I told them I was not a Han, they looked at me with their eyes wide open.

I am a Manchu. I am very happy that I belong to the minority group. I always tell Westerners that I am in the same ethnic group as the last emperor of China, so I am a princess.

Once at an international conference, I said in my speech the Han people all wish they were ethnic minorities. The audience all looked at me with a puzzled expression. I said if one of the couple belongs to an ethnic minority, their child would choose to be a minority instead of a Han. My son is an example.

There are more than 10 million Manchu people in China. The Miao ethnic group has less than one million people. My younger brother is a Manchu and my sister-in-law is a Miao. Their daughter Liu Hongye could be either Manchu or Miao. I suggested that my niece follow her mother's nationality. But she was determined to follow that of her father. I said that there were too many Manchu people and it was more distinct to be a Miao. She argued that there were more Miao people than Manchu people in Guizhou. It is true. The Manchu mainly concentrate in north China while the Miao mainly live in the southwest.

In fact, Manchu and Miao are two of the major ethnic groups in China. In order of population, the major ethnic groups are Han,

Zhuang, Manchu, Hui and Miao. Due to some political reasons, some Westerners know there are Tibetan and Uygur people in China, but they don't know China is a big country with 56 ethnic groups and has ethnic minorities all over the country.

In China we always say that the 56 ethnic groups are a big family.

Influenced by the Western media's biased views on issues related to Tibet and Xinjiang Uygur autonomous regions, many Westerners think ethnic minorities in China are deprived of religious freedom, are not allowed to preserve their traditional culture and customs, and are persecuted by the Han people. In fact, the Han and ethnic minorities have the same destiny. They share hardships as well as joys. The destiny of all these ethnic groups is closely associated with the prospects of the country. Every ethnic group suffered during the 10 years of the disastrous Cultural Revolution, just as they all benefited from the country's reform and opening-up. The country does not treat any ethnic group differently, saying turkey to one and bazzard to another. Only when the country is prosperous, the 56 ethnic groups will all be prosperous; if the country is on the wane, they will be all on the wane. The 56 ethnic groups are in the same boat. They share the benefits of the country's correct decisions as well as the disasters of the wrong decisions.

As an ordinary Chinese, I believe that in China every ethnic group needs more democracy and freedom. However, although some Chinese people may not approve of the government's way of dealing with some matters, no one will support the Tibetan and Uygur separatists; no one will approve of the splitting of our country.

Many many years before I was born, Tibet and Xinjiang had been an inalienable part of the Chinese territory. I believe people in Tibet and Xinjiang Uygur autonomous regions just like people of other minority groups, hope they can live happily and peacefully in the big family, enjoying democracy and freedom. What the government should do is to give the ordinary people more democracy and freedom and let them live in true harmony.

I am not the only one who has the idea. The great majority of the ordinary Chinese people have the same idea.

According to historical data, in the mid-13th century, Tibet was officially incorporated into the territory of China's Yuan Dynasty. Since then, although China experienced several dynastic changes, Tibet has remained under the jurisdiction of the central government of China.

In 1653 and 1713, the Qing emperors granted honorific titles to the fifth Dalai Lama and the fifth Bainqen Lama respectively, henceforth officially establishing the titles of the Dalai Lama and the Bainqen Erdeni as well as their political and religious status in Tibet. The Dalai Lama ruled the bulk of areas from Lhasa while the Bainqen Erdeni ruled the remaining area of Tibet from Xigaze.

In the Yuan (1271-1368), Ming (1368-1644) and Qing (1644-1911) dynasties, the central government exercised jurisdiction over Tibet. Despite the fact that incessant foreign aggression and civil wars weakened the central government of the Republic of China, it continued to grant honorific titles to the Dalai Lama and the Bainqen Erdeni. On many occasions the Dalai Lama and the Bainqen Erdeni expressed their support for national unification and for the central government. In 1940, the chairman of the national government issued an official decree conferring the title of the 14th Dalai Lama on Lhamo Toinzhub. The installation ceremony was conducted in Lhasa under the supervision of Wu Zhongxin, the commissioner from the central government, and Raiqen Khutuktu, the Regent after the death of the 13th Dalai Lama. The 14th Dalai Lama took over reins of government on November 17, 1950, and became one of the leaders of Tibetan Buddhism at the age of 16.

The national government was founded on July 1, 1925 and dismissed on May 20, 1948. It was the central government and the highest organ of state administration during that period of China's history. The People's Republic of China led by the CPC was founded on October 1, 1949. On May 23, 1951, the agreement between the central people's government and the local government of Tibet on *Measures for the Peaceful Liberation of Tibet* was signed in Beijing. The Dalai Lama sent a telegram to Chairman Mao Zedong on October 24, 1951, declaring his support of the agreement and his readiness to implement it. In the autumn of 1954 the Dalai Lama came to Beijing to attend the First Session of the National People's Congress of the People's Republic of China and was elected a vice-chairman of the NPC Standing Committee.

In the beginning of 1955, when the Dalai Lama returned to Lhasa from Beijing, he wrote "Ode to Chairman Mao" in which he compared Chairman Mao to the sun, a loving mother who protected the Tibetan people and a roc that had defeated imperialism and liberated Tibetan people from bondage and directed them to the way to peace. He wished our great leader would shine forever like the world's torch.

On April 22, 1956, the Preparatory Committee for the Tibet Autonomous Region was set up and the Dalai Lama was elected chairman of the committee. He was fully trusted by the central government and loved by the people.

In late November of 1956, the Dalai Lama was invited to attend the Grand Summons Ceremony on the occasion of the 2500th anniversary of Sakyamuni's Nirvana in India. He stayed there for three months surrounded by the separatist forces. Since then, he has been at the mercy of the separatist forces whether he wants it or not.

After 1957, the Dalai Lama acted in concert with the upper-class separatist forces in Tibet. They tore up the 17-Article Agreement and launched a full-scale armed rebellion against the motherland. On March 17, 1959, the Dalai Lama exiled to India.

For more than 700 years, the central government of China has continuously exercised sovereignty over Tibet, and Tibet has never been an independent state. Now millions of files in both Chinese and Tibetan recording historical facts for more than seven centuries are being kept in the archives of Beijing, Nanjing and Lhasa. No government of any country in the world has ever recognized Tibet as an independent state.

On our company's 2010 Training Session, I invited a high-ranking official to give us a presentation on religions in China. I also invited

American and European clients and friends to the presentation and prepared simultaneous interpretation for them. The government official had a great sense of humor and explained the complicated political background in simple language with some funny jokes. It was a refreshing experience and the audience broke into applause and laughter from time to time.

Most of the participants studied English when in the university and have worked with Westerners for a long time. They could well represent China's intellectual class. They had high opinions of the speech delivered by the government official.

I was secretly watching the facial reaction of the Western guests. They looked very serious from beginning to end. When we all burst out laughing, they still kept a poker face. I think there are two reasons. First, simultaneous interpretation could convey the meaning, but not the Chinese-style humor. Second, Westerners are not used to Chinese people's talking in such a way.

I feel kind of sorry. We are all friends and partners with profound friendship between us. But they felt uncomfortable after hearing only one speech of a Chinese government official. Have the Westerners ever thought how Chinese people feel when they hear the Western media or their government officials' prejudiced opinions of China every day?

With regard to the Tibetan issue, the Chinese government and scholars refer to the historical data to prove that Tibet has been a part of China's territory since the Yuan Dynasty over 700 years ago. But ordinary Chinese people prefer to tell the West China's sovereignty over Tibet in some other way.

The following paragraph by Wang Xiaodong, one of the authors of *China Is Not Happy* which was published in 2009, is representative of the opinions of the majority of the Chinese.

Granted that the Tibetan separatist forces and some Westerners could prove China had only suzerainty instead of sovereignty over Tibet before 1959, so what?

470

Will the majority of the Chinese people accept the independence of Tibet? Still no. I can tell the Westerns that the opinion of most of the Chinese people is reflected in the video "Tibet was, is and will always be a part of China" made by a 21-year-old Chinese youth who now studies in Canada: If Westerners pick up their bedrolls and withdraw from America, Oceania, Africa and Asia and return to Europe, we will withdraw from Tibet. Otherwise, don't talk about it with us. This is the opinion of the majority of the Chinese people. In terms of political strength, the United States occupies Afghanistan and Iraq and disintegrated Yugoslavia. So today, is the United States ready to disintegrate China? The Tibetan and Uygur separatist forces and some of the Chinese intellectuals indeed count on Americans to disintegrate China. But are Americans ready? Are Americans willing to go to war with China, a nuclear power, for Tibet? It seems the United States is not ready yet according to the American free press. In that case, Westerners can arouse nothing but the Chinese people's disgust and contempt if they continue to question China's sovereignty over Tibet.

I always tell my Western friends that they don't necessarily have to share my political views, but they should think about the will of the majority of Chinese people. The solution of any political problem should comply with the public opinion. Otherwise, there would be big trouble and those who suffer in the end would still be the people.

Before intervention by foreign forces, it was like fighting between two brothers when the Han had disagreement with the Tibetan or the Uygur. But now, things are much more complicated. When I was on a business trip in Xinjiang Uygur Autonomous Region, the local people would tell me that it used to be very common for the Han people and the local Uygur people to have a fight, just like brothers of a family would quarrel and fight. But now, they keep each other at a respectful distance because any conflict would be magnified to become a problem of the nation. When I was a child, I often heard of stories about intermarriage between the Han and the Tibetan or the Uygur people. It's said such marriages are getting fewer now.

No matter in Tibet or in Xinjiang, I enjoy the brotherly affection the local people and I have for each other. It depends on your personality instead of your ethnic group whether or not you can get along well with the local ethnic minorities. In the Grape Valley in Turpan area, the Uygur brothers and I sat on the ground, drinking wine and eating meat. They liked me and I liked them too. A Han official who had been transferred there to support Xinjiang was also present. He proposed a toast to me. Obviously, he was not popular. Two Uygur brothers who sat beside me said something to me in their local language. I couldn't understand it. A Uygur colleague whispered in my ear, "They ask you not to pay attention to that Han man. He won't stay here for long." I was touched at their words. I was a Han too (I didn't tell them I was a Manchu), but they trusted me and liked me and spoke ill of another Han man in front of me without any scruple. It thus indicates what matters is what kind of person you are rather than what ethnic group you belong to.

On March 14, 2008, violence broke out in Lhasa that astonished people home and abroad and the Tibet Autonomous Region was closed to tourists. On May 1, the city reopened, but had few tourists. When I arrived at the Lhasa Airport on May 11 and met my friends Puntsok and Nyma, I was surprised to realize that I was the first guest from the hinterland of the country they received after the 3.14 Incident, which meant I might be the first from the interior's tourism circle to visit Tibet after the incident. In the days that followed, the people who received me were all Tibetans. There was no gulf between us and we talked about everything.

I visited many monasteries among which Relong Monastery impressed me most. The former grandeur could be savored from the ruins of part of the monastery that was destroyed in the Cultural Revolution. When I had a chat with the abbot, he told me he was in prison during the Cultural Revolution. He said he couldn't stand the persecution against monks during the campaign of "destroying the four olds" and ran away, and was caught when he tried to escape "there" and was put into prison. "Where is 'there'?" "India." I was again touched by his sincerity and trust in me. In such sensitive period, the old abbot confided to me that he tried to run over "there". He didn't treat me as an outsider. This should be the normal relationship between people of different ethnic groups. What he experienced during the Cultural Revolution was not uncommon. Many Chinese people, regardless of religious belief and ethnic group, suffered the same pain.

There were more than 20 monks in the monastery. I met eight or nine of them. The rest had been invited by local Tibetans to chant scriptures at their homes. The family could pay them according to the family's finance. I wanted to do some contribution to the monastery, so I asked the abbot if Relong Monastery could chant scriptures and pray for my company Xiang and the Olympic Games which would be held in Beijing soon. The abbot said their pray was for all mortal beings, not a specific event or a person. If they knew the name of the person or the event, they could include them when chanting scriptures. Nyma wrote down my name, the name of my company and the full name of the Beijing Olympic Games in Tibetan. I contributed 1,000 yuan for the maintenance of the monastery. Later I asked Puntsok if the 1,000 yuan meant something to the monastery. He said the monastery was not well-funded and 1,000 yuan was a big sum of money for them. I was glad that I could do something for them.

The world will become a better place if people are sincere with and trust each other. It sounds easy, but not everyone can do it.

I have been to many ethnic minority areas and got on well with the local people. I would take a lot of pictures wherever I went. I did not just show the people their pictures in my digital camera. After I returned to Beijing, I would always develop and send all the photos to them, no matter how far away they were from Beijing.

My slight effort has brought them a lot of pleasure. Since the reform and opening-up policy was introduced, the economic development in minority areas has been greatly promoted and the people's living standards have been improved. But photo taking is still a luxury for them. Many tourists take pictures of them, but few would send them the pictures. I send them the pictures every time, so they like me.

On this Chinese New Year's Eve, my cellphone received a message from a Tibetan monk. I met his parents when visiting the Potala Palace. His mother was a very attractive woman. I asked her if I could take a picture of her and promised I would send her the picture. They were very simple people, and I kept my promise. They asked their son to call to express their thanks to me as soon as they received the pictures.

Protection of ethnic minority culture is a long-term challenge and mission in China.

The spoken and written languages of ethnic minorities are well preserved in our country. Even if there are defects, they are not restricted to minority groups. In recent years, a campaign for protection of intangible cultural heritage has been launched all over the country. To protect and develop the country's culture, tradition, customs and history is a common challenge that the 56 ethnic groups must face.

When I traveled in Yunnan Province, in July, 2008, I happened to be in Yuanyang County, Yi and Hani Autonomous Prefecture on the traditional "Torch Festival". I saw groups of local people in their ethnic minority costumes such as the Yi people and the Hani people. The Hani people have their own spoken language but no written language. What surprised me was that not only the old but also the young spoke the Hani language. In this way, their language is passed down orally from generation to generation. I tried to talk with some Hani girls, but they could hardly speak mandarin. I also found that all those who couldn't speak mandarin had very little schooling. Those better educated could speak both mandarin and their own language. It seems that the local ethnic minorities are much less sinicized than I expected.

Manchu people are considered to be the most sinicized. Twenty years ago, a Manchu autonomous county was established in Kuandian, Dandong City where Liu Family River Village is located. There are several Manchu autonomous counties in the northeast where the Manchu culture and customs are better preserved and developed.

The minority ethnic groups will inevitably be assimilated by the Han people just as China and other developing countries have gradually been Westernized. They must open up and increase exchanges with the outside world if they want to develop their economy and live a better life. To protect the cultures of different ethnic groups and ensure cultural continuity is a big challenge for the Chinese government. It is also a problem for countries inhabited by many ethnic groups.

Guizhou, where I grew up, is a multi-ethnic province and home to Miao, Bouyei, Yi, Dong, Shui, Hui, Gelao, Zhuang, Yao, Manchu, Bai, Qiang and Tujia and so on, altogether 17 ethnic minorities besides the Han people. Most of the minority ethnic groups live in remote and inaccessible mountains. Life is hard for them.

When I was on an inspection tour in the Miao and Dong areas in southeast Guizhou, I found the beautiful Miao and Dong villages along the way deeply impressive. But what's behind the beauty is poverty that the developed Western countries can hardly imagine. Since the reform and opening-up, the rural surplus labor force flocked to the cities to earn money so that they could build new houses when back home. More and more ugly and obtrusive white ceramic tile buildings have sprung up in the beautiful villages. I couldn't help thinking that the beautiful villages might disappear in the near future. However, to preserve the beauty of the villages doesn't mean they have to farm by the slash-and-burn method and live in poverty forever.

Guizhou Province protects the non-material cultural heritage of ethnic minorities through development of local tourism. Over-exploitation of tourist resources has become a serious problem in our country. The development of China has been a process of making mistakes and correcting these mistakes. Chinese people are learning from the practice of the economic reform and have paid prices when achieving successes.

The following story happened in Xingyi City of Guizhou. Miao village A was developed as a tourist attraction. The villagers became rich and began to build new houses. They built multi-storey houses and tiled the exterior wall white. They didn't know the townspeople only used the white tiles to pave the wall in the bathroom. The local government asked them not to tile the wall with white tiles, but no one listened. When more and more white buildings appeared in the village, fewer and fewer tourists came. The government helped the neighboring village B develop their tourist resources and the tourists were all attracted to Miao village B. The villagers of Miao village A then realized their mistakes. They removed the white tiles and restored the exterior of the houses to its original appearance.

The houses in most of Guizhou's minority areas are uncomfortable. It's the local people's right to improve their living conditions after they get rich. More and more villagers have realized how important it is to preserve the traditional culture of their own ethnic group. I know a family in Shiqiao Village, southeast Guizhou. They got rich from paper making by indigenous method and spent 200,000 yuan (an astronomical figure in rural Guizhou) on a new house. The exterior of the house is the same with that of traditional Miao architecture. The interior decoration is very modern with a flush toilet and a shower.

The central government should provide guidance and support to local governments in improving the local people's living conditions while protecting the non-material cultural heritage.

My good friend Yang, general director of Guizhou Tourism Administration, and anthropologist Zhang Xiaosong have made great achievements in the protection of the intangible cultural heritage of Guizhou's ethnic minorities.

Take the Miao embroidery as an example. The Miao embroidery has a history of several hundred years. Every Miao girl could do embroidery. They began to learn it from their mothers, elder sisters or sisters-in-law at the age of four or five. When they were seven or eight years old, their embroidery could be used in their dress. With the advance of urbanization and the changes in people's aesthetic tastes, fewer and fewer young people of Miao wear their traditional dress. The faster the modern culture develops, the faster the traditional craft of the Miao embroidery would disappear. To prevent it from happening, Yang and Zhang Xiaosong visited many Miao villages for investigation and found that many Miao embroidery stitches and skills are in danger of extinction. They applied for special fund from the State Development Bank and held training classes for the women in the village who could learn all kinds of Miao embroidery skills from the one or two old women masters. They also developed market for the Miao embroidery products and led the Miao women on a road to prosperity so that more of them could sit down and pick up needles. As a government official, Yang has devoted herself to calling on the villagers to build capacity for self-development and to take the path of sustainable development. It is a comfort to see that our country has paid more and more attention to the protection of the intangible cultural heritage. On May 20, 2006, the Miao embroidery was included in the first list of national intangible cultural heritage items issued by the State Council.

My company and People to People Ambassador Programs jointly donated a three-storey school building to Changjiao Village Primary School, Bouyei and Miao Autonomous County, Anshun City of Guizhou. Most of the villagers are Bouyei people. Because of our repeated request, the school building was built in Bouyei style. Our purpose was to arouse the local people's attention to the protection of their ethnic culture.

The ethnic minorities in China enjoy quite a lot of preferential policies.

As I have mentioned previously, many Chinese Han people wish they were ethnic minorities.

I believe there is bourgeois sentimentality behind many girls' yearning for life in minority areas. The ethnic minorities have beautiful costumes and romantic cultures. Most of the minority groups live in places with green hills and clear waters, which help to nurture outstanding personalities and beauties.

On the other hand, the Chinese government has provided special support to and adopted preferential policies for ethnic minorities.

First, the family planning policy.

Family planning is a basic state policy in China. Westerners may know about the so-called "one-child policy", but they don't necessarily know a more lenient childbirth policy is adopted towards minority peoples. An ethnic minority family that lives in the city may have one or two children. Minority families with special living conditions, such as living in the pastoral area on the Qinghai-Tibet Plateau, in the mountainous area in the southern Ningxia Hui Autonomous Region and the agricultural and pastoral areas in the Xinjiang Uygur Autonomous Region, may have three children. Under special conditions, a minority family may have more than three children. For example, according to the local policy in the Xinjiang Uygur Autonomous Region, families that belong to the minority group with a population below 50,000 may have four children; families in the agricultural and pastoral areas may have one more child if they have three girls. Families of Oroqen, Ewenki and Daur ethnic groups in the Inner Mongolia Autonomous Region and families that belong to the ethnic minorities with a population below 100,000 in Yunnan may have as many children as they like. In Tibet, the family planning policy is implemented among officials, government employees and urban residents that account for only 12 percent of the total population of the region, while 88 percent of the population there is not restricted by the national family planning policy.

Another preferential policy is related to the college entrance examination.

To ensure that all minority students enjoy an equal right to education and to develop talented personnel for minority areas, a preferential policy is implemented in the college entrance examination, whereby extra marks from four to 20 have been specially awarded for minority students according to different areas. Minority students in Beijing can enjoy

was born behind this blue door (photo on the right) in July 1955. The house was still there when visited it in 1994. The photo above is my home in ianyungang City in Jiangsu Province when I was vo and three years old. Our neighbor has lived iere for more than 50 years.

The above photo on the left (taken in 2009) is the bedroom where I stayed with my three year old son, a pregnant roommate and her mother when I worked for the H Ministry. Now it is the dormitory for migrant workers.

A lot of Chinese people still live in small houses like the one in the above photo on the right. The family of my brother-in-law's uncle has lived there for three generations in Beijing.

ly home today is always crowed with friends.

The photo on the left is the only one of Liu Yanxiang's childhood. Yanxiang, who was born in 1977, is president of Xin Xin Yi Yang. Yanxiang's happy family in the photo on the right.

Zheng Han, Xin Xin and Bao'er, Yanxiang's son.

Liu Family in the early 1990s. My grandmother is the one sitting in the middle, to her left is Big Uncle and to her right is Third Uncle. More and more family members have left Liu Family River Village.

Chen Family in 1994 when I took my parents to visit the hometown. The one in the middle wearing a fur hat is my mother's brother, the only boy of Chen Family.

My nephew, my cousin's only son who bears the responsibility for keeping the Chen Family line.

In 2009, I invited Tom Crossan, an American friend, to visit my hometown. He is the first Westerner to visit Liu Family River Village. When Big Uncle got to know that Tom used to serve in the US Army, he said he used to be a Chinese People's Volunteer Army soldier fighting against American soldiers during the War to Resist US Aggression and Aid Korea (1950-1953).

This is the tomb of my great-great-grandfather Liu Qingtai who was buried separately from the family graveyard. My grandmother did not allow her children to move this tomb to the family graveyard because a *fengshui* master had said this tomb was blessing her second son. The second son is my father. Third Uncle and his son my cousin Liu Shuan (next to the tomb stone) are the only two still staying in Liu Family River Village with their wives. Liu Shuan's son (squatting by my side) just graduated from university in July 2010 and got a job in Singapore. The photo was taken in May 2009 when I paid a visit to my hometown.

This photo was taken at my cousin Liu Shuan's house. My brother Liu Gang is holding the portrait of my grandmother. People in Liu Family River Village always admire the closeness and affection of Liu Family members.

I have been to the Tibet Autonomous Region for three times. I like to take pictures of those beautiful women and always try to send the photos to them.

In a Miao village in Guizhou, the province where I grew up.

Accepting the greeting gift *hada* (a piece of white silk) from the abbot of Relong Monastery (left) on May 15, 2008 in my second visit to Tibet.

Dancing with a Uygur brother when visiting Xinjiang Uygur Autonomous Region in July, 1999.

Children of Miao ethnic group in Guizhou Province.

The Catholic church in Changjiao Village, Guizhou Province. The girl showed me her cross. The polo-shirts the students wear are gifts from People to People Ambassador Programs which donated a three-floor school building to the village school together with Xin Xin Yi Xiang.

Wearing jeans or suits and living in apartment blocks, modern Chinese people are generally very different from what the Venetian traveller Marco Polo saw over seven centuries ago. But in Guizhou Province a group of Chinese people still adhere to the culture, clothing, language, customs, religions and architecture of 14th century China. These people call themselves "Old Hans" and bear witness to the great westward migration that took place early in the Ming Dynasty (1368-1644).

Women of Bouyei ethnic minority in Changjiao Village in Guizhou Province.

At the theme party of Xin Xin Yi Xiang Training Session 2010. The elegant lady in the middle is Kitty Wong, my personal friend, colleague and business partner in Taiwan.

The image of Sister Jiang, my hero complex.

For the first time ever, the whole family got together without anyone absent to celebrate my father's 80th birthday during the Chinese New Year of 2009 when my father was 79. It is a tradition for a lot of Chinese people to celebrate the 80th birthday one year earlier for good Luck.

My parents, 2010.

In January 2010, I paid a visit to Kaiyang Phosphate Mine with Juhua. The building behind us is the No. 13 Apartment Building, which bears too much of our joy and hardship.

10 extra marks. My son is one of the students that have benefited from the preferential policy. My brother lives in Guizhou, and his daughter enjoyed five extra marks.

The preferential policies towards minority ethnic groups have triggered corruption in our society. Some government officials or ordinary people descend to abuse of power, backdoor dealings or bribery to tamper with ethnic status in order to have a second child or enable their children to enjoy extra marks in college entrance examination.

I am proud to be an ethnic minority member in China.

My Hero Complex

People of our generation got to know many heroes from our textbooks, novels and movies. Most of the heroes emerged from the Long March, the War of Resistance against Japanese Aggression or the Liberation War. We grew up with the stories of the heroes. Almost all the artistic works we could get were about these heroes when we were young.

Many people of our generation have a hero complex or a red complex. In China, there are a group of film directors who were born in the 1950s or 1960s. They also have the hero complex and have made some "Red Classics" movies that touch our heart.

The heroes sacrificed their lives for the cause of communism. Today, I am still moved by their spirit, belief and pursuit no matter I believe in communism or not.

Sometimes I would ask myself if these heroes deeply inspired me when I was growing up. The answer is yes.

The hero that has influenced me most is Sister Jiang.

Sister Jiang was an underground Communist Party member. On

June 14, 1948, Sister Jiang was sold by a traitor and was imprisoned in Zhazidong near Chongqing. She was put through the severest tortures such as tiger bench (binding the legs of the victim on a bench and put bricks one by one under the victim's feet until the victim confessed or until the legs were broken), hanging up by iron chains, beating by steel whip with thorns, electrocution and the most brutal one of hammering bamboo nails into 10 fingers by the Kuomintang special agents. They attempted to wring useful information from the young woman Party member to destroy the underground Party organization in Chongqing, but all in vain.

We came to know Sister Jiang from the novel *Red Crag*, the stage and the movie. These artistic works have had a big influence on us.

When we were children, who we hated most was the traitor. If someone betrayed his classmate or report to the teacher or the parents, his classmates would call him "Pu Zhigao", the traitor that sold Sister Jiang.

Being cruelly tortured, Sister Jiang faced the enemies with dignity, "I know the name of my superior. I also know the name of my subordinate. I won't tell you because they are the secrets of our Party." My blood boiled whenever I saw it in the movie.

The enemies hammered bamboo nails into Sister Jiang's fingernails. Sister Jiang said, "All torture is nothing but the slightest test. Bamboo nails are made of bamboo, but the will of the Communists is made of steel and iron." What belief could make a woman so strong?

What moved me most was the story of Sister Jiang and her fellow sufferers embroidering the red flag in the prison.

On October 1, 1949, when Chairman Mao Zedong proclaimed the birth of the People's Republic of China on the Tian'anmen Rostrum, a large part of the southwest China was still occupied by the Kuomintang army. Sister Jiang and a group of revolutionaries were still imprisoned in Zhazidong.

One day, Sister Jiang got a secret letter sent by the underground organization, saying that "the People's Republic of China was born. A grand ceremony was held at Tian'anmen Square to inaugurate the People's Republic of China and the first Five-star Red Flag was raised". After reading the letter, Sister Jiang who had never dropped a tear in front of the enemies, couldn't hold her tears. She was too excited. She immediately told the good news to the comrades-in-arms in the same cell. One of them suggested, "Why don't we make a five-star red flag to celebrate the victory?" The idea was eagerly taken up. Sister Jiang carefully took out a bloodstained red flag from under her quilt. It was left by a comrade who died a heroic death. They embroidered four little stars and one big star on the red flag. Sister Jiang spread the red flag, raised it high and said solemnly, "Let the red flag be raised on every inch of ground of our motherland!"

They didn't know what the Five-star Red Flag looked like. So they put a big star in the middle and four small ones at each of the corners.

Even today, when I sing "Embroidering the Red Flag", an aria from the opera *Sister Jiang*, I would feel a fever of excitement and get emotional.

Thread is long, needlework is dense,
Embroidering the red flag with warm tears,
Warm tears following thread after thread.
They are not tears of misery but of joy.
So many years, so many generations,
Finally today the time has come.
All my passion, all my love,
Turn into the golden stars on the red flag.
No danger could make me wink,
But now my heart is beating violently.
Needle by needle, thread by thread,
A new world opens up in front of my eyes.

One time when singing karaoke with my friends, I picked the song.

A friend who was a veteran Party member said, "You are not a member of the Communist Party, but you sing the revolutionary song with so much feeling. It's a pity you didn't join the Party."

My admiration for Sister Jiang has nothing to do with whether or not I believe in communism. I admire Sister Jiang and her comrades-in-arms for their belief. Only people with belief can be so strong and steadfast. Belief is what some of us lack today.

The song *Embroidering the Red Flag* is an artistic creation. In the true story, a comrade wrote a poem for the occasion. "A bright flag, a red flag, a flag that has been paid for in our blood…. On the day when the Liberation Army comes, we will walk out of the enemy's concentration camp together, holding the red flag high and shedding tears of freedom."

Some young people may think I have been brainwashed when they read my article. Won't you be touched when you read "Shed tears of freedom and walk out together"?

On November 14, 1949, a few days before Chongqing was liberated, Sister Jiang was murdered by the Kuomintang special agents at the age of 29. She gave her life for the cause of communism she firmly believed in.

Sister Jiang and her comrades-in-arms died when the People's Republic of China was born, the cause that they had been fighting for. I cannot help thinking how regretful they would feel in the last moment of life.

In China, almost everyone knows Sister Jiang and Zhazidong prison in Chongqing. This period of history is well known to Chinese people.

Chinese tourists won't miss Zhazidong if they have the opportunity to come to Chongqing. Few foreigners visit there. Normally, the visit to Zhazidong is not included in the tour programs for foreign tourists, especially American tourists. One of the reasons is Zhazidong has something to do with the United States, so the Chinese travel companies hesitate to let Americans visit it.

Zhazidong prison grew out of the Sino-American Special Technical Cooperative Organization. It was jointly created by the United States and the Kuomintang in 1943 during the Second World War to gather intelligence against Japan. After winning the war in 1945, the Americans handed over all the equipment to Kuomintang. Since then, the Sino-American Cooperative Organization became a prison where the Kuomintang imprisoned revolutionaries. Many Kuomintang special agents who persecuted revolutionaries had received training from the Americans.

In the summer of 2003, I visited the Zhazidong prison with my American friends Ralph Baard and Dustin Daugherty. They carefully visited and observed the place and listened to me telling stories about Sister Jiang and other revolutionary martyrs. They were touched by my hero complex.

Ralph worked for People to People Ambassador Programs. He suggested the visit to the Zhazidong prison be included in the itinerary of the professional delegations. He thought the history was very interesting.

Our local agent in Chongqing replied that they never recommended it to the foreign tourists who wouldn't be interested in it.

However, they tried once as I insisted. A young tour guide showed an American delegation around the Zhazidong prison. The feedback I got was it was not interesting at all and the visit to the Zhazidong should be cancelled. I was not surprised. Not everyone, especially the young generation, has the hero complex I have. The young tour guide told the story unemotionally, so he failed to catch the American tourists.

The Sister Jiang I know is a combination of the true story, the movie, the novel and the opera. I like the image of Sister Jiang when she is wearing a blue *qipao*, a red cardigan and a white long scarf around her neck.

In 2008, before the Beijing Olympic Games, our company received over 100 Americans who came to Beijing to attend the "Sino-American Nursing Forum". On the farewell party, we staged a performance

"Olympic Games Melodrama" in which every historical stage from the late Qing Dynasty to the year 2008 was presented. It was my creativity and all my employees participated in the performance. I played Sister Jiang and the historical stage was the War of Liberation. It had been my dream to play Sister Jiang on the stage someday. Finally, I made my dream come true.

It was not long after China was hit by the Sichuan earthquake. Our performance ended with the chorus "Ode to the Motherland" to show that the Chinese people were of one mind in the earthquake relief work. The first lyric of the song is "The Five-star Red Flag is fluttering in the wind".

Everyone was singing passionately with my conducting. I was so moved that tears blurred my eyes. As we began to sing, all American friends stood up. Many of them were also moved to tears.

As a mother, I am always touched by the heartrending story Sister Jiang entrusted her cousin to take care of her son before she was executed. She wrote a letter to her cousin Tan Zhu'an.

"Please take care of Yun'er for me if something bad happens. Teach him in a proper way so that he will follow his parents' steps, consider building a new China as his lifelong goal and devote himself to the cause of communism. Children should never be pampered. A simple living is enough."

Her son Peng Yun was only three years old when she died. In the opera, when Sister Jiang is walking to her execution, she expresses her expectations on her son.

When the day of national liberation comes and the red sun shines brightly,
Please take care of my child for me.
Tell him that the victory is hard-won;
Tell him not to forget the hard times of struggle;
Tell him to work hard as a successor to the revolution;
Never fail to live up to what the people and the Party expect of him.

In the late 1970s, Peng Yun, sponsored by the government, went to study in the United States. He has settled down there and become a tenured professor in the computer science department of the University of Maryland.

Many people find it hard to accept that the descendant of a Communist has become a citizen of a capitalist country. In my opinion, Sister Jiang would smile in heaven as long as she knows what her son does is beneficial to mankind.

Modesty and Confidence of the Chinese

When I was in school or in my work place, people's negative comment on me was that I was too proud. For a long period of time, "proud" was a derogatory term in China. Since childhood, we have been educated to be modest. As a result, we never dared express our individuality. When I worked in the state-owned enterprise, although I kept my head down, I was still considered as someone who liked to show off and became a target of public attack.

Chairman Mao's teaching "Modesty helps one to make progress; conceit makes one lag behind" has become my motto.

When I was a teenage girl, many people especially boys thought I was too proud. But none of my good friends thought so. At that time, it was improper for boys and girls to get too close with each other, so the boys had no opportunity to know me.

Many years later, whenever I met some childhood friends, I would ask them, "Why did you think I was proud?" "At that time, you walked with your head up high in a snubbing way."

At that time, we didn't know the word "confidence". Now as I think about it, it was not arrogance but confidence I had then. I was singing and dancing in the Mao Zedong Propaganda Team and was admired and praised by people. Naturally I would feel confident.

In the past, when Chinese people introduced themselves, they would first show modesty, saying that they were not good enough, there was still a long way to go before they could catch up with others and they must learn from others and something like that.

If someone was praised for good looks, being good at singing or dancing, doing well in studies or job, he or she would say modestly, "No, no, no. I am not good enough. I am not good enough."

The Chinese-style modesty is heartfelt sometimes. At other times, it is hypocrisy. Some people can criticize themselves. But they would feel offended if they are criticized by others. It is easy for them to behave modest when being praised, but it is hard for them to accept criticism.

Now, we must publicize ourselves, promote ourselves, package ourselves and say we are the best, which was unthinkable in the past.

In the early 1980s, the H Ministry invited several companies from the United States, Finland and France to submit their bids for the pre-feasibility study of the processing project of phosphate mines in Hubei, Guizhou and Yunnan. When the project leader of the American company Jacobs Engineering introduced his company, he said, "We are the best!" in front of all the competitors. The Chinese people present were surprised at his boastfulness. The Chinese counterpart in charge said with an obvious strain of criticism, "You are not being modest." I looked up. The American man was still smiling without realizing he had said something improper. I didn't interpret the criticism. Otherwise he would be puzzled.

More than 20 years has passed. Now, we respond with an easy smile when being praised. We expect to be appreciated. We would say "Thank you" to those who praise us and appreciate us. We educate our children to give full play to their individuality and to be different. Many college graduates spend a lot of money on their resumes and brag about themselves.

As China has been shifting from a planned economy to a market economy where competitions are fierce, every company or individual is getting used to telling people "I am the best".

Chinese people have long been respectful to foreigners. We believe in Confucius "It is a delight to have friends coming from afar".

I came into contact with many Westerners because of my job in the late 1970s and the early 1980s when foreigners were rare in China. We were good to Westerners genuinely and sincerely. Our country was poor at that time. Whenever we had Western visitors, we would try our utmost effort to entertain them with the best food and drink we could offer. Westerners were well looked after by the people around when they were in China, regardless of their status. It was partly because of the traditional Chinese hospitality. Another reason was that China was underdeveloped in all respects; Westerners would be unable to do anything if there was no one to help them.

Westerners came to China to seek business opportunities. But their Chinese clients took care of their meals, lodging, transportation and touring. We did not have any ideas of utilitarianism. "Since the foreigners come from afar, they are our guests. How can we leave them alone?" There was another objective condition behind it. We had strict disciplines related to foreign affairs and regulations on foreigners' activities within Chinese territory when China was still quite isolated to the outside world. The Chinese host had to be responsible for the reception of the foreign guests from beginning to end.

When we worked in the United States in the mid 1980s, the host company treated us strictly according to the conditions stipulated in the contract. We found it hard to accept. "We have treated you with the cordial hospitality in China. But now in your country, you treat us like business is business." Our conclusion was that capitalism was truly impersonal.

Actually, the Americans treated us quite well. In return, those who had been to China invited us to watch baseball games, to enjoy performances, to have meals at home and to visit schools and communities, all at their own expenses. When they were in China, all the entertainment was funded by the government. Even if we wanted to entertain them personally, on the one hand, we had no money; on the other hand, it was not allowed according to the discipline.

At that time, we were very curious about Westerners. They stood for civilization and wealth. We were astonished to hear that even poor families in the West had TV sets. Once we saw a documentary film about Deng Xiaoping's visit to Japan in 1978. He was invited to visit a worker's home. There was a large TV set in the living-room! An exclamation of surprise and admiration escaped every mouth. What a difference! A worker's family had a large color TV.

Although Japan was an Asian country geographically, to the Chinese people it belonged to the Western camp.

When I was in the United States in 1986, an American told me her daughter was going to college and it would cost a lot, therefore the family had to eat eggs and chicken to save money. I was shocked at her words. Only poor Americans ate eggs and chicken! In China, even the wealthiest families couldn't have eggs and chicken every day. I was filled with longing for life in America.

Probably because of the curiosity and longing, Chinese people were particularly modest and respectful to Westerners, regardless of their status and position. We actually believed that all Westerners were rich people.

Chinese people were not only modest but humble in front of Westerners. I think it had much to do with our country's poverty.

It was difficult to go abroad then. Some people cringed before Westerners in the hope of getting the opportunity to go abroad or to send their children to study abroad. Most of those who were allowed contact with foreigners were not the men on the street. Therefore, what they did had a bad influence.

In 1986, I went with a delegation from the Mining Bureau of the H

Ministry to visit the United States. When we stayed over in San Francisco on our way back to Beijing, the relative of a delegation member sent him a trunk of old clothes. He was proud of having a relative in America and said triumphantly, "These clothes are not enough for everyone in my family. My younger sisters will fight for the clothes."

With the deepening of the reform and opening-up and the rapid development of China's economy, the material life of Chinese people has been greatly improved and the country's position in the world has also been notably raised. Delicate changes are taking place in the relationship between the Chinese and Westerners.

In the mid 1990s, one of my Chinese friends held an important position in a European company. When he was in Shanghai, a European employee accompanied him to an international brand hotel to check in. The receptionist of the hotel was extremely warm to the blond employee, smiling obsequiously, but treated my dark-haired and yellow-skinned friend coldly. He was terribly irritated. The European employee was very embarrassed and hastened to explain, "This is my boss. This is my boss."

His experience was not an uncommon one at that time. When a Chinese boss of foreign nationality came with his Western employee, the Chinese host would often make a mistake in the seating arrangement and would let the Western employee sit by the host.

I had the similar experience. In the early 1990s, I accompanied some Western clients to visit a hotel. The hotel staff bowed and scraped before the Western clients but was cold and indifferent to me.

Such kind of things seldom happens today. People are not judged high or low by the color of their skin or hair.

Today, it is so common that foreigners work for the Chinese.

In the past, my classmates envied me because I worked for Westerners. Today, they admire me because I have Westerners work for me.

The five-star hotels with international brands in China are no longer the privilege of Westerners. Especially today after the outbreak of the financial crisis, the luxury hotels that used to be crowded with Westerners now have Chinese everywhere.

Many Westerners choose to settle down in China after they stay here for some time. They have been fascinated by China and become "China Fans". I think there are several reasons. First, there are opportunities for gold rush in China. Second, China is a vigorous and lively country. Third, Chinese people are extremely hospitable to them.

Chinese people are too good to Westerners and many Chinese people think we have spoilt them.

Although we are no longer curious about Westerners, we are still good to them. It's due to the tradition of hospitality of the Chinese people. Many Westerners wish to make more friends, to build contacts, to learn the Chinese culture and tradition to facilitate their work and life in China. The overall opening-up and economic development of China has created favorable conditions for foreigners' living, working and traveling in our country. When the popular enthusiasm for learning English is still growing in China, more and more foreigners are beginning to learn Chinese.

The relations between China and the Western countries are on an equal footing. To some extent, harmony has been achieved between East and West, which is based on mutual respect. Nowadays, we often hear some Westerner has been lectured and taught a lesson by Chinese people for being rude, which would never happen in the past.

I think it is the common wish of the Chinese and Westerners to respect each other and to learn from each other.

I have entertained many Western friends at my home. Some of them have lived with my family. Although my home is not luxurious, it is cozy and comfortable. During the 2008 Olympic Games, my American friend Greg Marcinkowski sent his daughter to Beijing to be a volunteer. His daughter stayed with us. Greg's house in America is big and sumptuous, far better than mine. Even so, the living conditions today can enable me and my family to live a life with dignity.

Now it has been much more convenient for Chinese people to go abroad. No matter you are a government official or ordinary person, as long as you are a law-abiding citizen and have some source of income, you can go abroad. Last year, my son Zheng Han got a multiple entry visa with a validity period of one year for the United States the first time he went abroad. When I was his age, it was inconceivable.

We are still modest and respectful. After all, we are Chinese. But we are more confident than ever before.

Where Are You from? Why Don't You Queue?

I had an unpleasant experience when I flew from Barcelona to Paris by Air France in November 2009.

When I was waiting to board, I met someone who was in the same business in China. I chatted with her and didn't notice what was going on around me. When boarding started, two tall Western men didn't queue and went straight up to check in. I thought it was time for passengers in first class and business class to board, so I followed them and passed my ticket to the clerk. Suddenly, a European woman who was standing behind me said abruptly and rudely, "Where are you from?" Then she repeated, "Where are you from? Where are you from?" I looked at her confused by her anger. "Why don't you queue?" she asked again. I suddenly realized what she meant.

When she asked me where I was from, I was totally at loss and just looked at her in surprise. I didn't realize she was condemning me until I heard "why don't you queue".

"I am sorry. I am in business class."

"Me too."

"I am terribly sorry. I think I made a mistake. I didn't realize you are queuing here. I followed the two men who went by just now. You go first. I will go back to the line," I apologized sincerely.

Since I had already checked in, the airport clerk asked me to board first. I insisted others should go first. The people who stood behind said, "Don't argue. Just go."

I didn't like the European woman's manner of speaking. I couldn't resist the temptation and said, "I don't like your way of speaking." To my surprise, she didn't retort. Everybody could see I didn't jump the queue deliberately.

On the plane, the European woman was sitting behind me. I had thought to turn around and say to her, "I am Chinese. What does my jumping the queue have to do with where I come from?"

But I held my tongue. I felt helplessly vexed. I hate people who cut in line. I am the sort of person who observes public order and volunteers to keep order. If there is someone I know in the line, I wouldn't take advantage of it. Neither would I let someone who knows me take the advantage. I am very strict even impersonal in this respect. What irritated me was not that the European woman criticized me for jumping the queue but she asked me where I came from. How did it have anything to do with my jumping the queue? If it was an American or a European, would she ask "where are you from"? Why didn't she ask the two Westerners who boarded ahead of me? I am generally acknowledged as a broad-minded person. But I felt hurt being treated so and couldn't help harboring resentment against the European woman. When waiting to get off the plane, I stood up, turned around and looked at her in her eyes. She looked at me for a while and then turned her gaze somewhere else.

I don't know if Westerners understand it. What Chinese people hate most are Westerners' prejudices. When I came back, I told my colleagues about it. They had the same feelings.

Recently, I had a lot of contact with the son of an overseas Chinese. He was born abroad and has worked and lived abroad all the time. His colleagues are all Westerners. Strictly speaking, he is not Chinese and he cannot even speak Chinese fluently. But he always said "we Chinese people", which moved me very much. He got very emotional when speaking of Westerner's prejudices against the Chinese. He was often wronged because he was yellow-skinned and black-haired. He even warned me not to be misled by superficial phenomenon when I told him my partners in the West were good to me.

The Westerners who are prejudiced against Chinese people really should think about it themselves.

I was not so indignant as he because it was indeed my mistake. It is common to see Chinese people jumping the queue, home and abroad. As a Chinese, I have to be very careful when I am abroad. Don't adjust your shoe in a melon patch, or your hat under a plum tree. Otherwise, misunderstandings will easily be caused because they are prejudiced against us. Although I get on well with my partners in the West and are respected by them, occasionally I will feel humiliated and indignant at being wronged or prejudiced.

Today, we should be more careful with our manners and speech because we attract more attention than ever before with the economic development of our country.

Whenever I see my countrymen can't wait to leave their seats before the plane has come to a complete stop and hasten to unfasten their seat belts, get their luggage, turn on their cell phones and chat away and flock to the gate to get off the plane, I would feel angry and shame. I would feel more embarrassed if there are foreigners present. My sense of national pride is stronger when I am abroad.

When waiting in line in the public bathroom at airport or in shopping center, there would always be someone who turned a blind eye to the long queue and walked straight to the front of the queue. I would always be the one who stepped forward to stop them. But now I was mistaken for a queue-jumper. I felt wronged. I even felt guilty because I couldn't explain it clearly and brought shame to Chinese people.

Chinese people have left a bad impression on the world for some uncivilized behavior. Therefore, I am particularly careful with what I say and what I do. I often go abroad and have become well-known internationally in our industry. I don't think how great I am. I try hard to be an excellent Chinese and to change Westerners' prejudices against Chinese by my proper behaviors. A lot of Chinese share the same feeling with me.

I have two different attitudes and a double standard towards my compatriots' jumping the queue. What I hate to see most is the well-educated urban white-collars jumping the queue. However, I am lenient to ordinary people, especially those who live at the foot of the social ladder. The reasons for jumping the queue are complicated. Too many people and inadequate resources are one of the important reasons. Who can have the heart to condemn the peasant workers who are anxious to return home for the Chinese New Year and cut in line to get a ticket that is extremely difficult to get? It is the government's responsibility to improve the transport system and to strengthen public order.

I come from the lower social class and I understand the sufferings of ordinary people. Today, there are still numerous people in our country who live in deep poverty. The hardships in their life are more than I can bear. I seldom take the bus, the subway or the train. My current financial situation enables me not to compete with ordinary people for the limited resources. I have no right to criticize such undesirable behavior caused by resource scarcity.

I can always remember the spectacle when we queued up in the school canteen for meals in the 1970s. The food was bad. Whenever there were meat dishes, the students would push and shove towards the window, pass their lunch boxes and food coupons to get braised pork or hairtail. Then, they would lift their lunch boxes ahead of their heads and squeeze out with all their might. It was common to see the lunch box knocked over and the meat dish pouring down on someone. I remember a girl classmate who had several pieces of hairtail hanging in her hair and vegetable soup dripping from her face still forced her way towards the window. It is difficult to require people to be civilized when they are inadequately fed and clothed.

Now there are all kinds of food available in the cafeteria in today's universities. Who would jump the queue for food?

To solve the problem, education and administration are needed. It is important to strengthen administration before the quality of the Chinese people has been improved.

I lost my luggage when I came back from Europe recently. I went to register at the Lost and Found office of the airport. Five or six people were waiting there in line. Then, an airport worker led a girl to the counter ahead of the queue. Apparently the girl knew the airport worker. I said, "There is a queue." The clerk behind the counter also said, "Several customers are in front of you. I will serve them first." I think it's good for the customers and the staff to supervise together. More importantly, it should be included in the administration that it is the staff members' responsibility to maintain order. Sometimes, they know someone is jumping the queue but choose to ignore it. They are actually abetting the evil-doer by turning a blind eye to bad behavior.

I find it hard to tolerate the crew members' blindness to such a behavior. They don't take measures to prevent it or just remind the passengers through gentle announcement. As a result, this kind of misconduct is becoming more and more prevalent. In fact, if all the airlines in the country join hands to deal with the problem, it will be easily solved. I once saw a flight attendant loudly and stoutly urging the passengers who stood up before the plane had come to a complete stop to sit back. All the passengers listened to her. No one stood up. A young girl could do it. How hard is it?

If the government strengthens its administration and puts an end to the behavior, people will form the habit of queuing up.

Chinese people and the Chinese government are aware of the problem and have made efforts to deal with it. On January 18, 2007, the Beijing municipal government marked Queuing Day on the 11th of every month, a date chosen because of the two straight 1s, to raise public awareness of queuing up and to create a favorable public order. More than three years have passed. How many people still remember what a special day the 11th of every month is? I don't know if any government department has followed up to examine the continuity and effectiveness of the measure.

In today's China, both the people and the government talk a lot about raising the soft power of China. We should keep in mind that everyone of us can contribute to the soft power enhancement of our country.

Chapter Seven

My Business Values

I didn't really go into business until I gave up my iron rice bowl in 2001. I always believe I have the kind of EQ and the mode of thinking that make me suitable for service industry. I want to devote a whole chapter to writing about business values because there is a big difference between doing business in China and in Western countries. The stories in this chapter happened in the tourism industry, but they could be significant reference for other industries in China.

Before 1980, there were only two state-owned travel companies in our country, China Travel Service and China International Travel Service. Tourism at that time served politics more than economy. There were strict limitations that the government placed on who was allowed to visit the country and who was not.

When China Youth Travel Service was founded in 1980, it cornered the travel market together with China Travel Service and China International Travel Service.

In 1984, the Chinese government decided to carry out the reform of the travel service system, to break the monopoly and liberalize the market. But travel services still had to be state-owned enterprises.

Private travel enterprises didn't appear in China until the beginning of the 21st century.

My Dream

When I entered tourism in 1992, I knew nothing about it in the first year. I just bent over work and paid no attention to what was going on around me. When I was dealing with the detailed matters, I felt the defects in the corporate system and operational mode, which made me disappointed with the famous large state-owned enterprise.

When I changed from a layman to a professional, I found there were many administrative problems in state-owned enterprises. Many of the problems were clear, but it was hard to solve them due to the limitation of the system. The failure to solve the problems led to inequitable distribution of income and employees' worry about personal gains and losses, which ultimately influenced the quality of service and the interests of customers.

I always dreamed that maybe some day I could have my own company and I would manage my company with international standards. It was but my illusion back then. There was a wide gap between the ideal and the reality. I even doubted if I could live to see my dream realized.

In about 1999, China accelerated its WTO (World Trade Organization) entry negotiations. I felt my chance was coming, but I was still not sure.

In the first half of the year 2001, I kept thinking maybe it was time to act. I was already 45 years old. At my age, people were supposed to be content with their lot and live a stable life. I could not be reconciled to the tradition. I have only one life to live. I should do at least one thing I really want to.

At the end of 2001, I resigned from the state-owned enterprise and embarked on the journey towards my dream.

During the three and a half years from January 2002 to July 2005, I was making preparations for setting up my own company. Xin Xin Yi Xiang (hereinafter referred to as Xiang) was founded in July, 2005. There were five shareholders. I was the absolute holding shareholder. I wanted to be the absolute holding shareholder not for economic benefits but for power. I knew I would encounter a lot of resistance and obstacles for setting up a company by international standards which would be against the Chinese traditional practice. I would need absolute power to make my dream come true. When the company was founded, I suggested we not distribute dividends within five years to accumulate a reserve for the company's development. It won the support of the other shareholders.

I was right, as what happened later proved.

The most realistic issue was about the rights and interests of the shareholders. If my decision temporarily influenced the shareholders' allocation of equity, I would be the one who suffered the biggest loss. If I took the lead to sacrifice, it would be easier to persuade other shareholders to follow me.

What should we do to build a travel service of international standards? We need to go out to learn the advanced experience of other countries, even at a high cost. If we didn't make the investment but put the money into our own pockets, we wouldn't have achieved today's success.

From 2002 when the team gathered together to 2005 when our company was founded to 2010 when our Shanghai company was established, our business has increased year by year with more market input and our company has become more and more internationalized.

Most of the people who resigned from the HO ran their business in the form of *guakao*. Some of them were waiting for the opportunity of independent operation. More of them considered *guakao* as a shortcut to maximize personal benefits.

Several years later, there is a big difference between *guakao* and independent operation. Those who run their business in the form of *guakao* might have realized their personal interests to a maximum degree; but they haven't made much progress in market development and brand building.

There is a typical example. Fu Jun resigned from the same company as mine, taking a big American client with him. He reached a *guakao* agreement with a travel company. The American client brought a business of about 10,000 American tourists to China every year. Fu Jun and his team entirely depended on the client and led a comfortable and wealthy life. This was typically "putting all one's eggs in one basket". Suddenly, one day, the American client was taken over by some other company. All of Fu Jun's eggs were broken and his team was also dissolved. Fu Jun has worked in tourism for over 20 years, but how many people still remember his name and his team?

Independent companies have built brands, expanded their market share and international influence. Every step Xiang has taken towards its success shall be written into the history of China's development of travel service industry.

Before Xiang was founded, there was no clear market segmentation in the travel companies in the Chinese mainland. Xiang is the first company to specialize in incentive travel and later has developed into a DMC (Destination Management Company) and a PCO (Professional Conference Organizer). We became a company engaged in MICE (Meetings, Incentives, Conventions and Events) industry, which has broadened our business scope.

DMC and PCO are still relatively new concepts in China today. So we caught hold of the opportunity and pioneered in China's MICE industry.

I feel it is so ridiculous whenever I recall the sanction that the HO imposed on me at the beginning of my new career to restrict my development. I am taking totally a different road. We are not competitors at all.

PCOs are companies that supply the service of meeting planning and organizing, coordination with the government, marketing, sponsorship procuring, registration, financial management, quality control and any other professional services related to meetings and exhibitions.

DMCs, who must be the local experts in the industry, take care of the local service including accommodation, transportation, banquet, theme party, entertainment and tours as well as offering the services of planning and organizing meetings, seminars, summits and training sessions.

In practice in China, part of DMC function overlaps with that of PCO.

Xiang is a complete DMC and a partial PCO. We are still learning.

Before Xiang, there was no internationally influential incentive travel company in China's mainland except two or three with international background whose decision makers or top managers were Westerners or Hong Kongnese, not mainlanders. Through years' hard work, Xiang has begun to rise onto a par with them in the world market.

Before Xiang, there was no internationally influential Chinese PCO in the Chinese mainland. Many conferences were undertaken by PR companies or done by professional associations themselves. The service quality was far behind the international standards.

As an emerging PCO, Xiang is still learning and growing. Starting off on the right foot to catch up with the advanced world levels, Xiang has achieved double results with half the effort and made rapid progress. Xiang will surely play a role in breaking the stereotype in doing conferences and promoting the professionalization of China's meeting industry.

Xiang's development has enabled the world incentive travel and meeting industry to see the progress China has made and the prospects in its high-end travel and meeting industry.

Does it mean I have realized my dream?

Not yet.

The progress we have made only proves that we have chosen the right way. We are moving along and still fall far short of our expectations. We need to keep on going forward.

By July, 2010, it was five years since our company was founded. Although we shareholders have sacrificed dividends temporarily, what we achieved is a sound economic base of the company which proves to be extremely important under the present economic crisis.

An entrepreneur, especially an entrepreneur of my age, should have accomplished personal capital accumulation. But I haven't. What I am doing now should have been achieved when I was in my thirties or forties. But at that time, there was no overall climate for individuals to pursue their ideals. People of our generation started late. Our destiny has changed with the change in our nation's destiny.

As a person of lofty ideals, I think the capital accumulation of the company is more important than that of individuals. "The temple is getting poor while the monks are getting rich" is a Chinese idiom used to describe profits of enterprises going into private pockets. What I pursue is sustainable and sound development of the company. The relation between the company and the employees is "the big river with the small rivers"; the water will flow to the small rivers when the big river is full of water.

Standing on the World Stage

When I was still in the HO, a European partner said to me: "Ping, you should join an association named Site (Society of Incentive & Travel Executives).

I hadn't joined any industry associations until I built up my own business and became a decision-maker. I joined Site at the beginning of 2005 and became one of the few Site members in China. I went to attend the Site international conference in Toronto in the same year and I was the only member from the Chinese mainland among several hundred members.

I joined Site with a sense of mission. China's tourist enterprises had no reputation in the international high-end tourism industry. It was agreed that there was no professional DMC in China's mainland. Although there were up-and-coming private enterprises like Xiang, they were not known to the world. I wanted to change the situation.

Tourism is considered a rising industry in China. China didn't start to have foreign tourists until the late 1970s. People who worked in travel companies only knew the six factors of food, accommodation, transportation, sightseeing, shopping and entertainment. The majority of travel companies in China still focus on leisure tour products.

When I worked in the HO, the main business was leisure tour. There was only one department dealing with incentive travel groups, which served as a local agent for a Hong Kong DMC and did not have its own market development. During the 10 years there, I handled only a few incentive groups. I was intensely interested in the more challenging tour programs with high requirements and high profits. I decided that my future business should be in high-end tourism. The incentive travel products were not as good as today's. We had no creative ideas, just tried to satisfy customers' needs passively. Compared with leisure tours, the only difference of the incentive travel then was the time was shorter, the hotels more luxurious and the restaurants better. We did not have any knowledge or experience in handling incentive groups. We didn't know there was a professional association for incentive travel.

For a long period of time, most of the incentive groups from Western countries were handled by travel companies in Hong Kong. No travel company in the Chinese mainland knew how to do incentive travel, so Hong Kong travel companies held the largest market share of the incentive travel and other high-end tourism in China's mainland.

With the rapid development of China's tourism industry, many professionals from Hong Kong or foreign countries have come to seek opportunities in the Chinese mainland. The threshold for setting up travel companies was high and only few foreign enterprises could reach the conditions for setting up joint-ventures or exclusively foreign-funded companies in the mainland. Some foreigners ran travel business with Chinese partners. The legal persons were the Chinese who shared profits with their foreign partners based on the agreement between them, but all the sales and marketing were done by foreigners. Some travel companies from Hong Kong, the United States and Europe set up offices in cities like Beijing and Shanghai. According to relevant law in the Chinese mainland, the offices couldn't directly engage in receiving travel groups, so the travel companies must find local partners in China's mainland to handle the land service of their travel groups. The Hong Kong and foreign companies had their brands in the international market, while their partners in the Chinese mainland were not known to anybody.

With the deepening of China's reform and opening-up, a group of professionals in high-end tourism have grown up. Changes are taking place in the situation of China's incentive travel market which used to be cornered by travel companies from Hong Kong or with Western background.

Unlike the professionals from Hong Kong and Western countries who have been active on the international stage, the incentive travel companies in China's mainland are not internationally recognized in the industry. To take part in the annual conferences or activities of international associations is the effective way to display and promote oneself in a short time.

I was elected an international board director of Site in 2008.

From being a layman in 1992 to running for international board member of an international professional association in 2008, I could not believe that such a great change had happened with me. More importantly, I was the first member from the Chinese mainland to be elected to the International Board of Directors since Site was founded in 1973. Before, the seat was always assumed by members from the Asia-Pacific region excluding China's mainland. It means that Chinese mainland has won a place in the international incentive and meeting industry.

I have also found that many Site members are at the same time members of MPI (Meeting Professionals International) and ICCA (International Congress and Convention Association).

At that time, our company co-organized one or two professional conferences with an American client every year. Most of our employees had no meeting expertise, so they constantly made mistakes.

The meeting industry has been developing fast in China and there is a shortage of meeting professionals. If we could develop into meeting professionals in a short time, we would have a competitive advantage.

I joined MPI in 2006 and my company became the member of ICCA in 2008.

Site and MPI are for individual members and ICCA for corporate members. Among all the travel and meeting companies in China, our company has the most Site and MPI members. We have five Site members and three MPI members and our company is one the first private companies in China's mainland to join ICCA. We have developed more than 20 Site members in our local agents in the main incentive travel destination cities such as Beijing, Shanghai, Xi'an, Guilin, Suzhou, Kunming and Hong Kong.

The three associations ICCA, MPI and Site were founded in 1961, 1972 and 1973, respectively, when Chinese people were suffering from hunger and poverty, or indulged in crazy personality cult, or rebellion or fighting with each other. But today, I am an active member of the international industry associations, sharing experiences with professionals from all over the world and discussing important matters concerning the development of the incentive and meeting industry with international colleagues. It is indeed a tremendous change.

China's incentive and meeting industry started late and lagged behind the developed countries for many years. China suffers from a shortage of professionals with international standards. Therefore, only through constant learning can we catch up with advanced world levels.

Some people joined the international associations for quick success and instant benefits. They expected they could get business as soon as they became members of the associations. This is why they were disappointed soon after they joined the organization with great enthusiasm. It reflects their short-sightedness. After I joined the international associations mentioned above, I attended professional seminars, listened to speeches, consulted counterparts from other countries and exchanged ideas with them, which all increased my knowledge. The annual international conferences of these associations are supported and sponsored by the local government, tourism department, hotels, scenic spots and venues. Therefore, the meetings, theme parties and gala dinners are all world first-class and most creative. Every activity is a unique experience and a chance to learn. If I didn't go out of the country or join the international associations, I would never have had such opportunities.

More and more members of the three associations tell me, "Ping, you are famous now. Everybody knows you."

I am an active member. I do not only try my best to join the international conferences of the three associations personally but also take my colleagues with me. We share ideas and make contacts with incentive and meeting professionals from all over the world and build a business network to reach the goal of cooperation. We met our American sales representative at the annual meeting of Site. Many businesses during the Beijing Olympic Games were brought by him.

I should say I have benefited a lot from joining the associations. I have learned knowledge, broadened my horizons, built a network of relationships and increased our recognition in the industry.

The cost for attending the international conferences of the associations is quite high. Air travel expenses, registration fees and hotel rates add to a large sum of money. In terms of investment in education and training for employees and marketing, few travel or meeting companies in China can compare with my company. We can do it because I am the policymaker and I can make the final decision. This is also why I am more suitable to be an international board member of Site. International board members are actually volunteers of the association. We are not paid for our work. Instead, we have to put in a lot of time, energy and money. Besides, there are several board meetings to attend every year at the cost of my own company. Even so, I have my own way of calculating the rate of return on investment. The knowledge I learned, the experience, the friendship and the network of relationships have profoundly influenced me and my company.

We need to take a shortcut to build name recognition in a short time. To join professional associations and be an active member is the shortcut. Since we joined the three international associations, we have met many counterparts from other countries. A formerly unknown small company has been recognized by more and more international colleagues. The business we are in is interpersonal. People won't develop friendship and trust unless they meet each other and communicate with each other. Friendship and mutual trust are the basis for cooperation.

Due to the different national conditions of China, the meeting industrial structure of our country is different from that of other countries. Therefore, there is another more important task for me to join the international associations. We will bring back the knowledge and ideas we have learned and spread them to more people to promote the development of China's meeting industry.

One of my top honors is the IMEX Academy Award granted at the IMEX (Worldwide Exhibition for Incentive Travel, Meetings and Events) in Frankfurt in May of 2009. The awards are presented to outstanding individuals in four geographical regions who are judged to have served the meetings and incentive travel industry exceptionally well and achieved consistently high standards within their chosen profession. I, representing the Asia-Pacific region, became the first Chinese to receive this award.

I hadn't had any idea that I would be granted the honor beforehand. Paul Flackett, Managing Director of IMEX sent me an e-mail and said, "Just to let you know that we have you seated at my table for the IMEX Gala Dinner in Frankfurt …. A fun table which I think you will enjoy…"

It was a gala dinner like the one of Oscar Academy Awards. I enjoyed it so much and watched around and thought what we could copy if we would do the same thing in China. Suddenly I saw my old black and white pictures of my childhood on the screen and heard Paul Flackett said something about me. I was totally puzzled and did not know what to do until someone whispered to me and woke me up, "Go to get your award!" I walked like stepping on cloud when the spotlight followed me all the way to the stage. I received my award from Mr. Ray Bloom, Chairman of IMEX Group, who has high integrity and prestige in the industry.

IMEX people had contacted my colleague and asked him to "steal" a couple of my old photos for the award ceremony. My colleague did a good job to keep the secret.

Furthermore, with the help of relevant government department, a Site chapter was founded in China's mainland in 2006. Through the joint efforts of the local government and the chapter, Beijing won the bid for hosting the international conference of Site 2012.

I have a great sense of accomplishment.

The Woman in Red

In February, 2005, Site held its summit in Beijing. I got the news from newspaper. Site members could join the summit free of charge, but non-members needed to pay a registration fee. I was thinking of joining Site at that time. To attend the summit free of charge, Yanxiang, then vice president of the company, and I joined Site several days prior to the meeting. It was a new experience to me. I didn't know what it would mean to me or what I should do.

Most of the Site international board directors came to Beijing to attend the summit. At the question-and-answer time, Chinese people were too shy to raise their hands.

Although I have been to many big occasions, it is still not easy for me to ask questions beneath the gaze of so many eyes. Whenever I tell my friends or colleagues that I am in reality a shy person and would be nervous when raising my hands, they don't believe it.

I asked myself, "Why did I join Site? Why am I here for the summit?"

The answer was I needed to learn, to show myself and to get more people in the industry to know me and my company.

I encouraged myself and Yanxiang to ask questions. We seemed to be the only two Chinese participants that asked questions. Most of the questions were asked by the foreign hoteliers or foreigners working in the travel industry in China. I asked several questions. One of the questions was very silly.

I pointed to the panelists sitting on the stage and asked, "What qualification do you need to sit on there?" "They are all Site international board directors," answered Brenda, CEO of Site.

"I wish that one day I could sit there like them," I said.

I was noticeable wearing a red coat that day. I put up my hands so many times that I left a deep impression on Site international board directors and other participants.

They didn't remember my name and referred to me as the woman in red. They appreciated me for being active, though my questions might be silly.

At international meetings, Chinese people are shy and silent. When foreign speakers are invited to China for seminars, some Chinese hosts would remind them beforehand that most Chinese people are not used to asking questions or interacting with other people.

Our company has the annual training session and invites international speakers every time. I would arrange several colleagues to prepare questions beforehand in case it would be embarrassing if nobody asks questions after the speech.

Now I have many opportunities to attend all kinds of international meetings, many times as a speaker or panelist sitting or talking on the stage. Three years after I asked the silly question at the Site Summit in 2005, I was elected to the International Board of Directors of Site.

People remember my name today even if I am not in red.

At international conferences or seminars, I always encourage my Chinese colleagues to speak and to be involved in the discussions. The good thing is that more and more Chinese colleagues can raise their hands to ask questions and speak confidently on every occasion.

If we want to make us or our companies known to the outside world, we should show ourselves nicely on different occasions and get people to remember us. It is contradictory to the traditional education we have received. We have been brought up to be modest and prudent and not to be in the spotlight because one who sticks his neck out gets hit first. Another psychological barrier is that we are afraid of making mistakes and losing face. In fact, we are here to learn and to exchange ideas with others. It is normal that we may say wrong things or ask silly questions. Just take it easy.

Whenever I was too shy to speak, I would ask myself, "Why did I spend so much money to come to this meeting? I am here to learn, to show myself on the international stage. I must get my money's worth."

Later I shared my experience with many Westerners. They told me they were also nervous and needed to overcome shyness to speak in public.

At the 2009 Site International Conference in Aruba, as an international board director, I attended the meeting for first attendees. Site CEO Brenda asked each participant to introduce himself and tell the story of his first car or tell people what talent he had. They all told the story of their first cars.

When it was my turn, I said, "It was in recent years that Chinese people began to have private cars. My first car is a long story. I think I'd like to tell you what talent I have. I am good at revolutionary dance. Let me show you."

I stood up, walked to the front of the venue and did a small part of a dance. My performance wowed the audience. Everybody remembered me. Many people even asked me to teach them the dance. My colleagues in the board came over and said, "You did an excellent job. You make people remember you right away."

It is very important to get people to remember you in a short while. If they remember you, they will think of you when there is a cooperation opportunity.

At the group discussion session of this year's Site China Chapter Annual Conference, the foreign moderator said to me beforehand, "Ping, I hope you will take the lead to ask questions if nobody else does."

I was the first to ask questions. The discussion went on well and many questions were asked. I was most impressed by Li Yan, my former colleague in the HO and president of a private travel company, who soon fit in although she didn't join Site for long. She asked a lot of good questions that day.

With Chinese people playing more and more important roles on the international stage, they are becoming more confident to present themselves as a part of the big world community.

I still love wearing red when attending meetings. Red gives me courage.

A Single Flower Does Not Make a Spring

My team and I have done much volunteer work and devoted a lot of time, human resources and energy to increasing China's influence in the international associations of incentive travel and meeting industry. Before Site China Chapter was founded, our company had helped organize and sponsor many activities for Site members to promote friendship. Quite a few Site members have established partnerships through the networking.

At first, some people didn't understand why I was so active in the activities of our industry. They thought there was some personal purpose behind it. Someone said to me frankly, "Your ultimate purpose is for the interests of your own company."

I never denied it.

I once made a speech at a conference held by the Beijing government. I said, "An incentive travel and meeting company in Beijing wouldn't possibly attract people's attention unless the city becomes a most-watched incentive travel and meeting destination. No one would believe a city with underdeveloped incentive travel and meeting industry would have professional DMCs or PCOs."

Someone has to be the pioneer in developing the incentive travel and meeting industry in China. Besides, our team has gained a lot of valuable experience when doing the seemingly money-losing volunteer work. We do not lose anything.

I am more than willing to share with Chinese professionals in the same industry the knowledge and ideas I have learned during the activities of the international associations. Someone found it hard to understand and asked me, "You have paid for it. Why do you share it with others, especially your competitors?"

I don't have a nobler character than any other person. I might have a little more wisdom.

I don't consider competitors as enemies. As a leader of China's incentive travel and meeting industry, my aspiration is to form a good academic atmosphere in the industry which has huge potential. A lot of professionals are needed to make the cake bigger.

The generosity will also increase the credit of the individual or the enterprise. The following example can fully prove it.

There was a "silent auction" at the annual conference of ICCA held in Victoria, Canada in October, 2008 with the proceeds going to ICCA Education Fund. An auction corner was set up at the meeting. Each member had a "silent auction" number.

One of the items for sale was ICCA CEO Martin Sirk's 24 hours (including four hours of sleep). The bidding started at 800 euros. I got it at 1,600 euros. Besides, I had to pay for Mr. Sirk's round air ticket of business class from Amsterdam to Beijing and his stay in Beijing. It was not a small investment.

The reason why I decided to bid Martin's 24 hours was that I had too many questions to ask and my employees had too much to learn in the field of meeting industry. We are eager to learn because China lags behind Western countries and other countries in the Asia-Pacific region in its meeting industry. We must pay for the "schooling" if we want to catch up with them.

I also wanted to take the opportunity to introduce my company to Martin so that he would know there is such a good incentive travel and meeting company with great potential for development in China. It was a good way to enhance the image of our company to let the CEO of a world famous professional association, which has more than 850 corporate members in over 80 countries, know my company Xiang. For someone like Martin who had numerous affairs to deal with every day, if I didn't buy his time, I would never have had the chance to get him to know me enough and a Chinese private company well.

When the chair announced at the closing ceremony that Xiang won CEO Martin Sirk's 24 hours, many people remembered the name of Xiang, a Chinese company that attended the annual meeting of ICCA for the first time.

Despite all the benefits, it still made my heart ache to spend so much money. Actually, every single investment made me feel so. It was by no means as easy as I appeared when making every decision.

When I thought I did this for social responsibility and my company could benefit from it at the same time, killing two birds with one stone, I felt much better.

In September, 2009, Martin Sirk came to Beijing as scheduled.

When I won the bid for Martin's 24 hours, many people asked me jokingly how I was going to use the 24 hours. I tried to make a good use of his 24 hours and share some of his time with a university and some Chinese professionals including my competitors. I liked and respected Martin more when he told me that his favorite element was actually lecturing to university students. I, like a slave driver, made him work hard continuously for 20 hours even if some of those hours were spent at pleasant meals sharing ideas and experiences. My team and I learned a lot from him.

Martin and his ICCA colleagues were deeply impressed by me to share Martin's 24 hours. When they went to other countries in the Asia-Pacific region, such as Japan, India and Thailand to give lectures, they would use my case to illustrate that rivals were not enemies. It's said many people didn't believe it because they thought rival companies in China killed each other. At the 2009 ICCA Congress in Florence, I met many members from the Asia-Pacific region who were eager to tell me how they appreciated me for my generosity.

I always think if Xiang had no rivals, we wouldn't have made progress. We clearly know who our rivals are. When we lose to our rivals, we will find out our weaknesses, analyze our rivals' strengths, sum up our experience and learn from the failure.

To learn from one's rivals is a wonderful way to improve oneself. I have made friends with some of my rivals. We often share experiences and resources and I have learned much from them.

As a Site international board director, I ask myself not to use the advantage to seek benefits for my own company, but for the whole industry. If what we do could promote the development of the industry as a whole, it should be our contribution to the development of China's economy.

As the Chinese saying goes, "A single flower does not make a spring."

Fragrant Both Inside and Outside the Wall

There is a Chinese saying, "Flowering inside the wall and fragrant outside the wall," which means when someone has made some achievement, it is often more appreciated by outsiders than insiders.

I often say that Xiang's main business is inbound tourism and we are better known abroad than at home. We are flowering inside the wall but fragrant outside the wall.

As a private enterprise which has officially been in the business for only five years, we need to work out a series of sustainable development strategies to expand our market and to win fame both at home and abroad.

To attend trade shows is one of Xiang's main marketing methods.

Reed Travel Exhibitions, a British company, holds CIBTM (China Incentive, Business Travel & Meetings Exhibitions) in Beijing every year.

CIBTM had been held in Beijing for three times when Xiang was appointed as exclusive DMC to offer the land service to the buyers of CIBTM in 2009.

Reed Travel Exhibitions' choosing Xiang as its official DMC showed its recognition of the company's qualifications and strength. Our international counterparts all congratulated us on being appointed as official DMC of CIBTM.

Three years ago, Mr. Graeme Barnett of Reed Travel Exhibitions in charge of CIBTM asked me if I was interested in becoming the DMC for CIBTM. I said yes. But after that, nothing more was heard about it again. I thought if CIBTM needed us, they would come to us. If they didn't come to us, it meant we didn't reach the standard required.

After Mr. Graeme Barnett and I knew each other better, he told me he thought I was different. Normally DMCs would pursue it relentlessly when they heard of such an opportunity. But I just said "I am interested in it" and did nothing.

Indeed I should have been more active. But I was glad that our client came to us before we promoted ourselves, which showed that Xiang had strength and competitiveness.

A month prior to the opening of CIBTM 2009, Mr. Graeme Barnett asked me if I was interested in sponsoring the welcome reception. For some reasons, the details of 2009 CIBTM were confirmed at the last minute. There was not enough time for some other potential oversea sponsors to do anything. But how could a small private enterprise like Xiang sponsor a cocktail party for 500 guests? I asked him how much money it would need. Considering the cost was not more than we could afford, I thumped the table and said, "Ok, we will do it."

I was not as relaxed as I appeared. I often invest a large amount of money in market development; therefore I am a bold person who could do something big in people's eyes. In fact, all such decisions were not easily made. I thought to sponsor the welcome cocktail party of a world well-known exhibition brand would help Xiang raise its name recognition.

Due to the limited budget, we made best use of our resources and creativity and tried to get more done with less money. We designed kites with Chinese traditional characteristics. Dozens of kites were flying in the air with Xiang logo. We invited dozens of Beijing citizens to perform Chinese folk sports such as Taijiquan, shuttlecock kicking and diabolo at one corner of the party to create a relaxing atmosphere.

Certainly, one had to have economic strength to make the patronage decision. Xiang is an enterprise with sound development and has accumulated a sum of development fund. Otherwise, we wouldn't have made such a big investment under the global financial crisis.

When people walked in the exhibition venue of CIBTM on September 8, 2009, they could see the name and logo of Xiang everywhere. Many people inquired about us.

The company profile and logo of Xiang could be seen in the brochure and on the website of CIBTM.

CIBTM made Xiang become known in China's incentive travel and meeting industry overnight. Many people came to our booth to ask what kind of company Xiang was. When my colleagues exchanged business cards with other people, they would exclaim, "Wow, you are from Xiang!" Reporters of all media also chased the managers of our company for interviews.

Since it was founded, Xiang has been making efforts to build its brand. We hope to make Xiang a famous brand. A famous brand is a brand that is known to everyone, at least everyone in the industry. A famous brand should be known not only abroad but also at home.

In recent years, Xiang has done many meetings. We are not only a DMC; we have developed into a good PCO. We provide service for the international meetings that are held in China. Our customers are the Chinese hosts of the international meetings. Therefore, Xiang needs to increase its exposure and popularity domestically.

As for the international buyers, whether or not they will bring us business soon, they enjoy the high quality service of Xiang. When they talk about us to other people in the industry, it is actually word-of-mouth advertising for us. When they need a DMC in China, they will think of us.

Besides, the exhibitors from both home and abroad could serve as the publicity team and sowing machine for Xiang. We work in the same industry. The word-of-mouth publicity will be the best promotion for Xiang and will make more and more people get to know Xiang.

Xiang is an ambitious, competitive and forward-looking enterprise. We are ready to give, therefore we have achieved more. We will continue to develop along the healthy track.

Xiang is a young enterprise with advanced ideas, scientific management, a professional team and high quality service. It needs to make itself better known in the shortest time possible.

Xiang has been very active on the international stage of the industry for years. It has gained certain popularity abroad. The CIBTM in 2009 has given Xiang an opportunity to fully show itself domestically.

Finally Xiang is flowering inside the wall and fragrant inside the wall as well.

Doing Business in China

Many Westerners think it is difficult to do business in China. The conditions of China and the interpersonal relations are too complicated for people from Western countries to understand.

Maybe you will feel much better if I tell you that it is not easy for us either, a native Chinese enterprise to do business in our own country.

The following story happened in the meeting industry. I believe the stories of other industries are much the same.

My friend Lili is deputy secretary-general of an association in

China. She told me so-and-so society entrusted her to do its first international forum on so-and-so research. Mr. Li, an entrepreneur from Henan Province who has very strong economic power, wanted to invest in some research work in so-and-so culture and would exclusively sponsor the forum. All he wanted was a world first-class forum. Money was not a problem.

I was very excited. I didn't expect that someone would sponsor a first-class international meeting at any cost under the circumstances of financial crisis. On the one hand, we could make a good profit from the meeting; on the other hand, it was a good opportunity to fully display our talents.

According to Lili, so-and-so society was a newly established association. The office and the expensive wood furniture were also sponsored by Mr. Li. The society had no experience in doing meetings, so they asked Lili's association to handle the forum.

Xiang signed a cooperation agreement with Lili's association and prepared a written offer. Lili asked us to start working on the meeting after she confirmed it and paid a deposit of about two million yuan according to the agreement.

One day after we worked for a period of time, Lili suddenly came to our company and said that so-and-so society thought our price was too high and wanted to have a face-to-face talk with us.

We reached so-and-so society as scheduled.

Seven or eight people met us. The older ones were vice-president, secretary-general and deputy secretary-general of the society. One of them, relatively young, was the son of the society president who was absent. The son was the chief negotiator.

"We think your price is too high."

Normally we offer breakdown of the price for each item and our profit margin is transparent. Because of many uncertainties on the side of the society, many items in the offer were to be confirmed. Due to the time limit, we started to work on the first part such as the meeting visual image design and the hotel and air ticket reservation. Besides, we didn't start work until we got Lili's written confirmation.

"We will work out a more detailed offer to explain how the price came into being. We can do some adjustment according to your requirements and lower the price," I said.

"Your price is too high. We reserve the right to replace you with another meeting company."

The son of the society president spoke as if he were not negotiating but delivering the ultimatum.

"You are being unprofessional. We offered the price of a first-class meeting with international standards as you required. You confirmed the price and signed an agreement with us. If you find our price unacceptable, why didn't you let us know before we reached the agreement? Since we didn't violate any provision of the agreement, there is no reason for you to break the agreement."

I realized so-and-so society was not sincere. They just wanted to break the agreement. We signed the agreement with Lili's association, so we had no direct contact with so-and-so society. This was the first time we met the people from the society.

After the meeting, we worked out a very detailed written report to explain our price. Lili handed it to so-and-so society. We asked the society to tell us which item's price was too high.

We got no reply. Our report was like a stone dropped into the sea. Although Lili kept urging them, so-and-so society didn't give us an affirmative reply. Our written report was perfect. There should be no reason for so-and-so society to break the agreement.

Lili told us the truth in the end. Too many people wanted to use the meeting to seek personal gains. If the meeting was given to a canonical company like Xiang, they would gain nothing.

So-and-so society decided not to use us. But they had no reason to break the agreement. The son of the society president begged Lili to persuade us to terminate the agreement and give them back the advance payment.

I said we would return the advance payment as long as they explained to us why they decided to terminate the agreement. Besides, expenses incurred and cancellation fees would be deducted from the advance payment.

So-and-so society still couldn't give us any oral or written explanation. I felt so-and-so society would rather lose the nearly two million yuan of advance payment than cooperate with us. There must have been some dirty secret for them to allow such a ridiculous thing to happen.

I didn't want to make it difficult for Lili. We returned the advance payment after deducting the necessary cost.

So-and-so society was satisfied with our visual image design. They used our design though they didn't give us the meeting.

Later I knew that so-and-so society formed a temporary meeting company especially for the forum. The total cost of the meeting was over 10 million yuan, more than double the price we offered. The meeting company disbanded as soon as the meeting was over.

The meeting was a failure with low class and low quality. The sponsor was very unhappy. I felt sorry for him. He was fooled. Who knew how much money went into the pockets of the individuals? In his fury, the sponsor did not make the full payment and hauled away all the furniture he sponsored for the office of the society.

So-and-so society complained our price was too high. Our price was only six million yuan, but our service standard was much higher.

The following examples show how poor the quality of the meeting was.

With such a high budget, so-and-so society arranged double rooms for all the invited guests sponsored by Mr. Li. The domestic guests accepted it reluctantly. But the foreign guests firmly refused to share rooms with strangers and refused to check in the hotel until they got their own single rooms.

A good friend of mine happened to be invited to the meeting. She told me she hadn't shared a double room with someone else for many

521

years. She shared a room with a stranger this time.

The badge had no delegate's name on it, but was marked A, B, or C. During the discussion session, the delegates couldn't choose the topic based on their interest. Instead, they were divided into different groups according to the A, B or C on their badges. The delegates were not allowed to take part in other sessions. My friend wanted to join the discussion of other groups, but she was stopped by a guard with rude manners.

The meeting was poorly organized. The host committee asked all the participants to assemble at 6:00 a.m. to save time for the security check in the Great Hall of the People. But when they reached there, it was not open yet. Several hundred delegates had to wait in the snow which was the biggest snow for years.

When the meeting was over, no news could be found on the internet, which meant it had no influence at all either at home or abroad. The sponsor's money was wasted.

It might be an extreme case. But it happened under my eyes. I just want to use the case to tell you the difficulties you may meet when doing business in China. Corruption is not a problem that can be solved in a short time in China.

Doing inbound tourism for many years, we understand the Western culture and Westerners' mode of thinking. We know how to deal with them. They choose Xiang as their partner because they value our strength, lawful operation and credit. Only in this way can the two parties build trust and friendship.

When we entered the meeting industry to provide service for the international meetings to be held in China and to cooperate with our own compatriots in the local associations or government organizations, we began to feel things were difficult even for the native-born people like us.

We went to bid an international conference which was to be held in Beijing. The person who was in charge of the conference host committee asked us, "Who is your higher level authority?"

"We are a private enterprise. There is no competent authority at a higher level. The relevant governmental department of the industry just exercises administration and supervision on private companies."

"You are a private enterprise. Then how can we trust you?"

In China, some government organizations and associations are not used to working with private enterprises. In fact, private businesses are playing a more and more important role in many industries, especially the service industry. Many private enterprises are doing better than state-owned enterprises, which is for everyone to see.

"You can investigate our company's legitimacy and check our credit and cash flow in the bank. Our financial situation is more favorable than most of the state-owned enterprises in the same industry."

Although the relevant international association and the Chinese host committee thought we were the best, we lost the bid. In fact, the host committee had already decided which company to use before the bid invitation. The invitation of bids was just going through the motions.

We are still full of confidence though such things repeatedly occur.

A funny thing happened later. One day the host committee called me and asked for an urgent meeting. We were told that the company chosen by the decision maker decided to quit for it did not know how to handle an international meeting and how to deal with the problems. The host committee wanted Xiang to take over. We did.

Over the past 30-odd years since the reform and opening-up, China has achieved great results in economic development and social progress. Great changes have also taken place in people's mind. Many of those who are in high positions in government departments, state-owned enterprises or associations have studied abroad or have many opportunities to go abroad to attend academic exchanges or activities. They have seen the world and know what international standards are. It is much easier to communicate with them.

Besides, the Chinese government has intensified its efforts to combat corruption and build an honest government. The laws and regulations are being gradually improved. Some decision makers will not take the risk of losing their jobs for personal gains.

In China, the environment of fair competition is gradually formed, though the process is very slow.

We have the following experience to share about doing business in China.

Take the meeting industry as an example.

When Westerners are researching China, they always get a conclusion that one has to depend on *guanxi* to get anything done in China. In my opinion, *guanxi* is important, but not everything.

First, we have to do our homework well.

We work out a bilingual proposal without being requested by the host association. The proposal includes any necessary information available – company profile, qualifications, honors and cases, the project leading team and main staff, the range of services for professional meetings, briefing about the venues, hotels, tour programs and transportation during the meeting. The host association can find whatever they need in the proposal. We will also write a letter to show our sincerity and send it together with the proposal and a unique company brochure to the host association.

When the host association receives our professional and eye-catching proposal and brochure, we will follow up to contact them by telephone. Since they already have a favorable first impression of our company, they wouldn't refuse us at once. Therefore, it would be much easier to communicate with them.

We ask them to give us a chance to pay a formal call on them. We are good at presenting ourselves. We are confident because we have very good slides and videos to prove our qualifications. As far as I know, some companies, even some large state-owned enterprises pay no attention to accumulating and sorting materials even if they have scored many big projects. They cannot convince people if they say how experienced they are.

At the same time, we do spend a lot of time and energy building *guanxi*. Our purpose of seeking *guanxi* is to get equal opportunities to compete with other meeting companies. We just need our *guanxi* to lead us into the door and we will do the rest by ourselves.

If we establish a connection with the decision maker through our *guanxi*, we should never let our *guanxi* down. We should do a good job to make our *guanxi* proud of us. Only in this way will our *guanxi* continue to help us in the future.

If we fail in the competition because we are not good enough, we will never use the *guanxi* to intercede for us. Otherwise, we are making trouble for the *guanxi*.

Sometimes we lose the bid, but the organizer still says we are the best. Due to some reasons, they have to choose some other company that is not so competitive as us. Sometimes, we know there is little chance of success; we will still participate in the tender. We want to use the opportunity to promote ourselves, to increase our influence and to lay a foundation for cooperation in the future.

Even if we don't get business, it doesn't mean our work is useless. The rising of meeting companies of international standards like us will pose a threat to those unqualified meeting companies or PR companies. If they want to stay competitive, they must change and improve themselves instead of just building *guanxi*, which is good for the healthy development of the meeting industry in China.

Chance favors only the prepared mind. With the constant improvement of the legal system and increased supervision, the power of *guanxi* will get weaker and weaker. *Guanxi* will be more useful only when you are dynamic and competitive. Nowadays, some meeting companies spend a great deal of time and energy on *guanxi* instead of improving their abilities. They are putting the cart before the horse and making the road ahead narrower and narrower.

Another important thing is to educate your clients. Take the meeting industry as an example. Many people think no professional knowledge or expertise is needed to do meetings. Some meeting hosts break down the service, leaving the easy and profitable part to themselves and giving the difficult and time-consuming part to the meeting companies. Several companies are involved in one event. As a result, many unexpected problems will arise as there is no overall coordinator. The meeting hosts have no professional knowledge or experience, and have no ability to foresee the problems or solve them.

Once the host committee of a meeting appreciated Xiang and said they would ask the meeting company which won the bid to subcontract part of the work to us. We refused it. The meeting company was of a low standard. We wouldn't work under an amateur. We would rather lose business than cooperate with a company which is not professional for the sake of our reputation.

Foreigners or foreign companies will meet with more difficulties doing business in China.

I have the following experience to share with them.

To do meetings or events in China, foreigners should make a good use of the local resources and establish partnerships with local or localized international DMCs or PCOs.

First, language barrier is still a big problem. Though more and more Chinese people are learning English, few decision makers can speak fluent English. Foreign businessmen need the local resources to open the door to the decision makers.

Second, the local resources are needed to go through relevant formalities to get the support from the local government.

Third, most of the large-scale venues in China are owned by the state. To use the venues for big events, one has to go through official procedures. Many of the venues are not of easy access to foreigners.

Fourth, the local resources know the bureaucracy and inefficient work style of relevant departments and can mobilize their social resources to facilitate and coordinate the process.

Fifth, Chinese people value personal relations very much which can help further the communication. It is very hard for foreigners to directly build personal relations with Chinese decision makers. They have to rely on the local resources to build up personal relationship with the decision makers, so that they can make themselves clear and avoid misunderstanding caused by cultural difference or language barrier.

The biggest challenge for foreigners is to control the degree when dealing with Chinese decision makers. If they don't do enough, it won't work. If they overdo it, the result may turn out to be just the opposite of their wish. Foreigners really need to be modest if they do not know China enough. We have some Western partners who believe that they can deal with all the problems in China and are always dominating during the cooperation with us. They do not listen to us until they knock into the wall.

The last and most difficult thing is to find the right partner.

The competition among enterprises is the competition for talents. I have noticed some employees of certain Western enterprises in China, who are hired at high costs, are incompetent. I am worried for them. To be honest, I have no good ideas about this because of the big shortage of professionals in MICE industry in China.

Chinese cities like Shanghai and Beijing have developed into destination cities for international conferences. Some Western meeting companies have seen the tremendous potential and come to register business in these cities. They have great sales force in the international market and can get business directly from the source, the headquarters of international associations. In this case, they should pay attention to building a good relationship with the local hosts of the meetings, the relevant Chinese associations. Some associations in China also function as PCOs. Western companies get business from the source, which means that they take away the cheese from the relevant Chinese associations. To have meetings in China, a lot of coordination is needed. Without the help of the relevant Chinese associations, Western meeting companies would have headache every day.

It is very important for a foreign meeting company to find a reliable partner in China. Otherwise, they will encounter more difficulties than they can imagine.

Both Chinese people and Westerners need to learn to do business in China. Chinese people should learn to keep up with the trend of globalization while Westerners should learn how to adapt to the business environment in China.

Serve the People with Heart and Soul

The nature of my job is to serve people. For international travel companies that specialize in inbound tourism like Xiang, what they do is to serve foreign people. Working in the same industry, someone does a good job, someone does a great job, while someone only does a so-so job. Someone stands out soon while someone remains mediocre for many years. No secret of success or know-how is needed to do well in the service industry. The essential thing is whether you work with your heart and soul and whether you care about your clients who you serve.

People often ask me, "What's your secret of success?" I am no better than my colleagues in any way. On the contrary, they have many advantages I wish I could have. My advantage is that first, I work wholeheartedly; second, I pay attention to details and third, I care very much. Anyone can do the above three points as long as he really wants to. No special knowledge or skill is needed.

The following story will tell you the difference between "care" and "not care" and how much you have to care.

At 8:00 a.m. on August 21, 2008, I was driving to the Bird's Nest to see the Olympic Games. It was the first time I went to the Games since it opened on August 8. It was raining heavily. I was worried about the American couple who were going to visit the Great Wall today. The couple were introduced to me by Stephanie Quesada, the secretary of Mr. Peter Ueberoth, the president of US Olympic Committee, in the American House. I only met the couple once when we hurriedly greeted each other. I assigned a sales manager named Chao to be in charge of this request.

The guide was supposed to pick up the couple at their hotel at 8:30 a.m. When I was in the car, I was thinking about calling the guide to ask how it went. I didn't want to seem nervous and told myself I should trust my staff, so I resisted the attempt to make the call. When I reached the Bird's Nest, it was past 8:30. I was more worried by the heavier rain with thunders, so I finally called the guide.

"Have you picked up the guests?"

"Yes, I have."

"It is really a bad time to visit the Great Wall."

"I am not going to the Great Wall today. I am sending the guests to the airport."

I was utterly confused. We were short of tour guides during the Olympic Games. The guide was actually an office staff of our company. I had asked her personally if she had time to accompany the couple to the Great Wall on August 21.

"Aren't you supposed to accompany two American guests who stay at Grand Hyatt to visit the Great Wall today?"

"No. I am not."

I immediately called the operation manager to ask who was assigned to pick up the two guests.

"We have no guests going to the Great Wall today," said the operation manager.

I hung up the phone and said, "Shit!"

I called Chao who was also on the way to the Bird's Nest.

"What is the tour plan for the two American guests who are visiting the Great Wall today?"

"It is not today. They are visiting the Great Wall on the 28th."

"I clearly remember it's a Thursday. Is today Thursday?"

Chao confirmed it was Thursday.

"Shit!"

I uttered "shit" like four or five times. It was not directed against anyone, just a way to express how I felt at that moment. I asked the driver to return to the company soon.

On the way back, I called Stephanie to ask for the names and telephone numbers of the two guests. All the information about the clients was in the computer in my office. I finished my job after I handed the case to Chao. As a CEO, I usually was not involved in the details of operation. Stephanie was in a meeting and said she would call me back later. I said it was really urgent and I needed the cellphone numbers and full names of the two American guests. Without their names, I could not find their room number. I could not remember the full names of the two guests because I was handling a lot of last-minute requests those days. When Stephanie was looking for the telephone numbers, I tried to contact the reception desk of Grand Hyatt Hotel to check if there were two guests waiting in the lobby. Nobody answered the phone. I decided to try my luck. I asked the operator to put me through to the guests' room when I got their names from Stephanie. It was nearly 9:00 a.m. The guests couldn't have been in the room.

Thank God! The husband was still in the room.

I lied to him. I said the car broke down on the way to the hotel. I asked them to wait for a few minutes and I would arrange another car to pick them up.

Twenty minutes later, a car and a tour guide reached the hotel from two different directions.

A close friend who was in the same car with me said, "You are CEO. If you do so many detailed jobs, you are more likely to make mistakes." I only got involved in the operation during the special period of the Olympic Games. There was no spare hand in the office. I was responsible to take care of important public relations and close friends of the company. Most of the needs were urgent and the last-minute requests, but I hadn't made a single mistake in all the arrangements, even under the pressure of the Drum Tower attack incident.

I didn't retort. I was quite sure I didn't make any mistakes since I cared about the clients so much. But I never draw the conclusion until I find where the problem is.

It turned out Chao made a mistake.

I checked the tour schedule made by Chao. The date of the visit to the Great Wall was the 28th instead of the 21st. I immediately realized where the problem was.

According to the Chinese grammar, next Thursday should be the Thursday of next week. The American couple sent me an e-mail on Tuesday and asked us to arrange a tour to the Great Wall on next Thursday which according to the English grammar should be the Thursday of the same week. Chao's major is English; he should know this difference between English and Chinese, which he had learned as early as in the high school.

I didn't criticize Chao harshly. He was actually a very good staff and worked very hard during the Olympic Games. But I hope everyone can learn something from it.

If I didn't care so much about the client, I wouldn't have called the tour guide when I saw the bad weather. If I hadn't called the tour guide, we would have made an irreparable mistake because the American couple only had time to visit the Great Wall that day. What is worse, it would have ruined our company's reputation.

During that period, all the programs we did were related to the Olympic Games. By the day of August 28, the Olympic Games would have been over. It should not be difficult to judge the guests couldn't possibly visit the Great Wall several days after the games. Chao wouldn't have made the mistake if he had given more care to it.

Chao said he also had some doubt about visiting the Great Wall on August 28 when he was working out the program for them. Since he had doubt, why didn't he ask? The nature of our work decides we shouldn't take any chance.

Maybe someone would ask me, "Do you care so much about all clients?"

Yes, I do. For me, there are no important clients or unimportant clients.

Besides, I don't advocate lying. I lied to the guest because I didn't want to make it complicated before the problem was solved. I told him the truth when he came to the company to pay for the tour.

To admit one's mistake is an effective way to solve the problem.

He gave me his card in my office. He was quite somebody.

He said he was still in the room because he was delayed by an early morning meeting. His wife was waiting in the lobby. He went back to his room to get something. When he was about to leave, he heard the telephone ringing...

This client later introduced business to us.

Not Only for Money

Our company attends several international trade shows for incentive, business travel, meetings and events in most cases with the National Tourism Administration or Beijing Tourism Administration every year. Most of the Chinese exhibitors are state-owned enterprises. The National Tourism Administration or Beijing Tourism Administration provides equal opportunities to all the companies. In the center of the Chinese booth is a speech area where all the companies can take turns to do presentation by using slides or videos. During the three-day exhibition, some companies uses the speech area once, some twice, some not even once. We are the only company that would never miss any opportunity. Our slides and videos are also the most exquisitely made.

I met a department general manager of my former employer at an exhibition a couple of years ago. When he saw I was so active at the show, he said approvingly to others, "You see the difference between working for others and working for oneself. One can really work hard to earn money for oneself." I concluded that he wouldn't do anything great when I heard his remark. When I was working in the state-owned enterprise, I worked no less hard than now for my own business. No matter who you work for, the government or an individual, as long as you accept the job, you should abide by the professional ethics and work hard for your employer. Nobody forces you to work there. If you cannot accept it, you can leave. You should be loyal to your employer as long as you remain an employee. Although I didn't enjoy my job in the state-owned company, I devoted 10 years' loyalty to the company because I chose it myself. Now I have my own business and I still work very hard. It has nothing to do with who I work for and how much money I earn. The only difference is that being self-employed, I have more decision-making power to avoid in-fighting and bureaucracy and to do things better.

During the Beijing Olympic Games, I had the chance to meet the American gymnastics team. Many people were envious of my meeting with Nastia Liukin and Shawn Johnson. Actually it was nothing much for me. Though I was happy to meet them, I was not a fan chaser.

Our company provided some service to the American Gymnastics Association, all hard work but little profit. We helped the American Gymnastics Association make a reservation for the celebration dinner at a roast duck restaurant. The dinner would be paid by the American Gymnastics Association CEO directly to the restaurant. We had no profit at all. Presumably, we had no obligation to provide any service.

Today Show of NBC (National Broadcasting Company) decided to broadcast it alive from the roast duck restaurant. A large generator and a Satellite News Gathering had to be placed in the restaurant. I understood that it was impossible for the American Gymnastics Association to coordinate with the restaurant. The program team asked me to help them with the coordination. I took it as a mission.

The American Gymnastics Association asked me to find them a restaurant the day before the dinner party. They first told me 70 people would attend the party. On the afternoon of the day of the party, they told me there would be 90 participants. But actually there were 100 participants. The only room available in the restaurant could only hold 70 people. It was thus obvious that the Americans would have been in trouble without our coordination.

The CEO of the American Gymnastics Association invited me to the party. I didn't want to attend it because I hadn't had a good rest since the opening of the Olympic Games. I could have said no. We did not charge for anything, so we didn't have the duty to offer any more service. But I thought the Americans might need help, so I went in the end.

As expected, I was busy with the coordination throughout the party. The CEO apparently didn't treat me as a stranger and "ordered" me to do this and do that. The gymnastics stars and their families certainly had no idea who I was.

I was invited to the party, but I didn't eat anything and stood for three hours. The CEO had no time to eat either. But he was the host and should serve his guests.

Certainly, I am not a fool who always does a hard but thankless job. Moreover, we are a profit-seeking enterprise. No profit, my team would go begging.

Certainly I would figure out the cost. If my service generated cost, I wouldn't do it for nothing unless it was part of the marketing strategy.

The cost of my service at the party was my own time and energy. I was willing to do something for the Olympic Games and for Beijing. I had no complaint if I took all the unpaid service as the duty of a volunteer.

Strictly speaking, a CEO's time and energy can be measured in money. However, don't forget you get public praise and a good reputation from your readiness to give.

What I got for my free service was a plaster on the waist.

Any Better Solution than Returning the Quality Guarantee Deposit?

One day at the end of 2008, a reporter from *China Daily* called me to ask my opinion on "the National Tourism Administration's decision to return part of the quality guarantee deposit to travel companies to help them cope with the global financial crisis". It was the first time I heard it and I replied, "If a travel company especially a company that has been in the business for many years has to depend on the quality guarantee deposit to cope with the financial crisis, it is not far from going bankrupt."

Quality guarantee deposit is the mandatory fund travel agents pay to the tourism administration department to safeguard lawful rights and interests of tourists. Travel agents shall compensate tourists who suffer losses in the following cases:

The travel agent fails to reach the service quality standard as agreed upon in the contract due to its own fault;

The travel agent fails to provide services up to the national standard or trade standard;

The travel agent causes loss of traveling expenses paid by tourists in advance due to its bankruptcy.

I have never advocated appropriating the quality guarantee deposit for other purposes.

It is known in the industry that the profit margin of travel companies is low. It is also a common phenomenon of "monks getting rich while the temple getting poor".

Whenever a crisis is approaching, many people in the industry would say that it is a good opportunity for the tourism industry to be shuffled. They expect the superior travel companies will prosper and inferior ones be eliminated in the mighty wave of economic rules. But after each crisis, everything remains the same.

A travel company with healthy development must have a reserve plan to cope with crises and emergencies. Now the financial crisis has just begun. If a travel company has to use the quality security to survive, what can they do next if they use it up? According to the *Beijing Youth Daily*, the National Tourism Administration has declared the local tourism offices across the country would return 50 to 70 percent of the quality guarantee deposit to travel companies so that they have enough working funds to cope with the calamity caused by the sharp decline in the number of tourists. It also said "this year (the year of 2008), business has been bad for travel companies influenced by the snow disaster, the earthquake and the Olympic Games (fewer regular tourists came to China)". The quality guarantee deposit cannot help them overcome the real problem of bad business. Some private travel companies have already run into financial difficulties. In this case, nobody can help them. I wonder if the managers of those private travel companies face personal financial trouble too.

The measure of returning the quality guarantee deposit should help those companies who are stuck in emergency but could not help those who are poorly managed.

According to *Metropolis Times*, "The financial crisis may hit tourism harder than SARS. To return the quality guarantee deposit to travel companies can effectively help some companies overcome the lack of working fund, especially outbound travel services that require more working fund." The representatives of several travel companies in Shanghai said in an interview that "the measure to return the quality guarantee deposit in 2003 cushioned the travel companies from the impact by SARS and helped them pull through. If the measure is really put into effect, it would undoubtedly give a cardiac stimulant to the gloomy tourism industry".

I agree the current financial crisis may have a heavier impact on the tourism industry than the SARS outbreak. But the so-called cardiac stimulant will not necessarily cure the disease. Heart failure may still happen after its short time effect. SARS lasted for several months. When it was over, tourism recovered soon. But nobody knows when the financial crisis would come to an end.

Xiang is well prepared for the financial crisis because it has learned a lesson from SARS.

Not long before the outbreak of SARS, I signed a letter of intent on acquisition with travel company B. Before the acquisition was completed, I was running my own business in the form of *guakao*. I didn't spend a penny of the quality security returned to travel company B. It was all used by the general manager of travel company B to pay the company's debts left before I took over the operation of the company. The company didn't pay back the quality guarantee deposit until long after SARS was over and was warned by the government department concerned several times.

I just started my own business for a year when SARS broke out. I was under great economic and mental pressure leading a team of more than 20 people and with no accumulation of funds. I made up my mind that we must have built up a capital reserve enough for at least two years in the shortest time. But I was not sure how long it would take to achieve the goal.

When Xiang was officially founded in July 2005, the five shareholders reached an agreement not to distribute dividends for five years for the accumulation of a reserve. After several years' efforts, we have achieved the goal. Our reserve will help us pull through even if the financial crisis lasts longer than we expect. Besides, the financial crisis doesn't mean there is no business at all. Actually the company is doing quite well under the financial crisis because of the timely adjustment to the marketing strategy.

We are grateful to the government for being considerate and helping enterprises overcome the difficulties. But we will not depend on the returned security to solve the problem. For enterprises like Xiang, what we really need is tax reduction or tax rebate so that we can put more into market development. Only in this way can the travel companies with healthy financial conditions be stimulated. Otherwise everyone wants to put the money into his own pocket. Our accumulating reserve resulted in more taxes. Although we did it willingly, we still felt uncomfortable when other travel companies enjoyed the same treatment even if they earned little profit, paid no or less tax.

We adopted the following measures to cope with the financial crisis.

First, broadening sources of income and reducing expenditure. Although we have kept a reserve for rainy days, we still need to practice economy and reduce costs so that the reserve can last for a longer time.

Reducing the salary of the management 20 to 50 percent from January 2009. My salary had a 50 percent drop.

Not renewing contract with incompetent or disloyal employees.

I need to do some explanation as to the last point. No matter how bad the financial crisis becomes, we will never dismiss employees who are working hard and loyal to the company. On the one hand, we need to maintain strength to wait for the economic recovery; on the other hand, it is our social responsibility to help the government solve the employment problem. But we are not a charity. For those employees who don't work hard or who are incompetent or disloyal to the company, we may give them a chance or more time to correct their mistakes when the economy is doing well. But in recession, we will not waste time and money on them for the interests of other employees.

Lower salaries of the management will not influence the quality of their life. They just need to change their ways of consumption. We will never cut the salary of the employees unless it is absolutely necessary. In fact, since the financial crisis began, the pay of the employees has been increased for better business opportunities than we expected.

We reduced expenses in all respects in 2009 and 2010 except investment in market development and promotion which maintained the level of the year before or even higher. It is like everybody is selling stocks while we are buying more. When other companies cut their budget in market development and promotion, we do exactly the opposite to increase our overseas exposure to win more cooperation opportunities.

The business has increased rapidly since I resigned and started my own business in 2001. I have been busy with my work and have no time to sum up experience and to work out in details market development strategies and long-term development targets for the company. The financial crisis might be an opportunity for us to slow down to think, to make us known to more people especially those potential customers. We can have more time to train our staff to improve their professional qualities and to standardize customer files and human resources management so as to make the team more competent.

When the world economy is going from bad to worse, I am still confident because we have a powerful country behind us. The world has increased its attention to and interest in China. International cooperation and exchanges will not come to an end because of the financial crisis.

To support travel services to cope with the difficulties caused by the global financial crisis and other factors, the National Tourism Administration issued a notice in January 2009 that it would temporarily return part of the quality security to travel services which can be used for a term of two years and has to be paid back before December 31, 2010.

We put the returned money in the bank and have never touched it.

Fighting Alone

This is a topic I am reluctant to touch.

Like many other industries in China, there are also undesirable practice and hidden rules in tourism. For years, I have been struggling to find a balance between protecting the interests of the vested interest group and protecting the interests of the clients.

Many of my ideas were not accepted by my management team from the beginning until they have stood the test of time and proved correct. Many people have tried to persuade me not to be so obstinate and childish. Something couldn't possibly be solved in one or two days. Some people believe that laws would fail where the violators are legion, but I stand up for what I think is right. Those who once said I was obstinate now say I am persistent.

There is a team behind me and I am the leader of the team. Therefore, I am always the one who stands in the forefront of the struggle and is the target for attack.

Since I started my own business, some of the employees who were criticized or punished for breaking the rules of the company directed their hatred on me. Someone sent e-mail messages to my colleague to attack me with filthy language. But the colleague reacted slowly and made no counterattack for me. In fact, I just needed support. What I wanted from my colleague was a reply "It's stupid." Without the counterattack, the person who hated me thought I was alone and weak and doubled his revenge on me.

For a long period of time, I was fighting alone.

Several years ago, some senior staff members failed to resist the lure of money and violated the company rules.

I learned of it when I was on an inspection tour in Shanghai with two American clients. The two clients were good friends of mine and they knew a great deal about tourism in China. Seeing that I was always lost in thought, they asked me, "Do you think it has been hard for you?"

I told them I always felt lonely. I felt helpless when the person I trusted most betrayed me and violated company rules and disciplines.

I did nothing to the employees who violated the rules. One of them was G, vice president of the company. I didn't know how to deal with him. I had to protect his prestige. I just pointed out his problem frankly.

G was a nice person and was very popular among the colleagues. I often said that if we had a fight, those who didn't know the truth must think it was my fault.

His main problem was that he couldn't manage the company from an overall perspective as a company leader should, and failed to fight against bad influences because he himself benefited from them. As a guide with more than 10 years' work experience, he knew more about the hidden rules in the industry than me. It would have been much easier for me if he helped me manage our guides. No matter how hard we tried to protect the interests of the guides, we could do nothing about the temptation of the hidden rules and the influences around them.

G was a very good guide, but not a qualified leader. He wouldn't violate the rules when he worked alone. When he worked with other senior guides, he didn't check their malpractice but held a candle to the devil. They formed a clique against me for the interests of their small group. I was more weakened when G who was supposed to work with me turned his back on me.

The problem I encountered was a very complex one that has long existed in China's tourism industry. Today, I still have reservations when talking about the problem. I can only say I have been fighting against the excessive commercialization of the tourism industry for a long time.

Most of the guides in China are freelancers and have no steady income. Small and medium-sized travel companies, especially private companies, don't keep full-time guides for decreasing cost. But our guides are regular staff and have basic salary, benefits and insurance. Our purpose is to ensure the quality of our service and meanwhile protect the benefits of our guides. The average income of our guides is much higher than that of the sales managers.

In 2003 shortly after the SARS epidemic, a People to People alumni delegation of more than 70 members came to visit China as scheduled. Given the importance of the delegation, I assigned G and another two senior guides X and Y to take care of this group.

I went to Shanghai to visit the group before they finished their journey in China. I talked with the delegation leader and other members and expected that they would appreciate the excellent job by the guides. The comments I heard from the delegates were not as good as I expected. I was puzzled and didn't know why. The three guides were supposed to be a group of the best guides in China.

In 2006, when I attended the 50th anniversary of the founding of People to People in Sydney, I came across a delegate of the delegation. He told me the guides were too commercialized and always urged them to do shopping. Suddenly I realized what had happened. If you don't want people to know it, you'd better not do it. I got to know the answer three years later.

We would rather recruit college graduates than accept experienced guides with many bad habits. Once bad habits are developed, it is very hard to get rid of them. The corrupt practice has long existed among guides because there hasn't been an effective way to solve the problem.

I thought college graduates were a blank page where one could draw the newest and most beautiful pictures. They were not mentally polluted, so I thought I could train them to be guides with both integrity and ability.

Facts proved it was just my wishful thinking. I was like an ant trying to shake a big tree if I wanted to contend against the forces of the whole industry.

I trained the new employees personally. G, as the vice president in charge of guides, and X and Y, as senior and experienced guides also undertook the training program.

As the new guides took up their jobs, their conflict with the veteran guides began to emerge. When they worked with the veteran guides, they found what they did was contrary to what they taught them in the training. The veteran guides often violated the rules. They just managed to cover it up because they were experienced guides. The new guides told me what confused them. I never worked as a guide, so I didn't know all the underhanded activities in it. For many years, I was quite in the dark and did not know all the tricks of the guides. I found ways to deal with each of the problems as soon as I discovered it. I had rules while the guides had their own ways of getting around them. As time passed, the new guides picked up the veteran guides' bad habits. But they were too green and were easily complained by the clients. The veteran guides were not willing to work with the new guides. They have formed some tacit understanding among themselves. If they worked with the new guides, it would be harder for them to justify themselves when they violated the rules. The new guides were not willing to work with the veteran guides either. They felt they were bullied and often came to me with tearful eyes.

I realized it would be impossible to manage the guides well if we didn't solve the problem of the veteran guides. The local agents were also dissatisfied with G, X and Y because of their domination in the cooperation. They thought I wouldn't possibly make up my mind to deal with the guides because I couldn't do without them, so they concealed their violation from me.

According to the company rules, it is the duty of the local agents, the local guides and the national guides to supervise each other. If the national guide violated the rules and the local agent chose to keep silent, we would terminate the partnership once we found it out.

The national guides were in a more dominant position in their cooperation with the local guides. When they asked the local guides to join them in violating the rules, the local guides had to. Certainly it was what some of them wanted to do themselves.

Because I never gave up my supervision over the guides, what they did finally came out of the water. I was good to my employees and fair to my partners, so many of them could not tolerate it any longer to see I had been cheated all the time and finally told me the truth with a guilty conscience.

The biggest helper might be the biggest wrecker.

G, X and Y were the best guides in professional competence. Our American professional groups needed guides with high-level interpretation skills. Average guides couldn't reach the standard. This is one of the reasons why we keep full-time guides instead of using freelancers. Many people thought if I were too strict with them and pressed them too hard, they would quit and I would be the one who suffered losses.

I often feel hurt. I am a good boss and I care much about the interests of my employees, which is well known in the industry. I can sacrifice my personal interests for those of my employees. In fact, the pay of our guides is almost the highest in the guide circles in China.

Even so, some guides repeatedly violated the company rules for their vested interests. Not only common employees, G, the vice president of the company, who was supposed to oversee the guides and was a guide himself, set a bad example for other guides. When G violated the company rules working as a guide, our local agents thought we gave him silent consent, which made it more difficult for me to manage the company.

My strict management led to the three best guides G, X and Y's resigning en masse.

Y sold seals to the guests on the coach and violated the rules. I gave G a free hand to deal with it. I wouldn't interfere, but I was waiting to hear the result.

Instead of G's decision as to how to deal with it, what was waiting for me was the three guides' resignation.

It was the busiest time of the year. They knew clearly that their resignation would make me unprepared.

They had already been assigned many groups when they resigned. Normally, the national guide would have three months to prepare for the interpretation for the American professional delegations. It was difficult for me to find proper guides to replace them in the season. But I was determined to handle it no matter how hard it would be. I didn't know if they had deliberately planned it for a long time, especially X who had been assigned to accompany a professional delegation to Mongolia and had just got the visa. I had to find a guide to replace him and to get a visa for the guide within a short time. Their malicious resignation took away the last bit of good impression I had on them.

When they put their letters of resignation on my desk, I approved them immediately.

Their resignation was actually a relief for me. If they hadn't resigned, it would have been difficult for me to make up my mind to dismiss any of them. I told G more than once that I would have long dismissed Y if it was not for saving G's face. Y violated the rules many times and had a bad name among the guides and the drivers. If one man says "someone is not good", there might be personal bias; if everyone says "someone is not good", it must be true.

G said that one of the reasons for his resignation was I was too capable and he felt he couldn't give full play to his abilities working under me.

If a man cannot uphold righteousness, correct errors and take responsibility, he is not qualified to be a leader and will not give full play to his abilities no matter where he works.

One of our common American friend said that G wanted to be the second "Liu Ping". "He would never become the second Liu Ping," I said resolutely. A good leader should be just and fair and stick to principles, which are the qualities he lacks.

After they left Xiang, they started their own business in the form of *guakao*. I asserted that they wouldn't work together for a long time. When in Xiang, they formed a clique against the company. Now self-managed, I wondered how G was going to balance the interests among the three of them.

Later, I met G. He told me he began to understand me since he had his own business to manage. It was easy for him to say. But he had no idea what trouble he had brought to the management of the company because I had to spend a lot of time and energy to solve his problem first.

As I predicted, the small group split up soon.

I have been doing it for more than a dozen years to fight against those who intentionally violate the rules.

The following case happened when I was a division chief in the HO.

One day, the Finance Division chief came to my office and asked me to see a problematic bill. It turned out one of my sales managers juggled with the account and embezzled part of the cash the client paid. The sales manager was a young man. He didn't do well in his work, but was on good terms with the department head. I accepted him only because I was required by the department head.

I asked the department head what should be done about it. He didn't give me a definite reply. "If you don't want me to handle it, you must handle it yourself," I said.

I thought it was a serious matter. Since the Finance Division chief had pointed it out, as head of the department, he should make his view clear, otherwise how could he manage the whole department in the future? I appreciated the financial person for sticking to principles. If nothing was done about it, it would be unfair to those who stood for principles.

Later that day, the young man confessed his behavior and made a written self-criticism.

The next day, a meeting was called. All the leaders at or above division chief level of the department attended the meeting. It was not my suggestion that the young man should make a self-criticism at a department level. It was obviously the arrangement of the department head. At the meeting, the young man reversed what he had said the previous day and said that it was me who ordered him to steal the money to build up a coffer for the division.

My superior was unhappy that I insisted on dealing with the young man. He wanted to make concessions to avoid trouble, but he didn't expect I was a person with principle. When I was framed, he did nothing to defend me but said ironically, "Is Liu Ping happy now that she has brought trouble to herself?"

Although I was indignant at the young man's false accusation against me, I disdained to explain for myself. I just asked him to his face, "You said I ordered you to do it. Then why didn't you hand over the money to me but kept it to yourself?"

He couldn't reply.

I said to the department head, "I don't want him any more."

What the department head didn't expect was that all the division chiefs, no matter they liked me or not sided with me this time. The reason was simple: If anyone can frame up his superior so easily, how can they supervise their subordinates in the future?

The young man still worked in my division because nobody wanted him. The department head asked me to give him a chance. He was very young. Although he made a serious mistake, I didn't want to finish him off with a single blow. I was helpless. I knew the seed of vengeance had been sown.

Sometimes, I cannot help thinking why all these things have happened to me, being falsely accused, cursed, harassed, and attacked by anonymous letters.

I find a true reflection of my life in the following paragraph by Chinese philosopher Mencius (372 – 289 B.C.), "When Heaven is about to place great responsibility on a great man, it always first frustrates his spirit and will, exhausts his muscles and bones, exposes him to starvation and poverty, harasses him by troubles and setbacks so as to stimulate his spirit, toughen his nature and enhance his abilities."

I have been doing my own business for nearly 10 years. It has been a decade of struggle, of correcting mistakes and of remolding my colleagues. Sometimes I am exhausted by the struggle. Now Xiang has become more and more standardized, specialized, professional, closer to the international standards and has got more recognition in the international market. The result of the struggle is that our group has become more and more competitive. It is worth all the struggles and all the setbacks. The struggle of me alone has gradually become the struggle of the whole team with more people understanding me when they witness the progress the company has made.

In 2009, the complaint we had most was about the shopping trap. Our guests complained that they fell into the trap of shopping everywhere when they visited China. I couldn't understand it. According to the itinerary, there was only one shopping opportunity in each city and we always made the shopping transparent in the schedule. For some groups, no shopping was arranged at all. Why were there constant complaints about the shopping trap?

Recently, I went to Xi'an and Guilin on an inspection tour and I got to know the truth of the shopping trap.

There are shopping traps where the guides can get a rake-off everywhere in the tourist attractions even in the places of historical interest. I always wonder why the local government allows shops to be opened in the valuble historical architectures. For example, there is a shop in the corner tower on the City Wall of Xi'an selling antique, furniture, calligraphy and painting. If tourists go inside the tower, they will inevitably fall into the shopping trap. Then it occurs to me, for such a vast country, the government has to provide all job opportunities it could to solve the employment problem. The government would not allow this to happen if it has better choice.

The problem lies in the guides. The guides have two choices. First, they don't tell the guests about the shopping trap but watch them fall into the trap and share the benefit with the shop. Some guides even deliberately lead the guests into the trap. Second, they remind the guests beforehand that there are shops everywhere in the places of interest. If the guests are willing to do something for the local economy or for the interest of the guide, it is another story.

We cannot possibly solve the problem of the shopping trap, but we will make sure that our guests have the right to know.

A gentleman makes money in the right way. One should never turn to deception.

I don't understand why there are some guides who show a total disregard for the Chinese people's face for a bit of ill-gotten gains. What I can never tolerate is that a guest told me that he or she has been cheated.

The last thing I do not want to see is that foreign guests return home after their visit and say that they don't like China.

I know the struggle will continue. I am not fighting alone anymore. The struggle of an individual has developed into the struggle of a team and will develop into the struggle of an industry.

I think more and more people have realized the importance of standardization which will benifit everyone.

When I was fighting alone, my son Zheng Han was also growing up. He may not understand what has happened; he knows I have had a tough time. When I was writing this article, he walked past my desk and saw me typing "Sometimes, I feel lonely". He said he could understand why I felt lonely. It was because that I was idealist. He also said that he admired me for what I had achieved and he was not sure if he could be as persistent as I was.

The fight against the industrial wickedness will continue.

Who will go to hell if I don't?

Corporate Social Responsibility of Xiang

Corporate social responsibility is a relatively new concept in China. Although Xiang hasn't put corporate social responsibility into its development strategies as a specific objective, it has been fulfilling its social responsibility all the time.

Many people have misconceptions about corporate social responsibility. They think it is all about charity and public welfare causes.

To give back to the society is just a part of social responsibility.

Corporate social responsibility is divided into basic-level social responsibility and high-level social responsibility. Basic-level social responsibility requires that enterprises run their business according to the law, be honest and pay taxes as required. High-level social responsibility includes public welfare donation, charity, volunteer activities and being people-oriented.

A Chinese well-known entrepreneur once said, "Generally speaking, the first social responsibility of an enterprise should be to observe law and discipline and to make sure its operation is reasonable and legal, for example, there should be no contaminated milk powder, fake or inferior medicine or jerry-built projects. Quality guarantee of products and responsibility to your customers should be your first social responsibility. Your enterprise has no social responsibility at all, if you evade taxes, disobey the laws when hiring laborers and operating your business or dock insurances for the employees. As an entrepreneur, I would rather not have the highest profit, but the most long-lasting one, which can best guarantee the interests of the employees."

His words struck a sympathetic resonance in my heart. Take paying taxes as an example, I am not telling the truth if I say it doesn't trouble me at all to pay all the taxes with the money earned by hard work. But I feel much better when I think we are fulfilling our social responsibility. Besides, if an enterprise has no profit and doesn't pay taxes, it is not a financially healthy company.

Once I attended a Beijing tourism industry conference, the presidents of two state-owned enterprises were sitting beside me. When the speaker on the stage said something high about the private enterprises, one of them said to the other, "We should see who pays more taxes." I

My two benefactors Flying Swallow (in white) and Yang Shengming (in yellow).

Since I entered the tourism industry, I have always tried to do something creative and challenging. In 1999, I hiked on the Great Wall for 10 days with a group from Ireland.

At the 50th Anniversary of People to People International Worldwide Conference in Sydney in 2006 with Mary Eisenhower (left), CEO of People to People International, Jeff Thomas, CEO of People to People Ambassador Programs and Peg Thomas, president of People to People Ambassador Programs.

Xin Xin Yi Xang was officially founded in July 2005. The four in the photo are the management and shareholders of the company.

A delegation of Xin Xin Yi Xiang paid a visit to North Korea in 2006, led by Mr. Kees van Galen, a historian and CEO of VNC Asia Travel, the Netherlands. Kees was one of the first Europeans who opened the door of North Korea for European tourists. He had been to North Korea several times before he led a Chinese delegation there. He said that he had a different experience with a Chinese delegation there and was very interested in observing the reaction of the Chinese to whatever they saw in another socialist country.

Several of us in the delegation had some connections with North Korea because our family members of the elder generation were fighting shoulder to shoulder with the Korean People's Army during the War to Resist US Aggression and Aid Korea (1950-1953). Kees was smiling when we were singing " The Song of Chinese People's Volunteer Army " with the North Korea soldiers. Some of my friends asked me why I was following a European to North Korea. I told them it was because that the world was changing too fast.

Kees was my first client when I started my career in the tourism industry and became a very close friend of mine. Our friendship has extended to the next generation.

Performing at the reception of the 50th Anniversary of People to People at the Great Hall of the People in Beijing together with the children of the employees in 2006.

Interviewed by my son and his classmates who majored in mass communication in the Capital University of Economy and Business in 2008.

With Peter Ueberroth, President of American Olympic Committee, Peter's wife Ginny Ueberroth and secretary Stephanie Quesada, two days before the 2008 Olympic Games in Beijing.

Xin Xin Yi Xiang stood the test of emergency during the Beijing Olympic Games. Duan Rong (third left, second row) was injured in the accident on August 9, the second day after the opening ceremony.

Representing China in the parade of Site chapters at Site International Conference in Barcelona, 2006.

Martin Sirk, CEO of ICCA, with the leaders and teachers of Beijing International Studies University, 2009.

Receiving IMEX Academy Award from Mr. Ray Bloom, Chairman of IMEX Group in Frankfurt, May 2009.

In July 2009, I joined a community activity, planting a tree in this beautiful park, when I was in Salt Lake City for MPI WEC (Meeting Professionals International World Education Conference).

With Joost de Mayer, a client, partner as well as colleague in the board of Site at the cocktail party on the desert in Dubai during the Site Europe Conference in 2006.

At the gala dinner of ICCA conference in Florence 2009 with Jennifer Salsbury (left), a British working for China International Convention Center in Beijing and Richard Rheindorf (second left), a German working for Pacific World Beijing Office.

I was elected the international board director of Site in 2008 and became its first board director from Chinese mainland. The photo was taken in Aruba when we won the bid for hosting 2012 Site International Conference in Beijing. Liu Yanxiang (fourth left, back row), president of Xin Xin Yi Xiang and I joined the delegation from Beijing Tourism Administration to do the presentation to the board of Site.

My son Zheng Han and I at Xin Xin Yi Xiang Annual Theme Party 2010. It is the company tradition to have families involved in the company events.

I showed one of the postcards of old China we brought from Beijing to the audience at the Incentive Travel Show in Las Vegas in June 2010 and said: "I cannot believe that the baby in this postcard is now as old as my father who is eighty. Unfortunately, my father never had an opportunity to take a picture during his childhood for the family was too poor to afford it. However, I will show this photo to my father and tell him 'father, I found your baby photo'." All the audiences laughed.

don't know if private travel businesses pay fewer taxes than state-owned enterprises in China. As a private enterprise, Xiang and its employees pay taxes in accordance with regulations. I hope the tourism industry will take tax payment as one of its measures to evaluate the performance of enterprises to encourage them to pay taxes as required and fulfill social responsibility.

Xiang has been fulfilling its corporate social responsibility all these years; it is just we haven't realized it. In fact, being a law-abiding enterprise itself is fulfilling its corporate social responsibility.

Corporate social responsibility has suddenly become a fashionable thing. More and more enterprises are beginning to examine themselves if they have taken their social responsibilities.

Since Xiang was founded five years ago, we have tried our best to do something for our society, helping rural primary schools in poverty-stricken areas improve their teaching and learning environment, helping quake-hit areas in Sichuan and Qinghai rebuild their homes and providing financial aid to the children in poor families in Tibet so that they can go to college and so on.

Someone said, "Xiang must have earned a lot of money to be so enthusiastic in public welfare undertakings."

This is a misconception too. To work for the public good is not big enterprises' patent. Big enterprises can donate millions or tens of millions to charity events while small enterprises can only give several thousand or thousands of yuan. But there is no difference between their values. If you don't have money, you can devote your time and energy to help those who need your help. It is also fulfilling your social responsibility as an enterprise or an individual. What matters is not money, but attitude.

Influenced by the relationship of the cause and effect in Buddhism, I believe that good is rewarded and evil is punished. Therefore, I shall do all the good I can to bring good luck for my company, my employees and my family.

Postscript

I Love You, My Motherland!

I have finished this book at last.

I have been working on this book off and on for several years. I didn't write the book in time sequence. I just wrote what came to me. When I stringed all the articles together into a book, I found many of them in need of rewriting. This book covers the period from the 1950s to today. The problem lies in "today". China is changing with each passing day. I want to make comparisons between old and new, so I have to change the end of my book constantly to catch up with the change of my country. I was thinking about ending my book in a big event, first the Beijing Olympic Games, then the 30th anniversary of the Economic Reform and Opening-up, then the 60th anniversary of the founding of the People's Republic of China, and later the Shanghai World Expo. Today, I have finally finished it. I guess the English version would be published on the day of the 90th anniversary of the Chinese Communist Party.

With a private business to run, I wrote many of the articles by stealing moments of leisure under the pressure of busy work. Later, I felt I had to finish this book as soon as possible so that I could concentrate on other things; otherwise I would be under great pressure and can not be released.

I didn't worry about my writing skill. What happened to our generation is unique, so it would be good enough to tell the stories in a straightforward way.

I wrote about the 1950s and the Cultural Revolution at one go. The chapter about the 30 years during China's reform and opening-up was more difficult. This period of history is closer to today. If I didn't go deeply enough, there would be a lack of truthfulness. If I did, I was afraid it would bring trouble for me or the people I mentioned in the book. More importantly, I was afraid that I would have biased views which would mislead the readers.

The book is targeted for international readers, so I write some common sense articles such as "To Be A Good Person", "I Am a Non-Communist Party Member" and "I Am a Manchu Princess" together with my own stories. I think most of the books by Chinese or foreign experts and scholars on China's religion, political system and ethnic minorities are from the academic perspective and are difficult to understand for the average readers. When I was working on these chapters, I interspersed common sense with my own stories to make it more interesting and readable.

I have read the books by some Chinese who went to study abroad by the end of 1970s or in the early 1980s. They stayed abroad and had no first-hand experience of China's economic reform and opening-up. Their stories ended in the 1980s. Their life in the Western countries might be happy, free and democratic, which is the one I am yearning for. Due to some reasons, I didn't realize my dream to study abroad and settle down. At the same time, I am grateful that I didn't leave my motherland, but have been personally involved in the economic reform and opening-up, have personally experienced the sweetness and bitterness, have personally witnessed the tremendous changes of China, and have become a beneficiary of the changes.

One of my purposes for writing this book is I want to let readers abroad know more about China and Chinese people through these true and simple stories. This is also the problem that troubles me. I have kept asking myself, "Can I represent the majority of Chinese people?" The idea badly influenced my writing. I would spend a lot of time checking netizens' opinions on some matter or discussing with my colleagues or friends to see if my views were correct or unbiased. Later it occurred to me that what I was writing was about myself and those who were around me. I have been a worker, a teacher, a worker-present-soldier college student, a government official, a backbone of a state-owned company and CEO of a private company. I have walked out of the remote mountainous area to the capital city of Beijing and finally to the world! As long as my stories are true, I can represent the majority of the Chinese people with my rich experience even if I cannot represent all of them.

If you have the chance to meet Chinese people of my age, you will find the life experience of almost every one of them can make a book. However, few of them turn the stories into a book except some professional writers or celebrities. Many people have cherished the dream of writing, but few of them really sit down to realize it. It has convinced me more that I have done a significant and meaningful thing to leave my stories to the younger generation.

Another important purpose of this book is to express my love for my motherland. I am not sure if it is achieved in this book. When I am making a speech to the Western audience, no matter what the topic is, there are always some people who tell me that they can feel my love and passion for my motherland, though, during the whole speech, I usually don't directly express that feeling. I hope that this book can achieve the same effect.

Although it is not what I usually do, at the end of this book, I am still going to say from the bottom of my heart, "I love you, my motherland!"

Chronology

1955	Liu Ping was born in northeast China in 1955, six years after the People's Republic of China was founded.
1957	Liu Ping's family moved to the Jinping Phosphate Mine of Lianyungang City, Jiangsu Province in east China.
1958	Liu Ping's family moved to the Kaiyang Phosphate Mine of Guizhou Province in southwest China.
1959-1961	Three famine-stricken years
1959-1962	Four Clean-ups Movement, the first political movement in Liu Ping's memory
1966-1976	The Great Proletarian Cultural Revolution
1966	Red Guard organizations were formed.
1971	Liu Ping joined the working class and became a manual laborer.
1973	Liu Ping began her university studies.
1976	Premier Zhou Enlai and Chairman Mao Zedong passed away.
	Tangshan earthquake
	End of the Great Proletarian Cultural Revolution
	Liu Ping graduated from university and became a middle school teacher.
1978	Beginning of the economic reform and opening-up
1979	Liu Ping left Guizhou Province and became an interpreter in the Chemical Mining Bureau of the H Ministry based in Z County of Hebei Province (not far from Beijing).
1985	Liu Ping traveled outside of China for the first time.
1987	Liu Ping's son, Zheng Han, was born.
1989-1992	Liu Ping became an interpreter in the Foreign Affairs Department of the H Ministry.
1992-2001	Liu Ping began her career in the biggest state-owned

	travel company in China.
2001	China entered the World Trade Organization (WTO).
	Liu Ping resigned and started her own business.
2005	Xin Xin Yi Xiang was founded in Beijing and Liu Ping became one of the owners and CEO of the company.
	Liu Ping joined the Society of Incentive and Travel Executives (Site).
2008	Beijing Olympic Games
	Liu Ping became the first international board director of Site from Chinese mainland.
2009	Liu Ping received IMEX Academy Award.
2010	Liu Ping established her second company, Xin Xiang, in Shanghai.
	Liu Ping's son graduated from university and began work for the *Beijing News*.